BECOMING
AN ETHICAL
HELPING
PROFESSIONAL

BECOMING AN ETHICAL HELPING PROFESSIONAL

CULTURAL AND PHILOSOPHICAL FOUNDATIONS

RITA SOMMERS-FLANAGAN
JOHN SOMMERS-FLANAGAN

John Wiley & Sons, Inc.

Library of Congress Cataloging-in-Publication Data:

Sommers-Flanagan, Rita, 1953-
    Becoming an ethical helping professional : cultural and philosophical foundation / by Rita Sommers-Flanagan, John Sommers-Flanagan.
        p.   cm.
    ISBN-13: 978-0-471-73810-7 (paper/dvd)
    ISBN-10: 0-471-73810-7 (paper/dvd)
    1.   Human services personnel—Professional ethics.   2.   Human services—Moral and ethical aspects.   3.   Counselors—Professional ethics.   4.   Counseling—Moral and ethical aspects.
    I. Sommers-Flanagan, John, 1957- II. Title.
    HV10.5.S65 2007
    174'.9361—dc22
                                                                        2006011099

Printed in the United States of America.
10 9 8 7 6 5 4 3 2 1

Dedication ──────────────────────────

To those seeking help,
to those offering help,
and to all who refuse to simplify that interaction.

Table of Contents

Section Three: Specific Specialties and Professional Identities

Ten   Counseling in the Schools   235
(By John Sommers-Flanagan, Nancy Bodenhorn, and
Rita Sommers-Flanagan)

Acknowledgments

We owe many debts of gratitude to colleagues, friends, critics, and family members. We thank our contributing authors—you'll find their voices peppered here and there in the text. Tracey Belmont deserves credit for bothering us about this idea for years, finally starting the process that made it real. Lisa Gebo stepped in as our senior editor at a critical time, adding her warmth and wisdom to the mix. The rest of the incredible workforce at John Wiley and Sons also deserve our thanks, especially Isabel Pratt, Katherine Willert, and Judi Knott, who were always ready with supportive answers. Editors Susan Dodson and Sarah Sunderland were also very helpful.

Our friend and mentor, Deni Elliott, started us down the philosophical road (lo those many years ago) and provided essential guidance and support. Our reviewers all offered challenging and excellent ideas. We appreciated their efforts. We couldn't really ask Liz Welfel to review, since we are now officially competitors, but her ongoing devotion to ethics and her vision for how things *could* be will always provide inspiration to us.

Noah Kastelowitz-Leiberman is a DVD-making protégé with skill and style that we appreciate enormously and that will take him far. Our students and colleagues featured in the DVD, Mika Watanabe-Taylor, Brenda C. Binkerd, John McKay, Monica Carlson Roscoe, Deanne Bell, Nilda Bishop, Mehrdad Kia, and A. J. Johnson were all wonderful, and most generous with their time, insight, and good humor. Thanks, too, to Connie and Ross Keogh for moral and technological support.

Our families continued to support our writing with grace and love, even when weddings, holidays, graduations, college choices, and book deadlines ended up all stirred together like a big pot of family stew. We are indeed fortunate to live (together) through such interesting times.

Rita and John Sommers-Flanagan

About the Authors

Rita and John Sommers-Flanagan have been helping professionals for over 30 years. They currently serve as full-time faculty members in the Counselor Education program at the University of Montana. Trained most recently as clinical psychologists, they have held and currently hold a number of helping positions that provide them with insight into the many dimensions involved in helping relationships. Rita has held positions as a rehabilitation counselor, disabled student advisor, director of a Big Brother Big Sister program, acting director of UM's Ethics Center, and director of Women's Studies. She is also certified as a school counselor. John has held positions as a recreation therapist, psychologist in private practice, and executive director of a community parenting education organization. Both currently work as mental health consultants at Trapper Creek Job Corps.

Drs. Sommers-Flanagan provide continuing education training workshops nationally and internationally. They are the authors of *Clinical Interviewing,* in its third edition, and the popular *Counseling and Psychotherapy Theories in Context and Practice: Skills, Strategies, and Techniques,* as well as four other applied texts. They live in Missoula, Montana and enjoy gardening, parenting, writing, teaching, and considering the deep and ethical meanings of life.

About the Contributors

Nancy Bodenhorn is an Assistant Professor at Virginia Tech in Blacksburg, Virginia where she teaches School Counseling, Multicultural, and Ethics classes, and coordinates the school counseling program. She was a school counselor for twenty years in the U.S., in Thailand, and in Belgium. She maintains her professional and personal wellness with regular tennis games, music, laughter, and friendships.

Tim Bond BA (Hons), CQSW, Cert Ed, PhD is a Reader in Counselling and Professional Ethics in the Graduate School of Education, University of Bristol. He has written extensively on professional ethics for counselling and the caring professions. He has been actively involved in ethical development in the British Association for Counselling and Psychotherapy since the mid 1980s and was chair of the association from 1994–1996. He is a member of the Executive Council of the International Association for Counselling. His other major interests concern research ethics, particularly in the social sciences. He continues to work as a counsellor in a small private practice.

Mary Alice Bruce is an Associate Professor at the University of Wyoming where she coordinates the school counseling program. As a Fulbright Senior Scholar in Guatemala, she worked with school counselors as well as conducted cross-cultural studies on women's spirituality. Currently, she is a member of the CACREP 2008 Standards Revision Committee and cochair of the ACA International Committee. When not engaged in academia, yoga as well as cross country skiing and snowshoeing in the Rocky Mountains with her husband, children, family and friends offer fun times.

Aida Hutz is an Assistant Professor in Counselor Education at the University of Montana. She was born in Brasil and spent much of her early childhood there, and currently maintains family and personal connections there. She completed her doctoral studies at the University of Northern Arizona. Her research and writing interests include multicultural issues and counseling process variables.

Joyce Jarosz Hannula teaches Educational Psychology at Montana State University and Psychology and Advanced Placement Psychology at Bozeman Senior High School. She is first generation Ukrainian-American, and has recently been able to reconnect with her Ukrainian family members. Her work with high school and college students consistently wins her strong praise and she is the recipient of many teaching honors and awards.

Cathy Jenni began her sojourn into qualitative research when, at age 5, she began asking questions about the meaning of people, flowers, storybooks, religious statues, her Springer Spaniel Satan, and far-away cultures. She received her training in phenomenological research from Andy Giorgi and as a result has enjoyed many journeys into the inner experiencing of research subjects, students, clients, and friends. She is currently working on the absence of the body in contemporary traditional psychotherapy approaches.

Mika Watanabe-Taylor, MA is a Disability Services Coordinator at the University of Montana-Missoula. She is currently pursuing a doctoral degree in Education at the university. She also coordinates the summer program for youth with disabilities for transitioning from high school to postsecondary settings. She has been recognized for her leadership in the American Counseling Association and was the 2004 president of the Montana Counseling Association.

Preface

There are many ironies in writing a textbook, not the least of which is that the preface is written last. Maybe if we had written the preface first, this book would not have taken us on quite so many adventures. Not that we're complaining; we've been on some grand excusions and we are excited to share them with you. We've dug around in musty old philosophy texts, bemoaning things like Artistotle's gender problems, Kant's apparent rigidity, and the short shrift given to Joseph Fletcher. We've traveled a long ways back in time, and taken quick trips around this increasingly small planet we all call home to try and deepen the dialogue among the cultures. We've boldly (rashly?) waded into the middle of the helping turf wars: There are specialty and professional identity conundrums with no easy answers.

And the result? This text is appropriate (and important) for anyone considering a career in the helping professions. Not all professional helpers provide the traditional 50-minute hour of counseling or therapy—and those who do also provide other forms of helping. However, all professional helpers engage in the creation and maintenance of helping relationships that have therapeutic potential. We use the words counselor, therapist, mental health professional, and helper interchangeably, believing that the shared ethical domain is greater than the sum of the distinctions.

When we began this project, we had to ask ourselves a question you might be asking as well: Why another ethics text in the helping professions? There are a number of excellent texts already. Why is this one necessary or unique? We wrote it because we believe the gap between the theories about right and wrong and the application of helping skills has grown dangerously wide. We wrote it because most of us claim to value multicultural skills and awareness but often fail to exert the energy necessary to grasp other worldviews. Ethics (morality/right-and-wrong) *is* a central strand in our own and other worldviews. It isn't always easy to wrestle with this material. It is not comfortable to face our own ignorance, confusion, and biases, but it is the right thing to do.

Some who reviewed this text were concerned that graduate students would be unhappy with or resistant to the thinking required in parts of this book. Others worried that faculty might not be familiar with some of the material and therefore be intimidated. We can understand these reservations, but in our experience, graduate students and faculty are deeply concerned about our callings as professionals. These callings include developing the kind of wisdom and depth necessary to reach meaningfully across cultures and practices. In this book, we give faculty and students alike permission to explore new realms of thought—to consider controversial or foreign concepts together. At the same time, we've structured the book so this material can be minimized or even temporarily shelved without omitting any of the more pragmatic ethical concerns inherent in professional development.

Another valid criticism is the fact that we do not include all possible moral theories, and we do not rank the theories in terms of utility or perfection. What we hope to provide is exposure and ample food for thought. We are not proposing that helping professionals declare their allegiance to one moral philosophy, but rather that they become much more aware of the complexities in the ongoing evolution of ethical thought and behavior.

Because sometimes ethical material is so challenging, we've made liberal use of our hallmark almost-free associations, down-to-earth examples, and sometimes questionable senses of humor. Some will find this refreshing; others may use less complimentary descriptions. There is a method to our madness: Ethical concerns are everywhere and occasionally, it is just fine to, as our daughters say, *CHILL!* and just meander in the mundane or mull the outlandish.

Books like this one usually move through time in the form of newer editions. Even now, you can expand your sense of professional identity by entering into a dialogue with us. We would love to hear every reader's reactions throughout the book and are especially interested in feedback on the risks we have taken by including both intellectually challenging material as well as an irreverent writing style.

After an orientational first chapter, Chapter 2 provides a reader-friendly synopsis of moral philosophy and offers overviews of significantly divergent ethical worldviews. Chapter 3 specifically addresses the development of codes and standards and practice, and Chapter 4 rounds out this section by considering values as they interact with ethics. We hope these foundations will accompany the reader as the text moves into Chapters 5–9, covering the core ethical challenges in the helping relationship: confidentiality, boundaries, assessment, and competence.

In the final section of the book, Chapters 10–13, we write about specialties within the helping professions. With current lifespan expectancies, no one could live long enough to make use of all the specialty coverage this text provides. However, even if readers never, in their wildest dreams, consider trying to offer pastoral or addictions counseling, knowing what these fellow helpers face and what is expected ethically of them helps all of us broaden our grasp of the many facets of helping and mental health care. We also provide a short epilogue about the dynamics and practicalities of ethical misbehavior.

Our intention has been to write a book that is philosophically palatable and sophisticated, clinically sensitive, and personally meaningful and challenging. To this end, we've:

- supplied code quotes, practical applications, and clinical examples;
- included current topics, such as human rights and ethical concerns in crisis work;
- allowed ourselves to digress and reflect aloud (hoping to prod readers to do the same);
- convinced some of our most interesting colleagues to say a few words;
- and offered diversity concerns that move beyond the usual, overused examples.

Ethical practices evolve and hopefully improve with time and deliberate attention. More than ever, we realize that becoming ethical helpers is a lifelong interactive process greatly enhanced by soul-searching, frank debate, and intellectual integrity. We hope this book contributes to these endeavors.

Accompanying DVD to *Becoming an Ethical Helping Professional*

New copies of *Becoming an Ethical Helping Professional* come bound with a complementary DVD. We created this DVD to offer readers live and interactive perspectives on ethical considerations in professional helping. We believe that it is profoundly important to listen to persons from diverse backgrounds, life experiences, and philosophical positions in order to gain empathy and wisdom. Our intention in making the DVD was to create a conversational tone as together we consider common historic philosophical positions in ethics. We also hoped to bring thoughtful experts directly into your world, allowing you to listen in as they consider the cultural dynamics of ethical lives. We have provided hot links to the American Counseling Association (ACA) and the American Psychological Association (APA) ethics codes so that you can easily access these important codes. We hope that you find this DVD thought-provoking, instructive, and entertaining.

Becoming an Ethical Helping Professional

SECTION ONE

THE FOUNDATION

Chapter One

COUNSELING ETHICS AND THE BIG PICTURE

Let us toast twice. First to the older generation: May your days come to be many, full of comfort and understanding. May they be spent knowing that those days past have held a completeness uncommon and unknown to many, and that every detail of your beings continues in the lives of those who follow.

To the younger: May we accept these gifts, knowing that they are of this tradition, of this old-fashioned courage, of ethics, and that they can be carried along forever like rusting relics, or they can be worn as wings.

Let us wear them as wings.

—Terry Tempest Williams

CHAPTER ORIENTATION

To be perfectly honest (which we are compelled to be since this *is* an ethics text) we know this chapter and the next will present you with challenges, ideas, and material not commonly included in your run-of-the-mill applied ethics text. And we are not apologizing for this, although we will be very understanding if you contact us or complain to your instructor that you find little relevance in learning to pronounce *deontological* or *nonmaleficence.* We hope that by the end of this text, you will agree with us that this material is worth the time and brain expansion necessary to absorb a bit of it. For now, our overall explanation is this: We love our profession and believe it has a central role to play in the future health and well-being of many societies. Professional helping entails a powerful interaction that can be of great benefit or great harm. For the sake of our profession, those we serve, and the future nature of those interactions, we ask you to bear with us and delve thoughtfully into the content in these first two chapters. *You* are the next generation of practicing professionals and, knowingly or by default, you will shape the ethics and professional identities of future helping professions. As Alasdair MacIntyre (1998b) said, "Understanding the world of morality and changing it are far from incompatible tasks" (p. 2).

This chapter explores applied and philosophical connections between morals, ethics, principles, and values, and concludes by linking this inquiry to your professional identity as a counselor. You will be considering:

- the definitions of the words *ethics* and *morals;*
- the role of ethics in the professions;

- the role of morality in human culture;
- the concept of universal morals;
- the issues surrounding global human rights;
- the definitions of moral values, rules, and principles;
- common ground in the helping professions;
- the role of professional organizations and associations; and
- the definition of the client, or the people we serve.

DEFINING THE TERMS

Ethics and Morals

Will you be a moral professional? Will you be an ethical professional? Is there a difference? Can you be both? Etymologically speaking, these terms have ancient Greek and Latin roots, which we discuss in the following paragraphs, but the struggle to define the rightly lived life and the best ways to live together as a human community is even more ancient. Very early texts, such as the Hebrew *Torah* (Fasching & deChant, 2001) or the Hindu *Rig Gita* (Brannigan, 2005), include treatises on human relationships with each other, nature, and the sacred.

As Robert Wright explores in his book, *The Moral Animal* (1994), morality may even be a genetic adaptation, enabling human survival and evolution. Humans are social animals. Psychologically, spiritually, and physically, our survival depends on getting along with other humans to some extent. Customs or rules for how to best treat each other are evident in even the most loosely defined communities, but the rules themselves and the penalties for breaking them vary radically across time and culture. Chapter 2 provides a glimpse into some of these diverse customs, theories, and practices.

The terms morals and ethics have similar origins; both were related to norms or customs in society. More specifically, according to the *Oxford English Dictionary,* the word *morals* is derived from the Latin word *mores,* which means "manners, morals, character" (1981, p. 900). The word *ethics* comes from the Greek word *ethos,* which means character, or custom.

Although there is overlap in meaning, in general, the terms *morals* and *morality* have become more closely associated with values and matters of conscience, while the term *ethics* has come to be more closely associated with the business and professional world. For example, many trades and professions have codes of ethics, but not codes of morals. Another distinction between these two terms is that, in one sense of the meaning, ethics is the study of morality, much like political science is the study of politics, or theology is the study of religion. Thus, college courses in ethics are common, but you might do a double take if you were required to take "Morals 101"—or even worse, "Morals for Dummies."

Both ethics and morals refer to behaviors that some collective of human beings has agreed to be good, or right ways of being. *Ethics* tends to be the term used when professionals of some sort describe how "good" practitioners behave. *Morals* tends to be the term used more generally to describe good or right human behavior.

Morality, Ethics, and Essence

There is a parallel between professional ethics and the broader concept of human morality. Professional ethics defines professional identity—something we cover thoroughly in the second half of this chapter. At the very core, our ethics demand that counselors know how to effectively and safely use the skills and talents involved in offering counseling. From a constructivist perspective, ethics codes and practices articulate the good, effective, counselor narrative (Mahoney, 2003).

Following this parallel, morality defines the good human. Morality is the story of what it means to be fully human, realizing all that is good and true in human potential. "Good and just societies require a narrative . . . which helps them know the truth about existence and fight the constant temptation to self-deception" (Hauerwas, 1981, p. 18). Given this centrality, we should take a closer look at both professional ethics and human morality because "moral knowledge is necessary for the functioning of society" (Kavathatzopoulos, 2005, p. 277).

THE ROLE OF ETHICS IN THE PROFESSIONS

In the course of becoming professionals, people learn specific sets of skills. Dentists learn basic medical material and then learn all about teeth. Teachers learn about their subject area and specific skills for teaching others. Learning the *ethics* of how the skills are applied is an important aspect of this skill acquisition. That is, what is the best and most correct and effective way to use the knowledge that defines the profession? These rules define the heart of professional endeavor and identity. There are codes of ethics for attorneys, architects, chemists, counselors, dentists, nurses, scientists, zoologists, and many more.

Some argue that without a code of ethics, a profession has not yet fully come into being (T. Remley & Herlihy, 2005). Further, if professionals decide to ignore or violate their particular ethics code, they run the risk of being shunned, sanctioned, or removed from their profession. Learning to be an ethical practitioner has been compared to the process humans go through as they become members of a new culture (Handelsman, Gottlieb, & Knapp, 2005). Using Berry's (2003) model, which identifies four possible adaptation strategies people use when faced with joining a new culture, Handelsman, Gottlieb, and Knapp (2005) describe four ways you, as a new member of the counseling culture, might adapt. These include:

1. *Assimilation.* When people assimilate into a new culture, they embrace the new culture so fully they lose their connections to their original culture. Handelsman, Gottlieb, and Knapp (2005) point out that assimilated mental health professionals might overly identify with the external trappings of the profession, believing credentials are more important than the substance of the profession. They might follow the ethics codes religiously without ever grasping the broader principles involved. This can lead to simplistic or legalistic application of the codes, and a failure to seek the higher ground and the best possible ethical practices and solutions.

2. *Separation.* When new mental health professionals choose separation as their adaptation to their new professional culture, they allow their original personal val-

ues to overrule what they are learning as a new professional. They might be strongly committed religious people, or devoted environmentalists, unable or unwilling to integrate this new set of values into their ways of being in the world. They may discount the importance of the new ethics, believing their own moral systems to be preferable. Those who maintain this separation often fail to understand the harm that can come from applying their values under the umbrella of the new identity. The counselor/environmentalist who scolds clients for not recycling or the helping professional with religious values who shames parents for sending their children to public schools instead of home-schooling them are behaving unethically in their new professional culture.

3. *Marginalization.* "Marginalization is the most problematic acculturation strategy, comprising low identification with both cultures" (Handelsman et al., 2005, p. 61). Graduate students who have not developed an optimal sense of moral identity in their personal lives, and who minimize or ignore the ethics of the professional culture they are joining, are at great risk for unethical behavior. They might get along with an ethics-as-convenient style for some time, but without any real allegiance to the ideal of professional and moral excellence, they are highly likely to break as many rules as they can get away with.

4. *Integration.* Integration involves retaining your sense of self, as a person, while also adopting the new culture in an authentic way. Becoming an ethical counselor will include adopting some new values, new guidelines, and new goals. Integrated mental health professionals also find ways to maintain their own values and senses of meaning in the world. Integration allows "a richer, more sophisticated appreciation for the underlying principles of both cultures" (Handelsman et al., 2005, p. 59).

Obviously, integration is the form of adaptation we hope you eventually achieve. However, cultural adaptation is a process, not an end-state. You may see yourself in each of these descriptions, sometimes overidentified, sometimes underidentified, and sometimes just confused. Be patient with yourself as you explore this professional culture you are joining, and the new layers of ethical identity that come with it. But do not underestimate the importance of this ethical identity. In our opinion, it is what defines our craft. See the unusual example in Digressions for Deliberation 1.1.

THE ROLE OF MORALITY IN HUMAN CULTURE

Human communities are essentially units of morality.

—Warren Lancaster

As soon as infant humans are born into their respective cultures, moral instruction begins. Caretakers in different cultures react to infants' needs with a wide variety of responses, sending important messages about how and when to ask for food, comfort, or even diaper changes! As these children (and their consciences) grow and develop, they become increasingly aware of the rules for conduct in their families, communities, and societies. There are decades of research focusing on how adults can teach children

---

Digressions for Deliberation 1.1

Shooting Isn't Necessarily Hunting

Some years ago, we helped a (vegetarian!) colleague facilitate a workshop on Hunting Ethics. There were a number of hunters present who believed fervently that there were moral behaviors that distinguished ethical hunting from simply killing an animal. Merely shooting something did not make someone a hunter. Abiding by the rules of the hunt, having an attitude of respect and gratitude, obeying the law and the rules of safety, having the skills and training necessary, and putting these ethics above all else makes someone a hunter.

You may not believe in hunting. You may not even eat the cellophane-wrapped chicken, beef, pork, or lamb produced by the feedlot-slaughter cycle. But bear with us: The definitive value these hunters place on ethical practices offers an analogy for mental health counseling. Bartenders, hairdressers, and even the occasional mother-in-law offer a sympathetic ear; they listen, reflect, and offer thoughts or advice. Often, they are quite effective in their efforts to help. But are they mental health professionals? They do not have the training, the credentials, or a code of ethics guiding their "mental health" interactions and protecting those who receive their services. They might be natural helpers, but because they are not aware of, or obliged to, follow a code of professional counseling ethics, they are not professional counselors or psychologists. They might, however, have a code of ethics for bartending or hairdressing. This code would focus on the essence of safe, effective bartending and hairdressing—not on effective counseling or therapy.

Those who fail to follow hunting ethics are not considered to be hunters by those who do. Those who fail to follow the ethics codes and expectations of many other professions are also excluded from claiming membership in the profession. Ethical behavior is central to professional identity.

---

moral values most efficiently (Casey & Burton, 1982; Gibbs, 2003; Jensen & Buhanan, 1974; McGrath, 1923).

Just as ethical practices and codes define a profession, moral rules serve a defining role in human culture. People who cannot or do not behave in ways their culture has prescribed as good or right are sometimes seen as less than full members of their culture. In some cases their autonomy, freedom to move about, or access to the culture is cut off. Words that describe immoral behaviors include the word *inhuman*—an acknowledgment of the definitional power of morality. If you break central moral rules, your culture may cast you out, or define you as less than human (Allport, 1954; Craig, 2002).

When teaching ethics, we ask students to complete a survey (found in Chapter 2) about their own personal moral and ethical principles. For now, we ask you to consider this: "Who taught you about right and wrong?" Or, put another way, "Where did you learn about what behaviors are more acceptable and desirable and what behaviors are less acceptable and desirable in your culture, family, and society in general?"

In response to these questions, most students name their parents and other early adult caretakers or role models as original moral authorities in their lives. This tendency has been true for most students from diverse cultural backgrounds and different age groups. Although some students occasionally cite a religious authority (or religious text), the vast majority cite parents, followed by grandparents, siblings, or other family members. Sometimes, teachers or coaches make it on the list as well. These early figures are very influential. In fact, when he teaches the ethics of family therapy, Sam Gladding has his students do an "Ethical Genogram" (Gladding, 2005b) to compare and contrast the ethical approaches of our close family members.

As you study counseling ethics, you will find that you already have a moral and ethical foundation and that by taking an ethics course and reading this text, you are merely building on your existing foundation. In the future, when you are faced with an ethical dilemma, you will be influenced both by those original authorities in your life as well as the layers you have added since then. When faced with an ethical question or quandary, mental health professionals often turn to the following resources:

- an immediate colleague or supervisor (if available)
- a colleague who is also a friend
- former ethics professor or counseling/psychology professor
- a local authority (e.g., university professor, county mental health professional, school superintendent)
- the state counseling or psychological association (state associations sometimes will put you in contact with their attorney)
- a local attorney familiar with psychology and counseling practice law
- the ethics committees of various professional organizations

When you face a challenging ethical situation, to whom will you turn? Who do you think most professionals turn to? Check with your professors and classmates to see how your answers compare.

Obviously, human morality intersects directly with multiculturalism. If behaving morally is part of the definition of being human, and at least some moral rules vary across cultures, cross-cultural encounters might be confusing or even disturbing for those unprepared for these central differences. Further, as we discuss in the following paragraphs, most of us believe in at least some small degree of moral absolutism— the idea that there are moral behaviors that are the same for all times and all people. When our moral norms are violated by cultures very different than ours, we might be tempted to define whole cultures of humans as immoral or less than human. This is painfully evident in times of conflict, war, and terrorism, when enemies are dehumanized to justify the aggression directed toward them. The social psychology literature has articulated this dehumanization process (Craig, 2002; Festinger, Pepitone, & Newcomb, 1952).

So, to underline the parallel, professional ethics codes define the essence of what it means to be a good professional. Analogously, and in a much more profound way, morality defines the essence of what it means to be a worthy member of the human race—and this morality is at least partially defined by the particular cultures and communities in which we live.

We all have beliefs in accordance with which we judge actions and characters, our own and those of others, to be right or wrong, good or bad; we have aspirations which we strive to realize; and we have a conception, dim or clear, of the best way to live. (Albert, Denise, & Peterfreund, 1975, p. 3)

Pause for Reflection

At this point, do you think your sense of human morality will be compatible with your ethical responsibilities as a professional? Do you know, or can you imagine, a professional who is quite ethical at work, but behaves immorally after hours?

ARE THERE UNIVERSAL MORALS?

One reason we decided to write this text is our strong belief in the importance of human diversity in understanding ethics. Humans are, to add a bit to the psalmist's observations, fearfully, wonderfully, *and* diversely made (Metzger & Murphy, 1994, p. 793). The vast, intriguing expanse of human variation should feature prominently as we consider the ethics of professional counseling. On the other hand, if morality is intended to point us toward the best of what it means to be human, could we hope to find agreement across cultures regarding certain aspects of morality?

Tensions between Relativism and Absolutism

There are natural tensions between diversity and commonality that parallel the intellectual tension between relativism and absolutism. Both provide us with an ongoing, productive dialectic to consider (see the section below for an explanation of the concept of dialectic). As someone once said, "Everything is relative, and of that, I am absolutely certain." In the 1950s, interpersonal theorist and early constructivist Harry Stack Sullivan (1953) wrote

Man [*sic*] is much more simply human than otherwise. . . . We are really up against one of the most difficult of human performances—organizing thought about oneself and others, not on the basis of the unique individual **me** that is perhaps one's most valuable possession, but on the basis of one's common humanity. (p. 4)

As counselors, we need not deny our shared humanity in service of exploring and celebrating diversity, and we need not fear or minimize diversity as we seek to understand our commonality.

The Dialectic of the Moral Life

One definition of the term *dialectic* is "the Hegelian process of change in which a concept or its realization passes over and into and is preserved and fulfilled by its opposite" (Woolf, 1973, p. 350). The study of ethics and our attempts to live a moral life cause all of us to face many uncomfortably paradoxical or contradictory truths. Among them are:

- I know the right thing to do, and yet, I do not do it.
- There are two "right" things to do.
- There are no purely right things to do—the choice is between the lesser of evils.
- If I do the right thing, I will hurt the people I love.
- The right thing to do will turn out to be wrong and harmful because of an inadequate judicial system or lack of funding.
- If I tell the truth, I will hurt someone's feelings or will be misunderstood by others.

Humans have to contend with both heart and mind. Some are more inclined to set their moral compass by their intuitions and a deep, gut-level sense of morality. As Eleanor Roosevelt once said, "Do what you feel in your heart to be right—for you'll be criticized anyway." Others use the human gift of rationality. They reason their way to the moral choice. Either way, the human condition is such that we will never achieve perfect consistency. As Walt Whitman wrote, "Do I contradict myself? Very well then I contradict myself, (I am large, I contain multitudes.)"

Barry Lopez offers the following in his book *Arctic Dreams* (1986):

No culture has yet solved the dilemma each has faced with the growth of a conscious mind: how to live a moral and compassionate existence when one is fully aware of the blood, the horror inherent in life, when one finds darkness not only in one's culture but within oneself? If there is a stage at which an individual life becomes truly adult, it must be when one grasps the irony in its unfolding and accepts responsibility for a life lived in the midst of such paradox. One must live in the middle of contradiction, because if all contradiction were eliminated at once life would collapse. There are simply no answers to some of the great pressing questions. You continue to live them out, making your life a worthy expression of leaning into the light. (p. 413)

In Chapter 4, we encourage you to consider your own and your culture's values as they intersect with those of your clients. There is no doubt you will find significant differences in values between yourself and your clients, even when you share similar cultural backgrounds and worldviews. At times, this will be difficult. Even more difficult is grappling with the notion that two very different values can be worthy of respect *and* correct in their own context.

Pause for Reflection

Thomas Jefferson said, "The same act, therefore, may be useful and consequently virtuous in one country which is injurious and vicious in another differently circumstanced" (Boyd, 1950, p. 143). What is the most radical moral difference you can think of between your own culture and another culture? Dare we consider suicide? In the United States, suicide is most commonly considered a tragic or difficult ending to an unhappy, terminally-ill, or angry person's life (Cutchin & Churchill, 1997; Lester, 1997). While we may be understanding of, or experience compassion for, this act, there is little to no honor associated with choosing to commit suicide within the dominant culture in the United States. The mindset necessary to become a kamikaze (tokubetsu) *pilot or suicide bomber is a mystery to most Westerners, and the honor given to suicide bombers by their culture is horrifying to many. This example is provocative and extreme, but when you consider even mild differences, can you feel the tug to judge* our *way of doing things as right, or moral—and* their *way of doing things as wrong? Can you feel the door to inquiry and understanding slam shut when faced with such disturbing differences?*

Living with and tolerating ambiguity is part of professional life for most counselors. Scaturo (2002) wrote ". . . an ability to think and function within the finer gray hues of life, rather than either the black or white polarities, tends to be a job requirement of the psychotherapist" (p. 117).

GLOBAL HUMAN RIGHTS

The current focus on global human rights is an international attempt to articulate values common to *all* humans. Most of us have heard the term, but few have stopped to consider exactly what is meant by *human rights.* The United Nations Universal Declaration of Human Rights is provided in the Appendix. Eleanor Roosevelt played a key role in bringing this document into being. It was written under the auspices of the United Nations in 1948, on the heels of World War II and one of the most horrific of the genocidal holocausts humans have visited upon each other.

Over the years, other human rights documents have followed the United Nations Declaration of Human Rights, including a draft declaration on the rights of indigenous peoples, which can be viewed at http://www.unhchr.ch/indigenous/main.html, and one detailing the rights of children at http://www.unicef.org/crc/crc.html. Visit these websites and look around. These conventions and declarations are attempts to reach an agreement about how human beings should treat each other across cultures, races, nationalities, religions, and socioeconomic conditions. Not everyone agrees with these efforts. As you read through the original Universal Declaration of Human Rights or look at the text of the other declarations, think about which of the articles or statements you find yourself agreeing with. Which seem to reflect cultural bias or outdated ideas? Which seem hopelessly idealistic? Which ones do you philosophically disagree with? What is still missing?

Within the national professional mental and physical health organizations, there are divisions devoted to global peace concerns and social justice, such as APA's Division 48, the Society for the Study of Peace, Conflict, and Violence; NASW's division, Social and Economic Justice and Peace; or ACA's Counselors for Social Justice (CSJ). On their web page, CSJ is described as "a community of counselors, counselor educators, graduate students, and school and community leaders who seek equity and an end to oppression and injustice affecting clients, students, counselors, families, communities, schools, workplaces, governments, and other social and institutional systems." The web page indicates a list of commitments, some of which include:

- challenging oppressive systems of power and privilege
- disseminating social justice scholarship about sociopolitical and economic inequities facing counselors and clients/students in schools and communities

- maintaining an active support network online and in person for engaging in social justice activities in schools and communities

Influencing public policy at the local, national, or international level is increasingly seen as a dimension of professional practice—topics ranging from torture to environmental toxins have direct implications for our clients and the world in which we live (Koger, Schettler, & Weiss, 2005). Perhaps more than most professionals, counselors and other mental health professionals must directly face the demands of reaching across many cultural divides when offering services. In fact, if you cannot reach effectively across a given culture, you not only have nothing to offer the client on the other side, you may cause more damage than improvement. As counselors, we need to live in the tension between honoring diversity and seeking common connection. Dimensions of diversity include cultural, racial, religious, socioeconomic, gender and sexual differences, disabilities, and many others too subtle to easily label. Dimensions of commonality rest in the human-to-human encounters we experience—the essence of any counseling relationship.

MORAL VALUES, RULES, AND PRINCIPLES

The term *moral values* has been used frequently in recent public and political discourse. For our purposes, moral values reflect beliefs about how people *should* behave in order to coexist in a just society, and have a good or satisfying life. Of course, morality overlaps with religion, but *religious values* are not necessarily synonymous with *moral values.*

Moral values are pervasive. ". . . [B]ecause our every action has a universal dimension, a potential impact on others' happiness, ethics are necessary as a means to ensure that we do not harm others" (Tenzin Gyatso [the 14th Dalai Lama], 1999). It is hard to imagine many behaviors that have absolutely no moral dimension. General moral values include respect for others, compassion, tolerance, honesty, generosity, fidelity, kindness, fairness, forgiveness, and justice. However, achieving agreement on what constitutes specific moral behavior, such as what sort of action is a true representation of "compassion," is an ongoing challenge and sometimes the focus of heated arguments.

Pause for Reflection

"Our beliefs about ourselves in relation to the world around us are the roots of our values, and our values determine not only our immediate actions, but also, over the course of time, the form of our society" (Stapp, 1993, p. 209). Many believe that respecting and striving for equal rights for all is the core task of a moral government. Do you? Think for a moment about how you define morality and what exact behaviors you believe are representative of moral behavior.

Moral values can also be expressed at the community level. When moral values are shared, this can lead to the establishment of moral rules or laws for a given group of people. The rule is intended to ensure that the value is upheld in the community. Moral rules may or may not become laws that society is willing to enforce. Some moral rules are explicit, sometimes taking the form of law, while others are implicit. Societies vary widely in the form and extent of enforcement of moral behaviors.

Further complicating the situation, the term *moral principles* has a different meaning than moral rules or values. According to Michael Brannigan, ". . . moral rules are concrete expressions of underlying moral principles. Moral rules are therefore derived from moral principles and are of the second order. Moral principles are of the first order" (2005, p. 13). You catch the sense of this meaning in this 1853 quote by abolitionist and historian, William C. Nell (1852): "I have borne allegiance to principles, rather than men." For Nell, even though owning slaves was legal by human-made laws, at a higher level, it was wrong based on moral principles that transcended law. After reading Chapter 2, you will be articulate in overarching principles that flow from some of the various ethical theories and approaches in ways guaranteed to impress your friends and family.

In summary, *morals* have to do with defining right or good human conduct in general. *Ethics* has come to be associated more closely with professional conduct. In fact, having a set of behavioral guidelines called an ethics code has become a defining feature of professionalism. Therefore, professional identity is an important component of any ethics inquiry, and an important aspect of your development as a graduate student.

PROFESSIONAL IDENTITY: POWER AND PERIL

Developing a professional identity is an exhilarating, arduous, and intimidating process (Kreisler, 2005; Weinrach, Thomas, & Fong, 2001). Although many of us might feel ambivalent about the status and responsibilities associated with professional identity, there is no denying that being a professional brings a certain amount of social power. The following quote by Paul Starr in his book *The Social Origins of Professional Sovereignty* (1982) provides a view of the social process that gives professionals distinct power and authority.

> Power, at the most rudimentary personal level, originates in dependence, and the power of the professionals primarily originates in dependence upon their knowledge and competence. In some cases, this dependence may be entirely subjective, but no matter: Psychological dependence is as real in its consequences as any other kind. Indeed, what makes dependence on the professions so distinctive today is that their interpretations often govern our understanding of the world and our own experience. To most of us, this power seems legitimate: When professionals claim to be authoritative about the nature of reality, whether it is the structure of the atom, the ego, or the universe, we generally defer to their judgment. (p. 4)

While society may believe the power invested in professionals is legitimate, graduate students often struggle with the process of acquiring this power. Quite recently, one of our school counseling students began an advanced internship placement at a small school that was temporarily without a counselor. As our student was leaving after his first day there, the principal made a point to come out, shake his hand, and say, "It's sure nice to have an expert around here again." In class, the student told this story with a mixture of shock, fear, and awe in his voice. His fellow students laughed nervously as they considered how very soon, each of them would be finding jobs wherein they would be seen as experts. Taking on the authority imbued in you by virtue of your graduate degree may feel uncomfortable at first. You may feel like an imposter, trying to look and act like a professional while inside feeling uncertain, confused, or even a little afraid.

On my internship, I (RSF) admitted similar feelings to a wise and experienced supervisor, Dr. Orin Bolstad. He said, "Hang on to that insecurity. It isn't comfortable, but it's what will keep you safe. It's what will make you continue to grow and develop your entire life. It will make you seek consultation. I don't trust people who think they've arrived or know it all—and furthermore, I don't think they make the best counselors" (Bolstad, personal communication, November 1988).

The act of engaging in a helping relationship as a professional helper has ramifications for all parties involved. To become and remain an ethical counselor, you must continually examine your motivations for acquiring and using the kind of power described in the previous quote.

Pause for Reflection

Perhaps unfortunately, counseling graduate students are unlikely to have enormous monetary gain as their primary motive. So, great wealth aside, what other forms of power or authority do you associate with counseling? Does it seem strange to consider counseling as a powerful profession?

ATTRIBUTES OF PROFESSIONAL HELPING: COMMON GROUND

Defining exactly what is meant by "professional" is difficult, but there are a number of commonly agreed-upon attributes (Greenwood, 1983). These include:

- a set of skills defined or driven by a theoretical foundation and a prescribed level of educational attainment
- a degree of authority and autonomy in exercising the practice
- a code of ethics or a generally understood set of ethical expectations
- an orientation toward serving the common good
- organizations or associations that foster the culture of the profession
- state or community sanction evidenced by certification or licensure

Providing professional help through the provision of therapy, counseling, and/or social work services is a relatively new set of professional activities. Professional mental health and school counseling, at the applied masters level, embody a multitude of related professional skills and identities (Gladding, 2004; Heppner, Kivlighan, Wright, Pledge, et al., 1995). Both social work and nursing programs produce masters level graduates who provide mental health counseling to clients, and there are doctoral level psychology programs with clinical, counseling, and developmental applied emphases. We discuss these distinctions more fully in Chapters 11 and 12. Is there enough professional common ground to write an ethics book applicable across these domains?

Although exactly what should be taught in graduate ethics classes for helping professionals is still a somewhat open question (Urofsky & Sowa, 2004), we believe there is significant common ground to explore. At the core of this enterprise we call counseling is an attempt to be of professional help to other human beings. We might be helping them overcome a disability or trauma. We might be helping them become better students, finding their way toward fulfilling careers. We might be offering to help someone on his or her spiritual journey. We might be helping a family find healthier ways to communicate and get along. We might be helping people recognize the ways they are affected by society, empowering them to seek both healing and social change.

These counseling activities all share similar expectations for educational attainment. They also share the needs for theoretical foundations and a core of common skills (J. Sommers-Flanagan & Sommers-Flanagan, 2004b), as well as skills distinct to the disciplines and specialties. Professional helpers may vary in the tools they use and the types of needs they address, and they may have different orientations.

PROFESSIONAL ORGANIZATIONS AND ASSOCIATIONS

We are advocates of lifelong membership in professional organizations. There are a number of reasons that membership in national organizations, along with state and regional membership, is essential for the profession and the professional. Professional organizations define, develop, and defend the profession itself, and the members within them. Professional organizations are the source of ethics codes and promote the ongoing development of ethical thinking and revision. These organizations give the profession a voice in national debates over issues relevant to the profession—such as salary, insurance coverage and reimbursement, professional stature and limitations, and national and state policy affecting our clients' lives as well as our own.

The publications and conferences of national organizations provide forums for dissemination of research and scholarly endeavors and for connection with other professionals. They also offer opportunities for continuing education. Ethical professionals never stop growing, learning, debating, questioning, and developing—and professional organizations are central to these processes.

The American Counseling Association (ACA) began in 1952, although as it has grown and developed, it has gone through a few name changes. It began as an amalgamation of four independent associations: The National Vocational Guidance Association, the National Association of Guidance and Counselor Trainers, the Student Personnel Association for Teacher Education, and the American College Personnel Association. These groups joined together with the intention of gaining a larger professional membership and voice. They named this new organization the American Personnel and Guidance Association. The name later changed to the American Association for Counseling and Development and, in 1992, the American Counseling Association. ACA is a national organization encompassing 18 different divisions with one organizational affiliate. We encourage you to visit the ACA website and review the divisions and other information you will find there.

The National Association of Social Workers (NASW) was formed in 1955 by consolidating seven related professional organizations. These sister organizations had been formed for social workers who engaged in group, psychiatric, school, medical, and community social work practices (NASW, 2006). By combining into one large national organization, these groups gained strength to address the educational and political issues facing the social work profession overall. The NASW currently has 56 chapters in the United States and other countries.

The American Psychological Association (APA) began in 1892, founded by G. Stanley Hall, long before the professions of clinical or counselor psychology came into being (MacFarlane & Nierman, 2005). It currently has 53 divisions with interests and emphases ranging widely. As is true with ACA, it is possible to be a member of a division within the APA without necessarily being a member of the parent organization. Again, a visit to the website is a most interesting excursion for developing professionals.

Regardless of your training background or the kind of work you eventually do, professional identity is foundational to ethically informed and clinically responsible practice. The identity infighting among mental health professionals, which we discuss in later chapters, will probably continue throughout our professional lives. However, there is common ground to share in our efforts to responsibly and ethically meet the enormous mental health and educational needs in our cultures.

AND WHO IS THE CLIENT?

Now that we have explored various aspects of professional identity for those who provide professional counseling, it is time to turn our attention to those we serve. The heading for this section may seem a bit self-evident, but in reality this becomes an ethically salient question for many counselors.

Some time ago, we conducted a workshop on ethics for rehabilitation counselors. The participants worked for a variety of employers, including government, private for-profit companies, and nonprofit companies. One issue they wanted to discuss was: Who is our client? State or federal government? The company? Our community? Society itself? The person we've been asked to evaluate or counsel? Places of employment where people were injured? The person with a disability or injury?

School counselors frequently ask similar questions, generating a slightly different list of potential "clients." This list might include students, teachers, administrators, parents, or the community (Mitchell, Disque, & Robertson, 2002). It gets even more complex when one considers teaching, forensic work, consultation, and supervision. One reason the "Who is the client?" question is so germane to ethics is that ethics codes do not necessarily offer a clear definition of the term *client*. Consequently, counselors who wish to behave ethically need clarity on their legal and ethical obligations to all stakeholders in their professional work.

A common assumption is that a client is someone who pays a professional for a certain kind of services. "Counseling and psychotherapy clients purchase counseling ser-

```
════════════ Deepening Diversity 1.1 ════════════

                    Client or Visitor?
```

In Mandarin, as is probably true of many languages, there is no direct translation for the word client as it is commonly used in the mental health professions.
Some years ago, we discovered that our clinical interviewing text had been
translated into Mandarin when a few complimentary copies showed up in the
mail (J. Sommers-Flanagan & Sommers-Flanagan, 2003). Luckily, a bilingual
friend of ours was able to look through the text and share with us some of the
translation decisions that had been made. She indicated that the word client
had been translated into a word in Mandarin that would be translated back into
English as *visitor.* She explained that the options were limited. There is a Mandarin word for business relationships that would translate as client, but its con-
notations would not capture the sense of the helping relationship. There is a
Mandarin word for a person who is seeking medical help, similar to our word
patient, but that would not have conveyed the nature of the counseling relationship either. Counseling, as a professional activity, barely exists in China. As
the profession develops there, perhaps new words will capture a culturally appropriate meaning for the participants in a professional counseling relationship
in China. Until then, at least when it comes to the use of our text in China, clients will be known as visitors.

vices (either directly or indirectly)" (Welfel, 2006, p. 103). However, the reality is much
more complex than the old Nixon-era Deep Throat guidance of "Follow the money"
(Woodward & Bernstein, 1994). The English word *client* comes from the Latin root
clinare, which means to lean, or incline toward. We believe the true identity of the client is insinuated in this root meaning.

Our contention is this: While there are many stake-holders, employers, groups, and
institutions all connected to the work of the counselor, the true meaning of the word
client is the one who is in need of the counseling assistance—the person in the office
with you, or the people to whom you go to offer guidance and facilitation of growth
and development. Although you may be paid by a completely different entity, your primary ethical obligation is for the welfare of the human being(s) you have been hired to,
or have chosen to, assist.

We cover the specifics of ethical obligations to different kinds of clients later in this
book. However, it is important to note that you undoubtedly will have times in your
professional life when you will face an ethical quandary—your employer, or society,
has goals for, or wants an outcome from, your counseling work that does not match one
or more of the following:

- the goals or outcome desired by your client;
- the goals or outcome you believe to be better for your client; or
- the reality of the timeline and resources you have to work within.

Case Example: Cammy's probation officer suggested that she could end her probation earlier if she agreed to go to counseling. In fact, he located a community fund to pay your fee if Cammy agrees to get the counseling. However, the probation officer insists that he be provided with all case notes and regularly informed of Cammy's progress. You meet with Cammy and quickly realize that she has been in a number of abusive relationships, and comes from an enmeshed, intrusive family system. You firmly believe that Cammy will need to be able to disclose things from her past that you will not want to share with the probation officer. The probation officer found the money to hire you. Is he, in any way, your client? Do you owe him anything?

Case Example: Trey is a kindergartener who has occasional problems with enuresis. The kindergarten teacher is worried about the odor, stigma, and the disruption. She wants Trey to meet with you to solve this problem. Trey's mother, having been shamed as a youth due to her enuresis problems, insists there is no problem because wetting one's pants on occasion is perfectly normal. She wants you to work with Trey to understand that he should not be ashamed of wetting his pants. The principal at your school has a small discretionary fund that could be used for a medical consultation, but Trey's mother is unwilling to have Trey visit a traditional physician. She does not believe in "organized medicine." Trey doesn't like visiting you and refuses to engage in any conversation about his wet pants. Again, who is your client? Who are you working for? Who most needs your help?

If there were simple ethically and clinically correct answers to these scenarios, we would happily share them with you. However, there are many questions that would need to be asked and answered before a clinically wise and ethically sensitive decision could be made in each case. Our wish at this point is simply to raise the sticky issues associated with the work of the counselor for both the "identified" client and the other forces and interests involved. The clients in the previous cases, by our definition, are Cammy and Trey, but there are clearly many people and institutions affected by the interventions you might use, the direction the counseling takes, and the decisions you make.

Writing about the need for professional integrity, Mumford, Connelly, and Leritz (2005) note that social interventions and social exchanges involve multiple parties who have different concerns and different needs. The professional must decide whose needs and what needs must be served. "One of the ways to solve the ambiguity of competing needs and the tensions that arise between personal and social gains is to apply norms and codes of ethics" (p. 223).

Pause for Reflection

Robert Kinscherff, JD, PhD, former chair of APA's Ethics Committee, said: "Instead of worrying about the ways [they] can get in trouble, psychologists should think about ethics as a way of asking 'How can I be even better in my practice?' Good ethical practice is good professional practice, which is good risk management practice" (D. Smith, 2003, p. 50). Throughout this text, how can you translate ethics into identity and practice? Keep this quote in mind, and see, by the end of your ethics course, if you agree with Dr. Kinscherff.

CHAPTER WRAP-UP

In this chapter, we began the acculturation process that will hopefully result in integrated ethical professional counselors. These are the key points:

- The terms *ethics* and *morals* have common original meanings. A society is defined by its morality; a profession, by its ethics.
- Becoming an ethical professional is a process and a journey, requiring continuing thought and education.
- Professional identity involves socially sanctioned power and corresponding obligations. This can be a bit intimidating.
- Professional identity is stabilized and enhanced by professional membership in one's professional organizations.
- Counselors realize they serve a large constituency and are accountable to many, but must also keep in mind who the client is.

Stanley Hauerwas (1981) wrote:

The plurality of communities, moreover helps to explain the peculiar moral power of the traditional professions. If every polity derives from a corresponding training in virtue, the professions must be regarded as some of the few remaining coherent polities. That is why, in spite of claims of moral neutrality, medical and law schools survive as the closest modern analogs to the ancient schools of virtue. In the commitment to their clients' welfare through the practice of developed skills, they exemplify a training in virtue from which they derive profound self-esteem. That is why their professions become the source of their identity and justification, as occupation is one of the few areas in life which leads itself to exposition. (p. 126)

We hope this text and your ethics course serve to instill such a profound sense of professional identity and commitment to client welfare that counseling, too, will someday be listed among the professions that serve as "analog to the ancient schools of virtue."

Chapter Two

PHILOSOPHY AND CULTURE: ROOTS AND PRISMS

Ultimately ethics and morality are not about heroes and leaders and shining examples. They are about the day-to-day and moment-to-moment ways in which we conduct our own lives, and what our basic stance is toward those tendencies in our own minds that drive us toward greed, hatred, and delusion when what we most need is to tap the deeper resources of our own hearts for kindness, generosity, compassion, and goodwill.
—Jon Kabat-Zinn

CHAPTER ORIENTATION

To give you a glimpse of the tremendous sweep of human concern for the ethical or moral life, this chapter condenses stories of human moral development over thousands of years and across many cultures. In doing so, we run the risk of offending philosophers and historians by omissions and oversimplification. We also run the risk of boring or intimidating readers who have never studied moral philosophy. And, finally, we run the risk of failing to make this material accessible and relevant to the ethical practice of professional counseling. As kind and moral readers, you can significantly reduce these risks by doing the following: First, allow this chapter to simply *begin* your acquaintance with the moral positions we describe, but know that each deserves closer scrutiny as your interest develops. Then, when you read and work with the material in chapters following this one, reflect back on these moral theories and positions—begin making links between the practical details of our ethics codes and the moral reasoning they reflect. Someday, you may have the time and motivation to read original sources and current moral theorists, thus continuing to make links between your professional development as an ethical practitioner and evolving moral reasoning within our culture(s).

Specifically, in this chapter, you will have the opportunity to consider the following:

- character or virtue ethics, including the notions of character development, Aristotle's Golden Mean, the interactions of rationality, emotions, and habits, and current expressions of this approach to ethics;
- deontological ethics, including getting acquainted with Immanuel Kant and his beliefs about moral duties;
- John Rawls and his innovative approach to considering social justice;

- utilitarian or consequentialist ethics, including the contributions of early and current adherents to this view;
- the misunderstood and challenging notion of situation ethics;
- the definition and role of the principles approach;
- the diverse traditions within Asian ethics, including Hindu and Buddhist ethics, The Tao, Lao-Tzu, Chuang-Tzu, and Confucian ethics;
- African and American Indian ethical views; and finally
- feminist ethics and the ethics of care.

EXPLORING MORAL PHILOSOPHIES

Before reading this chapter, please take the Moral Orientation Questionnaire in Applications 2.1. We developed the items over years of teaching counseling ethics and facilitating professional workshops on ethics. Each multiple-choice item illustrates an aspect of one of the moral positions covered in this chapter. The questions at the end help you orient to other important considerations in moral development.

For millennia, humans have asked themselves both "Who are we?" and "What are we?" As we insisted in Chapter 1, the answers have direct implications for human morality. In the coming pages, we summarize a number of theoretical orientations (interchangeably referred to as positions, theories, or views) related to applied ethical and moral behaviors. For now, we put aside the finer distinctions between the terms *moral* and *ethical* discussed in Chapter 1 and consider them as synonymous. Many of the theories we discuss predate any distinction between the two, and were originally written in languages other than English. And the theories would not make a distinction between professional and personal behaviors. All human behaviors would come under scrutiny through these systems.

Some adherents to these positions might argue that the positions are mutually exclusive; but in our experience, it is much more complex than that. The moral reasoning entailed in the positions described in this chapter overlaps, contrasts with, and sometimes actually supports the other approaches. Rather than opposing, mutually exclusive theories, these orientations are like worldviews arising in different times, meeting different needs in the human drama. The philosopher, Santayana, said, "It is a great advantage for a system of philosophy to be substantially true" (Lewis, 1946, p. 451). The systems you will read about are substantially true, but they do not individually offer the whole truth. In your own life, both personally and professionally, you will find these orientations offering lenses through which to view a given situation. Knowing when and how to apply them is the essence of ethical wisdom. Michael Mahoney (2005) wrote:

> Psychotherapy is filled with complexity, suffering, and the challenges associated with assuming professional responsibility for understanding and counseling lives in process. Demands are placed on us by more than our clients. We may often feel as though we were playing ball on running water. Just remaining off the rocks is challenge enough. When we encounter rapids, philosophy may seem remote and irrelevant to what we are doing. It is not. (p. 338)

Applications 2.1

Moral Orientation Questionnaire

For each of the following items, choose the answer that best fits with your personal philosophy. Please note that your answers will likely reflect your current understanding of ethics; wherever you find yourself today, trust that it will change—and remember, there is no single "correct" answer. This quiz is designed to give you insight into yourself. After reading this chapter, be sure to check back and see which philosophical position your answers align with most closely.

1. The best way to accomplish good things in the world is to:
   a. emulate the best qualities of really virtuous people, while paying close attention to developing your own unique talents so that you can contribute positively to the world in your own way.
   b. make sure you do your duty in any morally demanding situation. Never, *ever* do anything that exploits other people. Never do anything that you wouldn't allow everyone to do if they faced the same decision as you.
   c. size up each situation you find yourself in, and do the most loving, caring thing possible, given the set of circumstances.
   d. take serious stock of the outcomes of your actions. Always choose to act in a way that will promote the best possible outcomes for the good of the community as a whole.
   e. do what God/Allah/your Deity would advise is right.
   f. do what will enhance your own life quality or situation.
   g. act in ways that enhance healthy, connected, human relationships
2. The worst possible evil in the world occurs when:
   a. people take the easy way out and do not do their duty.
   b. people do what seems to them as right, but they ignore the overall outcome and costs of their actions.
   c. people choose their own way, rather than considering the needs and wishes of those close to them.
   d. people ignore the will of God/Allah/their Deity.
   e. people ignore their own needs and happiness and defer to others.
   f. people waste their talents and fail to notice the great virtues possible in people around them.
   g. people fail to act in the most loving, kind ways possible, ignoring the demands of a given situation.
3. If you must make a very hard decision that affects the welfare of others around you, the best guide to follow is/are:
   a. the commandments of a supreme being.
   b. your own heart.
   c. to determine your duty, including the law, ethics codes, and so on, and then do that duty, no matter what the outcome might be.
   d. with others, to take the best guess as to what will bring about the greatest good for the most people, or for the community overall.

=== **Applications 2.1 (continued)** ===

    e. assess what will be best for your own needs in the long run.

    f. consider the implications of your actions on those closest to you.

    g. consult with the wisest, most morally developed person you know, and then do what that person would do.

4. Among the following choices, which maxim would you choose to communicate to a child you love deeply?

    a. Always do your duty.

    b. Submit to God's will.

    c. Always consider the costs of your actions on your family and those you love.

    d. Look out for Number One. No one else will.

    e. The only law is the Law of Love.

    f. Your character and reputation are your most valuable gifts. Never squander them.

    g. Act in ways that will bring about the greatest good possible in the world.

In terms of Truth, rank each of these statements from 1 (not true) to 5 (completely true).

_3_ Even if the outcome for you or your loved ones was going to be awful, you should do what you know to be the right thing to do.

_1_ It doesn't matter what happens to you, or me, or anyone else. What matters is doing God's will.

_1_ The truth of the matter is that all people will always choose to act in their own best self-interest. If we just admitted that, and stopped pretending otherwise, that would be great.

_5_ The world is imperfect. Our laws are imperfect. We have to always have an eye to acting in ways that will bring about the best overall outcome in the face of such imperfection.

_V_ Humans are born with an amazing "blue print" and are meant to become wiser, kinder, and more deeply moral as they mature. True morality consists of pursuing this maturity through self-discipline and imitation of great moral leaders.

_5_ There can be no absolutes, or even many hard and fast rules, because each human situation has its own unique characteristics and moral behavior must be constantly responsive to the circumstances and the details.

_X_ Humans are meant to live in close, caring, mutually respectful relationships. When relationships are trampled upon, justice is impossible.

Do you think most people behave morally most of the time? _2_

Do you think most people BELIEVE they behave morally most of the time? _4_

Who (or what) has been the greatest influence in your own moral development? _parents_

How do you believe most people decide what is morally acceptable behavior? _instinct_

We begin with the three orientations commonly discussed in applied ethical theory: *virtue, deontological,* and *utilitarian* orientations. We also cover a less common position called *situation* ethics, and explain principle-driven bioethics. Briefly, we highlight traditional Asian, American Indian, and African moral views, and include a short feminist critique, explaining the *ethics of care* that arose from feminist work in the field. Of course, there is a significant relationship between religion and ethics. There are other orientations of significant influence, such as social-contract and natural-law positions, that we will not cover in this text. Remember, you do not need to choose among the different theories or approaches. Your job is to determine how to best integrate the theories into your own professional work. Some people find their ethical perspective within religious or spiritual beliefs, while others find their ethical perspective without involving a deity or transcendental knowledge. No matter how adamant you might be about the accuracy of your own ethical perspective, rest assured, many others are just as adamant about theirs.

CHARACTER OR VIRTUE ETHICS

Those who generally use character (or virtue) ethics ask themselves the basic question, "What is a good person, and what does it take to become a good person?" Such questions have been posed for a very long time—from Homer, to the writers of the New Testament, to Ben Franklin (MacIntyre, 1998a). Even though philosophers and writers of moral teachings before and after Aristotle equated morality with who a person *is,* rather than what a person *does,* he is given credit for the earliest and most complete articulation of this position. Aristotle was born in 384 BCE and studied in Athens with his mentor, Plato, later founding his own school in Lyceum.

For Aristotle, the ultimate and highest moral outcome of existence is for people to become what they were meant to be, both specifically and more generally. At the pragmatic level, he believed that people have many diverse callings and gifts, and will therefore become craftsmen, military officers, scholars, and so forth. But beyond and above these careers, Aristotle believed that mature humans are meant to grow into their full potential, which will bring about profound happiness, or *eudaimonia.* As James Burtness (1999) explains, "When Aristotle talks about eudaimonia, he is talking about total well-being in which the whole self flourishes, including the total society in which that self is nourished" (p. 85). So how is it that humans achieve this state of happiness? They achieve it, at least in part, by becoming virtuous—because for Aristotle, the fully actualized or fulfilled human is a virtuous human being. In fact, being steadily and purely virtuous is evidence that the human has reached the highest pinnacle of human development. In this sense, as the saying goes, virtue is its own reward.

Most people can recognize at least a small tendency toward this view within themselves. Think about a situation in which you have done what you know to be "the right thing," even though it may have been a struggle. Often that action is accompanied by an internal feeling of pride and satisfaction. That's the action and feeling that Aristotle says we should strive to achieve.

Defining Virtue

At this point, you might be wondering exactly what Aristotle meant by virtue. Aristotle identified many moral virtues, or attributes of good character, but they weren't explained as stand-alone traits. Rather, Aristotle believed that virtue exists in the middle of human extremes. Digressions for Deliberation 2.1 offers examples of virtues, their sphere of action or feeling, and descriptions of deficiency and excess.

Many of the terms used to describe Aristotle's virtues are no longer in common usage, so we've taken some liberties in Digressions for Deliberation 2.1. If you take the

---

Digressions for Deliberation 2.1

ARISTOTLE'S ETHICS

A TABLE OF VIRTUES, DOMAINS and EXTREMES

Domain	Virtue	Too Much	Too Little
Responsiveness to what happens to others (good or bad)	Righteousness Indignation/ Empathic balance	Envy or retreat	Malice or indifference
Desire for Pleasure (Food/drink/sex)	Tasteful moderation Temperance	Self-indulgent Piggishness	No appreciation or recognition of good things
Sharing Resource	Generosity	Extravagant/ Show-off	Stinginess/ Meanness
Confidence in Self	Courage	Rash Risk Taking	Cowardice
Desire to connect with or please others	Friendliness	Groveling/ Ingratiating	Hostile/Bristly
Self Care and Pride	Ambition and valid pride	Vanity/ Boasting	Lack of ambition/ false humility
Emotional Regulation (especially anger)	Patience/Even-temper	Touchy/easily set off	Lack of spirit/ Apathetic
Self-representation	Honesty	Boastfulness/ Bragging	Fake modesty
Social Conversation or desire to amuse others	Goof-off at any cost/ Buffoon	Quick Witted/ Warmly funny	Boring/ unable to tell or understand a joke
Susceptibility to Shame	Modesty	Bashful/shy	Shameless/bold

revised from: Aristotle, 1955, p. 104.

time to consider the domains, the virtues, and the deficits or excesses, you might come up with your own terms for the same basic concepts. Aristotle's grasp of human nature has stood the test of time.

Character Development

After considering the dimensions of Aristotle's sense of virtue, the next question might be: How does a person become virtuous? For Aristotle, the answer is similar to the command issued to all aspiring musicians and athletes. Practice! Of course, this means a conscious, rational choice to act in a certain way, over and over again. For Aristotle, virtuous character development is accomplished when you exercise rational control over yourself and work consciously on developing virtuous habits. For example, you may find it difficult to be kind and nonjudgmental toward certain difficult clients. If you want to be a kind professional, offer kindness even when you are exhausted, haven't had your morning coffee, or the client needing kindness has just sworn vehemently at you. Over time, what feels difficult to do will become easier.

According to Aristotle, virtuous acts are part of the fabric of the person—part of the ongoing development of character that virtuous people undertake. That is why he thought that we could figure out what to do by watching people of sustained good character.

Pause for Reflection

Which virtues do you believe might be most important to being a morally advanced professional? Are there some that seem more difficult to develop? Which would you value most highly if you were choosing your own therapist?

The Golden Mean

As you can see from Digressions for Deliberation 2.1, a central aspect of Aristotle's description of the virtuous life is his notion of the Golden Mean. Aristotle believed that virtue lies not only in rational assessment, but also in moderation. For example, courage is a virtue. Too little courage leaves one in danger. Too much courage can be foolhardy, and just as dangerous. Generosity is a virtue. Too little generosity leaves one a miser, but too much generosity, especially without careful rational assessment, can leave one in need of other's charity, or can set one up for giving to unjust causes.

One of our favorite examples is Aristotle's explanation of a virtuous social skill he called "ready wit." You might run a tally in your mind to see which faculty members and which of your fellow students might qualify as ready-witted, using the following guide from Aristotle (1980):

Those who carry humour to excess are thought to be vulgar buffoons, striving after humour at all costs, and aiming rather at raising a laugh than at saying what is becoming and at avoiding pain to the object of their fun; while those who can neither make a joke themselves nor put up with those who do are thought to be boorish and unpolished. But those who joke in a tasteful way are called ready-witted, which implies a sort of readiness to turn this way and that; for such sallies are thought to be movements of the character, and as bodies are discriminated by their movements, so too are characters. (p. 103)

If Aristotle's thoughts were reduced to various sound bites or bumper stickers, "Moderation in all things" and "Be all you can be" would clearly be among them. These are mottos echoed by many later religious and moral thinkers and writers—and recently borrowed by certain advertising agencies as well.

Rationality, Emotions, and Habits

Although Aristotle took into account the impact of emotions on our actions, it is important to remember the emphasis on rational choice. As he wrote, ". . . the virtues arise in us neither by nature nor against nature. Rather, we are by nature able to acquire them, and reach our complete perfection through habit" (Irwin, 1985, p. 34). Aristotle counseled that we could only become virtuous people because of inborn potential, but that good character does not just happen. We have to consciously strive to develop that part of ourselves.

There is an interesting parallel belief expressed in ancient Indian thought. In a book exploring Hindu ethics, Roy Perrett (1998) discusses the notion of karma as it applies to the consequences of our actions. He states, ". . . we are bound by our actions (karma) insofar as we are the victims of our habits. The central (and plausible) assumption is we wish to replace a life of reaction with one of response" (p. 21). Perrett is speaking of lessons drawn from the Bhagavad Gita (Song of the Lord), which was composed about the fifth century BCE and is considered the centerpiece for Hindu thought. Perrett notes that in the karmic sense, without conscious, rational intention, our actions bring about consequences that then bring about further actions. Aristotle would agree. We must rationally choose virtuous actions and practice them—thus consciously becoming a virtuous person, while increasing our good karma! It is important to remember that habit without thought can lead us down the wrong path, but that rational practice of good habits leads to virtue.

Doing the Right Thing

Character ethicists readily acknowledge that humans often display lack of willpower. Aristotle addressed this weakness of will, or as his translators call it, *incontinence.* We all suffer from occasional incontinence in the Aristotelian sense of the word. Helping professionals might find themselves gossiping or making fun of a client. They might tell a lie in order to avoid admitting an error. Few people deliberately choose to become corrupt or unethical, but doing the right thing is not always simple or easy. Even though Socrates (who was Plato's teacher) believed that if we deeply and completely know what is right, we will always do it, most of us have experiences in opposition to this belief. Humans are famously able to rationalize their actions when they know the right thing to do, but fail to do it. In Chapter 3, we include a list by Pope and Vasquez (1998), detailing rationalizations for ethical incontinence by mental health professionals.

Although moral incontinence is not admirable, it is not, from an Aristotelian point of view, as bad as intended wrong-doing. There is a significant difference between the person who knows what is right, intends to do it, but is overcome by fear or desire, and a person who intentionally pursues excessive gain (like insurance fraud) or selfish pleasure (like sex with clients). With practice, it is possible to build up strength of character and come closer and closer to always doing the right thing. But if you intentionally ignore the right thing, aiming instead for quick gratification or self-gain, there is little hope of becoming a virtuous person or professional.

Another important aspect of Aristotle's guidance about becoming virtuous is this: To learn how to be courageous, you must find a person whom the community has agreed is courageous. Then, model yourself after this person who has such highly developed courage. This has direct relevance for those seeking the best education and supervision throughout professional life. To become the very best counselor you can be, find an excellent, mature, highly skilled counselor to emulate. Get the best supervision and continuing education available. And of course, practice!

Current Expressions of Character Ethics

Many books, Internet sites, and teaching curricula are devoted to encouraging character development through education and practice. Each offers a slightly different list of virtues and prescribes various methods for helping oneself or others become more virtuous. The increased interest in virtue, character, and moral values in our culture has not necessarily translated into increased moral behaviors. Research indicates that rates of cheating in high school and college are increasing (Mustaine & Tewksbury, 2005). Incidence rates of child abuse and rape remain disturbingly high (Sebre et al., 2004). Lying or misrepresentation of the facts in advertising and political campaigning is not only tolerated—it is now an expected phenomenon (Kilbourne, 1999; Winneg, Kenski, & Jamieson, 2005).

Against this backdrop, many authors, researchers, school counselors, and teachers are attempting to explore and enhance character and moral development in our society. Among the more notable is Robert Coles, a Harvard child psychiatrist who has studied the moral development of children for over 30 years. Those of you whose professional lives will involve helping families and children, and those of you who are or will be involved in raising children, will certainly come face to face with the complex questions of moral development in humans.

DEONTOLOGICAL ETHICS

Though you may not have heard the term, it is likely that you have either thought like a deontologist at some point in your life, or have had a deontologically based judgment leveled at you. Deontological ethics holds that there are moral duties that apply to all people in all times and places. From a deontological perspective, you would ask yourself: Am I making the kind of choice that fulfills my duty? Is this the action I would want everyone to take, regardless of the circumstances? The deontological stance is one that emphasizes doing what is right and doing one's duty, not based on outcome or preference. As children, in the Brownie Scout troop, Little League, or as members of 4-H, we

---

Digressions for Deliberation 2.2

Common Childhood Pledges (as remembered by authors)

The Brownie Scout Pledge (circa 1963): I promise, on my honor, to do my duty to God and my country; to help other people every day, especially those at home.

The 4-H Pledge (circa 1965): I pledge my head to greater thinking, my heart to greater loyalty, my hands to larger service, and my health to better living, for my club, my community, and my country.

The Little League Pledge: I trust in God. I love my country, and will respect its laws. I will play fair and strive to win. But win or lose, I will always do my best. Play ball!

---

remember reciting the pledges in Digressions for Deliberation 2.2, which provide examples of a deontological—or duty-focused—worldview.

Kant and Moral Duties

Immanuel Kant (1724–1804) is the name most directly associated with a deontological approach. Although reading Kant's original works can be daunting, we dutifully recommend his essay called *Lectures on Ethics* (Kant, 1963) because it so fully illustrates the core tenants and style of Kant's approach. Kant is the original "just do it" moral philosopher. Regardless of how one feels about it, and regardless of outcome, Kant believed there are some moral duties that are applicable at all times and in all places. Some actions are morally wrong, no matter where or when they are enacted, and some are right. Kant wrote, ". . . if a law is to have moral force, that is, to be the basis of an obligation, it must carry with it absolute necessity . . ." (p.276). For Kant, there could be no exceptions or mitigating circumstances interfering with pure moral law.

Kant also understood that we are mere mortals, incapable of doing the right thing all of the time. All he asks of us (and it is a lot) is to be aware of when we are failing to do the right thing. For example, Kant argues that lying *always* causes some damage, even if that damage is no more than the liar knowing that he is choosing to do something wrong. But Kant also knew that people lie. He did not expect humans to completely stop lying, but he did urge people to consciously admit that they were not making the most moral choice. For Kant, lying was never, under any circumstances, morally correct.

Of course, the big question is this: How do we know which actions qualify as always morally correct? Kant came up with a guide for judging moral actions, and in keeping with his overall worldview, he named this guide the *categorical imperative,* meaning that an absolute moral maxim can be neither hypothetical nor optional. The categorical imperative is the ultimate yardstick against which you could measure any action to check the morality of the action. One of his formulations of the categorical imperative is this: *So act that you could will your action to be a universal law for all humankind* (Abbott, 1998).

You can certainly hear echoes of the Golden Rule, the statement of Jesus recorded in Luke 6, verse 31, "Do unto others as you would have them do unto you" (Metzger & Murphy, 1994, p. 88), as well as echoes of your parents saying, "Now how would you like it if everybody acted like you're acting?"

As Kant develops the notion of his categorical imperative, he offers another version that, correctly applied, should yield the same guidance. It is this: *So act as to treat humanity, whether yourself or another person, as an end-in-itself, never as a means only.* In his essay, Kant uses four moral dilemmas to illustrate the use of both versions of the categorical imperative, including:

- Choosing whether to break a promise when it would advantage you to do so
- Considering suicide when in terrible pain
- Giving to the needy when you have more than enough
- Taking the easy way through life, rather than developing one's talents fully

Pause for Reflection

If you take a minute to reason your way through these choices, you will find yourself wanting to add details, contextualize, add caveats, and be less than conclusive. Kant would not let you off the hook. Is suicide a moral choice? Can you lie to a client to help save face? Remember, you cannot answer, "It depends."

Kant argued that even though there will be compelling practical or emotional factors in a given situation, it is our duty to consider the action through the lens of "always, everywhere, for everyone." Regardless of the circumstances, and regardless of the outcome, there are moral actions that are always right or always wrong. Of course, Kant recognized that we would not always be able to comply with what was truly correct, but he believed it is important that we not excuse our actions away, but rather take responsibility for our less than ideal choices.

Kant also believed that ethical principles apply to *anyone* capable of deliberation and reason. He believed there were three ways rational beings could interact with their duty, but only one would yield moral behavior.

1. They could act in ways that are clearly inconsistent with human moral duty—actions such as lying, cheating, stealing, or torturing people. Counselors deliberately exploiting their clients would be another example.

2. They could act in accordance with duty—holding to the letter of the law, but ignoring the spirit of the law (Fletcher, 1966). An example of this might be a counselor who works with a client from another culture because she wants to appear to be broad-minded and accepting. She would be doing the act for her own sake, not purely from her sense of duty.

3. They could act from, or because of their duty—if the counselor previously mentioned agreed to work with a client from another culture because she knew it was her duty to do so, even though she felt shy, or had to seek extra supervision to be knowledgeable, Kant would say she acted from her duty.

What it comes down to is the motivation behind your action: You can purposefully do what you know to be wrong, you can do what you know to be right but only because other people are watching, or you can struggle to do what you know to be right just because you know it is the right thing to do. Some people are simply not motivated to take moral action. And many people are much more invested in doing the right thing because others are watching them than they are in doing the right thing because it is the right thing to do. Or, they are more likely to do the right thing if it makes them happy, or they were naturally inclined to behave that way anyway, or it benefits them directly in some way. For Kant, acting morally is a question of both will and motive. The most ethically ideal acts are those you must will yourself to do. Do the right thing for the right motives. Then you have acted morally. In fact, the less benefit you derive from doing your duty, and the less you actually want to do it, the more you can be sure your action is truly moral. While Kant was sympathetic to the struggle involved in doing the right thing, he was clearly not a behaviorist!

Kant noted that the scriptures command us to love our neighbor as ourselves, and even further, to love our enemies. He commented, as cited by Abbot (1998):

> For love, as an affection, cannot be commanded, but beneficence for duty's sake may, even though we are not impelled to it by any inclination—nay, are even repelled by a natural and unconquerable aversion. This is practical love, and not pathological—a love which is seated in the will, and not in the propensions of sense—in principles of action and not of tender sympathy; and it is this love alone which can be commanded. (p. 282)

This quotation links Kant to a more recent philosophical position called situation ethics, which we will discuss later in the chapter.

In his book *The Elements of Moral Philosophy,* James Rachels (1986) writes that one of Kant's lasting contributions is the notion that individuals cannot make themselves into special cases. We cannot argue that we are morally allowed to do something while others are not. Rachels proposed that a perhaps less troublesome way to approach deontological moral reasoning would be to only violate absolute rules for reasons that everyone would agree to be acceptable.

John Rawls and Social Justice

In Chapter 1 we discussed the dialectic between universal absolutes and multicultural perspectives, citing the United Nations' Declaration of Human Rights. The problems in arriving at potential universals are monumental. John Rawls, recently deceased Professor Emeritus from Harvard, proposed a method that free and rational persons could use to establish a just society. His ideas provide another way of thinking about Kant's categorical imperative. What Rawls (1998) proposed was a hypothetical scenario where all those concerned were in what he called the original position, described here:

> Among the essential features of this situation is that no one knows his place in society, his class position, or social status, nor does anyone know his fortune in the distribution of national assets and abilities, his intelligence, strength, and the like. (p. 622)

Rawls imagined that if free and rational people could be temporarily separated from all the attributes that made them unique, and see the world from behind this "veil of ignorance," they would create a just society. Think about it. If you did not know your sex, race, financial status, size, sexual orientation, abilities, family situation, talents, and so on, and you were asked to make rules about how people should treat each other and get along, you would have no motives other than fairness. You would want to protect yourself, no matter who you were, where you lived, or what advantages or disadvantages you faced.

Of course, it is not possible to actually get ourselves into this original position or see the world through the veil of ignorance. However, the image provides another way to try and remove our self-interests in the pursuit of pure morality and a just society.

Kant and those who advocate a deontological position offer an important piece of the ethics picture. However, there is an insistent, idealistic flavor to this position that can be alternately irritating and comforting. Sometimes, when reading Kant, we are reminded of an old joke. Apparently, there were new arrivals on a tour of Heaven (or Nirvana, or the Enlightened Place). People from all sorts of backgrounds seemed to be mingling and enjoying themselves in one large area, which the tour passed happily through. Then the tour guide got on his tiptoes, motioned for the group to be quiet, and opened a door to let the new arrivals have a quick peek inside. "Shhhh," he said. "These are the _____s. They think they're the only ones here. We don't want to disappoint them."

We did not fill in the blank out of a wish to avoid offending any group, but sometimes the attempt to impose absolutes on ourselves or others can lead to a type of exclusionary ignorance. Absolutes are hard to define, and even at their best, absolute moral rules are messier and more complicated than their definitions might suggest. Rigid adherence to a set of "true all the time, true no matter what" kinds of rules may lead to perhaps questionable stances of moral superiority or narrow-mindedness. On the other hand, most humans feel the need for some small corner of moral assuredness—of stability. Most of us want to believe there are *Right* or *Correct* ways to behave—and wouldn't mind a guarantee and a rich reward in heaven, or a better reincarnation next time around. In the end, we are probably all a little deontological, whether we admit it or not.

Pause for Reflection

Although it might be nice if we were all perfectly and completely humble, such is not the case. When do you suffer from moral superiority syndrome? Which groups get your secret or overt scorn? Smokers? Health fanatics? The poor? The rich? Republicans, Democrats, environmentalists, ranchers? Of course, we are not suggesting that you must be equally accepting of everyone in the world. However, we are suggesting that you be aware of your occasional lapses of intolerance or your more damning judgments.

UTILITARIAN OR CONSEQUENTIALIST ETHICS

Taking a completely different tact in negotiating ethical concerns, a utilitarian or consequentialist approach focuses on the end result—the likely outcome of the act. The intention is to bring about the greatest good for the greatest number, so the question is: "Given this morally demanding situation, what action will make things come out the best for the most people?" Another term used for this position is *teleological* ethics, meaning the study of the end state or outcome.

The Contributions of Jeremy Bentham and John Stuart Mill

The utilitarian ethical position is obviously socially oriented. The greatest good is not considered via an internal equation that excludes others—one must create an equation that assesses the pain/pleasure ratio for all affected parties. The first name associated with this position is the Englishman, Jeremy Bentham (1748–1832), who was unapologetically straightforward in his assertion that pleasure or happiness was the "substance" that should be measured in this equation (T. I. White, 1988). To evaluate the moral merits of one action over another action, you have to assess how many people would be made happy, or be given pleasure by each action. Thomas White quotes Bentham, "Nature has placed mankind under the governance of two sovereign masters, pain and pleasure. It is for them alone to point out what we ought to do . . ." (p. 43).

Bentham's thinking was heavily influenced by the enormous social upheaval that gripped 18th-century England. He witnessed tremendous affliction all around him and sought a basis for morality that was both practical and social in nature (Barad & Roberson, 2001). Bentham's claim was that all acts and institutions must justify themselves by their utility—hence, the label "utilitarian."

John Stuart Mill (1806–1873) was Jeremy Bentham's godson and Bentham was a close friend of the Mill family. Mill was thoroughly indoctrinated with Bentham's views but came to believe that Bentham was wrong on one important point. Bentham believed that all pleasure was of the same kind and worth. Mill argued that some forms of human pleasure were of higher quality than others, and therefore worth more in the utilitarian equation. His utilitarian position argued for the betterment of all humankind. Mill believed that the potential for an orientation toward prosocial goodness was either inborn, or could be acquired as readily as speech or other learned human functions.

Paraphrasing Mill in his essay "The greatest happiness principle," one would argue that humans have a deeply rooted conception of themselves as social beings. People tend to want to be in harmony with their fellow human beings. When there are disharmonies, it is because of differences in "opinion and mental culture" (Albert, Denise, & Peterfreund, 1975, p. 249), but at their core people want the best for each other and are inclined to promote the common good.

Current Adherents and Approaches

Modern day consequentialists also no longer try to quantify or qualify pleasure in a specific equation. James Burtness (1999), openly Christian Senior Lecturer at Luther Seminar and an avowed consequentialist (teleologist), offers this definition:

> Teleological methods understand morality as having to do with actions thought to have high degrees of probability to bring about outcomes that will increase the common good and decrease human ills. (p. 76)

In contrast to deontological approaches, consequentialists abandon any claim to moral certainty. "Morality is a fluid and porous social institution" (p. 80). How could anyone assume moral certitude in an uncertain world? According to Burtness, the best we can hope for is finding the greatest balance of good over evil in a world that has no perfection, no absolute goodness.

Counselors who focus on practices and research that promote wellness are working for both the individual and the common good. Prevention and early intervention in life problems benefit the individual and cost society far less than later, more expensive interventions (Hillier, Fewell, Cann, & Shephard, 2005). Many social reform movements can be seen as expressions of broadly defined consequentialist thinking. The welfare of the weak and disenfranchised members of society is counted as having equal weight and import in the overall fabric of society. For instance, Mill (1992) along with his wife, Harriet Taylor, was an early and articulate advocate for equal rights for women.

> . . . the principle which regulates the existing social relations between the two sexes—the legal subordination of one sex to the other—is wrong in itself, and now one of the chief hindrances to human improvement; and it ought to be replaced by a principle of perfect equality, admitting no power or privilege on the one side, nor disability on the other. (p. 471)

Democracy, as a form of government, could also be seen as an expression of utilitarian orientation. Robert Bellah and his coauthors (1996) have pointed out that the right to vote in a democracy is one in which we ask the individual to assess and support the common good. If a politician makes decisions based only on personal gain, we consider that politician corrupt. This is equally true of the voter who votes not for the common good, but for personal gain. We are charged to decide what is best for the whole community.

In summary, consequentialists view the moral worth of an action based on an assessment of the impact and the outcome for those affected. This requires us to go beyond our own desires and preferences to an objective standpoint (Singer, 1993). Some actions may be judged to be absolutely right, or absolutely wrong, but this is because these actions will absolutely bring about misery for the majority, *not* because the action is inherently wrong in and of itself.

SITUATION ETHICS

In this short section, we cover an ethical position called situation ethics. Because of its name, many people assume this is just a term used to describe people who do whatever they feel like doing in any given situation. Instead, it is actually the name of a demanding moral position promoted by Joseph Fletcher in his book *Situation Ethics: A New Morality* (Fletcher, 1966). Fletcher's basic thesis is this: The highest moral act in a given situation is one that is based on love for everyone involved. Okay, we admit that he wrote in the 1960s, and yes, it sounds quite suspect, if not outright flaky, but after consideration, you will see that Fletcher's position is closely related to the other ethical positions, and not nearly as permissive or easy as it might seem. His use of the word *love* most closely approximates the definition of the Greek word, agape, which means selfless concern and compassion for all humankind.

The basic question asked by situation ethicists is this: Given all that I know about moral rules, and given the unique demands of this situation, what is the most selfless, compassionate, loving act possible? Fletcher believed that there was a loving action available in every situation. He rejected both *legalistic approaches,* rooted in law and tradition, and *lawlessness* (antinomianism), which may offer freedom and creativity, but has no foundation or basis for justifying one's actions. He wrote, "Our obligation is relative to the situation; but obligation in the situation is absolute" (Fletcher, 1966, p. 27).

Many philosophers and religious leaders throughout history, including Aristotle, Thomas Jefferson, and Fletcher, assert that humans are created with the capacity to behave virtuously. While the capacity to make loving, compassionate, virtuous choices is inborn, the abilities necessary to discern and enact these choices are learned. Fletcher presupposes the kind of virtuous development Aristotle advocated and a working knowledge of the rules and customs of one's culture. But Fletcher goes beyond the character development and the knowledge of the rules.

He points out that moralistic or legalistic people comfort themselves by "playing by the rules," paying attention to the finest details of the letter of the law while hypocritically pursuing their own interests or ignoring the bigger picture—similar to Kant's doing one's duty for the appearance of it. Fletcher's book is full of examples of how rigidly obeying rules and laws can lead to terrible, cruel outcomes. He provides a compelling argument for the inclusion of the particulars of any circumstance, noting that authentic morality will sometimes need to break the rules, in the name of the only universal law—the law of love. Fletcher also argues against antinomianism, or lawlessness, in moral decision-making, quoting William Temple, who wrote:

> Universal obligation attaches not to particular judgments of conscience but to conscientiousness. What acts are right may depend on circumstances . . . but there is an absolute obligation to will whatever may on each occasion be right. (1934; as cited by Fletcher, 1966, p. 27)

On the surface, the situation ethics edict to act in the most loving manner possible in all situations may seem easy. We need to cultivate the virtues, understand the moral maxims, *and* include the particular demands of any situation. We then need to explain how our action was the truest, most moral, and most loving action available to us, regardless of the rules or our own needs or desires. Some might even argue that Fletcher offers a sort of modern-day hybrid of Mill, Kant, and Aristotle. Rather than let us off the hook, the situation ethics orientation may be the most demanding of all.

THE PRINCIPLES APPROACH

Before we give an overview of bioethics, it is important to review the layered notion of morality covered in Chapter 1. There are high level, abstract principles in the ethical positions previously discussed. There are many ways to state them, but their essence stays the same. Always do your duty. Always consider what's best for people. Strive to

eeply moral, virtuous character. Out of these principles flow rules, laws, and
1 other words, in behavioral terms, the principles get operationalized as en-
equired, or prohibited action. However, it is actually a two-way street. The
and legal rules can be observed for radically different reasons. For instance,
you might give ten percent of your income to charity because:

- It is everyone's duty to give to charity. It would be a wonderful world if everyone gave ten percent of his or her income to charity.
- Giving to charity is a loving, selfless choice.
- Giving to charity is better than being taxed by the government, or than letting people go hungry. It is good to give ten percent because then most people can feel good about their efforts to help and many who need it will be helped.
- Giving to charity is an exercise in generosity, which is a key trait in the virtuous adult. Virtuous people like Mother Theresa and Gandhi provide great examples of generous spirits.

Pause for Reflection

Which of the preceding reasons for giving ten percent of your income to charity matches which orientation you just read about? Using two or more of the theories, try articulating a rationale for this moral rule: "Counselors should be honest with their clients." Notice how evaluating an action can flow back to the theory, just as the theory can flow out into action.

BIOETHICS AND MID-LEVEL PRINCIPLES

In the late 1970s, a subfield of applied ethics came into being that has been central in guiding ethical decision-making in the fields of medicine and biological research and application. This approach rests in between concrete rules and higher-level theory. Bio-ethics theorists identified mid-level moral principles that they use to enact the more general principles flowing from the ethical positions discussed thus far in this chapter. Having mid-level, or second order, principles is not the same as having a set of rules to follow. Rather, if you believe the mid-level principle is relevant to making a moral decision, you seek to develop an action that is in keeping with the principle. You still might subject the action to an assessment through the lens of one of the overarching theories.

As this specialty field has grown and developed, the number of mid-level principles named has varied according to author, but Tom Beauchamp and James Childress identified four in the first edition of their influential book *Principles of Biomedical Ethics* (1979, 1994, 2001). These principles are:

- Autonomy (Human beings should have authority over decisions affecting their health and well-being.)
- Beneficence (Decisions should be made on the basis of doing good and being of help to others.)

- Nonmaleficence (People should strive to do no unjustified harm.)
- Justice (All people should be treated equally and benefits and burdens should be distributed fairly.)

Other writers have suggested other principals (Kitchener, 2000), most commonly:

- Fidelity (In a professional relationship, there must be honesty, reliability, and good faith.)

Mid-level principles offer a guide for professionals who must make decisions that will directly and immediately affect the lives and well-being of patients, clients, and those seeking professional assistance or intervention. They do not offer concrete answers, but they provide a framework to begin the hard work of ethical decision-making in the face of competing needs and limited resources. Recently, some authors have suggested that perhaps these principles are better understood as values because they have intersubjective meaning and worth to us as humans, and not as objective as the term "principle" might suggest (Liegeois & Van Audenhove, 2005).

ALTERNATIVE CULTURAL VIEWS ON MORALITY AND ETHICS

So long as it is vital, the cultural tradition of a people—its symbols, ideals, and ways of feeling—is always an argument about the meaning of the destiny its members share. Cultures are dramatic conversations about things that matter to their participants . . .
—Bellah, Madsen, Sullivan, Swindler, & Tipton

In this section, we provide you with a glimpse into fascinating alternative approaches to life's meaning, the good life, and morality. Those discussed in the chapter thus far have origins that are predominantly Western European, male, and secular. This is not to say that the positions discussed are excluded from religious, feminist, or alternative practices. However, there are views, methods, theories, and practices that vary radically from the orientations discussed. But first, we should consider the role of religion.

Religion's Interactive Relationship with Ethics

Allah loves the doers of good.
—The Holy Qur'an Q:3.134

Within the wide-ranging world of spiritual and religious practices and beliefs, there are those who have a legalistic or fundamentalist orientation that informs their moral beliefs and behaviors. This might be best captured in the saying "God said it. I believe it. That settles it." Regardless of the particular religious affiliation, or the image of God, Allah, the Tao, or State of Enlightenment in question, some humans have their moral world wholly informed by their perception of what their deity (or their deity's representative) has told them to do. No other measures are invoked. No other considerations are on the table. This orientation is referred to as Divine Command theory.

For the rest of the human population in the world, the inclusion of God, spirituality, or a higher power is not such a rigid and literal enterprise. People from all over the world, with widely varying religious belief systems and cultural practices, include the notion of a higher being or consciousness in their determination of right and wrong. Further, many, if not most, of the ethical systems covered thus far have included assumptions and beliefs about a creator who functions as a central or original force in the human quest for morality. The ethicist with a religious orientation would most likely ask the same basic ethical questions named in each of the previous sections, but would add the dimension of God, or the Gods and Goddesses, and human beings' right relationship to this Being or Beings.

In the early Christian tradition, Thomas Aquinas (1225–1274) provided the basis of a moral system that draws its precepts from the created, natural order. In contrast to Aristotle's notion of natural law, Aquinas grounded the theory of natural law within the notion of eternal law, or God's perfect law. Some of the issues currently debated in our culture, including a woman's reproductive responsibilities and rights and the intended purpose of sexual intimacy and marriage, draw reasoning from Aquinas's natural law theory.

Early Islamic philosophers, like the early Christian philosophers, struggled with explaining an all-powerful, all-loving God in the face of known evil and suffering in the world. Writing a century before Thomas Aquinas, Islamic authors including al-Raghib al-Isfahani, Abu Hamid al-Ghazali, and Fakhr al-Din al-Razi blended philosophical and religious ethics, with Al-Ghazali noted as the foremost representative of this group (Fakhry, 1994). Al-Ghazali describes the road to moral and spiritual perfection as the quest for God, which involves two aspects. The seeker's actions must be governed by the prescriptions or ordinances of the "divine law" (al-shar'), and seekers must ensure that God is constantly present in their hearts. God's presence, according to al-Ghazali, means genuine contrition, adoration, and submission, born of the seeker's awareness of the beauty and majesty of God (Fakhry, 1994).

In contrast to the Christian and Islamic incorporation of Greek philosophy with religious doctrine, early Hindu philosophers predate or are writing concurrently with the early Greek systems. The earliest writings, called the Rig Veda, date back to shortly after 1500 BCE (Brannigan, 2000) and are among the first works to raise metaphysical questions concerning reality and existence. The writings include references to prayers, rituals, and right relationships to the deities named.

In 1998, Roy Perrett (1998), author of *Hindu Ethics,* wrote, "I take ethics to be fundamentally concerned with two questions: 'What ought we to do?' and 'Why ought we to do it?'" (p. 1). With this broad definition in mind, it is easy to see why the story of ethics and morality is interwoven with religious and spiritual practices and beliefs throughout history, and around the globe.

Traditional Asian Ethics

Continuing in our humbling quest to summarize vast literatures arising over centuries in cultures radically different than our own, we turn now to that enormously diverse part of the globe loosely referred to as Asia. People raised in cultures informed by Hinduism, Buddhism, and Taoism number in the billions. There are many branching doctrines and variations of the religious and philosophical practices, so just the bare basics are noted. Think of the differences in church congregational practices and beliefs, even within the same Christian denomination—even those just across town from each other. Then consider the differences between Catholic and Protestant doctrines. Then add thousands of years, vast racial, geographic, and national differences, and you begin to see how difficult it is to do justice to these general labels. Our intention is to give you wider exposure than the usual applied ethics text, and to acknowledge the wisdom and diversity in these ethical views and practices. We encourage you to take the time to read further if you would like more breadth and depth than is possible here.

Hindu Ethics

Early Hindu philosophical teachings were written down in a collection of works called the Veda, beginning approximately 3,500 years ago, with the Upanishads added in from 800 BCE to 300 BCE. Collectively, these works utilize story-telling and dialogue to describe "the nature of our relationship between our own existence and all of being" (Brannigan, 2000, p. 5).

Hindu teachings transcend time and personhood in ways unfamiliar to most Western minds. The Bhagavad Gita points out that knowledge and action should not be considered separately, but rather the wise see these as inseparable, understanding that both lead to eventual freedom (Kinnes, 2004). The ultimate goal of existence is enlightenment (*moksha*), but it is not easily attained. One passes through many lifetimes in the endless cycle of *samsara,* the wheel of birth, death, and rebirth. An important concept related to virtue is that of *karma,* which literally means "act or deed" (Brannigan, 2000, p. 23), and refers to a central moral force, or law, of cause and effect. Bad deeds and thoughts get you negative karma, while good deeds and good thoughts yield positive karma. The equation you have achieved follows you through life, into death, and influences your rebirth. The notion of karma transcends the partisan and imperfect application of justice by other humans, leaving individuals inescapably accountable for their actions.

The term *dharma* has to do with all that is morally commendable. Dharma has an emphasis on duty and obligation (Perrett, 1998) and is thought to be embodied by those said to be virtuous in society. Brannigan (2000) traces the meaning of dharma to the Hindu principle of *rita,* or universal order and harmony. He writes, "Belief in the moral order of human existence inspired a rudimentary trust that all things would eventually work out for the best" (p. 14).

Our journey through life, according to Hindu teachings, should ideally include four discrete stages. The first stage, *student,* is that of an orientation toward learning, especially learning about life's meaning and appropriate end goals. The second, *householder,* puts early adults in touch with the realities of life—children, material needs, and so on. Householders' tasks should be aligned in a way that allows householders to keep in sight life's higher meaning. After completing the stage of householder, the individual moves into the forest-dweller stage—symbolic of retreat, spiritual orientation, and the beginning of disconnection from the material demands of the world. Aging is not to be dreaded, or a time of shame and decline, but rather of renewal and the gaining of wisdom. The final stage, hermit, is one of complete withdrawal from all things material and social so that one can devote full attention to attaining moksha, or spiritual awakening.

Related to the four stages of lifelong development, Hindu beliefs teach us that there are four goals we must have in life in order to progress morally. First, we need to seek material comfort so that our basic needs are met. Should we attain wealth, we have a responsibility to use and distribute it wisely and justly. Second, we must incorporate pleasure into our lives. Third, we must always seek to live righteously, conducting ourselves with virtue in mind at all times; and finally, we should seek to fully grasp the meaning of all things—or in other words, spiritual awakening (Menski, 1996).

Probably the most famous practitioner of Hindu religion and philosophy was Mohandas Karamchand Gandhi (1869–1948). Utilizing his wisdom and commitment to nonviolence, Gandhi was central in securing the end of British rule in India, and did so out of a conviction that this arrangement was unjust and immoral. He is credited with having elaborated on the Christian concept of the seven deadly sins. He listed the following traits, which he considered to be the most spiritually and morally perilous to humanity (Houghton, Stricklin, & Morris, 1992).

- Wealth without Work
- Pleasure without Conscience
- Science without Humanity
- Knowledge without Character
- Politics without Principle
- Commerce without Morality
- Worship without Sacrifice

In contrast to the more segmented or discrete positions associated with Western traditions, Asian approaches generally, and Hindu specifically, take a much more holistic view of human character and behavior. We are but a small part of the natural order, and our essence passes through many lifetimes and life forms. All perceived reality is temporary, and our path to enlightenment is one of detachment, paved with an immutable sort of karmically determined justice.

> *Harmlessness, truth, absence of anger, renunciation, peacefulness, absence of crookedness, compassion towards beings, uncovetousness, gentleness, modesty, absence of fickleness, vigour, forgiveness, fortitude, purity, absence of hatred, absence of pride—these belong to one born in a divine state, Arjuna!*
>
> —Bhagavad Gita 16:2–3

Buddhist Ethics

During the 6th century BCE, Buddhism came into being through the teachings of Siddhartha Gautama. His enlightenment experience was one of oneness and selflessness, which led him to disavow the Hindu concept of an individual essence (atman) and multiple deities. This enlightenment occurred after trying many extreme measures, and thus Buddha referred to his path as the Middle Way, between the extremes of self-mortification and self-denial on one hand, and self-indulgence or hedonism on the other.

The central philosophical question asked by Buddhism is "Why do we experience so much dissatisfaction and suffering, and how is it possible to eliminate it?" (Zeuschner, 2001, p. 138). And the answer, in the most basic terms, is to live a moral life. The moral life entails many precepts that are offered to practitioners to seek purity of mind, speech, and body, but each individual must take full responsibility for his or her life. The fundamental cause of suffering is revealed in the Four Noble Truths:

1. All is suffering. Life, by definition, involves suffering.
2. The cause of suffering is craving, greed, or wrong attachment to goods and outcomes.
3. It is possible to stop this greedy, wrongly attached way. There is a cure.
4. The cure involves the Eightfold Path.

The Eightfold Path has precepts that are perhaps better understood as interdependent guides for developing moral and mental discipline (Brannigan, 2000). See Applications 2.2 for a summary of the Eightfold Path.

Perhaps the most famous current Buddhist is the Tibetan monk-in-exile, Tenzin Gyatso, the 14th Dalai Lama, who received the Nobel Peace Prize in 1989 for his humanitarian work, and his peaceful but steady resistance to the Chinese communist rule in his country, Tibet. His energy, wisdom, and compassion have made him a popular and well-respected global figure. His books and teachings on compassion and nonviolence are worldwide best sellers. Also very popular is Thich Nhat Hanh, a Vietnamese Buddhist monk whose teachings and books have reached many in the Western world. Currently exiled from his home country, he lives in France. He is the author of over 70 books of prayers, poetry, and prose, and was nominated for a Nobel Peace Prize. He calls his form of Buddhism "engaged Buddhism," which combines meditative practices with active nonviolent civil disobedience.

The Tao

> The movement of the Tao
> By contraries proceeds;
> And weakness marks the course
> Of Tao's mighty deeds.
>
> —Lao-Tzu, translated by James Legge

Born about the same time as the Buddha, in 551 BCE, some 70 years before Socrates, the man referred to as Confucius (K'ung Fu-tzu) began life as a son in an impoverished family of lower nobility. Long before his birth, Chinese civilization had flourished, but around the time of his birth, corruption in royalty and in the feudal leadership had led to social chaos and economic depression (Zeuschner, 2001). Born 20 years after Confucius, Lao-Tzu wrote a small book call the *Tao Te Ching,* translated as *The Classic of the Way and Its Virtue.* Rounding out the early influential Chinese philosophers is Chuang Tzu (396–286 BCE). These three philosophers offered contrasting ethical guidance, although all were linked by a common, ancient Chinese cosmology.

One important difference between Western approaches and Chinese approaches to

=== **Applications 2.2** ===

The Eightfold Path

In Buddhism, there is no God to judge, condemn, or forgive us. There is no free ride out of life's repetitive cycle of birth and death, nor easy escape from life's suffering. The justice of karma cannot be thwarted. However, if the individual is willing, there is a way out. Living morally entails the following:

Right View: All things are impermanent, and there is no self apart from the oneness of the whole of the universe. Four mistakes, or perverse views, include taking pleasure in someone else's suffering, seeing beauty in destructive or ugly things, trying to assert that we have a "self," or seeking permanence.

Right Resolve: The intention behind a deed is as important as the deed. We must have an attitude of helpfulness and compassion behind our actions. In order to have right resolve, we must constantly seek to detach from goods and outcomes.

Right Speech: Gossip is definitely unBuddhist! The moral person strives to speak kindly, wisely, and honestly. We must also strive to speak deliberately and not just chatter to fill the airways, and most importantly, we should not use our speech to harm others.

Right Conduct: Buddhists refrain from causing unnecessary harm to others, including people, animals, plants, the environment, and so on. The saying "Live simply so that others may simply live" captures the intent of both this precept and many of the others in the Eightfold Path.

Right Livelihood: Not only should Buddhist refrain from killing and harming people or the earth, they should also not earn their living in ways that contribute to harm. Obviously, it would be unlikely to find a Buddhist running a weapons factory. But even jobs that might entice others to engage in harmful behaviors are considered wrong as well.

Right Effort: Buddhists believe in free will and volition. To do right, to detach, to live compassionate lives—this takes great focus and effort. Effort expended toward these precepts is right effort, but effort expended toward avoidance, or failing to expend effort, spells trouble.

Right Mindfulness: In American culture, multi-tasking and channel-flipping are symptoms of an inability to focus on the here and now. Buddhists practice mental and bodily awareness through meditation and other awareness practices. Right mindfulness has been described as being so fully immersed in an activity that you have a sense of oneness with the activity.

Right Concentration: Finally, Buddhists seek to achieve a level of meditation wherein the mind becomes free of all thought and sensation, resting in a state of balance, oneness, and equanimity.

understanding life is the notion of causality. Western thinkers tend to link cause with effect in a linear, mechanical way. The Chinese perceive life to be more interconnected, with patterns of relationships creating order, rather than cause and effect. The word *Tao*, or The Way, describes the essential, final ordering principle of the universe. The principles of yin and yang provide an example. Yin and yang are terms used to symbolically describe pairings of what Westerners might describe as discrete opposites. Yin is the internal, hidden, dark, and receptive. Yang is the light, forceful, active, and aggressive. Nothing is entirely yin, or entirely yang. The pair cannot exist independently of each other, and the two act in harmony, not competitively (Zeuschner, 2001).

This deep, abiding harmony—the interrelationship between natural pairs in the universe, is the Tao. The highest moral attainment for a Taoist is to devote one's life to becoming wise enough to grasp the meaning of the Tao and to live life in complete harmony, attached to nothing but this harmonious Way.

Humans continually breach this harmony, causing ourselves to lose sight of this natural balance. We become fixed on judging and on valuing wealth and pleasure—all signs of false consciousness. Following the Tao is an inner process. If Western ethicists ask "How, then shall we live?" Taoists might ask "How do I live in harmony with life and with myself?"

The power of Tao has been translated as *te*, which also implies virtue. The Way is one of compassion and simplicity. When people struggle in life, physically or emotionally, Taoists believe that their ch'i, or life force, has been disrupted and is out of balance. While it is difficult for people raised in the United States to grasp this sense of harmony and balance, it might be useful for you to think about the last time you felt absolutely centered, focused, or in the zone. Athletes and artists describe the experience as "being in the flow" (Csikszentmihalyi, 2000; Voelkl & Ellis, 1998).

Confucian Ethics

The moral focus for Confucius was to reestablish the harmony of the past. His concept, *li*, was one of social order, which included respect, proper etiquette, and good manners. His concept, *jen*, was one of loving kindness, which included being benevolent, humane, and caring. It is from this concept that the Chinese draw their principle of *filial piety*, or the love, respect, and honor due to one's parent.

In the following quote, Confucius defines jen for his devoted student Chung-kung. Notice the similarities between this definition and Joseph Fletcher's Law of Love, or Immanuel Kant's categorical imperative.

> Chung-kung asked about perfect virtue, jen. The Master said "It is, when you go abroad, to behave to every one as if you were receiving a great guest; to employ the people as if you were assisting at a great sacrifice; not to do to others as you would not wish done to yourself; to have no murmuring against you in the country, and none in the family." (as cited in Brannigan, 2005, p. 296)

An important moral belief that Confucius held was related to public service. He believed all people of high moral character should seek to serve the public good. This was not to gain power or wealth, but to exercise virtue. He wrote that gentlemen understood what was moral, while "small people" understand what is profitable (Zeuschner, 2001, p. 163).

Lao-Tzu and Chuang Tzu

Both of these philosopher-poets stressed the meaninglessness and futility of trying to judge right and wrong, or good and evil, and then rid oneself of wrong or evil. These concepts do not exist without each other. If you could eliminate one, you would eliminate the other as well. Chuang Tzu (1970) wrote:

> Now do you say that you are going to make Right your master and do away with Wrong, or make Order your master and do away with Disorder? If you do, then you have not understood [ming] the principle of heaven and earth or the nature of the ten thousand things. . . . From the point of view of the Way, what is noble or what is mean? These are merely what are called endless changes. Do not hobble your will, or you will be departing from the Way. (p. 180–81)

In Asian ethics, as in the larger Asian worldview, nature and the individual are not seen as separate entities, nor are individuals seen as separate from their families and communities to nearly the extent as in Western worldviews. There is a flowing circularity and deep interconnectedness that allows a longer and wider view of life than we tend to have in Western traditions.

African Ethics

Presently, Africa is made up of 53 nations and approximately 1,200 diverse groups, each with a rich history and traditional ethos (Brannigan, 2005). Scholars of African ethics argue about the relative importance of religion in central ethical beliefs and practices (Ayantayo, 2005). While it would be impossible to delve into this debate too deeply in the context of this text, the debate itself reveals the importance religious practices hold for many Africans, with widely varied traditions.

Two intriguing ethical stances that scholars identify as common to most African cultures have to do with parenting and with relationship to one's tribe or community. In contrast to much of Western thought and practice, but reminiscent of Mill's utilitarian orientation, African cultures tend to value behaviors that are weighed with regard for the common good of the community. The very essence of identity is wrapped up in belonging to, and contributing positively to, one's group. An act is seen as immoral when it hurts or disrupts the community. Ethical systems will therefore be much more attuned to the obligations one has related to communal well-being.

A specific subset of communal well-being, of course, has to do with the way children are raised. African cultures often honor the aging process and elders much more readily than we do in our culture. Further, elders are believed to have a moral obligation to assist in the rearing of children of good character. Good character includes the ability to sacrifice one's own desires for the good of the village or community. "In learning that others come first, African children learn their most important moral lesson, and this lesson plants the seeds for the priority of community welfare over personal desires" (Brannigan, 2005, p. 328).

In African ethics there are traditional concepts very reminiscent of both Kant and the Christian "Golden Rule." From the Yoruba comes the sacred saying,

> You do it to yourself, you do it to yourself, it is to the person who throws ashes at other that the wind directs the ashes. You do it to yourself, you do it to yourself. For an evil doer succeeds only in doing half of an evil to others; the other half of evil he invariably does to himself. (M. Akin Makinde as cited in Brannigan, 2005, p. 318)

In African ethical development, there is a strong emphasis on the development of good character, but the emphasis is far more communal than Aristotle's, both in the reasons given for developing good character, and in the methods of acquisition. As you might predict, parents and elders are the source of moral instruction for the development of virtue. The virtues are learned at the feet of the elders and the parents. Also, one strives to develop good character for the good, and the health, of the community.

As a continent, Africa has faced centuries of moral and physical struggle—from people being stolen and enslaved to apartheid to genocidal wars. One amazing experiment in social justice and healing is South Africa's Truth and Reconciliation Commission. It is a story well worth knowing, and we recommend Desmond Tutu's (1999) book, *No Future without Forgiveness.* In it, he writes:

> We contend that there is another kind of justice, restorative justice, which was characteristic of traditional African jurisprudence. Here the central concern is not retribution or punishment. In the spirit of *ubuntu,* the central concern is the healing of breaches, the redressing of imbalances, the restoration of broken relationships, a seeking to rehabilitate both the victim and the perpetrator, who should be given the opportunity to be reintegrated into the community he has injured by his offense. (p. 54–55)

In this quote, it is possible to sense concern for communal well-being that connects much of African ethical thinking. The individual is not ignored, or left out of the equation, but there is equal weight given to the notion of restoring and balancing the relationships affected by crime and moral failings.

American Indian Ethics

Like Africans, American Indians span many tribes, national identities, and cultural customs. Officially, there are approximately 550 tribes currently recognized by the United States Federal Government, so of course, there are many contrasting ethical practices and beliefs. However, American Indian attorneys Gloria Valencia-Weber and Christine P. Zuni state that through their exposure to tribal commonalities, they are comfortable asserting that American Indian societies generally hold a common world view that seeks to achieve balance or harmony in all relationships (Valencia-Weber & Zuni, 1995). Published in a book that was produced and illustrated by the students of Pleasant Hill Community School in Saskatoon, Saskatchewan, and later published in the Inter-Tribal Times in 1993, the Ethics Code in Applications 2.3 captures many of the ethical practices common to American Indian and Alaskan Native tribes. However, it

---

Native American Indian Traditional Code of Ethics
(Bopp, Bopp, Brown, & Lane, 1985, p. 77–85)

1. Each morning upon rising, and each evening before sleeping, give thanks for the life within you and for all life, for the good things the Creator has given you, and for the opportunity to grow a little more each day. Consider your thoughts and actions of the past day and seek for the courage and strength to be a better person. Seek for the things that will benefit others (everyone).

2. Respect: Respect means to feel or show honor or esteem for someone or something; to consider the well being of, or to treat someone or something with deference or courtesy. Showing respect is a basic law of life.

   a. Treat every person from the tiniest child to the oldest elder with respect at all times.

   b. Special respect should be given to Elders, Parents, Teachers, and Community Leaders.

   c. No person should be made to feel put down by you; avoid hurting other hearts, as you would avoid a deadly poison.

   d. Touch nothing that belongs to someone else (especially Sacred Objects) without permission, or an understanding between you.

   e. Respect the privacy of every person; never intrude on a person's quiet moment or personal space.

   f. Never walk between people that are conversing.

   g. Never interrupt people who are conversing.

   h. Speak in a soft voice, especially when you are in the presence of Elders, strangers, or others to whom special respect is due.

   i. Do not speak unless invited to do so at gatherings where Elders are present (except to ask what is expected of you, should you be in doubt).

   j. Never speak about others in a negative way, whether they are present or not.

   k. Treat the earth and all of her aspects as your mother. Show deep respect for the mineral world, the plant world, and the animal world. Do nothing to pollute our Mother, rise up with wisdom to defend her.

   l. Show deep respect for the beliefs and religion of others.

   m. Listen with courtesy to what others say, even if you feel that what they are saying is worthless. Listen with your heart.

   n. Respect the wisdom of the people in council. Once you give an idea to a council meeting it no longer belongs to you. It belongs to the people. Respect demands that you listen intently to the ideas of others in council and that you do not insist that your idea prevail. Indeed you should freely support the ideas of others if they are true and good, even if those ideas are quite different from the ones you have contributed. The clash of ideas brings forth the Spark of Truth.

3. Once a council has decided something in unity, respect demands that no one speak secretly against what has been decided. If the council has made an error, that error will become apparent to everyone in its own time.

====== **Applications 2.3 (continued)** ======

4. Be truthful at all times, and under all conditions.

5. Always treat your guests with honor and consideration. Give of your best food, your best blankets, the best part of your house, and your best service to your guests.

6. The hurt of one is the hurt of all; the honor of one is the honor of all.

7. Receive strangers and outsiders with a loving heart and as members of the human family.

8. All the races and tribes in the world are like the different colored flowers of one meadow. All are beautiful. As children of the Creator they must all be respected.

9. To serve others, to be of some use to family, community, nation, and the world, is one of the main purposes for which human beings have been created. Do not fill yourself with your own affairs and forget your most important talks. True happiness comes only to those who dedicate their lives to the service of others.

10. Observe moderation and balance in all things.

11. Know those things that lead to your well being, and those things that lead to your destruction.

12. Listen to and follow the guidance given to your heart. Expect guidance to come in many forms; in prayer, in dreams, in times of quiet solitude, and in the words and deeds of wise Elders and friends.

is not a code that speaks for all tribes. In fact, this code may be inaccurate for some, and not go far enough for others, as stated in the following quote, by Liz Gray, a Shawnee and Cherokee woman and publisher of Native American Times:

> One of the ethics I was taught, which is causing me hesitation, is that Native tribes do not speak for one another in their beliefs. I was taught that each person gives his or her own thoughts and beliefs and does not speak for anyone else. There are no shortcuts to finding out what the ethics of different tribes and tribal people are without researching and gathering opinions from various tribes. By saying this is a code of ethics for all tribes shows that it is not authentic. There is no such thing in the [American] Indian community. You can pick a few tribes as an example and go after a person within that tribe that can say what their beliefs are. But it may be difficult to get someone to speak for the whole tribe and especially all of the tribes.
>
> After saying that, the Code of Ethics that you sent could work, in general, for most tribes . . . the one about touching another person's belongings—that is very true. But the code leaves out one prominent courtesy among many traditional people—that is to not look people in the eye when they are talking to you. Many Native people look down at the ground or straight ahead out of respect. Looking a person in the eye resembles a challenge or an invasion. (Personal Communication, Feb. 5, 2005)

Like the other non-Western philosophies discussed previously, American Indian world views tend to be less individually oriented, with more focus on the good of the community and the respect we owe each other, our elders, and our ancestors. Family, hospitality, an active prayer life, and service to others are all central features of these moral worldviews.

Feminist Ethics and the Ethics of Care

It is true that we still are far from fully represented in decision-making bodies and that politics remain a male game; but that's no excuse for failing to use the power we have to make this a more livable world.

—Harriet Woods

As readers, you should stop and admire the restraint exercised in this chapter thus far by at least one of the authors. Regardless of the far-flung and disparate views on ethics and morality summarized to this point, most originally had a very disturbing aspect in common. Given the heading of this section, you can probably guess what it is. With the exception of the writings of John Stuart Mill (1912), to lesser and greater degrees, females are ignored or feminine virtue is achieved by women performing well in assigned positions of less influence and authority than their male counterparts. Aristotle believed that females were defective males, and the dire consequences of doing badly in life as a man might be to come back as a female next time. Taking his cue from Aristotle, St. Thomas Aquinas (Aquinas, 1993) wrote that in women, "reason flourishes very little because of the imperfect nature of their body" (p. 432). Freud believed that women lacked superego development, and were therefore morally inferior. There is no shortage of such examples from religious and philosophical writings. For thousands of years with few exceptions, it has been morally permissible, or morally encouraged, to view and treat women as second-class, adjunct, inferior, and/or subjugated to men.

For example, many brilliant women have been writing moral philosophy and psychology, often from a starting point very different from their male colleagues, at least since the time of Socrates, Plato, and Aristotle. But unless you take a course in the history of feminist ethics, the wise and articulate voices of these philosophers—Sappho, Hypatia, Hildegard, Heloise, Wollstonecraft, Harriet Taylor Mill, and Charlotte Perkins Gilman, to name but a few—are likely to be unrecognized and ignored (Petroff, 1986).

Of course, the current versions of the main ethical positions have become, at least on the surface, gender-neutral. Good character is no longer the sole domain of free, white males. Further, feminist theorists and ethicists have begun to have a voice in the critique and evolution of most of the ethical theories we've covered thus far. And finally, arising from Carol Gilligan's pioneering research and thinking, feminists have added yet another lens through which we can explore and pursue moral lives.

The Feminist Critique

In a word, the feminist critique of most traditional theories of morality is *power*. Margaret Urban Walker (2001) writes, "The most obvious way feminist ethics and politics connect morality and power is in examining the morality of specific distributions and exercises of power" (p. 4); and Hilde Lindemann Nelson (2001) adds, "The coercive forces within an abusive power system—patriarchy, for example—create the identities that are required by the system. These oppressive identities then determine the degree to which those who bear them may exercise their moral agency" (p. 45).

Applications 2.4

An excerpt from the Feminist Counseling Code of Ethics

II. Power Differentials

    A. A feminist therapist acknowledges the inherent power differentials between client and therapist and models effective use of personal, structural, or institutional power. In using the power differential to the benefit of the client, she does not take control or power which rightfully belongs to her client.

    B. A feminist therapist discloses information to the client which facilitates the therapeutic process, including information communicated to others. The therapist is responsible for using self-disclosure only with purpose and discretion and in the interest of the client.

    C. A feminist therapist negotiates and renegotiates formal and/or informal contacts with clients in an ongoing mutual process. As part of the decision-making process, she makes explicit the therapeutic issues involved.

    D. A feminist therapist educates her clients regarding power relationships. She informs clients of their rights as consumers of therapy, including procedures for resolving differences and filing grievances. She clarifies power in its various forms as it exists within other areas of her life, including professional roles, social/governmental structures, and interpersonal relationships. She assists her clients in finding ways to protect themselves and, if requested, to seek redress.

© Copyright 2000, Feminist Therapy Institute, Inc.
50 South Steele, #850, Denver, CO 80209
Administrator: Polly Taylor
128 Moffitt Street, San Francisco, CA 94131

Sometimes feminist counselors have struggled with the power inherent in professional relationships, and sometimes feminist clients have as well (Evans, Kincade, Marbley, & Seem, 2005; Hayward, 1994). As a core tenant, feminism seeks to empower people. Some theories and techniques of counseling and psychotherapy can overtly or subtly invite misuse of professional power (J. Sommers-Flanagan & Sommers-Flanagan, 2004b). See Applications 2.4 for an excerpt from a feminist counseling code of ethics, produced by the Feminist Therapy Institute in Denver, Colorado.

The moral use of power is a complicated endeavor. Many philosophers envisioned political hierarchies wherein the more powerful were the more virtuous, and thereby free from corruption, bias, and self-serving practices. The reality with which most of us are familiar is quite the opposite. The more power someone has to influence others and the social order, the more susceptible they become to misuse of the power. Wisdom and virtue are not necessarily commensurate with attainment of status or political office, but access to shared power is a global moral issue (Savage, Harley, & Nowak, 2005). As Madeleine Albright (Woods, 2004) stated in Beijing at the U.N. Conference for Women, "Enter any community in any country, and you will find women insisting—often at great risk—on their right to an equal voice and equal access to the levers of power" (p. 451).

Pause for Reflection

What is your experience with and attitude toward power? Have you seen individuals wield power in mostly positive ways or mostly negative ways? William Glasser and other psychological theorists believe that the need for power (or recognition or achievement) is a natural human need (Glasser, 1998). What is it like for you when you have power over others? What do you think is necessary so that power does not have a corrupting effect on people?

Ethics of Care

Western ethical theories have been said to be driven by concern for individual rights, rather than informed by the intricacies of human relationships. Originally dubbed "feminist ethics," the addition of a relationally oriented moral viewpoint was ushered in (in the mid-20th century Western rendition) by the work of Carol Gilligan. Gilligan worked with Lawrence Kohlberg, famous for his hypothesized six stages of moral development (Kohlberg, 1979). Subjects in Kohlberg's research had most often been boys, as he sought to further his theory and understanding of human moral development.

In early studies that included girls, Kohlberg and associates found that girls were scoring statistically lower than boys in terms of moral development on their measures. This finding intrigued Carol Gilligan, and thus her groundbreaking research began. Gilligan conducted in-depth interviews with young women to better understand the moral substance of their reasoning and choices. She reported this research in her best-selling book, *In a Different Voice* (1977). Although her work has opened many new avenues in ethical reasoning and research, ironically, the original assumption of a difference between boys and girls, like many such assumptions, turned out to be false (Hyde, 2005). Males and females both attend to justice concerns at roughly equal levels in most research projects (Garrod & Beal, 1993). Further, more current research shows that there is inconsistency in the ways all adults make moral choices, depending on the dilemma, and each person's social and personal goals in that moment (Krebs & Denton, 2005).

Care ethics argues that moral decision-making should directly include concern for others and their well-being. Emotions of love, compassion, and empathy motivate us toward the care of others, thereby enhancing the relationships around us, and some would argue, the general condition of humankind. Those who research and advocate an understanding of care ethics draw sharp distinctions between care reasoning and the more traditional approach reflected in Kohlberg's work, called justice reasoning. They believe the two reflect very different orientations toward morality. Propensities toward one or the other orientation were initially purported to fall along gender lines, but research has not always borne this out. Males can be morally guided by concern for relationships and other's welfare, and females can be morally guided by concepts of justice (Rooney, 2001). Of course, there are many differences in the ways people orient their solutions to moral dilemmas, and researchers often find differences between groups on social class, gender, contextual, and cultural dimensions (Garrod & Beal, 1993; Ryan, David, & Reynolds, 2004; Sevenhuijsen, Bozalek, Gouws, & Minnaar-McDonald, 2003).

Care ethics place *relationship* in the center of the moral vision. At a meeting of the American Society for Social Philosophy, ecofeminist theorist, Karen Warren, (1991) stated:

> If we dare to care, if we dare to enter into community with others through an honest recognition of our commonalities and differences, we will be poised to create generally respectful, nonviolent, care-based, intentional communities where commonalities and differences are just that. . . . Such intentional communities are a creative alternative to violence-prone communities where order is imposed from outside through unjustified domination.

We have already noted how Western philosophical orientations are generally far more individualistic than Asian, African, and American Indian orientations. Many worry that Western dominant culture is continuing on paths toward greater individualism, isolation, and commodified, single-purpose relationships, rather than communally oriented and traditional, complex relationships. In an editorial, Jeremy Rifkin (2004) reflects on the moral power of traditional relationships:

> Traditional relationships are born of such things as kinship, ethnicity, geography, and shared spiritual visions. Social contracts are steeped in the notions of indebtedness to ancestors, unborn generations, the Earth and its creatures, and a benevolent God.
>
> Membership in traditional communities also brings with it restraints on personal action. Obligations to others take precedence over personal whims, and security flows from being embedded in a larger social organism. Commodified relationships, on the other hand, are instrumental in nature. The only glue that holds them together is the transaction price. (p. 5)

Care ethics offers a moral alternative to an overemphasis on individual notions of fairness and justice. It is centered both on immediate relationships and on the "web of relationships that extends beyond immediate personal relationships to people of other races and nations and to all living things" (K. Taylor, 1995, p. 2). Indeed, Gilligan (1977) argues at the end of her groundbreaking book that the morally mature person will use the tools related to an ethics of justice and those related to an ethics of care.

> To understand how the tension between responsibilities and rights sustains the dialectic of human development is to see the integrity of two disparate modes of experience that are in the end connected. While an ethic of justice proceeds from the premise of equality—that everyone should be treated the same, an ethic of care rests on the premise of nonviolence— that on [sic] one should be hurt. In the representation of maturity, both perspectives converge in the realization that just as inequality adversely affects both parties in an unequal relationship, so too violence is destructive for everyone involved. (p. 174)

CHAPTER WRAP-UP

Take a deep breath. We have just been on the intellectual equivalent of a whirlwind tour of the world. We have attended to summaries and briefly considered disparate views from across thousands of years, from Greece, India, Prussia, Germany, Africa, the Americas (before white settlers appeared), and many parts of Asia. We have considered love and care, contrasting these with duty and justice. We have tried to grasp cultures in which the individual plays second fiddle to the community or the family. It was not an easy chapter to write, and we are fairly certain it has not been especially easy to read. You may still be wondering exactly why we believe this chapter is important enough to be included, given its difficulties and shortfalls. Here are some of our reasons:

First, because most of us live in a comparatively wealthy and dominant culture, we can get away with being naïve and ignorant about other cultures and other histories. Our personal moral life can be unidimensional, without reflection or critical scrutiny. Our professional ethical awareness and concerns could be as shallow and limited as simply worrying about avoiding lawsuits by irate clients.

Second, being an ethical helper of any kind includes having multicultural competencies, which we discuss in many later chapters. There is no better place to start than with the amazingly diverse considerations of right and wrong through historic and cultural lenses. You will be a wiser, more reflective and accepting counselor if you wrestle with understanding different views of right and wrong.

Finally, counseling and professional helping are evolving professions, with ethics codes and standards of practice that need ongoing revision and attention. We would love to see a whole new generation of professionals involved in adding deeper and more informed moral dimensions to our professional identity as counselors and professional helpers. We hope you will dare to ask hard moral questions of each other and of our cultures as you bring your voice fully into the choir of these professions.

> *The challenge, then, is to recognize that the world is about two things: differentiation and communion. The challenge is to seek a unity that celebrates diversity, to unite the particular with the universal, to recognize the need for roots while insisting that the point of roots is to put forth branches.*
>
> —William Sloane Coffin

Chapter Three ——————————————————————

ETHICS CODES, CODES OF CONDUCT, EMPLOYER POLICIES, AND THE LAW

I do not accept any absolute formulas for living. No preconceived code can see ahead to everything that can happen in a man's life. As we live, we grow and our beliefs change. They must change. So I think we should live with this constant discovery. We should be open to this adventure in heightened awareness of living. We should stake our whole existence on our willingness to explore and experience.

—Martin Buber

CHAPTER ORIENTATION

Some of us are more comfortable being told clearly what to do and not do. Others prefer the freedom to figure out the best ways to act. This chapter explores the reasons professional codes exist, and the distinctions between Ethics Codes, Codes of Conduct, Standards of Practice, Employer Policies, and the law. Also, we cover the educational, judicial, and aspirational aspects of codes and standards (and how to tell the difference). We include guidance for how to continually update your knowledge base and resources in this area, as well as ethical decision-making models. Finally, we venture into a relatively new domain—ethical guidance for emergency and crisis mental health work.

More specifically, in this chapter you will have the opportunity to consider:

- the moral dimensions of our professional knowledge and the legal concerns that influence our codes;
- the functions of various codes and sets of rules;
- the large and small distinctions between professional codes and laws;
- the role and influence of policies and institutional practices;
- the important contributions of guidelines, codes of behavior, and mission statements;
- various ethical decision-making guides; and a relatively new area,
- ethical considerations in crisis and humanitarian interventions.

WHY CODES?

Official codes of ethics are becoming commonplace among professions. This is not without controversy, and it certainly has not always been the case. Why are codes becoming more common? We offer various reasons and ideas, but stop for a minute and take a guess or two for yourself. Then, based on your guesses, think of why you might be in favor of codes, or why you might question their proliferation. Maybe you will find yourself agreeing with the upset writer in Digressions for Deliberation 3.1, or maybe you are more inclined toward the philosophy expressed in Abby's response to her disgruntled reader.

Recognizing the Moral Dimensions of Professional Knowledge

With our rapidly advancing technology, professional knowledge is readily available, comprehensive, and constantly changing. Ethicists are concerned that we are not developing the ethical depth necessary to apply our knowledge and technology with benev-

---

Digressions for Deliberation 3.1

An Ethics Code for Cell Phone Users?

(Missoulian February 17, 2005, p. B6)

Dear Abby: I have just had an upsetting experience. I walked into my local public library this morning to find a man angrily confronting one of the librarians. I don't eavesdrop, but there was no way to miss what he was saying because he was shouting.

Apparently when it was his turn to be helped, he was on his cell phone and refused to hang up. Part of his problem, according to him, was that he was so involved with his cell phone call that he hadn't heard what the librarian said! I don't feel that was the librarian's fault. I don't see why she and the other people in line should have been expected to wait for him to finish his call, and I certainly don't understand why he felt entitled to intimidate this woman. His anger upset me, and I wasn't even involved, so I can only imagine how she must have felt. She was visibly shaking after he left.

Isn't it time for some rules of conduct for cell phones?

Courtesy, Please
in Springfield, MO

Dear C.P.: It should not be necessary to have written rules of conduct for cell phone users. Common sense and basic good manners should apply. The librarian was within her rights to take the next person in line if the one in front of her was preoccupied. And if the man was belligerent and intimidating, she was also within her rights to have a security guard escort him out.

olence and justice (Anchin, 2005). Many thriller movies feature the misuse of knowledge. Sometimes, the plot draws from the physical or technological domains—robots run amuck, body parts going to the highest bidder, or biological weapons intentionally released into the world. But on occasion (both in the movies, and in real life) psychological knowledge is used without regard for basic morality. For instance, consider advertising, and efforts to cause significant psychological insecurity in order to sell a product, or the ongoing concerns about the use of torture to obtain information.

We cannot simply acquire knowledge for knowledge's sake, pushing the moral considerations off to the side or ignoring them entirely. Of course, this is especially true for mental health professionals. **Vulnerable human beings entrust themselves directly into our professional care.** Please reread that last sentence and let the magnitude sink in. We hope this profound but simple truth will inspire you to take your education, your work, and your self-care very seriously.

Unfortunately, recognizing the moral dimensions of knowledge and producing ethics codes cannot adequately address all the moral quandaries that might arise, but they provide a starting point. If you have not already done so, please read at least two of the ethics codes relevant to our field by visiting the websites in Applications 3.1. Compare the tone, clarity, and overall message(s) you get from each code.

Legal Concerns and Fears as a Driving Force

Professionals can be held legally accountable for the application of their skills and knowledge (Henggeler & Schoenwald, 2002; Hughey, Gysbers, & Starr, 1993; Stone, 2005d). Whether you consider trial lawyers to be villains or heroes, the fact remains that clients, patients, and consumers use courts of law to seek justice if they feel harmed or treated unfairly. In a civil society, the rule of law provides a neutral mediating structure so that such claims can be evaluated. There are extremes in both directions: On one hand, there are civil suits that seemed to hold businesses or professionals culpable for accidents or human failings that could not possibly be managed or controlled. On the other hand, there are terrible misuses of power or professional negligence that ruined or ended lives, with no consequences for the professional or business.

Ethics codes are not ordinarily or largely enforced by the blunt instrument of law. Morality *can* be legislated, but only at the most basic and general levels. Ethically ideal behavior in the professions is a matter of identity, duty, and honor. Morally ideal behavior in the human community is the beating heart of civilization. Our laws are the safety net underneath both professional ethics and moral conduct.

Ethics codes give the public and professionals a set of guidelines to judge and calibrate professional behaviors. This helps everyone have similar expectations for behavior and similar understandings of the limits of the knowledge and skills at their disposal. And while ethics codes are not legal documents, they *can* be used by attorneys in legal suits as evidence of malpractice. To add to the confusion, some ethical obligations are also reflected in law in many states. For instance, it is both unethical and illegal to have sexual relationships with current clients in many states. In contrast, most codes consider it unethical for professors to offer to become their students' counselors, but there are few, if any laws addressing this unethical behavior.

FUNCTIONS OF THE CODES

Ethics codes vary in clarity, purpose, and specificity. The Internet has provided a direct and immediate method for reviewing professional codes of ethics. We encourage you to acquire the habit of checking codes relevant to your practice because codes change and evolve over time. It is very important for you to stay current—more current even than this textbook! It is also important that you have a voice in this evolution. Most codes are readily available on the organizational websites, many of which we provide in Applications 3.1.

Most ethics codes have at least three functions (Elliott-Boyle, 1985):

- The codes paint a picture of the truly moral professional. At the aspirational level, they contain statements about the ideals of the profession at its finest.
- The codes have an educational function. They define the profession and those served, and give the public and the profession a condensed story of what behaviors can be expected in interactions between both professionals and clients and professionals and other professionals.
- The codes have a legislative, or mandatory, function. Many people think of this as the main function of ethics codes. The codes contain many statements about what the professional must or must not do. Organizational consequences of violating these mandatory portions are usually spelled out in the professional organization's bylaws. However, violations can have many legal and moral consequences that extend beyond the domain of the professional organization.

Some professions have both ethics codes and standards of practice. This is more often true of professions that have ethics codes that define the moral principles related to the profession, and standards of practice that speak to the level of performance, or expertise, expected. Standards of practice are more pragmatic, descriptive, and operational, or behaviorally oriented. Until the most recent edition of their ethics code, the ACA had a separate ACA Standards of Practice (American Counseling Association, 1995). If you took time to read these standards, you would have noted that they were an operationally oriented reiteration of the ethics codes. The amalgamation of the ACA Standards of Practice into the ACA Code of Ethics has served to reduce the overall amount of material ACA members have to contend with as they strive to become and remain ethical practitioners.

Besides formalized ethics codes, there are many other collections of rules, policies, and guidelines that exert influence over the moral choices you will grapple with as a professional. These include:

- Laws at the international, federal, state, and local levels
- Codes of conduct and behavioral guidelines
- Employer and agency policies
- Implicit or explicit mission statements

We discuss each of these and how they are related in the following pages.

Websites for Mental Health Professional Organizations

- American Association for Marriage and Family Therapy (AAMFT): The AAMFT homepage is at www.aamft.org/index_nm.asp. Specific legal and ethical information, including the AAMFT Code of Ethics and free ethical consultation information, is available at www.aamft.org/resources/LRMPlan/index_nm.asp.
- American Counseling Association (ACA): The ACA homepage is at www.counseling.org. ACA Code of Ethics as well as additional information about ethics for professional counselors is at www.counseling.org/resources/ethics.htm.
- American Group Psychotherapy Association (AGPA): The homepage for AGPA is www.agpa.org. The specific Guidelines for Ethics is at www.agpa.org/group/ethicalguide.html.
- American Psychiatric Association: The main website for the American Psychiatric Association is www.psych.org. You can find ethics information, including the Principles of Medical Ethics with annotations especially applicable to psychiatry and the Ethics Primer of the American Psychiatric Association, at www.psych.org/psych_pract/ethics/ethics.cfm
- American Psychological Association (APA): The APA homepage is at www.apa.org. The APA ethical code and contact information for the APA ethics committee is at www.apa.org/ethics/homepage.html.
- American School Counselor Association (ASCA): The ASCA homepage is at www.schoolcounselor.org. The ASCA Ethical Standards for School Counselors is at www.schoolcounselor.org/content.asp?contentid=173.
- Association for Specialists in Group Work (ASGW): The ASGW is a specialty organization that follows the general ACA Code of Ethics and Standards of Practice. Their homepage is at www.asgw.org. The ASGW has its own set of Best Practice Guidelines located at www.asgw.org/best.htm.
- British Association for Counselling and Psychotherapy (BACP): Most readers won't be held accountable to this code or the next in this list, but both provide great contrasting approaches. www.bacp.co.uk/ethical_framework.
- Canadian Psychological Association (CPA): www.cpa.ca/cpasite/userfiles/Documents/Canadian%20Code%20of%20Ethics%20for%20Psycho.pdf.
- International Association of Marriage and Family Counselors (IAMFC): The IAMFC homepage is at www.iamfc.com. The IAMFC Ethical Standards is at www.iamfc.com/ethical_codes.html/
- National Association of Social Workers (NASW): The NASW homepage is at www.naswdc.org. The NASW Code of Ethics is at www.naswdc.org/pubs/code/default.asp.
- National Rehabilitation Association (NRA): The NRA homepage is at http://www.nationalrehab.org/website/history/index.html
- Division 22, Rehabilitation Psychology, American Psychological Association. The homepage is http://www.apa.org/divisions/div22/

DISTINCTIONS BETWEEN CODES AND LAWS

There are international, federal, state, and local laws that you need to know to be a safe and effective mental health professional. While we cannot provide you with a list of pertinent laws in every locale, we can provide you with a list of areas to which you need to attend throughout your professional life. In addition, in the upcoming chapters, we point out legal implications within the various areas of concern. Elected legislators make the laws, but the actual interpretation of the law is an ongoing evolution of court cases that define and refine the legal ramifications of various professional actions. This process is often referred to as case law. You cannot simply read federal, state, and local law and assume you know the legalities of a given action. If you are faced with making a tough decision with legal implications, our best advice is to consult a good attorney.

Common areas of legal concern follow.

- Confidentiality is an overarching concern, both in what must be kept confidential, and in what must *not* be. This includes questions such as the following: Must you report a past felony that a client tells you he committed? How would you handle finding out your client is an illegal alien? Must you report instances of unreported child or elder abuse within a certain amount of time? Must you contact an intended victim? Are you liable if you disclose someone's HIV status with the intention of preventing a partner from being infected?
- Dual or multiple roles, especially any roles you have in clients' lives, that may cause you to be seen as exploitive can pose serious ethical/legal challenges.
- The rights of minors and the elderly in the counseling relationship are of concern.
- The rights of illegal aliens and their children are a recently contentious concern.
- Competence and concerns about malpractice remain important across setting.
- Insurance reporting and record-keeping practices have always been an area of ethical and legal concern. The advent of the federal set of laws referred to as the Health Insurance Portability and Accountability Act (HIPAA) has added exponentially to the concerns in this area (see Applications 5.2 in Chapter 5).

It is not unusual to work with clients who have legal concerns in conjunction with their counseling concerns. These concerns might include the rights of gay and lesbian couples, parental rights or property distribution in the event of a divorce, protection rights in the event of intimate partner violence, and so on. State laws vary widely in these areas. In some countries, and in a few states in the United States, gay and lesbian couples can make a legal commitment to each other in civil unions or marriages. In others, they cannot. States vary in their laws for divorce and child custody. The availability of protection from an abusive intimate partner varies, even from city to city. Unless you are employed in an agency that provides legal information, you should not do so. And even if you provide legal information, it should never be construed as legal advice.

Perhaps understandably, many people assume that professional ethical and legal responsibilities will be compatible, mutually supportive, and never in contradiction. They would be wrong. From the mundane to the profound, there are times when an ethical stance or action is illegal, and there are times when an unethical stance or action is perfectly legal. While ethics codes are more extensive and have far more directive material for practicing professional helpers of all types, sanctions associated only with ethical violations are limited. Violations of the law have more far-reaching consequences. However, there are instances when the law actually takes into account the ethics codes of a given profession.

Legal issues fall into two general categories: Civil matters and criminal matters. Civil law is likely the domain that has led to the many jokes and judgmental attitudes toward the term "trial lawyer." Civil suits are brought by people (or in the case of class action suits, groups of people) against other people, professionals, corporations, or governments. These suits are brought because of a perceived failure to meet basic, expected responsibilities humans have for each other in civil society. For example, Remley and Herlihy (2005) comfort(!) professionals who need legal advice by stating the following: "Lawyers are required to stand behind the advice they render. You can sue your lawyers if you are harmed as a result of relying on their incorrect advice" (p. 350).

The truth is that anyone can try to sue anyone for anything. While it is not always illegal in the criminal sense to act unethically, ethics codes can certainly come into play if a client decides to sue. Acting in an unethical manner can then become a legal issue, even if the unethical act was not covered by legal statutes. In Chapter 4, we discuss personal and professional values. On rare occasions, professionals may choose to engage in civil disobedience because of profound values that run counter to prevailing law. This is a serious undertaking. Engaging in civil disobedience involves an expectation of being fined, sanctioned, or jailed—being willing to have this happen to bring attention to the injustice of the law in question.

POLICIES AND PRACTICES

In the excitement of your first internship placement, or the even greater excitement of your first job, it is easy to forget this crucial rule: *Read the fine print. Ask the hard questions before they are excruciatingly and immediately relevant.* Besides laws and ethics, there are policies that develop over time in any given agency or school and there are practices expected in any given community.

Policies within Schools and Agencies

School, government agencies, and nonprofit organizations can all have many layers of official policies and practices to which all employees may be held accountable. These policies are often a reflection of a given administration, and can change radically when there is a change of principal or business manager or president or legislative body. Sometimes, the policies are written down and more or less codified. Other times, they are only stated orally, or are recorded in some obscure document you would not ordinarily see.

The domain of any given policy is obviously the institution that has written or adopted the policies. By becoming a part of the workplace, you are agreeing to uphold the policies. Thus, in many respects, when violated or misapplied, policies can have the weight of law (and the impact of a freight train) for you and your clients.

Case Example: Randy was hired by a small school near a large urban area. He was the counselor for the entire school, which had 200 students, K–12. Randy had just finished his Master's degree in school counseling. He was proud of himself for finishing, as he was a single father of a toddler. The mother of his child had left the state, having started using cocaine again after the birth of their child. Randy had legal custody of the baby, and was grateful to have fulltime employment with good dependent benefits.

Randy's internship had included work with both middle school and high school students in a much larger school. He had worked primarily with social skills groups, career choices, and had helped with group testing. There were a number of senior counselors, and Randy had not experienced many emergent, nor deeply emotive, situations.

Kelsey, a 16-year-old student, stopped by Randy's office the first week of school. With a rather casual air, she informed him that she was having an abortion the next day. Kelsey was hoping that Randy would arrange for a medically excused absence since she was not planning to tell her parents about this pregnancy. Randy's emotions surged, and he panicked. He did not know if the school had a policy about parental rights to be informed, and he wasn't sure about state law. In the back of his mind, he knew this issue had been in the news lately.

Randy decided to consult Mr. Jones, the principal, who was very public about his opposition to abortion. Mr. Jones told Randy to disclose the name of the girl. He stated that it was school policy to notify parents of such disclosures. Randy reluctantly told him the student's name, and then was quickly besieged with guilt. He was sure he should have resisted the principal's wish to know, but felt confused and emotionally drained. He decided to find Kelsey and let her know about the conversation with the principal. Not surprisingly, Kelsey was very angry with Randy. After their conversation, she not only stormed out of the counseling office, she also fled the school. Meanwhile, the principal had chosen to contact Kelsey's parents. Although not necessarily opposed to abortion, they were shocked and worried. They wanted to talk to Kelsey, but at this point, no one knew where she had gone. Randy wondered if he should try to speak with the parents. He wondered if he should try to drive around town to find Kelsey.

Finally, Randy realized he was in full-throttle reactive mode, and called a former professor and supervisor for consultation. He also called an attorney to ask about state law and reviewed the school's policies manual. He found that in his state, currently, there was no requirement for parental notification or consent. School policy was worded in a way that was open to interpretation. Randy also reviewed ACA and ASCA ethics codes.

And so what is the moral of this story? Although there are many, for now, the main message is *know the basics* of every possible law and policy that will affect your work with clients. And for those of you who need to know the end of the story, Kelsey had driven herself to the clinic, slept in her car on a side street, had the abortion, and had come home. Her parents were much more distressed at the lack of trust than they were about Kelsey's abortion. They sought family counseling. No one sued anyone. Randy kept his job, much wiser, more cautious—having aged a few years rather quickly. You will find further coverage of this area in Chapter 10.

We wish we could reassure you that dramatic examples like this are rare, or that this one was exaggerated, but they aren't and it wasn't. As counseling interns or new employees, you will need to be inquisitive, attentive, and thorough as you get to know everything you possibly can about your new environment and the rules and regulations to which you are accountable.

Standard of Care or Acceptable Practices

Related to agency policies is a concept applicable in any counseling setting, whether agency, governmental, nonprofit, or independent practice. This concept has been variously referred to as standard of care (e.g., Quattrocchi & Schopp, 2005), community or customary standard of care, and/or acceptable practice. The essence is this: The standard of care is what our most moral, trustworthy, and expert colleagues would do. In the worst case scenario, it is conceivable that these colleagues would be asked to give their opinions about your actions in a civil or criminal court of law.

The trust placed in professional consensus is another compelling reason to be a member of an ongoing collegial consultation or supervision group. There *is* wisdom and safety in numbers.

GUIDELINES, CODES OF BEHAVIOR, AND MISSION STATEMENTS

In settings such as residential or private schools, prisons, the military, or faith-based communities, counselors, social workers, and other employees will be considered part of the larger corporate or communal identity. Members may wear uniforms or badges or other external signals of membership, rank, or status. In addition, there may be guidelines for behavior and codes of conduct that everyone must adhere to. These may not have the force of law or enjoy the power or status of a professional ethics code, but they can define the rules of membership. Similar to agency policies, those who violate the code or guidelines may find themselves excluded from the community. As members of these communities, employees are expected to adhere to the rules and guidelines, but they must do so with an eye to the codes and laws relevant to their unique profession. When there is a conflict among these expectations and rules, members of any of the helping professions would need to seek consultation, try to resolve the conflicts, document these efforts, and ultimately decide on the ethical path, knowing that complying with one set of codes will not shield them from the consequences of violating the other.

Just for fun, (and to remind you there *is* life after graduate school) in Digressions for Deliberation 3.2, you will find a portion of the guidelines for hikers on the Appalachian Trail. See if you can identify the deontological, utilitarian, and situational threads in these statements.

Digressions for Deliberation 3.2

From The Thru-Hiker's Handbook, Guidelines for Thru-Hikers:

1. Rules on the Appalachian Trail are relatively few and far between, and the ones that do exist have been designated by dedicated Trail workers to protect the Appalachian Trail while allowing as much freedom to as many people as possible. You will be tempted to ignore a seemingly pointless rule somewhere along the way. Before you do, ask yourself, "What will happen if a thousand other thru-hikers do the same?"

2. The Golden Rule—*Do unto others as you would have them do unto you*—is a good standard to live by on the Appalachian Trail, and the relatively few problems that develop among thru-hikers could be eliminated if this simple rule were observed. It requires that you consider the effect your actions will have on those around you and, equally important, on those behind you. Remember that "Trail magic" for you is usually the results of good impressions left by your predecessors.

3. Community spirit develops among thru-hikers as the miles go by. You can seriously diminish this sense of community if you are openly judgmental or critical of others . . . (Bruce, 2000, p. 172).

Mission Statements

As described by many ethicists, most ethics codes have an aspirational section that describes the highest calling and mission of the profession (G. Corey, 2005; Elliott-Boyle, 1985). For instance, read the mission statements that follow. Notice the use of words, the emphasis, and orientation of these mission statements.

From the American Counseling Association: The Mission of the American Counseling Association is to enhance the quality of life in society by promoting the development of professional counselors, advancing the counseling profession, and using the profession and practice of counseling to promote respect for human dignity and diversity. . . .

The American Counseling Association is an educational, scientific, and professional organization whose members work in a variety of settings and serve in multiple capacities. ACA members are dedicated to the enhancement of human development throughout the life span. Association members recognize diversity and embrace a cross-cultural approach in support of the worth, dignity, potential, and uniqueness of people within their social and cultural contexts.

Professional values are an important way of living out an ethical commitment. Values inform principles. Inherently held values that guide our behaviors or exceed prescribed behaviors are deeply ingrained in the counselor and developed out of personal dedication, rather than the mandatory requirement of an external organization.

From the National Association of Social Workers: The mission of the social work profession is rooted in a set of core values. These core values, embraced by social workers throughout the profession's history, are the foundation of social work's unique purpose and perspective:

- service
- social justice
- dignity and worth of the person
- importance of human relationships
- integrity
- competence

This constellation of core values reflects what is unique to the social work profession. Core values, and the principles that flow from them, must be balanced within the context and complexity of the human experience.

From the American Psychological Association: The objects of the American Psychological Association shall be to advance psychology as a science and profession and as a means of promoting health, education, and human welfare by

- the encouragement of psychology in all its branches in the broadest and most liberal manner
- the promotion of research in psychology and the improvement of research methods and conditions
- the improvement of the qualifications and usefulness of psychologists through high standards of ethics, conduct, education, and achievement
- the establishment and maintenance of the highest standards of professional ethics and conduct of the members of the Association
- the increase and diffusion of psychological knowledge through meetings, professional contacts, reports, papers, discussions, and publications thereby to advance scientific interests and inquiry, and the application of research findings to the promotion of health, education, and the public welfare.

The aspirational sections of most ethics codes are essentially mission statements; they are necessarily brief, and practicality argues that they stay well within reasonable bounds. Mission statements as discrete, stand-alone documents, can have guiding, inspiring functions in the lives of dedicated professionals (Covey, 1990). We encourage you to consider writing and maintaining a professional mission statement as part of your ongoing journey toward both proficiency and definition as a mental health professional.

Pause for Reflection

Have you ever written a personal or professional mission statement? Most people have not. It is almost as threatening as writing your own obituary. We suspect the resistance comes from this: Both activities force us to face life's meanings and limits. What are your ideas about the value and/or dread associated with personal and professional mission statements?

A different path—history of professional ethics for counselling in the United Kingdom

by Tim Bond

This short piece is an insider's account of the development of professional ethics in the British Association for Counselling and Psychotherapy. I have grown increasingly interested in how our respective national professional associations have reached such different approaches to ethics as we enter the 21st century. My hope is that these reflections will stimulate continuing global dialogue about morality and professional ethics for our area of work.

Initiating phase: 1980–1990

The professional body for counseling in the UK was founded in 1977. It had a distinctive ethos in comparison to the established professions in health care, social work, and education. Although the early members came primarily from these backgrounds or from the charitable sector, such as the national Marriage Guidance Council (now known as RELATE), there was a radical edge and social agenda that wanted to change the ways services were provided and the relationship between service user and provider. At that time the dominant ethos in professional services was paternalistic fidelity; the public were expected to trust that a professional was well-intentioned and competent. To question this ethical assumption out of anxiety or grievance was unacceptable. Compliant gratitude was the generally expected attitude of service users and this is how most people behaved.

The established professions were changing more slowly than the rest of society, persisting with a form of social regulation based on duty and compliance: the cultural legacy of two world wars. The development of a new profession provided an opportunity for those with more radical intent to come together, inspired by the youth culture and radical politics of 1960s and 1970s and informed by the more egalitarian values of humanistic and existentialist therapy. The vision of "new ways of being" found ethical expression in a short inspirational Code of Ethics and Practice for Counsellors that promoted a vision of respect for client autonomy, actively engaging clients in strategic decisions about how they would be counselling (Baca & Cervantes, 1984). Commitment to the personal and social experiment of asserting the possibility of being autonomous, self-governing people was more important than conformity to rules within the association during this early phase.

It is hard to know precisely what tipped the balance toward a more conventional professional infrastructure. It was probably the combined impact of a number of factors. The public appetite for talking therapies had grown and there was an emerging struggle for this work between counsellors, psychotherapists, and psychologists. The association became increasingly concerned with livelihood rather than lifestyle. There were also issues of internal governance and management as the membership had rapidly grown to about 10,000 with corresponding legal and financial responsibilities. Greater media exposure and questions about how counselling fitted within the law all tended to focus attention on professional responsibility.

Regulatory phase: 1990–2000

The presentation of ethics changed during the late 1980s from being inspirational to being more educational in terms of ensuring greater understanding of areas of potential difficulty, legal responsibilities, and disseminating learning from any disciplinary procedures. The replacement of the short aspirational code with a much lengthier code of prescriptive rules, systematically setting out the implications of respect for client autonomy (BAC, 1990), marked a major shift in the collective ethic. A profession's childhood had given way to adulthood, at least insofar as there was a determination to take on collective responsibility for counselling. Throughout this decade the published ethics looked very like those that would be familiar to any members of the American Counseling Association or the American Psychological Association. The codes of ethics grew in length and detail in response to issues considered in professional conduct adjudications, which were simultaneously growing in legal and ethical sophistication.

Membership continued to grow throughout this phase and doubled to 20,000 by the end of the decade. The public demand for counselling also flourished and it was increasingly made available on a commercial basis and through statutory and charitable organisations.

Notwithstanding this success there is a growing sense of unease that the professional ethic is becoming oppressive and, ironically, may be ethically counterproductive. With hindsight, it is easy to see that counsellors found themselves working in increasingly constricted ethical space. They were occupying the diminishing space between respect for client autonomy, the ethical priority, and an increasingly powerful and regulatory professional body. This created an ethical crisis because the profession was developing more rapidly than a large organisation could keep up with. The members were responding to the challenges of providing services across an expanding range of cultures and contexts, each requiring ethical adjustments to meet new legal requirements or to meet the needs of the client group. What was needed was not uniform compliance to a shared set of rules but an ethical framework that informed and supported counsellors in grappling with the ethical intricacies of responding to new contexts.

For me the turning point was when I realised that the inquiries from members to the professional help line no longer asked, "What is ethical?" but "What am I allowed to do?" Mere compliance is ethically questionable as an adequate

Digressions for Deliberation 3.3 (continued)

basis for any profession. "I was only obeying orders" is a characteristic defense of gross atrocities such as those tried at Nuremberg concerning the Holocaust. There needed to be a better balance between setting minimal standards to protect client safety and supporting the ethical resourcefulness and resilience of counsellors to respond to the ethical challenges as they arise with individual clients in local circumstances. This seemed particularly important in a listening profession that needed to be able to respond to the increasing moral and cultural diversity to be found in the British population. The profession was reaching a new stage in its development in which it was not merely sufficient to grapple with diversity within the client work, arising from responding to the challenges of diversity in morals, identity, and context; but, also to begin to rebuild the ethical capital within the profession that had been inadvertently undermined by a centralised ethic based on rules. My own academic work turned toward considering the conditions for promoting ethical mindfulness (Bond, 2000).

When I started to voice my concerns about the ethical path we were following in the Association, I discovered widespread support. The adequacy of professional rules as a way of regulating professions had become widely questioned because of the failure of rule-based systems to prevent major accountancy scandals in the UK and the United States with far-reaching adverse impact on peoples' savings and pensions. There was a wider social concern to find alternative methods to rules alone for fostering ethical practice. We looked at the North American tendency to produce ever longer and more elaborate codes of rules for the talking therapies and thought "This is where we are headed" and we did not like the prospect. We needed to find some other way of honouring our radical vision of personal empowerment evident in the initiating phase with our concern to promote ethically mindful practice that was the outcome of the more regulatory-minded second phase. It was time for radical reconsideration and ethical reorientation.

Establishing an ethical framework for ethically mindful counselling: 2000 onward

One of the challenges of writing ethics and ethical guidelines is ensuring that what is produced is considered relevant and meaningful by the practitioners who will be the primary implementers of what is proposed. However, there is a danger of losing the critical and imaginative edge if the ethics are solely composed from within the professional community for which they are intended. In this case, we experimented with having a panel of expert consultants who are specialists in applied moral philosophy who would be willing to test ideas, pose challenging questions, and suggest new possibilities. Only toward the end of the creative process did we consult lawyers to ensure that what we were proposing was shaped to be compatible with existing law.

Digressions for Deliberation 3.3 (continued)

I was appointed to lead the development work and the writing of what became the Ethical Framework for Good Practice in Counselling and Psychotherapy (BACP, 2002). I always approach these tasks with mixed feelings. I enjoy the intellectual challenge at a conceptual level. I am much more ambivalent about the writing in the form of a code or ethical guidance. It requires all the hard work of finding the right words to express what is being communicated with the accuracy of a poet but without the aesthetic satisfaction. Also few poems would survive the carefully judged compromises required by the politics of the approval and implementation process.

The outcome of the process that took place over the next 2 years was a Framework written in three parts. The first sets out various ethical positions around six principles and how these might relate to issues that arise in counselling. The principles are autonomy, fidelity, beneficence, nonmaleficence, justice, and self-respect. A further innovation was the introduction of personal moral qualities (typically referred to as virtues in moral philosophy) as another point of ethical reference, both for counsellors who think of ethics as an aspect of their identity and moral aspirations and for some traditional communities that do not identify with principles as a form of moral discourse. The aim is to promote ethical thinking and to give counsellors the language in which to consider ethical dilemmas and challenges as they arise and in which to explain their actions. The educative aspect of professional ethics is prioritised and this section has become widely used in supervision as a point of reference. The second part provides basic guidance on client safety and good practice and is more prescriptive although less so than the codes that preceded it. The final part sets out the professional conduct procedures. These require a counsellor to be ethically accountable for actions and decisions made rather than merely being able to demonstrate compliance or noncompliance with the rules. Throughout the document counsellors are directed to consider what would be contextually appropriate practice rather than imposing a universal general rule except over some basic requirements like avoiding sexual exploitation and the obligation to have supervision or professional mentoring.

The ethical framework was subject to an induction process involving background articles and workshops across the UK. This elicited over 1,000 written responses. The overall sense of the responses was of a profession relieved to be treated as responsible adults rather than children who needed to be controlled by rules, thus releasing a great wave of ethical energy that had previously been held back by a dam of rules or had only found expression as dissident thoughts on the margins of an authoritarian regime. This framework clearly spoke to the ethically committed and competent counsellors reinvigorated by the recognition of their active role in meeting the considerable ethical challenges of their work.

This move away from rules had profound implications for disciplinary and professional conduct hearings within the profession. Adjudicators would no

---

Digressions for Deliberation 3.3 (continued)

longer be evaluating conduct against the literal interpretation of rules but considering whether the counsellor's actions were justifiable against general ethical principles as meeting the requirements of a reasonable standard of practice. The adjudicators found relief in being able to concentrate on what they considered to be just for the people appearing before them without straining against the interpretation of specific rules in order to produce a fair outcome. With over 40 cases considered under the new system, this remains true.

The next ethical development

The process of ethical development is one of continual learning. The process of consultation on the last series of developments reinforced our sense of the value of distinguishing fundamental issues of client safety, which justify general rules, from matters of ethical concern that are encountered by ethically well-intentioned and competent counsellors who want support in making contextually appropriate decisions. With hindsight we could have made this distinction clearer and more explicit in the original Framework and this may be something to do when it is due for review. However, pursuing the needs of the counsellor who works above the safety line has revealed an ethical void. There is a missing ethic. Principles provide useful points of reference that are extrinsic to the counselling relationship. What would an intrinsic ethic look like? This seems to be the missing ethical discourse that could inform and provide meaningful ethical points of reference from within the ethical relationship to respond to the intricate issues of psychological intimacy and reciprocity that characterise the therapeutic relationship. This is the focus of the next step in what appears to be a creative vein of ethical thinking and practice on this side of the Atlantic.

Ethical Decision-Making Guides

When faced with making a decision that has ethical ramifications, you need to find a way to systematically consider all the angles. Such considerations include basic moral concerns, laws, ethics codes, agency or school policies, and your own values. Many authors have offered decision-making models. We were tempted to create our own, but the similarities of the existing ones led us to believe that this terrain has been well-covered. In fact, Cottone and Tarvydas (2003) developed a table detailing seven different models, all of which bear a strong resemblance to each other. The model in Applications 3.2 is Tarvydas's integration of these seven models. You will find a school counseling ethical decision-making model in Chapter 10.

Decisions about Decisions

The notion of a decision-making model may seem simplistic and unnecessary as you read this text in the safety and security of your own mind, with your main concern

Applications 3.2

Integrative Decision-Making Model of Ethical Behavior (Cottone & Tarvydas, 2003, p. 89)

Before even beginning to list the stages and components, Vilia Tarvydas encourages us to: (a) Maintain an attitude of reflection; (b) address balance between issues and parties to the ethical dilemma; (c) pay close attention to the context(s) of the situation; and (d) utilize a process of collaboration with all rightful parties to the situation.

Stage I. Interpreting the situation through awareness and fact finding

Component 1   Enhance sensitivity and awareness.
Component 2   Determine the major stakeholders and their ethical claims in the situation.
Component 3   Engage in the fact-finding process.

Stage II. Formulating an ethical decision

Component 1   Review the problem or dilemma.
Component 2   Determine what ethical codes, laws, principles, and institutional policies and procedures apply to the dilemma.
Component 3   Generate possible and probable courses of action.
Component 4   Consider potential positive and negative consequences for each course of action.

Stage III. Selecting an action by weighing competing, nonmoral values, personal blind spots, or prejudices

Component 1   Engage in reflective recognition and analysis of personal competing nonmoral values, personal blind spots, or prejudices.
Component 2   Consider contextual influences on values selection at the collegial, team, institutional, and societal levels.
Component 3   Select the preferred course of action.

Stage IV. Planning and executing the selected course of action

Component 1   Figure out a reasonable sequence of concrete actions to be taken.
Component 2   Anticipate and work out personal and contextual barriers to effective execution of the plan of action, and effective countermeasures for them.
Component 3   Carry out, document, and evaluate the course of action as planned.

being to pass your ethics class. However, we hasten to assure you that when faced with the complex ethically loaded situations in your internship, or in your professional positions, these models will offer a pragmatic lifeline for your racing thoughts and provide a calming effect on your potential impulses.

These decision-making models also have clinical and philosophical aspects. The way you conceptualize the problem, and the method you use to sort it out, reflects your own ethical framework. Cottone (2003) and other authors have offered important relational and constructivist approaches to the ethical decision-making process. Cottone writes:

> When concerns arise at crucial moments of professional practice, the social constructivist obtains information from those involved, assesses the nature of relationships operating at that moment, consults valued colleagues and professional expert opinion (including ethical codes), negotiates when necessary, and responds in a way that allows for a reasonable consensus. (p. 105)

Often, ethical dilemmas also have significant clinical ramifications. Feminists and social constructionists urge professionals to take into account the relationship and the context, involving all affected to whatever extent may be possible (L. S. Brown, 2001; Worell & Remer, 2003). For an example, see Steigerwald and Forest's article using a social constructivist model of ethical decision-making with a family (Steigerwald & Forrest, 2004). When you involve your client, and/or your administration, you are modeling respect and serving as a guide in helping others understand the moral dimensions of a given situation. This is a morally admirable, but professionally challenging goal. The following scenario provides an example.

Case Example: Sue is an attractive, funny, warm 23-year-old counseling student. She is an intern at her campus Career Services. Jerod, a 24-year-old athlete, stops by during open office hours to ask Sue about taking some interest inventories. He explains that he has been feeling a little lost, since his sport's season just ended. He considered seeing a counselor at the Health Service, but decided what he needs to do is work on his future. Sue compliments him on his positive attitude. She also comments on having seen him play very well in the last few games. Jerod seems pleased. He becomes quite flirtatious, and after making an appointment for the testing, he asks Sue to join him for a latte on her next coffee break.

What are Sue's options? What are the ethical and therapeutic, or clinical, implications of these options? How might Sue responsibly and ethically include Jerod as she solves this ethical dilemma? While Sue would certainly be technically correct if she simply told Jerod that she would violate her ethics code if she accepted his request, such a response lacks depth, sensitivity, and nuance. It may not even be completely accurate. It also runs a very high risk of making Jerod think people training to be counselors, and maybe most counselors themselves, are uptight and strange in their interpersonal interactions.

Counselors, therapists, and social workers are as diverse as the clients they serve. We have colleagues who use checklists and linear models for interviewing, treatment, and ethical decision-making. We have colleagues who work strictly within one theoretical orientation, or exclusively with one kind of life problem. We also have colleagues who are avid postmodern thinkers, aware of the many ways reality is constructed and construed. As a student, you not only have the responsibility to develop your theoretical orientation (Ivey, D'Andrea, Ivey, & Simek-Morgan, 2002; J. Sommers-Flanagan & Sommers-Flanagan, 2004b), your clinical skills, and your knowledge base, you also need to know yourself well enough to find an ethical decision-making process that fits your philosophical orientation, your personality, and your clinical setting. If you fail to do so, you will most likely fall victim to at least some of the items in the list provided in Digressions for Deliberation 3.4.

Finding an ethical decision-making model or practice congruent with your professional setting, theoretical orientation, and personality is an important part of preparing for your career. In fact, thoughtful preparation can prevent many inadvertent but serious ethical missteps. For instance, because of the increasing globalization of mental health services, and the ongoing needs presented by the many natural and/or human-caused disasters, you may find yourself volunteering to help in crisis interventions.

Often, the ethical guides for such activities, if they exist at all, are in the form of behavioral guidelines or codes of conduct. They may not even be readily available to the volunteers. In these cases, attention to the basics in the codes will help guide professional behavior. Over 25 years ago, Redlich and Pope (1980) suggested seven general principles applicable across many helping disciplines. They are as follows:

1. Do no harm.
2. Beware of the boundaries of your competence.
3. Do not use your power to exploit.
4. Respect all human beings.
5. Keep confidentiality.
6. Obtain informed consent.
7. Practice within the bounds of social justice.

More recently, Kenneth Pope applied these guides in an article advocating the development of ethical standards for primary prevention (K. Pope, 1990a). In the next section, we use a principle perspective to build on similar basics, and offer further guidance to consider in the event of emergency or crisis mental health assistance.

ETHICAL CONSIDERATIONS IN CRISIS COUNSELING

Someone viewing humans from another planet would notice that our species clings tenaciously to life, striving to improve our lot for ourselves and our offspring. They would discern that humans help each other in good times and horrific times, and sometimes put themselves in harm's way for the sake of others. They would observe that humans are capable of great sacrifice and of recovering from enormous setbacks and trauma, whether caused by fellow humans or other natural forces.

Most people drawn to the helping professions are drawn by a sincere desire to help

A List of Excuses for Ethical Misconduct

The following list (which we edited for brevity) was created by Ken Pope and Melba Vasquez (1998, pp. 13–15).

1. It's not unethical as long as a managed care administrator or insurance case reviewer required or suggested it.
2. It's not unethical if we're victims.
3. It's not unethical as long as we can name at least five other professionals right off the tops of our heads who do the same thing. (There are probably countless thousands more we don't know about or we could name if we just had the time.)
4. It's not unethical as long as there is no body of universally accepted, scientific studies showing, without any doubt whatsoever, that exactly what we did was the sole cause of harm to the client.
5. It's not unethical as long as we weren't really feeling well that day and thus couldn't be expected to perform up to our usual level of quality.
6. It's not unethical as long as no one ever complained about it.
7. It's not unethical as long as our clients' condition (probably borderline) made them so difficult to treat and so troublesome and risky to be around that they elicited whatever it was we did (not, of course, to admit that we actually did anything).
8. It's not unethical as long as we don't talk about ethics.
9. It's not unethical as long as we don't know a law, ethical principle, or professional standard that prohibits it.
10. It's not unethical as long as a friend of ours knew someone that said an ethics committee somewhere once issued an opinion that it's okay.
11. It's not unethical as long as we know that legal, ethical, and professional standards were made up by people who don't understand the hard realities of psychological practice.
12. It's not unethical as long as we know that the people involved in enforcing standards (e.g., licensing boards, administrative law judges) are dishonest, stupid, and extremist; are unlike us in some significant way; or are conspiring against us.
13. It's not unethical as long as it results in a higher income or more prestige.
14. It's not unethical as long as it's more convenient than doing things another way.
15. It's not unethical as long as no one else finds out—or if whoever might find out probably wouldn't care anyway.
16. It's not unethical as long as we're observing most of the other ethical standards.
17. It's not unethical as long as there's no intent to do harm.
18. It's not unethical as long as we don't intend to do it more than once.
19. It's not unethical as long as we're very important.
20. It's not unethical as long as we're busy. After all, given our workload and responsibilities, who could reasonably expect us to obtain informed consent from all our clients, keep our chart notes in a secured area, be thorough when conducting assessments, and follow every little law?

others. As we emphasize throughout this book, ethical counselors realize that authentic help is a complicated endeavor. This is especially true in crisis situations. Never can we force those in need, simply because of their need, to accept what we have to offer or expect them to use interventions incompatible with their needs. The responsibility flows in the other direction. The person offering help must continuously seek to make this assistance

- culturally acceptable,
- developmentally appropriate,
- interpersonally sensitive,
- politically neutral, and
- attuned to the real life parameters of the environment and situation.

Analogous to sending candy bars or soda as food aid to starving people, there are forms of counseling, professional attitudes, and demeanor that do more harm than good in crisis situations (Chiang, Lu, & Wear, 2005). People in crisis, in the aftermath of trauma, are especially vulnerable. Their coping abilities are diminished (Fullerton & Ursano, 2005). The costs of physical and psychological survival are high and the last thing needed is ineffective or iatrogenic help. Harmful "helping" in crisis and the aftermath can take many forms (Chiang et al., 2005).

- The helping professional can explicitly or implicitly demand that the one helped see the world or themselves differently, behave according to the professional's rules, or in some other way, meet the helper's needs.
- Professional helpers may be drawn to crisis situations for selfish reasons, with questionable motives.
- And finally, professionals can underestimate the effects the crisis exposure will have on them, thus adding another casualty to the crisis and a resulting burden on the recovery process (Gladding, 2002; Motta, Chirichella, Maus, & Lombardo, 2004).

Consider the following case examples. Each is fictional, but has factors drawn from actual incidents.

Case Example: Mr. W. was a school counselor in an urban area. He offered to do overtime crisis counseling in an inner city school where a favorite teacher and three students had been shot in front of an entire assembly. Mr. W. was Asian-American, raised in an upper-class family in San Francisco. The school where the shooting took place was predominantly African American, as were three of the four victims. The shooter, who had not been apprehended yet, was said to be from an Asian gang, although he had been wearing a hood, so this wasn't verified. Mr. W.'s first assignment was to facilitate a small group of students who wanted to talk about what they had witnessed. The group members were very angry and seemed bent on insulting Mr. W. because he was Asian. Mr. W. knew better, but he could not stop himself from defending himself and his heritage. He insisted that group members acknowledge their own racism, rationalizing that this would help them heal and become better people.

Case Example: Dr. X. volunteered to travel from California to Oklahoma following the tornado there. She had occasionally participated in Critical Incident Stress Debriefings, so argued that she did not need to attend any special Red Cross training. She was unprepared for the sights and sounds of the physical devastation wrought by the tornado and needed to rest a great deal. She also felt very uncomfortable interacting with survivors. The situation was chaotic. It wasn't possible to have structured meetings, there were no ways to ensure confidentiality, and no therapy rooms. She wanted to find someone to work with; someone she could listen to and reassure. She planned to help them with their anger or despair, but her own anger and despair were too overwhelming. She often snapped at other volunteers, refused to get out of the vehicle, and to the relief of other volunteers and survivors, finally asked to be sent home.

Case Example: Mr. Y. was a midlife clinical social worker who loved to travel. He had an opportunity to join a volunteer organization that sends mental health professionals to India to work with young girls and women. The organization's stated intent was to offer interventions that helped girls who were likely to end up in the sex trade industry find alternatives, and to help those in the trade get out. Although Mr. Y. did not admit it to himself, his motives for volunteering were (a) adventure; (b) funded travel to a country he wanted to visit; and (c) a belief that he had superior skills to offer these women, since his professional work in the United States had included work with women leaving violent intimate relationships.

Case Example: Ms. Z. had chosen a secular graduate school, only with reluctance. Her deep faith led her to want to help others, and she had always hoped she could work within her faith system's boundaries. In graduate school, she learned that she could not ethically use her counseling skills to overtly try and convert clients to her faith. She still fervently believed that the main source of other people's sufferings was their lack of faith, but she understood that as a licensed counselor in a public agency, it could not be her role to explain this to them. In her work, she mainly did intakes and brief assessments for court-ordered families. When she read about the opportunity to go to New Orleans to work with the poor who had lost everything due to Hurricane Katrina, she felt called to do so. She was convinced she was being sent to give these people a chance to find healing through converting to Ms. Z.'s faith system.

These hypothetical case examples point to serious ethical problems. Consider them in light of the following principles, as well as through the various ethics codes in our profession.

USING ETHICAL PRINCIPLES TO GUIDE CRISIS WORK

Mental health professionals who volunteer in crisis situations are obligated to their own ethics codes which have general, but not specific, applicability to crisis work (Hanson, Kerkhott, & Bush, 2005). Some will volunteer for organizations that have codes of conduct, such as the Code of Conduct for the International Red Cross Red Crescent, which is provided at the end of this section. However, some will volunteer without exposure to ethical concerns particular to crisis volunteer work. These considerations will help professional crisis volunteers contemplate the ethical quality of their interventions. We use the midlevel moral/ethical principles (Beauchamp & Childress, 2001; Kitchener, 2000) described in Chapter 2 as a general guide.

Beneficence

Beneficence refers to promoting good for others. It does not involve promoting your own best interests.

Assess your motives.   Before volunteering to help in a crisis, professionals need to assess their motives—engage in some honest, serious soul searching. The dominant motive should be a desire to be of help. If curiosity, boredom, or a desire to express rage or indignation dominate, the professional must meet these needs in ways other than offering mental health crisis assistance. Other unacceptable primary motives include

- wishes for media exposure
- opportunities to grandstand one's expertise
- hopes of converting traumatized people to a certain faith system or philosophical orientation—even if the professional believes such a conversion would offer comfort

In the case of Ms. Z., using counseling skills in a secular context to convert clients to a faith system would be unethical, even if a crisis were not part of the scenario. Similarly, it is unethical to have "conversion to atheism or agnosticism" as one's primary or underlying goal.

Seek necessary skills.   If the desire is sincerely to be of professional assistance in crisis or disaster work, then training, supervision, and extra readings and/or coursework are in order (H. B. Smith, 2002). This may surprise you. It takes time to develop specific skill sets and crises demand instant responses, right? It is rather arrogant to think that just because we have basic counseling skills, we are ready to be crisis workers. Beneficent professional interventions are based on doing good and helping others. To have the best chance of actually doing good, being of real help, professional crisis counseling requires preparation. Collins and Collins (2005) write:

> Individuals who provide single-session crisis intervention should be proficient in utilizing beginning helping skills, knowledgeable about common crisis reactions, and the dynamics of specific crises, and familiar with relevant community resources. The more complex process of assisting individuals in the long-term struggle to resolve and integrate crises in their lives requires a helping professional with even more advanced professional skills and knowledge. (p. 45)

Monitor self-care.   Crisis workers can themselves be traumatized by trying to help those ravaged by trauma and crises (Pearlman & MacIan, 1995). This is to be expected to some extent (Ursano, Fullerton, Vance, & Kao, 1999). However, volunteers must self-monitor so that they do not become so traumatized, the help they offer is ineffective or even damaging.

Nonmaleficence

Nonmaleficence refers to doing no unjustified harm. This is a challenging principle in crisis or disaster situations because the potential for unintentional but significant harm is exceptionally high in attempting any intervention. In most crisis situations, every resource is precious. Simply taking up space while having nothing to offer is a form of harm. However, misapplication of professional skills or authority is worse (H. B. Smith, 2002).

Problems with conception and diagnosis. Humans react and adapt to crisis and trauma in individually and culturally diverse ways. Some may seem more adaptive than others. While a subset of survivors may develop symptoms that warrant a mental health diagnosis, most will not (Caffo & Belaise, 2005). Further, the assumption that pathogenic—or diagnostic-based—interventions are called for can be detrimental in many ways. It heaps insult on injury by insinuating the survivor is weak, permanently damaged, or mentally ill (Yehuda & Bierer, 2005). It might also impose a sick role on the individual, bringing on further symptoms in a self-fulfilling prophecy (Violanti, 2000).

Problems with intervention models. Mental health professionals come from diverse training backgrounds and theoretical orientations. The imposition of one's theory or intervention model on traumatized people can cause harm. To give an absurd example, it would be a terrible waste of time and resources to try and desensitize very recent tsunami survivors from their fears of high waters or the sounds of the ocean, or to begin work on their experiences of early parental abandonment and resulting lack of trust in authority figures. Intervention models for crisis work have many steps and dimensions (Weine & Henderson, 2005). They are pragmatic and include social, environmental, and individual concerns and interactions. Outcome research is difficult and controversial, but essential for the ethical professional to follow. For instance, critical incident stress debriefings, while still practiced, have been shown to be of little efficacy, and to perhaps cause damage (Rose, Bisson, Churchill, & Wessely, 2002).

Problems crossing cultures. Crisis volunteers often come from all parts of the country or world, and are not even privy to the usual community understandings, let alone the deeper concerns of race or culture within the community (Jackson & Cook, 1999). They are strangers. As such, they can make terrible mistakes born of simple but inaccurate assumptions of commonality or stereotypic traits. They can also easily misunderstand signals of distress, fear, or even strength. Multicultural competencies (see Chapter 9) are expected of all mental health professionals (D. W. Sue & Sue, 2003), and under ordinary circumstances, the professional has time to do research, get supervision, and utilize cultural gatekeepers when adding knowledge about an unfamiliar culture. Crisis allows little time for such research and adjustment. The Department of Health and Human Services provides an online article entitled "Developing Cultural Competence in Disaster Mental Health Programs" that is helpful for both volunteer professionals and those assembling the necessary services in the given locale (Athey & Moody-Williams, 2003).

Further complicating the task of culturally sensitive assistance in crisis work is the fact that traumatized humans search for meaning in the tragedy or crisis (J. L. Herman, 1992). "Such meaning is inevitably culturally embedded, yet the role of the cultural idioms and meaning systems in trauma adjustment is seldom fully explored" (Eagle, 2005, p. 202). The role of social support, too, cannot be understated in crisis recovery and general well-being (Cohen & Wills, 1985). Any intervention that inadvertently reduced a survivor's social support system would most likely be quite damaging (Norris & Kaniasty, 1996). Counselors could easily fail to recognize cultural norms and beliefs about psychological distress and the relative stigma attached to various patterns of symptom expression (Shinfuku, 2005).

Justice

Justice refers to a group of norms used to distribute benefits, risks, and costs fairly, or *equal treatment for equals* (Beauchamp & Childress, 2001). However, it may also be interpreted as unequal treatment for those with unequal status. For example, physicians and hospital staff struggle with this principle when they must decide which person in the emergency room should receive treatment first or when they must decide which sick patient should receive the next liver, kidney, or heart (Richard, Rawal, & Martin, 2005). Obviously, not every individual has an equal need for medical or counseling interventions and the struggle to provide services in a fair and just manner can be excruciating.

Crises and traumas violate our sense of security and justice in the world. Terrible things happen to innocent people. The poorest, youngest, and least able are often hardest hit by natural or human-caused disasters (Caffo & Belaise, 2005). Crisis workers can be sorely tempted to play favorites, or to try to secure goods or services in ways that are not fair. Mental health volunteers are generally not in a position to determine fair distribution of goods, but may, unfortunately, be in positions to obtain goods or offer services. While understandable, it is not ethical for professionals to use their status or influence to secure special favor for some traumatized clients and not others.

Crises bring out the best and worst in people. In the aftermath, humans often seek someone to blame (Janoff-Bulman, 2004). Benyakar and Collazo (2005) write that helpers tend to create small groups that often compete with each other, thus recapitulating the environment's injustices and disorganization. Mental health professionals must use their understanding of human blaming tendencies to manage temptations to project blame on any survivors—even those who may be behaving in obnoxious, threatening, or blaming ways.

Autonomy

The ethical principle of autonomy suggests that humans should have authority over decisions affecting their health and well-being (e.g., Thornicroft & Tansella, 2005). In theory, this principle also can apply to persons from collectivist cultures; they have the right to decline their individual authority to make decisions in favor of communal authority. In practice, the autonomy-based ethic can sometimes be experienced as supplanting a family-oriented approach (Chiang, Lu, & Wear, 2005).

Crisis situations can severely limit autonomy (Rosenstein, 2004). When people are moved to shelters and forced to leave behind all their worldly goods, they probably do not have much of a sense of personal autonomy. In fact, in the face of natural disaster, war, rape, or train or plane crashes, people understandably question how much control they really have over their lives (Bonanno, 2004). This is all the more reason for the mental health crisis worker to be understanding and respectful of peoples' rights to self-determination. Certainly, in times of immediate crisis, mental health work may be directive and authoritative. However, interventions should never be insistent, combative, or punitive (Foa, 2000). When possible, crisis counselors allow people in crisis to make choices. They offer support and reassurance in this choice-making process.

Fidelity

Fidelity in counseling and related forms of assistance and intervention involves honesty, reliability, and good faith. It includes loyalty, personal commitment, and integrity in one's actions with clients (Teddy D. Warner & Roberts, 2004).

Crisis situations will seriously challenge or transform many of the ethical practices you read about in this book. Informed consent may be trimmed from many thoughtful pages and detailed questions and answers to a 5-minute exchange designed to provide only the barest essential parameters of the counseling contact, or it may disappear entirely. Confidentiality may be extremely limited due to meeting in tents, along the seashore on a log, or in someone's front room. Records may be kept in scant ways on decidedly nontraditional materials (scraps of paper, napkins). Certain customary boundaries may be suspended. "As assisting and assisted persons are under the same threats, it is especially difficult for the therapist to establish a proper therapeutic distance" (Benyakar & Collazo, 2005, p. 82). However, crisis counselors must make valiant efforts to hold themselves to the spirit of ethical, professional interactions—this is the essence of fidelity.

The survivors and the systems created to help survivors cannot easily protect themselves from fraud and exploitation. Therefore, fidelity takes on the weight of the entire ethics code. It has been said that the truest test of morality is how people behave when no one is looking and no one will know. The chaos of crisis obscures accountability. The compelling human dimensions of crisis heighten every human emotion. The combination can be most difficult. In *Disasters: Mental Health Interventions,* John Weaver (1995) writes:

> Sometimes the combination of a stress response (especially an adrenalin rush) and the strong bonds that form in times of disaster can lead to confused feelings and emotions. People under severe stress may be inclined to misinterpret the events that are occurring around them. (p. 94)

In crisis work, ethical professionals exude compassion, wisdom, and skill while maintaining absolutely unambiguous boundaries. They may find themselves the love objects

========= Deepening Diversity 3.1 =========

The Fundamental Principles of the International Red Cross and Red Crescent Movement (http://www.ifrc.org/publicat/conduct/index.asp)

Humanity: The International Red Cross and Red Crescent Movement, born of a desire to bring assistance without discrimination to the wounded on the battlefield, endeavors, in its international and national capacity, to prevent and alleviate human suffering wherever it may be found. Its purpose is to protect life and health and to ensure respect for the human being. It promotes mutual understanding, friendship, cooperation, and lasting peace amongst all peoples.

Impartiality: It makes no discrimination as to nationality, race, religious beliefs, class, or political opinions. It endeavors to relieve the suffering of individuals, being guided solely by their needs, and to give priority to the most urgent cases of distress.

Neutrality: In order to continue to enjoy the confidence of all, the Movement may not take sides in hostilities or engage at any time in controversies of a political, racial, religious, or ideological nature.

Independence: The Movement is independent. The National Societies, while auxiliaries in the humanitarian services of their governments and subject to the laws of their respective countries, must always maintain their autonomy so that they may be able at all times to act in accordance with the principles of the Movement.

Voluntary service: It is a voluntary relief movement not prompted in any manner by desire for gain.

Unity: There can be only one Red Cross or Red Crescent Society in any one country. It must be open to all. It must carry on its humanitarian work throughout its territory.

Universality: The International Red Cross and Red Crescent Movement, in which all Societies have equal status and share equal responsibilities and duties in helping each other, is worldwide.

of some crisis survivors, and the hate objects of others (see our suggested self-care image for projective attacks in Chapter 7).

In Deepening Diversity 3.1, we provide the Fundamental Principles for the International Red Cross Red Crescent organization. These principles help volunteers grasp the significance of their interactions with disaster-stricken survivors. Other volunteer organizations will have behavioral guidelines and codes of conduct, all of which are important to consider before and during any professional volunteer affiliations.

Remember, your own professional code of conduct is the starting point for ethical conduct in many related professional situations. You are never *not* accountable for the basics, but beyond the basics, many specialties and situations call for additional ethical consideration (Hanson, Kerkhott, & Bush, 2005). Because of the nature of crisis work, there are many ethical concerns in both clinical service and potential research, but this seems an area that would benefit from further inquiry. Once their lives are stable again, asking the recipients of crises counseling about their experiences of ethics and efficacy can be most instructive for all concerned (Chiang et al., 2005).

CHAPTER WRAP-UP

From a "Dear Abby" writer distressed by cell phone rudeness, to a brief history of the British Counselling Association's ethical ponderings, to the International Red Cross Red Crescent Movement striving to alleviate human suffering, this chapter has explored the fascinating enterprise of encoding of moral guidance. Humans use both intuitive/emotional and critical/evaluative methods for discerning ethical dilemmas and deciding on courses of action (Gladding, 2005b). In other words, just like the legendary cowboys (and cowgirls) of the wild west (Owen, 2004), we use our heads and our hearts. This chapter covered the rational, written, legal, and legalistic side of ethical decision-making. Staying familiar with and contributing to the codes as they evolve is a very important part of being an ethical professional.

Chapter Four

PROFESSIONAL IDENTITY DEVELOPMENT: VALUES AND DEFINITIONS

It would be difficult indeed for anyone who has had a long clinical experience as a psychoanalyst to belittle the destructive forces within man.

—Erich Fromm

Do all the good you can, by all the means you can, in all the ways you can, in all the places you can, at all the times you can, to all the people you can, as long as ever you can.

—John Wesley

CHAPTER ORIENTATION

In this chapter, we cover personal and cultural values as they influence the formation and maintenance of helping relationships. Our professional activity is not an inert substance; wrongly enacted, helping relationships can be quite harmful. The whole notion of helping deserves careful scrutiny. In addition, we'll explore "differences" including cultural, sexual, age, and socioeconomic as they impact the helping relationship. Self-care and burnout, though they may seem to be premature topics, are covered as well. We hope you will read and reread this chapter. This information takes significant time to consider and absorb. It includes topics and materials that we find ourselves and our seasoned colleagues talking about and coming back to over the years. Specifically, the main topics we will consider together include:

- exploring the complicated intricacies of helping;
- reasons people become counselors, therapists, and professional helpers;
- that place where motivations and values intersect; including when values contrast, clash, or are shared;
- moral sensitivity as it interacts with clinical concerns;
- anxieties, such as the imposter syndrome and the invisible knapsack, that are common to graduate students; and very importantly,
- burnout awareness and prevention.

THE INTRICACIES OF HELPING

The concept of help may seem fairly simple to most of us, but just for argument's sake, let's assume it is not. Here are some provocative hypothetical statements that speak to the subtleties of complex helping interactions. Feel free to argue about these with your colleagues:

- In the act of helping, the person offering the help gains more than the person being helped.
- The helper always has a personal or political agenda.
- Being able to help is an indication of power and privilege.
- The one in need of help is vulnerable because of the need and because of the vagaries associated with seeking and receiving assistance.
- Helping people can diminish their autonomy and sense of control.
- There is no such thing as selfless helping.

Consider your own experiences of offering and seeking help. Have you ever needed a plumber, medical care, or a compassionate listener in the middle of the night? Have you ever found yourself all wrapped up in someone else's problem, wondering how you got yourself there? How many times have people said to you, in offended voices, "I was only trying to help," as if that let them off the hook for whatever they had done?

One of us (and that would be JSF) wanted to grow up to be a superhero. The notion of having unlimited powers with which to offer help was wildly appealing. This may explain why he chose to become a mental health professional instead of an oceanographer.

Pause for Reflection

Do you think of yourself as a natural helper? Are there people in your life who especially like to talk to you because you're an excellent listener or because you seem to understand people so well? How is it for you to be the one in need of help? Do you find receiving help to be harder than offering help?

As a rehabilitation counselor, I (RSF) learned that people with disabilities are especially cognizant of at least two essential truths about helping. The first is this: The human condition is such that we need each other's assistance to survive and thrive. As Bill Wither's (1972) song, *Lean on Me,* says so well, "We all need somebody to lean on." Many of us deny, fear, or ignore this human interdependence. However, the fragile myth of independence is shattered when one is faced with a serious disability. Learning to ask for and accept help is part of coping with human frailty and limitation. But the second truth is this: Some forms of "help" become more debilitating than the original need (Rooney, 2001). The one in need can be made to feel out of control, humiliated, weakened, overpowered, and helpless. Real needs and real solutions are ignored in favor of the helper's preferences and worldview. In the end, efforts to help can contribute to or cause an "illness" or problem (Bootzin & Bailey, 2005). This makes helping—especially professional helping—a much more demanding and delicate endeavor than one might initially assume.

Pause for Reflection

Have you ever experienced a situation where someone genuinely tried to help you with a problem, but the help offered actually contributed to a worsening of the problem? Have you experienced the inverse of this situation—when you tried to help someone, but somehow your efforts backfired? As you reflect on these experiences, consider what may have caused these efforts to fail.

Why People Become Professional Helpers

Liz Welfel wrote, "Real compassion for human problems and an unwavering commitment to be of service are essential for ethical sensitivity" (2006, p. 26). We concur wholeheartedly, and add that these same ingredients, compassion and commitment, are essential to any effective mental health interventions. If asked why you chose to become a helping professional, we assume that among your top ten reasons would be a desire to help other people. If not, you should reconsider your career choice. A desire to offer effective help to others is essential to the helping professions, and it is especially central in mental health work. So it is safe to assume you want to help other people. But *why* do you want to help other people? And how does this desire form the bedrock for ethical sensitivity? This is where it begins to get interesting.

Most helpers have both admirable and less-than-admirable motivations. Aristotle's conception of the Golden Mean, discussed in Chapter 2, provides another way to consider these helping impulses. Striving for the Golden Mean between the extremes in helping motivations can become a very practical ethical endeavor. For instance, our students are often a little insulted when we insist that they are, or should be, nosy. We do not mean that our students seek gratification by peeking in other people's bedroom windows, or prying into other people's private business, but we do mean that good mental health professionals actually enjoy peering into and knowing about other people's inner lives and struggles. Enjoying this deep exposure too much could easily lead to ethical trouble (see Chapters 6 and 7) but, on the other hand, not enjoying it at all would most likely lead to cynicism, disinterest in listening to clients or students, and early burnout. The first step in achieving a Golden Mean balance is acknowledging that being intrigued with human lives is, indeed, part of the motivation to become a counselor, but that intrusive curiosity or boredom are both signals of excess.

Motives for Helping and the Golden Mean

Some motives for helping others are listed in the following. Which of these seems a healthy balance between too little and too much? Which make you uncomfortable? Which reflect too little or too much motivation?

1. My life is such a mess, I need the distraction.
2. My own struggles have given me something to offer others.
3. I feel sorry for people.
4. Other people's troubles are more interesting than the best books or movies.

5. I want to be important to someone.

6. It makes me feel great when I can tell others how they could improve their lives.

7. I am deeply gratified when I get to be part of someone's healing.

8. I have been given many good things in my life. I want to give back.

9. I want to understand what makes people tick.

Besides the desire to help others and a genuine curiosity about human being's lives, at least two other common motivations draw people to the counseling profession. Obviously, neither involves earning a six-figure salary, although the first is related to the status accorded rich people in our culture. The first common motivation has to do with professional status or achievement. Achieving a master's or doctorate in a professional helping field, assuming a title, and obtaining a license carries status. Naturally, this prestige is part of the draw for individuals pursuing this calling. Sometimes counselors are uncomfortable with the power they have in the therapeutic relationship, and want to disavow both this power and the responsibilities that come with it. Others experience it as a rewarding aspect of the profession. Either way, the title usually carries prestige and power.

The other common motivation mental-health-professionals-to-be usually have is to achieve self-understanding, or even self-healing (Enochs & Etzbach, 2004; Jordan, 2002). No one is without childhood disappointments, teenage insecurities, or adult angst about life. Studying how to help others is also simultaneously an exploration of how to help oneself. Again, a glance at the extremes helps shed light on the ethical Golden Mean. To a greater or lesser degree, all healers are wounded healers. Consider this quote by Annie Dillard (1974) from *Pilgrim at Tinker Creek.*

> I am a frayed and nibbled survivor in a fallen world, and I am getting along. I am aging and eaten and have done my share of eating too. I am not washed and beautiful, in control of a shining world in which everything fits, but instead am wandering awed about on a splintered wreck I've come to care for, whose gnawed trees breathe a delicate air, whose bloodied and scarred creatures are my dearest companions, and whose beauty beats and shines not in its imperfections, but overwhelmingly, in spite of them. . . . (p. 242)

Given that we are all nibbled and frayed, the counseling profession would not exist if the entrance requirements included being perfect, whole, and pain-free. The question is not perfection, but rather what we have done and will continue to do with our imperfections, traumas, addictions, and rough edges. Wearing them as a badge of identity or honor represents an imbalance. Simply having survived something awful or challenging does not make you an expert. Self-focused wounded people or survivors often superimpose their experiences and solutions on their clients, and fail to listen and grasp the unique nature of each human's experiences (Sherman & Thelen, 1998). This focus on our brokenness is quite natural. Theologian and monk, Henri Nouwen, (2000) wrote:

> When people come together they easily focus on their brokenness. The most celebrated musical composition, the most noted painting and sculpture, and the most read books are

often direct expressions of the human awareness of brokenness. The awareness is never far beneath the surface of our existence because we all know that none of us will escape death—the most radical manifestation of brokenness. (p. 70)

Even though it is normal and even comforting, too much focus on your own struggles can be a harmful extreme, both for yourself and for those you will serve.

On the other hand, assuming a cool professional demeanor and denying one's own past and current struggles can be quite damaging as well (Gilroy, Carroll, & Murra, 2002). Such segmentation and denial risks creating gaps and avoidance, as well as an impersonal, sterile interpersonal style. There is nothing wrong with the motivation to grow in self-understanding or to find that the act of offering counseling and assistance to those in need also brings about healing in the counselor or helper. There is also nothing wrong with setting aside your own woundedness to focus on the pain of your client. However, taking either side of an extreme can end up being unethical and damaging. As noted in Deepening Diversity 4.1, there are clinical, individual, and cultural dimensions to consider in finding the right levels of self-disclosure.

THE INTERSECTION OF MOTIVATIONS AND VALUES

Alan Tjeltveit (1999) began his book titled *Ethics and Values in Psychotherapy* with this statement: "Psychotherapy, once viewed as value-free, is now widely acknowledged to be value-laden" (p. 1). Just as your motives for becoming a counselor must be examined and balanced in order to be an ethical counselor, so too must your values. In fact, if you examine your motives carefully, you will probably gain insight into your values as well. By values, we mean culturally shared and constructed concepts and materials that have physical or psychological worth to an individual. In this sense, one can value loving relationships with other people, one can value freedom, one can value all things purple, one can value a sunny day, a shiny car, a certain fashion look, birth control, heterosexuality, and so on. Values have a positive valence in one's life (Glasser, 1998). They are interrelated, layered, and often overlap, so that it is hard to articulate, or even be fully aware, of one's core values unless they are threatened or challenged.

As an illustration, let's say you place a high value on shiny, clean cars. After some thought, you realize that for you, shiny cars indicate pride of ownership and a certain classy way of being. So, under the shiny-car value are the values of responsibility and being respected in a certain way. To take it one step further, perhaps your mother shined her cars with care, and expressed her strong, warm, approval of you when you helped keep the car shiny. So, perhaps a core value expressed in the valuing of shiny cars is the value of honoring your parents, and attaching merit to their approval.

It is unlikely that valuing shiny cars, per se, will pose many ethical issues for you as a counselor. However, the next layer down can certainly come into play in your work with clients. If you value behaving responsibly in the world, and have a counseling practice that includes teenagers who are far more likely to value freedom or independence over responsibility, you may find yourself in one of the many, many, *many* counseling situations wherein counselor and client values clash (Glasser, 2002). If you have any

---

Deepening Diversity 4.1

Cultural Differences in Transparency

Researchers and writers in the area of negotiation and conflict management often consider the concept of "face."

> Face is a multi-faceted term, and its meaning is inextricably linked with culture and other terms such as honor and its opposite, humiliation. Saving face or giving face has different levels of importance, depending on the culture or society with which one is dealing. Perhaps the most familiar term to many is "saving face," which we understand simply to mean not being disrespectful to others in public, or taking preventive actions so that we will not appear to lose face in the eyes of others. (Rosenberg, 2004, p. 20)

Sue and Sue (2003) note that Asian people often experience emotional problems as shameful, and as a sign of personal weakness that brings disgrace on the entire family. Vast as they are, Asian cultures are not the only cultures that contrast starkly with the dominant culture in the United States with regard to self-disclosure—and, of course, it is always a mistake to assume individuals have *all* the general characteristics attributed their race or culture (Kim & Omizo, 2005). However, certainly some Caucasians in the United States are more likely to "let it all hang out."

Besides a general reticence to openly admit weakness, there are also other cultural differences in expressing need. The person or institution considered appropriate to turn to in times of pain or trouble vary as well. In many cultures, religious or spiritual guides are the ones to whom families or individuals turn in times of loss, confusion, trauma, or trouble. It is less shameful or awkward to seek spiritual guidance or forgiveness than to seek assistance from a secular professional who is a stranger. Similarly, the amount of professional self-disclosure expected or tolerated will vary based on client ethnicity, age, sex, and personal preference (Constantine & Yeh, 2001; Munely, Lidderdale, Thiagarajan, & Null, 2004). The sensitive multicultural professional will adjust levels of self-disclosure and formality accordingly (Lowe, 2005).

---

doubts about this, peruse (and add to) the noncomprehensive list of current value-conflicted domains in our culture in Digressions for Deliberation 4.1 and add your own ideas as you go along.

No list of human values will ever be complete. Further, any hierarchy of values will be different across cultures, age, and time. Some values obviously have more moral weight than others.

Many philosophers have attempted to make a clear distinction between moral and nonmoral actions, preferences, and values, (Annas, 1991; Pojman, 1995; M. White, 1988). However, James Rest, a moral development researcher, has argued that an action has *moral (or ethical)* implications *if* the behavior in question will have an effect on others

Digressions for Deliberation 4.1

Domains Where Values Reside and Rumble

Religion: Humans have an amazing variety of religious values. These are core values, often associated with beliefs about life and death, including how to live, eat, dress, interact socially and sexually with others, one's proper relationship to nature, and so on. These values are all linked to one or more deities and/or sacred texts or philosophical systems. These values can present counselors with compelling value challenges, from being asked to pray with a client of a completely different (and antithetical) faith, to being asked about beliefs regarding heaven, hell, and the true meaning of life.

Health: Rights to basic health care, mental health care, and end-of-life care are value-laden areas. In addition, health education, especially when it includes sex education, aspects of mental health, or family relationships can be quite controversial and laden with values. For instance, should we teach children that soda pop is unhealthy and an unwise use of their money, while accepting large grants from soda companies that guarantee their products are available to these same children in the halls of the school?

Marriage and Family: You'd have to have been sound asleep the past few years to be unaware of the value-based battles over who can legally marry in our culture, who can reproduce and why, and the myriad struggles surrounding the rights of parents, embryos, biological and adopted children, and even grandparents as we wrestle over the definitions of family, commitment, and divorce.

Education: Who gets free education? Why? How much should taxpayers pay to educate the next generation? Who writes the textbooks? Who gets to sell them and make money? Who determines what is "true" for the time being? Which tests, if any, are culture-free and what do test results really mean in terms of knowledge acquisition or intellectual ability?

Limits of Government/Limits of Freedom: In the world today, values clash dramatically over how much government is needed for people to be safe. How aggressive should our country be with other countries or toward its own citizens? What should our collective resources be devoted to, and how much of our resources should we give to the environment, the poor, oil companies, and economic stimulation?

Birth and Death: When does life begin? Who decides the right course of action in the event of a pregnancy? Is sex primarily an act intended for procreation? Recreation? Spiritual connection? Is birth control wrong? And on the other end of life, should we legally prohibit people from taking their own lives? Or should we prohibit professionals or family members from assisting in a chosen suicide? Should we protect our elders from lives of poverty and meaninglessness? Why do we embalm bodies? Is cremation wrong?

Digressions for Deliberation 4.1 (continued)

Honesty/Deception: Under what conditions is lying expected and/or acceptable to you or to others? Is deceptive advertising acceptable? How about misleading political promises? Is it acceptable for citizens to "fudge" on their income reporting to save money on taxes or for determining how much to pay using a sliding fee scale? Are little lies to save self-esteem, time, or money acceptable? Is it okay to lie to your clients so they won't know you're on a particular kind of vacation?

If you made a similar list of value-laden topics, what would you include? What are the glaring omissions to this list? Interestingly, this list reflects our focus as authors, and the domains we emphasized, and those we neglect to mention here say something about us, just as the domains you noticed missing or the domains you would omit or express differently say something about you.

(Rest & Narvaez, 1994). The word *evaluate* literally means to determine the value of a given person, place, object, action, or idea. Without consciously thinking about it, we make value judgments almost incessantly, in our choices about the food we eat, the clothes we wear, the transportation we use, the way we spend our time and resources, and the ways we treat others. As the subatomic physicists, Buddhists, and many other spiritual and scientific thinkers assure us, we are all interconnected. It is hard to imagine many human actions, or values, that have absolutely no connection to other people and their welfare. It is also readily apparent that some choices and values have more immediate moral implications than others.

Another important dimension of values and valuing is this: Our values shift over time, and change with exposure and education (Erikson, 1963). Remember what you most wanted to own when you were a teenager? Who you most wanted to impress? Was being respected more important than being caring? Or was it the opposite for you? Remember what you valued the most your first year of college? Have you always valued honesty? Courage? Faithfulness to your family? Have your concerns about the environment, financial well-being, or personal health habits changed over the past 10 years? For a thought-provoking view of aging, see Joan Erikson at age 90 in a video produced by Frances Davidson (1995). Sometimes, our values are so central to us, and change so gradually, that we would have a hard time readily naming and prioritizing them if someone asked us to.

We have used the exercises provided in Applications 4.1 and 4.2 as a way for all of us to come to grips with our values, fears, and those biases we all have but hate to face or admit. We hope you will take time to do these exercises, preferably in a small group, or in class, and then talk together about the experience of doing them.

As a professional in the mental health or counseling world, your work will bring you into close proximity with other people's values day in and day out. Some of these values will be deeply held, deserving of your respect. Other values your clients hold may be subject to change and development in the process of their work with you. These values will sometimes contrast with yours in interesting ways, sometimes conflict with yours

---

Applications 4.1

Uncovering Values Exercise

If you were going to adopt a child, rank order from first to last, which you would adopt?

___ A child with cerebral palsy
___ A child with AIDS
___ A child from a mixed racial background
___ A child with a physical handicap
___ A child with Down syndrome
___ A child with an alcoholic mother
___ A child that had been abused for the first 2 years of life
___ A child that is deaf
___ A child that is blind
___ A child that was born with a horrible, permanent disfiguring birthmark
___ A child born addicted to cocaine
___ A child born to a schizophrenic mother (she got pregnant while hospitalized)
___ A child born in a rural area of country racially or culturally very different from your own, raised for 2 years in an orphanage there

---

Applications 4.2

Facing Our Values Exercise

Name the disability you most fear for yourself.

Name the "difference" in others that you find most frightening, upsetting, and/or disconcerting.

Name the "difference" within you or about you that you would be most ashamed to admit.

Name the "difference" within or about you that you feel most proud of.

Under what circumstances would you wish for death?

What class/group/cultural set of people do you believe to be the loneliest people in the world?

What actions in the world, done by yourself or other people, would you be comfortable labeling as sin? As evil? As wrong?

Are there any types of people or belief systems you would label as just plain wrong or even evil?

in troubling ways, and sometimes match up so closely that it actually makes you uncomfortable or confused. The following three examples will illustrate these possibilities.

When Values Contrast in Interesting Ways

Shortly after Sam's seventeenth birthday, his 19-year-old girlfriend, Bindi, told him she was pregnant. Sam decided to quit school and work full-time at Oil Can Henry's, where he could make $8.00 an hour with decent health benefits. He wanted to marry Bindi, and wanted her to have the baby. Bindi's parents were wealthy African-American business people. Sam lived with his mother, who described herself as a starving artist. Sam described her as a flaky Catholic. Sam's father lived in another state and was not often in touch with Sam. Bindi no longer lived at home, but was very close to her parents, who very overtly begged her to get an abortion and take her time thinking about her relationship with Sam. Sam was extremely distraught, and his mother worried that he might be suicidal. Sam's mother got him to agree to meet with a counselor.

As luck would have it, Sam ended up with Ms. Benson, an openly feminist clinical social worker in a community practice. Ms. Benson found herself quite taken with Sam's devotion to Bindi, and his desire to marry and have Bindi have the baby. Ms. Benson believed quite strongly that the decision about whether or not to bring the pregnancy to term was primarily Bindi's. However, she found herself in sympathy with Sam, admiring his willingness to make sacrifices, and touched by his wish to have this pregnancy continue, and to be a father.

When Values Clash

Connie, a seasoned school counselor, thought she had talked with children about every subject known to humankind, but she was wrong. And though she was a vegetarian, an active member of the Humane Society, and the owner of two dogs, three cats, and a gerbil, she also believed she was very balanced and understanding when children told her about going hunting, skinning the wild game to tan the hides, and so on. After all, she lived in a small town in Wyoming. But when Duane, the new boy, came to see her based on his teacher's urging to talk about his misbehaviors in sixth grade, Connie was handed quite a set of challenges. Duane explained that his family was very poor, and that his mother often put out cat food in the alley to catch stray cats. "She sneaks up on 'em and grabs their tails, and snaps their necks. Like this," Duane said, making a breaking motion with his two hands. "Then we skin 'em. Make stew. I don't like it much, but it's what we eat sometimes." Connie could barely keep her mind in the room and her focus on Duane. The images were strong and horrifying. She knew if her face showed her horror, she would be of very little help to Duane.

When Shared Values Present Challenges

Diasku was a first generation Japanese-American. He was the first-born son, and took very seriously his duties to his aging Japanese parents. He saved every dime he possibly could so that he could cover his parent's needs. He worked as a rehabilitation counselor in an urban area, and was often asked to work with clients whose first language was Japanese. One day, a young man named Abe came in for an evaluation. He had been badly burned in a cooking accident at a local restaurant. He very much hoped his disability payments would continue, allowing him to provide care for his aging father. Diasku found himself drawn to the young man, because often, the Japanese-American youth he interviewed wanted to be free of the familial obligations of "the old ways."

Abe's injuries were significant, but Diasku knew he would be making a judgment call in terms of the overall length of recovery and other factors that had financial implications for Abe. He could feel himself pulled to maximize the situation to Abe's advantage.

MORAL SENSITIVITY AND CLINICAL CONCERNS

As you may remember from the last chapter, ethical decision-making models either specify or assume moral sensitivity as a starting point for ethical behavior and decisions (Welfel, 2001). One could reasonably ask, "How does someone become morally sensitized?" We hope that taking ethics courses and reading ethics texts such as this one contribute to adult, professional moral sensitivity. Many who study cultural practices and child development have offered theories of moral development based on reason, instruction, and cognitive maturation (Krebs & Denton, 2005). Diverse thinkers have hypothesized that our values and morality are products of our capacity for and engagement in meaningful relationships, or our spiritual commitment, or our ability to reason. Still others believe that our values have evolved due to natural selection. Matt Ridley (1996) quotes Charles Darwin, who wrote in his 1871 book, *The Descent of Man:*

> A tribe including many members who, from possessing in high degree the spirit of patriotism, fidelity, obedience, courage and sympathy, were always ready to aid one another, and to sacrifice themselves for the common good, would be victorious over most other tribes; and this would be natural selection. (p. 172)

Regardless of the origins of our values and the direction our development takes, it is clear that values vary widely across cultures, change over time, and are influenced by life experiences and relationships. In fact, we are willing to wager that simply reading a quote by Charles Darwin raised value issues for some of you. There is absolutely no doubt that your values will influence the ways you work with people professionally. The question is not *if,* but *how.* The essence of professional ethical behavior centers on the welfare and betterment of the client *from the client's point of view.* Therefore, the imposition of your values directly onto your client is questionable, and needs to be closely examined before you allow yourself to engage in something that direct. In fact, coercive attempts to influence have long been shown to negatively affect perceptions of the influencer (Raven, 1983). Therefore, even if your values correspond with what would be objectively "good" for your client, such as weight loss, more careful sexual activity, or curbing of an addiction, you could harm your therapeutic alliance by allowing your values to seem coercive to your client.

On the other hand, you cannot hide your values nor keep them from being part of your work. Your values are part of who you are and what you have to offer to clients in your professional work. Many believe that psychotherapy's attempts to be value-free have failed and been damaging in the process (Doherty, 1995; Tjeltveit, 1999). In the next chapter, we cover the rich concept of informed consent and informed refusal in the counseling relationship. The interactive process of informed consent provides an important starting point for the counselor and the client in examining values pertinent to their work together. However, except in settings explicitly defined by a particular set of values, such as a pastoral counseling center, the direct *promotion* of your values will likely be ineffective as well as unethical.

CHOICES ABOUT DISPLAYING VALUES

In the United States, we live in a secular democracy. We deliberately separate church and state, and we have worked over time toward a pluralistic society based on justice and equal access for all. Large segments of our population hold deep religious and/or philosophical beliefs that define much of the meaning in their members' lives. The first amendment of the Constitution of the United States guarantees that faith systems and various ways of believing and living are not penalized or discriminated against (S. Welch, Gruhl, Comer, & Rigdon, 2004, p. 645). As a society, we try to uphold this value—with varying degrees of success.

Most likely, many of you reading this text hold some emotionally charged and central values, springing from your faith, political affiliations, or philosophy. How do you negotiate the ethical challenges of having strong beliefs *and* a mandate to offer a safe, nonjudgmental counseling environment for young and old, rich and poor, gay and straight, feminist and fundamentalist, disabled and temporarily able-bodied? Do you owe it to your clients to reveal who you are? Just exactly how authentic did Carl Rogers (1957) intend for professional helpers to be? Is it okay to post the Ten Commandments from the Hebrew Bible in your office? Or to have the Qur'an prominently displayed on your office coffee table? Do you wear crucifixes, head scarves, or yarmulkes to signify certain religious affiliations?

These are complicated decisions because these overt symbols carry great meaning for both your clients and for you. The symbols might carry similar meanings for you both, or they may be surprisingly dissimilar. You may be a mystically oriented, liberal Catholic with a beautiful rosary that you keep on your desk. You may be comfortable with birth control, gay marriage, and abortion rights, but your client has no way of knowing this. Your client could easily see the rosary and assume you were not the person to talk with about an unwanted pregnancy. We will discuss these important dimensions of your practice in the next chapter, as we explore the particulars of informed consent.

Besides overt symbols of religious, political, or philosophical orientations, your office and work setting send many other messages. We have a personal preference we overtly try to convince our students to adopt regarding photos and other personal materials in offices. Our preference is to *not* display any family photos in counseling offices; the following are some of our concerns.

- Displaying family members in photographs in your office reveals the family members' identities. Your clients know who your children, spouse, or friends are, but of course, your loved ones cannot be told who you work with. Therefore, you expose your family to being known and identified in ways they cannot know about or respond to.

- Displaying your personal life too fully gives clients the message that you have created a personal space for them to enter. They are likely to feel free to ask who is pictured in the photo, and to follow up with questions about your familial relationships. Perhaps not many clients will ask, but they nonetheless register this familiarity and it therefore weakens an important professional boundary.

You may or may not agree with us on this preference, but it is worth considering that the most basic communication principle is that *you cannot not communicate* (Wilmot & Hocker, 2000). Your values are revealed every step of the way, from first contact with clients, to the final good-bye. And sometimes they are revealed inadvertently and interpreted incorrectly. The more conscious and deliberate you are in the ways you reveal or choose *not* to reveal your values, the better.

Pause for Reflection

Think of the most central symbols of your identity. It might be a flag, a Star of David, a mountain bike, your membership in Alcoholics Anonymous, a gift from a departed loved one, or a memento from your best vacation ever. With whom do you share the meaning of these symbols? Have you ever had someone make fun of or desecrate a symbol of great meaning to you? Can you see ways in which the personal must be kept separate from the professional?

CARE FOR THE CARING

Here is an unabashedly judgmental value statement for you: We believe that *all* developing mental health professionals and anyone seeking to help others professionally should take good care of their minds, bodies, and psyches. They should, to use an old idiom, practice what they preach. We are not alone in this belief. Gilroy, Carroll, and Murra (2002) write, "We believe that the key to [burnout] prevention lies in establishing a professional ethos in which self-care is viewed as a moral imperative" (p. 406). There are four very important reasons for our stance.

1. First, we believe all humans will live more fulfilled lives if they take care of themselves in mind, body, and spirit (Hattie, Myers, & Sweeney, 2004; Jane E. Myers, Sweeney, & Witmer, 2000).
2. Second, the most valuable tool most professionals have to work with is themselves (Rogers, 1961; Hubble, Duncan, & Miller, 1999; Kottler & Brown, 1996). Keeping the self well-tuned, rested, psychologically balanced, and educated is as important as any theory or technique a counselor might use.
3. Third, good counseling involves empathic exposure to more human misery than would naturally come into the lives of most people. It is the profession of listening to or intervening in the fallout of natural and human-caused pain, disappointment, outrage, angst, and despair. Without good self-care, professional helpers run the risk of vicarious (secondary) Posttraumatic Stress Disorder (PTSD), overload, burnout, and cynicism (Pearlman & MacIan, 1995).

4. Related to the third point, even the most admirable helpers are necessarily imperfect, with our share of pain, traumas, disappointments, and unfinished business. If we leave our own psychological wounds unattended to, they are quite
likely to intersect with our work in conscious and unconscious ways that can be
damaging to all involved (Goleman, 2003; Luhrmann, 2000).

Most graduate mental health programs encourage graduate students to get counseling as part of their professional development. Often, they highly suggest both group
and individual counseling. No one enters any professional field with absolutely pure,
altruistic motives. Humans are a mixture of prosocial and selfish motives. The safest
way to handle your self-serving motives is to understand them and keep in touch with
them. If you weren't, at least sometimes, more preoccupied with understanding and/or
solving your own problems, you wouldn't be human.

If you didn't anticipate, at least to some extent, enjoying the authority that comes
with professional title and credentials, you wouldn't be pursuing your degree. But it is
never ethical, in the helping relationship, to let your own needs take precedent over the
welfare of your clients. Of course, managing self-serving motives isn't the only reason
to seek counseling. While studying diagnosis, multicultural materials, and other related
topics, students often discover that they have unresolved psychological conflicts, under-
developed areas of personality, old family issues, and many other good reasons to do
some personal work in counseling. Perhaps the most basic reason of all is to insure
deeper empathy for your clients by taking time to experience counseling yourself.
Research indicates that for graduate students, finances, time, and worries about confidentiality are all common obstacles (Dearing & Maddux, 2005).

In urging that all professional helpers take care of themselves, we stop short of *insisting* that this self-care take the form of personal counseling—at least at any given
time in one's life. Of course, being in the business, and considering the consistent research findings regarding how much counseling helps (Seligman, 1995; M.L. Smith &
Glass, 1977), we wonder why anyone would choose to become a counselor while at the
same time, never sitting on the other side of the desk. If you are training to offer a service you never seek yourself, you may want to explore your deeper attitudes toward
those who *do* seek counseling. On the other hand, sometimes it is not realistic or practical to obtain personal counseling. Other forms of self-care and growth are available
and offer meaningful healing and insight. This is a great topic for a group discussion.
Think about and share all of the ways you or close friends and family have found for
self-care, growth, and healing. You will find a list reflecting a recent group of graduate
students' thoughts on this matter in Digressions for Deliberation 4.2.

ANXIETIES THAT ARE (OR SHOULD BE) COMMON TO
GRADUATE STUDENTS

Just as stress is not all bad, a certain amount of anxiety can serve useful functions in
our professional development. As mentioned in Chapter 1, professionals-in-training
are often uncomfortable with the power and prestige that come with the titles associated with professional counseling and helping interventions. There are solid reasons for

---

Digressions for Deliberation 4.2

Ideas on Self-Care

Human healing and moral and psychological development occurs in many settings and through many channels. This list includes ideas students and colleagues have generated for psychological self-care and healing.

Marianne: I would say that everyone should seek therapy once in a while, but I also have found great challenge and a sort of deepening of my soul by going on a vision quest, and by doing direct work on my sense of calling and meaning in the world.

Monica: I have a wonderful spiritual advisor. I was raised Catholic, and while I don't agree with everything in the church, there is a rich tradition of mysticism that intrigues me.

Tri: As a first generation Vietnamese-American, I have found that both pursuing some of my family's traditional values, and actually visiting Vietnam, has brought about a kind of balance in my life. I plan to do more of it. And, there's always soccer!

Joyce: I need a lot of alone time. I've been an introvert forever, so I like to go on retreats, learn new techniques by experiencing them myself, and sometimes, I actually feel that I am healed directly by my work, if I just take time to let it sink in.

Deanne: For me, as an athlete, working out is essential. I played tennis in Jamaica almost daily throughout high school and college. After a series of injuries, I've had to turn the intensity down a bit, but it is still essential for me.

Greg: Even though I grew up on the reservation, I never really understood the power of my ancestors' spiritual practices. Now I participate in sweats and in other activities that help me walk in both worlds reasonably sanely.

Karin: Growing up, my family didn't have the resources to do much but buy groceries. Now I get an occasional pedicure, a massage, or something like that and I feel like the Queen of the World. Life is precious and short. I think we should give ourselves a treat now and then.

Tina: Art. For me, poetry, music, and fine pieces of oil or watercolor all stir something healing and wonderful in me. I dabble in all of those things myself, but it's really other people's work that gives me that sense of something good beyond myself.

Rob: In my other life, I'm a carpenter. I think all people need a hobby or two that grabs them—that they feel passionate about. You have to get out of your head occasionally, so that when you get back in your head, you see things more clearly.

Nancy: I meditate. Sometimes it's mountain walking meditation, or gardening meditation. I'm a secular Jewish woman with Buddhist leanings, and a lot of Christian friends. I think clearing the mind and meditating is a

---

Digressions for Deliberation 4.2 (continued)

wonderful practice—it can't replace getting some counseling when you need it, but it sure helps me lead a more balanced, mindful life.

Eli: For me, nature is the most healing thing on the planet, except for maybe my pets. I love caring for my dog. I love walking and hiking. I need to find that grounding, that sense of being part of a greater plan, or I get really antsy and unfocused. And I like to travel, too . . . when I can afford it. You know, James Baldwin (2005) said, "I met a lot of people in Europe. I even encountered myself" (p. 48).

This is a personal, noncomprehensive list that we hope helps broaden your own ideas about self-care and potentially growth-producing and healing human activities.

---

this discomfort. Rather than deny it or become overly reactive to it, it is best to acknowledge these various anxieties and gain guidance and wisdom that can come from facing and addressing our fears.

The Imposter Syndrome

Research into the *imposter syndrome* first began in 1978 by researchers Pauline Clance and Suzanne Imes (1978), who studied successful, high-achieving women. They found that these women suffered from significant self-doubt and had not internalized their successes as their own. The women believed that other people had been deluded into thinking of them as competent, and that their accomplishments were due to good contacts or luck. This was true even though the facts indicated the exact opposite. The women reported fearing that they would be found to be phonies, and were often filled with self-doubt.

In our experience, many graduate students, regardless of sex or gender, struggle with imposter syndrome. Seeing your first client, starting work on your first internship, or seeking your first professional position will likely raise fears of inadequacy and incompetence (J. Sommers-Flanagan & Sommers-Flanagan, 1989). Humans tend to cope with this kind of anxiety along a continuum with dysfunctional extremes on either end. The continuum might be described as the following:

- One extreme: Absolute self-deprecation, coupled with false humility, used to excuse one's lack of participation and knowledge.
- Middle ground (or Golden Mean): Appropriate humility and willingness to ask for help, seek outside resources, and put in the extra effort to feel confident and responsible.
- Opposite extreme: Bravado and overconfidence. "Fake it 'til you make it" sort of attitude. Misuse of authority, unwillingness to admit mistakes or uncertainties, and refusal to seek the extra help or spend the extra time necessary to know what one needs to know.

We cover issues in competence in more depth in Chapter 9. For now, we encourage you to embrace your beginner's anxieties, and the feelings of inadequacy that naturally come with being new in the field. Further, we hope you realize that you will never "arrive" and be a totally actualized, completely educated, and fully mature professional. Continuing education, collegial supervision groups (e.g., Thomas, 2005), and a determination to be a lifelong learner are all essential to a healthy, ethical counseling practice.

The Invisible Knapsack

There is another problem sometimes present in developing mental health professionals, but less commonly known to be associated with sleepless nights—although it should be. The phenomenon, in one form or the other, has most likely been around as long as humans have graced the earth. Peggy McIntosh (1998) was the first to name this problem the invisible knapsack. Members of any dominant culture have one, but most of us are unwilling to admit it, and even less willing to open it, dig into the contents, and decide what to do about it. In our knapsack, we have all the little benefits and commonalities that make being a member of the dominant culture enviable and secure. Some of these include:

- I can, if I wish, arrange to be in the company of people of my race most of the time.
- I can turn on the television or open to the front page of the paper and see people of my race widely represented.
- I can arrange to protect my children most of the time from people who might not like them.
- I can swear or dress in second-hand clothes or not answer letters without having people attribute these choices to the bad morals, the poverty, or the illiteracy of my race (p. 148).

As a class, or on your own, make your own personal list. If you are a member of the white dominant culture, make your list from that perspective. If you are a member of a nonwhite race or culture, make a list of advantages you believe are operational for your white counterparts.

Whites have the luxury of being the normative group. Social psychologist, Susan Fiske, reports that when asked who they are, her white students rarely, if ever, begin with a statement of their race or ethnicity. However, almost to a person, her students of color spontaneously include their racial or cultural identity (Hackney, 2005).

Most of us would like to believe that we have overcome the learned biases and prejudices of our families and culture, but such unlearning is a lifelong process, and often we suppress our prejudices long before we overcome them (Rutland, Cameron, Milne, & McGeorge, 2005; Smedley & Smedley, 2005). In the Rodgers and Hammerstein's (1949) musical, *South Pacific,* they sing a snappy little number that insists that children must be taught to fear and hate—such emotions directed at others do not come about naturally.

In Chapter 9, we provide you with a guide for multicultural competencies. Such competence is closely related to personal and professional identity development (Christopher, 1999; Munely et al., 2004). Most accredited graduate mental health professional programs have significant course work devoted to multicultural counseling and a concern for multiculturalism is infused in the new ACA ethics code, as well as a frequent topic of entire journals in the field (American Psychological Association, 2003). However, the road to the kind of identity development that embraces diversity is a long one.

One model for the cultural identity development journey includes six stages (L. J. Myers et al., 1991) beginning with *individuation,* which is described as identifying rather cluelessly with mainstream culture, displaying little insight into self or others. In the second phase, *dissonance,* there is the beginning of personal identity as different from the masses—often involving the individual noticing parts of self that are real, but have been ignored or devalued by others. The third phase, *immersion,* occurs when people begin to identify with those similar to themselves, especially those having similar traits to those devalued by the culture around them. This allows the individual, in the fourth phase (*internalization*), to have the courage to begin to give a positive valence to those parts of self previously devalued. In phase five, *integration,* the positive valence contin- ues, with recognition that there are many assumptions we make about the world that are inaccurate and that can be changed for the better. In the last stage, *transformation,* the shift in worldview is profound. There is a reflective recognition of the interrelated- ness of all people, with an appreciation of the unique cultures and histories we share (Munely et al., 2004).

Pause for Reflection

It is important to look at the invisible knapsack concept from an alternative angle: Imagine you decided to seek counseling for yourself or your family. Imagine a situ- ation where you absolutely cannot hope to see someone from your own race or cul- ture. What race, other than your own, would you prefer? What attributes about your potential counselor might make you uncomfortable? How would you compensate for the differences in background?

BURNOUT AWARENESS AND PREVENTION

Burnout is a relatively common experience for people in the helping professions (Bak- ker, Schaufeli, Sixma, Bosveld, & Van Dierendonck, 2000; Skovholt, 2001). Researchers Maslach and Jackson (1981) define burnout symptoms as (a) emotional exhaustion, (b) depersonalization, and (c) reduced personal accomplishment. All three of these symptoms spell trouble for mental health professionals and their clients. Emotionally exhausted therapists cannot center themselves and maintain the balance needed for empathy and containment of the client's emotions. Depersonalized counselors develop negative, cynical attitudes toward clients and cannot offer positive regard, neutrality, or perspective. Helpers suffering from a sense of reduced personal accomplishment are plagued by feelings of ineffectiveness in their professional role.

As graduate students, you may not want to grapple with thoughts about burning out in a profession you are just beginning, but it is likely you have already experienced some form of burnout in your life—and may even be experiencing a bit of graduate student burnout right now! Living a balanced, healthy life means taking steps to minimize or prevent burnout throughout your personal and professional life.

Factors and Symptoms of Stress and Burnout

Burnout results from mishandled and excessive stress. Stress, itself, is a fact of life. Hans Selye (1974) was one of the first to point out that stress has many positive qualities. A certain amount of physical responsiveness to life's demands is necessary to motivate and energize people. Selye referred to this energy source as positive stress, or eustress. As Holmes and Rahe (1967) pointed out many years ago, any change in the routine of our lives—even welcome ones—can be stressful. Digressions for Deliberation 4.3 provides the list that Holmes and Rahe used when they asked nearly 400 respondents to rate the relative stress introduced into someone's life by these events.

There are vast individual differences in stress tolerance and coping style among humans. There are differences in mind, body, and cultural beliefs that influence both what we find stressful, and the ways we then cope (Ray, 2004). It is important for you to learn about yourself, your stress tolerance, and your own personal signs of too much stress. The Holmes and Rahe scale (1967) helps identify possible stressors for middle-class members of the dominant culture. There are many other sources of socioeconomic and culturally determined stress that you might add to the list. In addition, Thomas Skovholt (2001), in his excellent book, *The Resilient Practitioner,* provides a 20-item list he calls "Hazards of Practice" (p. 76) and elaborates on each one (see Skovholt, Chapter 6). These hazards include:

1. We work with clients who have unsolvable problems that must be solved.
2. Our clients and students are not necessarily "honors students."
3. Our clients and students have motivational conflicts.
4. There is often a readiness gap between our desire to help, and see change, and our clients' or students' readiness to change.
5. Sometimes, the people with whom we work project negative feelings onto us.
6. Sometimes, we cannot help because we are not good enough, or we are the wrong person.
7. Our clients have greater needs than we, our social services, and our education and health systems can meet.
8. Mental health practitioners have a difficult time saying "No."
9. Our profession involves living in an ocean of stressful emotions.
10. We must often face ambiguous professional loss—clients and students who leave abruptly and we never know why, nor have time to process the loss.
11. Our work is confidential and we cannot talk about it openly and readily with whomever we might wish.
12. Our work involves providing constant empathy, interpersonal sensitivity, and one-way caring.
13. We cannot easily measure our success.
14. We can all too easily see our failures or shortcomings.

The Holmes and Rahe Stress Scale

Death of spouse	100
Divorce	75
Marital separation	65
Jail term	63
Death of a close family member	63
Personal injury or illness	53
Marriage	50
Dismissal from work	47
Marital reconciliation	45
Retirement	45
Change in health of family member	44
Pregnancy	40
Sex difficulties	39
Gain of new family member	39
Business readjustment	39
Change in financial state	38
Death of close friend	37
Change to different line of work	36
Change in no. of arguments with spouse	36
Major mortgage	31
Foreclosure of mortgage or loan	30
Change in responsibilities at work	29
Son or daughter leaving home	29
Trouble with in-laws	29
Outstanding personal achievement	28
Partner begins or stops work	26
Begin or end school	26
Change in living conditions	25
Revision of personal habits	24
Trouble with boss	23
Change in work hours or conditions	20
Change in residence/schools/recreation	19
Change in social activities	18
Small mortgage or loan	17
Change in sleeping/eating habits	16
Change in no. of family get-togethers	15
Vacation	13
Christmas	12
Minor violations of the law	11

15. We face chronic regulation oversight and control by external, often unknown, others.
16. Our work can become routine, yielding cognitive deprivation and boredom.
17. We must put up with cynical, critical, and negative colleagues and managers.
18. We must face ongoing ethical and legal challenges and fears.
19. In repeatedly witnessing and hearing of the trauma endured by others, we become traumatized ourselves.
20. We live with the awareness of potential physical trauma from angry clients, students, or family members.

At the risk of causing you to consider an abrupt career change, we include one last list. Drawing from our own professional experiences and the research of many in our field (Bakker et al., 2000; Holmes & Rahe, 1967; Skovholt, 2001), this list details possible signs of burnout and related indicators of professional imbalances, such as overidentification and/or underidentification with one's work (Emerson & Markos, 1996).

Symptoms of Underidentification
- the-organization (or world)-owes-me-this-job attitude
- unwilling to seek continuing education, defensive about counseling style
- socializing with students (Just one of the guys, lack of professional identity) *or*
- aloofness from students—puts most of them at a judgmental distance
- plays the numbers game but is *outta there* whenever possible
- secretly scorns people in need of help, compares them to self (one-upmanship)
- cynicism and callousness

Symptoms of Overidentification
- hero syndrome (needing to save someone/everyone at all costs)
- taking the work, worries, and stories home
- failing to keep boundaries between professional identity and core/personal identity
- willingness to rob friendships and family relationships on behalf of the job
- repeatedly using personal resources (time, money, books,) to serve "the cause" at work
- socializing with students inappropriately (secret mentoring)
- having your job as central or complete identity
- inability to envision doing something else with your life
- seeing self as above the rules of the profession, due to your "high calling"
- ignoring numbers game because personal devotion is obvious, should be enough
- giving beyond the point of health or wisdom
- failure to seek unbiased consultation or supervision
- chronic shame and doubt

Symptoms of Burnout
- dreading going to work
- feelings of relief if you have no-shows or get "rained out"
- difficulties concentrating
- difficulties listening
- chronic irritability with students and colleagues; cynical derogatory attitude
- recurrence of physical or emotional symptoms from past
- reduced immune system functioning
- failure to bounce back after usual breaks/vacations
- break-down of observation of rules, guidelines, paperwork (or rigid adherence)
- inability to accept constructive feedback
- physical, mental, emotional exhaustion (across life settings)

It can be quite overwhelming to consider all the stresses and strains common to the helping professions, and threatening to consider the ways this stress might translate into our work with clients. However, mental health professionals, more than most, should also realize the central importance of how we actually think about and handle these inevitable truths.

> *The mind is its own place, and in itself*
> *Can make a Heav'n of Hell, a Hell of Heav'n.*
>
> —John Milton, *Paradise Lost*

In other words, the ways you choose to think about your work, and your life, can make a radical difference in your overall functioning, health, and professional longevity. We discuss this more specifically in the next section.

Resilience and Hardiness

Researchers in the area of professional stress have found many factors that apparently build up resistance to or prevention of burnout. The descriptors of these factors vary from author to author, and there are many similar operational definitions for these concepts. An early researcher in this area, Kobasa (1979), found three factors contributing to what she called hardiness: *Commitment, challenge,* and *control*. Professionals who feel a deep sense of commitment to their work and find it meaningful, who find their work challenging, and who have a sense of control over their work and their own professional destinies are far less likely to become overstressed, cynical, and eventually, burned-out.

We have expanded Kobasa's (1979) list to include other areas researchers have found to be important in burnout prevention. *Workload* is an obvious factor in burnout. To minimize burn-out likelihood, the workload should be within reason and the setting should include resources necessary to do the job. In many counseling and social work arenas, especially in rehabilitation and school settings, this may not be the case. Professionals facing limited resources and unrealistic caseloads are forced to find other avenues for avoiding burnout.

Adequate *compensation,* or reward, is also significant in job satisfaction and burnout. Not only should your work pay well enough to care for your needs and provide a sense of financial security, it should also be intrinsically rewarding. Opportunities for professional growth and development, as well as recognition and support from supervisors, are also essential (Hutman, Jaffe, Segal, Kemp, & Dumke, 2005).

A *sense of community* and predictable, if not trustworthy, colleagues also make a difference in stress levels and burnout. Of course, you need a sense of community outside your workplace as well, but it helps to have professional colleagues with whom you can share ideas, humor, praise, fears, and successes (Zeckhausen, 2002). Research has shown that positive emotions, laughter, and good humor are also associated with resilience (Bonanno, 2004), which of course, are enhanced by a sense of connection to others.

And rounding out our list, *congruency with basic values* is critical to most people working in professional settings (Mumford, Connelly, & Leritz, 2005). The risk of cynicism and psychological erosion is high when people are forced to violate basic personal or professional values in order to succeed at work, or avoid work difficulties.

In keeping with the concept of the dialectical nature of reality that we discuss in Chapter 1, we want to note that a stress-free and predictable environment is not necessarily ideal for either burnout prevention or professional growth and development. Consider the following quote as an aid for discussion of this perspective.

> Recently an acquaintance of mine who has searched for many years for a sense of direction and mission revealed that he was waiting for "an unshakable vision." I immediately thought of the work of the Belgian physicist Ilya Prigogine, who was awarded the Nobel Prize for his theory of what he calls "dissipative structures" part of which contends that friction is a fundamental property of nature and nothing grows without it—not mountain, not pearls, not people. It is precisely the quality of fragility, he says, the capacity for being "shaken up" that is paradoxically the key to growth. Any structure—whether at the molecular, chemical, physical, social, or psychological level—that is insulated from disturbance is also protected from change. It becomes stagnant. Any vision—or anything—that is true to life, to the imperatives of creation and evolution, will not be unshakable.
>
> We must therefore be willing to get shaken up, to submit ourselves to the dark blossomings of chaos, to reap the blessings of growth. Much of this is axiomatic: stress often prompts breakthroughs; crises point toward opportunities; chaos is an integral phase of the creative process; and protest abets the cause of democracy. The whole science of immunization is based on this wisdom: We introduce a little bit of chaos in order to prevent a lot of chaos. Just enough, but not too much. We shake up the system for the sake of helping it evolve and become stronger. (Levoy, 1997, p. 8)

WEAVING THE STRANDS TOGETHER

These first four chapters have presented you with a provocative and somewhat disjointed array of perspectives and dimensions related to both human and professional morality.

If you've been allowing yourself to take it all in, you are most likely confused and perhaps even a little bit impatient with both the content and style of this material. You may wish we would simply tell you what you must do to be a safe, ethical helping professional. Or at least you might wish we would tell you how to absolutely determine the correct ethical course in any difficult helping situation. You are not alone in your concerns. Contemporary moral philosophers are actively wrestling with these very same concerns.

Recently deceased philosopher, James Rachels (1986), offered his version of a satisfactory moral theory in the last chapter of his text. He called this theory "morality without hubris" (p. 139) and stressed humility and impartiality as the guiding basis. Dartmouth professor emeritus Bernard Gert (2004) has written of his belief that there is a common morality shared by all human societies. He details ten general moral rules that he believes "account for all of the kinds of actions that are morally prohibited and required" (p. 20). The rules are as follows:

1. Do not kill.
2. Do not cause pain.
3. Do not disable.
4. Do not deprive of freedom.
5. Do not deprive of pleasure.
6. Do not deceive.
7. Keep your promise.
8. Do not cheat.
9. Obey the law.
10. Do your duty.

Gert believes that violations of these rules without adequate justification constitute immoral actions.

It is unlikely that either Rachels or Gert have succeeded in providing the perfect moral theory, and in fact, both have readily acknowledged this in their writings. The truth is that as of yet, there is no perfect guide for moral or ethical behavior. However, there is professional consensus regarding many areas of concern in the realm of ethical helping. These areas of concern are the subjects of the next section of this text. Ethics codes are a starting point, but they will never be enough. Moral philosophies and practices from our various cultural backgrounds lend important light, but they are each flawed in some way, or simply do not go far enough. Our own values and faith systems add to the mix as well and must be balanced by earnest consideration of other views.

CHAPTER WRAP-UP

This chapter covers a wide range of topics centrally related to the professional persona of ethical counseling. Borrowing from the Eightfold Path of the Buddha, we offer an Eightfold Path to being value-balanced, burnout free professionals.

An Eightfold Path for Ethical Professional Helpers

1. Right level of interest in others' lives and struggles
2. Right attitude toward the power inherent in the professional role
3. Right determination to be of meaningful assistance
4. Right commitment to becoming and remaining ethically sensitive
5. Right understanding of your values as they interact with the values of those you serve
6. Right determination to maintain your own physical and psychological health
7. Right attitude toward being a lifelong learner
8. Right knowledge of one's culture and the blinders culture can entail

It's all about balance, patience, moderation, and honesty. Our values and self-care are component parts of personal satisfaction and professional efficacy, and contribute to a goal we probably all share—the well-lived life.

SECTION TWO

THE DAY-TO-DAY CHALLENGES COMMON TO ALL

Chapter Five

THE HELPING RELATIONSHIP: FROM BEGINNING TO END

You must learn to be still in the midst of activity, and to be vibrantly alive in repose.
—Indira Gandi

CHAPTER ORIENTATION

This chapter represents a turning point in the text. Until now, we have considered three important strands in the fabric of ethical practice:

- moral philosophy
- professional ethics and identity
- personal attributes and values you bring to the helping endeavor

Now (at last?) we turn to the work itself—the particular issues in the development of the professional helping relationship. This chapter provides an overview of elements especially relevant to the beginning and end of an ethical helping relationship, including informed consent, issues in basic competency and referral, and termination or ending well. We examine tensions between autonomy and fiduciary responsibilities that may, at times, seem paternalistic. Children, the elderly, and those deemed unable to act in their own best interests present specific challenges and opportunities for mental health professionals.

Later chapters delve into four dimensions essential to maintaining helping relationships:

- confidentiality and trust
- boundaries
- assessment
- competent professional practice

In this chapter we also begin considering technology in mental health service provision, but this topic spans the chapters and specialties, so the thread is picked up throughout relevant chapters. Specifically, this chapter will provide you with food for thought on:

- considerations before the professional relationship begins, such as your office and your professional persona;
- informed consent and refusal and all related concerns;
- anxieties and skills related to the first session;
- technological concerns; and
- issues to consider in ending the professional relationship well.

BEFORE THE BEGINNING

When does a professional counseling or helping relationship begin? This may seem self-evident, but it is actually more complicated than one might think. In schools or large agencies, you may be introduced as the "counselor" or "social worker" to hundreds or even thousands of people who are potentially your professional responsibility in some way. When a large group introduction occurs, have you started a thousand helping relationships simultaneously? These impersonal first impressions play a role in people's beliefs about and responses to counseling, and affect their willingness to seek help. It may be a stretch to claim that your professional relationship begins at the moment of a large group introduction, but you are on display as the professional and are therefore communicating about yourself and how you might behave in a more personal one-on-one contact.

Similar exposures occur in mental health, community, rehabilitation, and other types of professional positions. Mental health professionals are often asked to comment publicly on events of interest, or to offer psychoeducational programs or classes to the community. Your professional persona is on display and potential clients are sizing you up and taking in information about both you and the profession. The same is true about your professional listing in the local telephone book. Your ethical (and clinical) obligations begin long before you are sitting comfortably in your office, getting acquainted with someone seeking your assistance (J. Sommers-Flanagan & Sommers-Flanagan, 2003). In this section, we cover factors to consider in optimizing those important first impressions.

Portraying Yourself and Your Services

From paperwork, such as intake materials or graduate program descriptions (Bidell, Turner, & Casas, 2002) to assumptions about handshakes and personality (Chaplin, Phillips, Brown, Clanton, & Stein, 2000), first impressions are powerful (Gladwell, 2005).

Pause for Reflection

Do you recall how counselors and counseling services were initially introduced to you in your life? How did you come to know about your school counselor's existence? What assumptions have you made and do you make about people introduced to you as counselors? Have you ever tried to decide on a mental health counselor for yourself or family members? What factors influenced you? As you read this section allow your reflections to these questions to guide your thoughts on what is important to consider when presenting yourself as a counselor.

There is no single correct ethical way to make yourself and your services known to potential students and clients. However, here are a few points to consider:

- If you include a picture of yourself in the school literature, your literature, on your card, or in the advertising pages of the phone book, what do you hope to communicate? How would you assess if you have achieved your goal?
- If you use letterhead, what credentials do you include? Do you list a long set of abbreviated educational and professional memberships, degrees, or licensures after your name, which are designed to impress, but will likely confuse the general public?
- Do you allow your home address and phone number to be readily available to the public?
- If you agree to be introduced in a large group setting, do you provide the speaker with the correct description of your job and training credentials?
- What does your wardrobe communicate?
- What does your level of preparedness to speak publicly communicate?
- What does your choice in jokes or personal self-disclosures communicate?
- How do you let other professionals know about your professional orientation and preferences?
- How do you let students or clients know enough about you to make an informed choice about working with you?

Officing Yourself

The location, size, and décor of your surroundings contribute to your clients' first impressions. We are aware of school counselors who are forced to work out of converted storage closets due to space shortages. We have known social workers, rehabilitation, and school counselors who had large windows in their office doors, so that those going by in the hall could see who was visiting the counselor. We even knew one agency mental health counselor who believed it was best to keep the door open a crack when she was talking with clients so they would not think counseling was a "closed" process. Obviously, there are some serious status and confidentiality problems with these examples. You need to give careful thought to the location and physical attributes of the space in which you work, and exercise as much control as possible over the comfort, privacy, and accessibility factors.

Physical and psychological accessibility.   The Americans with Disabilities Act of 1990 has been invaluable to professionals who needed legal support in their quest to make sure all clients, regardless of their ability to climb stairs, read signs, or hear directions, could make it safely into their offices. In most situations, it is both unethical and illegal to offer services that are inaccessible. If you find yourself considering office space that is inaccessible, you are well-advised to make sure you can conform to both local and federal laws regarding serving the general public.

Besides being physically accessible and welcoming, mental health professionals need to consider the ramifications of psychological barriers as well. What do we mean by psychological barriers? These are office or décor attributes that might make potential clients uncomfortable before they've even met you. Examples might include:

- office reading materials that indicate a certain political or moral stance
- an office located in a high-crime area
- an office located in a very upscale area
- dim lighting in the halls or waiting room
- loud background noise that intrudes into the office space
- an office located so that a lot of people can watch someone approaching your door
- an office with a shared waiting area, or no waiting area at all
- a mental health office located in a building devoted primarily to other uses, such as businesses, probation offices, or medical offices
- a telephone system that allows clients to hear the phone ring, to hear the answering machine start operating, or to see when a call is coming in
- office staff who interact in dismissive, controlling, intrusive, or unpleasant ways with clients

Of course, all potential psychological barriers cannot be eliminated—they vary from person to person, and are often out of your control. However, ethical professionals take these barriers into account, talk about them if appropriate, and try to accommodate client needs as resources and other factors allow.

The Health Insurance Portability and Accountability Act of 1996, fondly known as HIPAA (see Applications 5.2), is a comprehensive set of federal regulations that includes regulations pertaining to office arrangements. Additionally, many preferred provider panels or managed care organizations require that participating providers have private offices that meet specific standards. Consequently, in addition to legal and ethical concerns about physical and psychological office accessibility, there are also practical or employability issues requiring minimal office standards.

Comfort and aesthetics.   Beyond the ethical, legal, and practical standards associated with the helping professions, to the extent possible, when we finally get an office, most of us want to personalize it. Furniture, art work, even desk size and location all contribute to overall first impressions. There are no absolute rules. Obviously, tastes and incomes vary greatly—and this is a good thing. Humans tend to be blessed with more or less awareness of the space around them and what it communicates. There are excellent professionals who furnish their offices with the most expensive furniture and elegant art available. There are also excellent helpers who furnish their offices by shopping at Goodwill, Salvation Army, and rummage sales. We even know a psychiatric nurse who keeps little gnome statues sprinkled around her office and manages to have a sound professional reputation. Colleagues or friends can provide an external perspective regarding what your office communicates.

If your work will focus mainly on young people or people with disabilities, your office furniture and set-up should take this into consideration. For children, soft, comfortable furniture that allows fidgeting or curling up can facilitate a sense of connection and trust (Thompson & Rudolph, 2000).

INFORMED CONSENT AND INFORMED REFUSAL

All professional counseling-related codes require some type of informed consent from clientele. Many professional groups include an entire section on informed consent within their codes, or repeat the guidance, depending on the nature of the relationship (assessment, counseling, or research).

ACA *Ethics Code*

A.2. Informed Consent in the Counseling Relationship

Clients have the freedom to choose whether to enter into or remain in a counseling relationship and need adequate information about the counseling process and the counselor. Counselors have an obligation to review in writing and verbally with clients the rights and responsibilities of both the counselor and the client. Informed consent is an ongoing part of the professional helping process, and professionals should appropriately document discussions of informed consent throughout the helping relationship.

ASCA *Ethical Standards for School Counselors*

A.2. Confidentiality

The professional school counselor:

a. Informs students of the purposes, goals, techniques, and rules of procedure under which they may receive counseling at or before the time when the counseling relationship is entered. Disclosure notice includes the limits of confidentiality, such as the possible necessity for consulting with other professionals, privileged communication, and legal or authoritative restraints. The meaning and limits of confidentiality are defined in developmentally appropriate terms to students.

APA *Ethical Principles*

3.10 Informed Consent

(a) When psychologists conduct research or provide assessment, therapy, counseling, or consulting services in person or via electronic transmission or other forms of communication, they obtain the informed consent of the individual or individuals using language that is reasonably understandable to that person or persons except when conducting such activities without consent is mandated by law or governmental regulation or as otherwise provided in this Ethics Code.

NASW *Ethics Code*

1.03 Informed Consent

(a) Social workers should provide services to clients only in the context of a professional relationship based, when appropriate, on valid informed consent. Social workers should use clear and understandable language to inform clients of the purpose of the services, risks related to the services, limits to services because of the requirements of a third-party payer, relevant costs, reasonable alternatives, clients' right to refuse or withdraw consent, and the time frame covered by the consent. Social workers should provide clients with an opportunity to ask questions.

As you can see from the preceding examples, the informed consent process begins before therapy or counseling actually begins. In many cases, informed consent paperwork is made available to clients seeking professional services not only before the helping relationship formally begins, but also before the client even comes for an appointment. Increasingly, schools, agencies, and those in group and independent practices have brochures and other paperwork available to potential clients. Many counselors are also developing websites with similar introductory information.

Although the term *informed consent* has a legal ring to it, it is also a political, personal, and value-laden concept. It has cultural overtones and implications and is an ethical counseling obligation of great import. Rightly enacted, it can be an empowering, relationship-building process that contributes directly to the healing and growth of our clients. Wrongly enacted, it can be insulting, frightening, damaging, and potentially dangerous to our clients and/or our practice. The astute reader may suspect that we have strong feelings about this concept. And we do. We discuss the reasons for this in the following paragraphs, but first we provide a definition and some background information on this concept.

Informed consent is a process by which the professional provides potential clients with what they need to know in order to make conscious and knowledgeable choices about the professional relationship and the therapy or helping process and procedures (Pomerantz & Handelsman, 2004). This process involves verbal interactions as well as written material. The written material might include intake forms, disclosure statements, release of information forms, and so on. Much of the informed consent process takes place at the beginning of the relationship, but as things progress, it may be revisited. Remley and Herlihy (2005) claim, "As an ethical obligation, the rationale for informed consent is simple—Clients have a right to know what they are getting into when they come for counseling" (p. 77). The rationale may be simple, but the legalities, politics and clinical implications of the informed consent and refusal process are not.

Autonomy for All?

The ethical principle of *autonomy* is featured prominently within our dominant culture and this has been so since the early colonization of North America. The French writer, Alexis de Tocqueville, visited the United States when it was barely 50 years old, eager to observe the functioning of this new democracy and its citizens. Robert Bellah and his coauthors discuss Tocqueville's observations, noting how early and firmly the self-made, autonomous, independent citizen came to be the ideal symbol of success in the fledgling United States (Bellah, Madsen, Sullivan, Swindler, & Tipton, 1996). Of course, this self-made and self-directed ideal was possible for a limited few, and was heavily dependent on the free or reduced-cost labor of women, slaves, and immigrants from other cultures.

Counterbalanced against this autonomy was an increase in specialization and the emergence of professional skills and expertise. As medicine and related helping professions grew increasingly complex, the authority of the professional grew. *Doctor knows best* became a mantra that obfuscated patient (or client) roles in participating in decisions that affected their health and well-being (Kottow, 2004). "Historically, the health care professions took a fairly arrogant and authoritarian position in regard to what the patient needed. Informed consent is a principle absent from the Hippocratic Oath" (K. Pope & Vasquez, 1998, p. 128).

Case law, custom, and the cultural endorsement of personal autonomy have all contributed to current ethical and legal standards guiding informed consent in health care and related professions (O'Neill, 2004). These standards require that helping professionals provide consumers with the information they need to make knowledgeable choices about their care. The letter of the law is fairly clear, but as always, the devil is in the details. The story included in Digressions for Deliberation 5.1 captures some of the problems in providing genuine informed consent.

Digressions for Deliberation 5.1

John's Hernia Story

Medical procedures can elicit a fair amount of anxiety and even dread. Within the realm of minor surgeries, repeated hernia examination and repair has to be among the worst—at least in my (JSF's) experience. So, when I dutifully went for my preoperative meeting with the surgeon, I was less than enthused. Unfortunately, this was not my first hernia repair and so I was already experiencing a range of negative cognitions when my well-meaning surgeon began his informed consent monologue. As he worked his way down the list of remote-but-still-possible horrible outcomes (including impotence, testicular amputation, etc.), I began feeling nauseated, dizzy, and disoriented. At one point I considered fainting, but eventually encountered an adaptive thought: "I don't have to listen to this." And so I began an internal version of placing my hands over my ears and humming. I willed his voice into the background of Paul Simon singing, "I've got a Niiiiikon Camera" [could be severe blood clotting] "I love to take phooooootographs" [In 1.2% of cases, mumble, mumble, mumble] "Momma, don't taaaaake my kodachrome away, yeah yeah . . ."

The good news is that I made it through the "informed consent" chat without vomiting, signed the forms, had the surgery, and survived without any of the complications. But that conversation taught me a lot about informed consent. Too much information, too fast, too threatening, without regard for what I really needed to know (or could handle) was far worse than no information at all.

Although informed consent originated in medicine, mental health assistance is not a medical science. In medicine, there are many physical variables to be considered and outcomes and risks that are not always predictable. But this predictability problem is magnified many times over in counseling and psychotherapy. There are many facets of the professional helping process that are neither easy to describe nor readily measurable. It is not possible to equate techniques or to predict outcome with any quantifiable certainty (Croarkin, Berg, & Spira, 2003). Also, certain theoretical orientations lend themselves more readily to a kind of process-oriented informed consent than others. Alfred Adler (1956), Carl Rogers (1958), and many feminist theorists (J. Sommers-Flanagan & Sommers-Flanagan, 2004b) have all provided—or even demanded—that clients be informed and included as equals in the therapeutic decision-making process. But even within these orientations, it is difficult to adequately describe all the important aspects that informed consent must cover. Beahrs and Guthiel (2001) wrote:

> To mandate a style of informed consent for psychotherapy that is more appropriate for physical procedures, like surgery, could reinforce a widely held misbelief that psychotherapy also is a formal procedure "done to" a passive recipient by an active agent rather than a collaborative process in which patients play a dominating role. (p. 6)

Keeping these complications and challenges in mind, we believe that the process of informed consent provides ethical security and clinical depth in the therapeutic relationship. As discussed in the following, even with very young, or cognitively limited clients, effort should be made to include clients in making active decisions about their treatment, thus involving and empowering them in their own growth and healing. This is a value-laden statement—one that admittedly reflects our own cultural training and orientation. In other cultures, the provision of such information and the expectation of direct client input into the process might be experienced much differently by both client and professional (see Deepening Diversity 5.1).

Informed Refusal

No discussion on autonomy and informed consent would be complete without mentioning the other side of the coin—informed refusal. We are indebted to Ken Pope and Melba Vasquez for this term (K. Pope & Vasquez, 1998). Informed refusal is *not* the same thing as simply ignoring the process or failing to provide enough information. As Bernstein and Hartsell (2004) write, "Uninformed consent is no consent at all" (p. 41). Instead, informed refusal has to do with the client's right to consciously refuse a certain technique, to resist a certain theoretical orientation, or to decide not to pursue professional assistance at all. Unfortunately, it is beyond the scope of this book to delve into the extremely important and disturbing domain of people's rights, or lack of rights, to refuse to take psychotropic drugs. It is certainly something all allied helping professionals should consider, as Bassman (2005) explains,

> Most people are allowed to make extremely foolish life decisions without facing government intervention. You can choose to smoke until you die. You can eat so much that you cannot get through the doorway to leave your home. Being a member of a recognized

---

Deepening Diversity 5.1

Approaching Informed Consent with Cultural Sensitivity

by Mika Watanabe-Taylor

I was born and raised in Japan. My mother and father still live there, but they visit my husband and me at least twice a year. My work in the United States, as a professional counselor in Disability Services, has opened my eyes to many aspects and intricacies in the informed consent process. I try to make sure it is a very respectful and mutual process with the students I work with and advocate for. As with many of the counseling practices I learned in graduate school in the United States, informed consent was relatively unheard of in Japan when I was growing up, although it is now at least a topic of scrutiny and discussion (Asai, 1996).

I have sometimes imagined what it would be like for my mother to seek counseling in the United States. With a translator, or even with the advantage of a counselor who could work with her in Japanese, the informed consent process would be challenging for both the counselor and my mother. In Japan, the directness of the usual informed consent process would not be reciprocal. Politeness and deference would override any urges my mother might have to ask questions or to overtly object to anything her counselor might suggest.

In the unlikely event that my mother would seek counseling, I would hope the counselor she chose would realize what an enormous step my mother was taking. I hope this counselor would find a way to be respectful, formal, and deeply understanding of my mother's needs. I would hope this counselor would minimize or carefully explain the complicated legal language, be very clear about the limits of confidentiality, and my mother's rights as a client.

Although Japan is slowly introducing the concept of informed consent, it would be wrong to assume adults from Japan would understand this process, or even appreciate it in some cases (Leflar, 1997).

---

religion allows you to make a health decision based on a tenet of your religion even if it may put your life in danger. But if you are a mental patient, there is an automatic bias to believe that you are incapable of making good decisions. Therefore it is necessary for the court to determine what is in your best interest regardless of your beliefs. The freedom to make poor choices is a privilege that is denied to the person who is labeled mentally ill. (p. 492)

Clients need sensitive and accurate information to make choices about the potential of refusing services or treatments. In a counseling setting, informed refusal might include considering the following:

1. Refusal to be in counseling has external consequences: Counselors commonly face situations wherein it was not exactly the client's idea to see a counselor. This might be true in addictions work, school counseling, rehabilitation work, marriage counseling, working with clients on probation, or any number of other situations and settings. It is clinically wise and factually true for you to explain to your reluctant

clients that they do, in fact, have options other than counseling. Granted, the options may not be very appealing—jail, detention, loss of disability payment, divorce, or simply being grounded the rest of their lives, but there *is* a choice involved. Helping your clients sort out the concrete costs and consequences of refusing counseling is an important dimension of informed refusal.

In addition, learning to work effectively with this reluctance is an important clinical skill. In other writings, we discuss a technique called "termination as motivation" (J. Sommers-Flanagan & Sommers-Flanagan, 1997, p. 106). Basically, the idea is to side with clients' reluctance, assisting them in making the necessary changes as quickly as possible, so that the length of time in counseling is minimized.

2. Refusal to be in counseling has psychological or physical costs: Sometimes, counselors are in the position of explaining the costs and benefits of counseling to an ambivalent client or set of clients. Getting help to change habits, to conquer addictions, to reduce stress or anger, or to lose weight are all examples of life problems that counseling might affect positively. Talking over the cost/benefit ratio of engaging in counseling versus *not* engaging in counseling is certainly part of the informed consent and refusal process.

3. Refusal to engage in certain techniques or continue on in counseling has potential consequences: Counseling and psychotherapy are dynamic processes. It is not uncommon for clients to begin with a certain goal or problem area in mind, but as the professional relationship develops, it becomes clear that there are other potential areas to work on as well. In addition, most counselors and psychotherapists are technically eclectic and may begin counseling using behavioral strategies to work on a given area, but then decide that Adlerian techniques are better suited for concerns that arise later in the counseling (see the excerpt from the ACA code for example).

ACA *Code of Ethics*

Section A.2.b. Types of Information Needed

Clients have the right . . . to participate in the ongoing counseling plans; and to refuse any services or modality change and to be advised of the consequences of such refusal.

NASW *Code of Ethics*

1.03

(d) In instances when clients are receiving services involuntarily, social workers should provide information about the nature and extent of services and about the extent of clients' right to refuse service.

Case Example: Years ago, I (RSF) was working with a 60-year-old woman who was having panic attacks whenever she tried to go shopping for groceries. We met a few times and began working with the customary techniques for addressing panic attacks. She also visited a psychiatrist to straighten out the rather unusual set of psychotropic medications her general practitioner had given her. In the course of our time together, it became very clear that she had unresolved issues related to loss, past domestic violence, and her current marriage, which was filled with neglect and disappointment. After six sessions, the panic attacks were subsiding, and my client was very relieved. I firmly believed that it would be wonderful for her to continue on in therapy, exploring some of the underlying issues that may have contributed to the onset of the panic attacks, but I knew it would be a longer-term commitment than she had planned initially. I also knew there were risks in opening up this material and working on it.

We had a frank discussion about the options, and she thanked me, indicating she would give it some thought. At our next session, she said, "I understand there are many areas of my life that I have just put up with, forgotten, or gotten beyond. I don't want to talk about them, and I don't believe in looking back. I appreciate your help in getting control over the panic attacks, and if I change my mind someday, I'll come back. But for now, I think I want to leave well-enough alone." I did one last in vivo session with her, and we bid each other farewell. I was disappointed, but I also respected her decision and believed that this final informed consent work with her was an act of empowerment.

The Nuts and Bolts

Assuming our enthusiasm has convinced you to take the informed consent process seriously, you are probably wondering how to get started—how do you reflectively create the paperwork, cultivate the right attitudes, and develop the best practices to use the informed consent process well? There are many check-lists available that detail the information professionals should consider including in their informed consent process and intake paperwork. We provide such a list in Applications 5.1. However, these lists can only go so far. Your paperwork should be setting-specific, and sometimes, population-specific.

You cannot have a generic set of intake and consent forms if you work with a wide variety of clients. The information you would want to provide gifted, depressed adolescents is probably very different than the information you would provide mid-life couples with relationship problems, or a client in immediate distress with whom you have, at best, tenuous rapport (Croarkin, Berg, & Spira, 2003). Counseling people with addictions or people with legal problems requires specific information that would be irrelevant to other kinds of clients and practices (C. Scott, 2000).

Some authors and supervisors suggest developing pamphlets or smaller descriptions of important information so that you can pick and choose what is important to cover in each situation (Bernstein & Hartsell, 2004; Welfel, 2006). For instance, you might have a general description of your confidentiality practices, adding the particulars as the need arises. You might develop a few paragraphs about yourself, theoretical orientation, and office policies, and again, have possible additions ready. If you work with a particular group or problem area, you will probably want to develop information specifically relevant to your work.

Putting all of this information in written form is time-consuming and tedious, but it can make an enormous difference in the safety and professionalism of your work.

There are three related and sometimes conflicting aspects to consider as you develop the written portion of your informed consent process.

1. Your forms need to take into account current legal practices and conform to agency policies. Like it or not, we are a litigious society, and the legal ramifications of informed consent are quite serious. Therefore, when you have a draft of your intake and informed consent paperwork completed, it is wise to have it reviewed by an attorney familiar with case law and HIPAA (see Application 5.2). Even though much of the informed consent process can take place primarily in conversation, you must also have an adequate form for clients to sign.

2. Your forms need to be user-friendly so that they don't intimidate or fail to inform. Many studies assessing the general public's reading abilities caution that health related materials should be aimed at the fifth grade level, and that often, clients read at a much lower level than their reported education level (M. Williams, et al., 1995). Further, for many clients, English is a second or third language.

3. Your forms need to reflect you and capture the warmth and optimism you feel about your work. This is probably the most challenging dimension of the three, due to the demands of the first two, and due to the fact that it is hard to capture your professional persona in the written word. Helping professionals might assume the paperwork can be intimidating, or off-putting, and they can later make up for it by being extra attentive, kind, and empathic. There may be some truth to this. Many people have grown weary of the defensively worded "legalese" they have to sign off on before proceeding to get their teeth cleaned or their eyes examined. Many of us have simply learned to scan and sign, without asking many questions. However, if the paperwork is written simply and sympathetically, the process can be an opportunity for the helping professions to shine. It *is* possible to meet the legal demands and, with some creative attention, also create understandable and welcoming intake and informed consent forms.

Pause for Reflection

How about creating your first informed consent paperwork in graduate school? You have a ready-made peer consultation group to give you guidance and feedback about your tone and the adequacy of your information. Finding the right voice is more difficult than you might imagine. Besides, articulating who you are, your theoretical orientation, and what you will expect from clients can help bring your imagined professional identity into focus in a very real way.

Applications 5.1 provides the list of possible information you might include in your paperwork. This list reflects the thoughts of many writers and professionals (Bernstein & Hartsell, 2004; G. Corey, Corey, & Callanan, 2003; Cottone & Tarvydas, 2003; T. Remley & Herlihy, 2005; Welfel, 2006) in addition to years of contributions from our students and peer consultation groups. Because our culture(s), professions, and laws are constantly evolving, it is entirely likely you will need to add even more information in some form, tailoring your work to your setting, or to your future dream job.

Informed Consent Process and Intake/Disclosure Information

1. The credentials, degrees, licenses or certifications you hold (not just a string of letters, but actual descriptions)
2. Any affiliations you have with managed care companies, insurance companies, or other sources of payment and/or reimbursement
3. Your fees, including your procedure for missed appointments
4. Your theoretical and philosophical orientation, including what you believe to be appropriate goals for counseling or the proposed intervention
5. Risks associated with being in counseling, or seeking assistance, and possible alternatives such as church involvement, self-help strategies, and/or medical interventions
6. Techniques and how you choose to use them
7. Length of your sessions and/or meeting times
8. The voluntary nature of the choice to be in the professional relationship
9. Your policies regarding testifying in court
10. Guidance regarding the primacy of the professional relationship and how boundary and multiple role concerns might be addressed
11. What you might expect from the client in terms of participation and homework
12. Your policies regarding contact with other professionals in your clients' lives, such as physicians, teachers, probation officers, and so on
13. How you handle emergencies and off-hour and weekend needs
14. What arrangements you have in the event that you are unavailable due to an accident, prolonged illness, or death
15. How long the client might expect to be in counseling, or involved in the assistance
16. What the client can and cannot expect with regard to confidentiality, including the exceptions and limits (see Chapter 6)
17. Supervision and peer consultation practices you engage in
18. Your policies regarding telephone or email contact, including charges and acceptable content, and a warning about the lack of confidentiality control with these options
19. Your policies regarding sharing information with parents if you are working with children or adolescents
20. Your record-keeping practices and policies regarding providing case notes or assessment findings and reports (including reviewing and keeping current with HIPPA requirements)

Legal Concerns

As you now know, informed consent is a process that includes both verbal interactions and written forms. The actual legal requirements vary from state to state, but there are federal laws that come into play as well. The Health Insurance Portability and Accountability Act (HIPAA) has generated new dimensions to the informed consent process, especially with regard to how records will be handled and stored. Bernstein and Hartsell (2004) recommend:

> Prepare a consent form to use in conjunction with a HIPAA "Notice of Privacy Practices," go over it with the client, have the client sign it in your presence, and send the client home with a signed copy of the consent. (p. 42)

Remley and Herlihy (2005) provide a cautionary list of areas that could conceivably generate legal trouble for health professionals who fail to negotiate the sometimes challenging complexities of informed consent. Besides ignoring the details of HIPAA, their list also includes:

- guaranteeing an outcome as a result of counseling, psychotherapy, or interventions
- agreeing to fee arrangements other than those listed in your paperwork
- physically touching clients, or having them touch each other, without explicitly getting permission first
- misrepresenting your credentials
- failing to adequately explain the nature and limits of the helping process
- failing to adequately cover possible risks, including the stigma that might be associated with seeking counseling, therapy, or related assistance

Laws requiring informed consent are usually concerned with three elements: knowledge, voluntariness, and competence (Brody, McCullough, & Sharp, 2005; Croxton, Churchill, & Fellin, 1988). All three have subjective dynamics that require sound professional judgment on your part. The actual information (knowledge) must be calibrated to the client's capacity to absorb and understand what you are saying. Because almost by definition professional helpers are working with distressed and thus vulnerable people, they must be extraordinarily careful not to seem coercive—informed consent must be given voluntarily. And finally, competence is both a legally and developmentally determined attribute, which we discuss in the next section.

Considerations for Particular Populations

Professional mental health assistance is an endeavor that includes offering services to people who may not be completely autonomous, may not be fully capable of grasping their rights or the consequences of their choices, or may not have freely chosen to seek assistance. For example, counselors commonly work with young people, people with disabilities, people in prison or on probation, and/or reluctant spouses or family members. Is it still possible to engage in a meaningful informed consent process? We believe this is not only possible, but is necessary from both ethical and clinical perspectives.

=== **Applications 5.2** ===

HIPAA—Health Insurance Portability and Accountability Act: Compliance and Facts—Ethical Common Sense

In any kind of practice, HIPAA affects all areas, including, but not limited to, business procedures, operations, and information technology methods. HIPAA has two objectives:

- To standardize the electronic exchange of information, thus improving the efficiency of healthcare delivery.
- To protect the security and privacy of healthcare information. Substantial fines and imprisonment can result if client information is handled improperly.

All health organizations should become knowledgeable about HIPAA and consider HIPAA requirements in their planning, management, procurement, and implementation efforts.

Protection and privacy of client information is vital. HIPAA doesn't specify how an organization should protect this information, but it does state that organizations and individuals are liable for noncompliance. Providers must internally justify the appropriateness of information in case notes and reports. Client charts left in public areas or computer work stations with client information showing could result in fines ranging from $50,000 to $250,000 and/or prison sentences.

If you follow the practices outlined in the ACA or APA ethics and in this text, you will be meeting the spirit of this act. In fact, HIPAA compliance, while important, will not in and of itself meet the ethical requirements for informed consent. Specifically related to informed consent, the essential elements for HIPAA compliance include making sure clients:

- understand that their records are protected by law, and will only be used for treatment, payment, and operations, such as contacting them about an appointment. To be HIPAA-compliant, you must provide one example.
- realize they can retract their authorization to release information.
- understand they can ask about any disclosures you make or have made.
- understand that you will keep them informed of any changes in the laws or policies that affect their records.
- understand what recourse they have if information about them is disclosed illegally.
- read and sign a "Notice of Privacy Practices" that details these elements.

There are a number of websites available to stay current. For instance, visit: http://www.hipaa.org. Simply searching the term "HIPAA" will give you access to more information than you probably ever wanted to know.

The following is a list of factors to consider as you create consent forms and processes that accommodate cognitive limits, developmental delays, constricted choices, or otherwise involuntary clients.

- age
- developmental level
- cognitive abilities
- legal rights
- consequences for refusing counseling or assistance
- acceptable alternatives to achieve the goal or meet the need
- possible choices available to the client *within* the professional assistance and relationship
- institutional or system-wide power

Legal dependents.   Age and developmental level are both very important to consider when working with young people. As children begin to engage in formal operational thought (between ages 11 and 12, usually), they can grasp significant informed consent components, but they still need age-appropriate explanations and examples (Sigelman & Rider, 2006). Children under 11 are not likely to grasp many abstract concepts regarding consent to treatment or consent to participate as research subjects (L. Taylor & Adelman, 2001). However, they still deserve careful explanations and the opportunity to ask questions, express concerns, and agree to participate in counseling or research (Harcourt & Conroy, 2005). For instance, they might know what it means to tell someone a secret, and to some extent, they understand that secret-keeping takes place in trusting or special relationships. Depending on their experiences with secrets, this may have a positive or negative valence. See the story in Digressions for Deliberation 5.2 for an example.

Developmental level is usually, but not always, correlated with age. Both cognitive and moral developments are relevant in creating an authentic consent process. Genuine informed consent involves:

- understanding the verbal materials,
- freedom from control or coercion, and
- enough of a sense of self to permit autonomous choice (Boucher, 2002).

Though they may not have the vernacular down, moral principles such as autonomy and fidelity are very important to adolescents. Finding the right balance between abstract concepts and concrete examples is important in working with young people and/or people with limited cognitive capacities.

Planning to obtaining meaningful consent from young people does not mean professionals are free to leave parents out. In general, parents still have the legal right and obligation to provide consent to treatment until their children reach the age of legal majority (Stone, 2005c) and, to some extent, can exercise the right to know the content of the counseling or consultation sessions as well. These are very important issues to sort out ahead of time. Therefore, when working with young people, it is important to pre-

---

Digressions for Deliberation 5.2

The Adventures of Secret-Lady

One of my favorite child consent clinical stories begins with an adorable, curly haired 6-year-old and his 8-year-old sister, whose parents brought the children for preventative counseling because of the divorce the parents were going through. In front of their parents, I explained to the children that their parents loved and cared for them so much that they wanted them to have a place where they could talk about their feelings without anyone else knowing. I said something like:

> We can talk about anything you'd like in here, and I won't need to tell your parents or anyone else. The only thing I would not be able to keep secret would be if somebody was hurting you and we needed to figure out how to keep you safe.

Both parents were fully cooperative, and both children were delightfully open. We saw each other for a couple of sessions before one day I stopped at my daughter's school, which happened to be the same school these young clients attended. My 6-year-old client spotted me from across the playground and came running toward me. His face was lit up and happy as he zoomed toward me shouting, "Hi, Secret-Lady! Hi, Secret-Lady!" I smiled, returned his enthusiastic hug, and told him I had to hurry to a meeting in the school so I could avoid having him reveal himself any further to other students—especially my daughter.

---

pare an informed consent form for parents and obtain their signatures, except in cases where the child is emancipated, or the problem area is one for which your state law allows you to work solely with the child.

Fortunately, many state laws recognize that in certain areas, young people need to be able to seek mental health assistance without first obtaining parental permission. In addition to court-ordered counseling, young people can often seek counseling independently for matters related to problems with dangerous drug use, sexually transmitted diseases, birth control and pregnancy, and sexual assault (Lawrence & Kurpius, 2000). These are areas of great import—even life and death matters—and it is generally recognized that young people may not seek help if parental consent was required (Mitchell, Disque, & Robertson, 2002).

If you are in a position to consider providing assistance to minors without parental consent, whether in an agency, school, or private setting, weigh the factors before proceeding. These factors include legal considerations, the child's age and maturation level, the problem area(s), the child's level of need, and alternatives for seeking help.

When professional help is not the client's favorite idea.   The reluctant or involuntary client requires a different kind of approach. The information he or she needs remains the same, but he or she does not have the experience of having chosen to seek assistance. As you discuss these limited choices, you can compliment the reluctant client on choosing to get some help rather than being grounded, serving more time, or losing a spouse.

For example, with a young man whose parents said he could either go to counseling or no longer live at home, you could say something like,

> I know this isn't at all easy for you. There are probably a lot of other ways you'd rather spend your time. But you chose to be here instead of getting kicked out of your house. I think that's pretty courageous. A very cool choice. And I hope I can be of help to you, so it won't be a wasted choice. Let me tell you a little bit more about how counseling works, and see if you have any questions.

From an existential perspective, humans always have a choice. In his search for meaning as a Nazi prisoner, Victor Frankl (1963) wrote, "There is nothing conceivable which would so condition a man as to leave him without the slightest freedom" (p. 133). Helping professionals who work with involuntary clients can take hope from this amazing statement, and perhaps find ways to transmit this truth to our clients. We can also create as many choices as reasonably possible within the counseling relationship. However, we can never truly mitigate the disempowering aspects of coercion (Gert, 2004). As one anonymous reviewer of this text noted, "the client with no rights knows what Frankl means, it's the student that often does not."

Couples, families, and groups.   Much of the basic information in the informed consent process is the same when you are working with more than one individual as your "client." A few key elements are different. The description of your theoretical orientation and techniques should reflect your couples, family, or group work. As we will elaborate on in the next chapter, the dimensions of confidentiality change, and the method by which you take and store your professional notes should be made clear.

Because the informed consent process involves both written forms and verbal interactions, you will probably need to schedule extra intake time for couples and families so that you can make sure everyone understands the informed consent and counseling process and has time to ask questions (Haslam & Harris, 2004). Depending on the presenting problem(s) and overall treatment goals, you may also find that you need to schedule individual time with each member of the couple, family, or group. There are other ethical and clinical reasons for this, but in the spirit of informed consent, individual time will help insure that each person has a chance to consider the commitment he or she is about to make, ask questions he or she may be hesitant to ask in front of others, and thus give more fully informed consent.

In summary, we want to emphasize that like many other aspects of effective counseling or therapy, adequate and ethical informed consent will take into account the individual attributes and needs of each client. There are legal, ethical, and clinical reasons to do the extra work of creating the right forms and going over the particular issues and ramifications related to each member of any special population.

THE FIRST SESSION: COMPETENCY AND REFERRAL

Let us assume you have gotten your office nicely set up, been properly introduced to your community, developed the right attitude and set of forms for your state-of-the-art informed consent process, and now you are all ready to work as a helping professional.

What does "ready" look like? Ethics codes are not at all vague about insisting that counselors and related mental health professionals know what they are doing. Competence is such a central and important ethical issue that we cover it in greater depth later (see Chapter 9). For now, we address the anxieties new professionals experience, and the judgment calls necessary throughout the counseling or helping relationship with regard to competence and referral.

From the first practicum experience forward, students struggle with how to present themselves properly and honestly—without apology, and certainly without overstatement. Consider the following case example with two different self-presentations.

Case Example: After meeting in the waiting room, Mr. Sanchez and his assigned counselor intern, Maggie Struthers, go to the counseling room down the hall. Mr. Sanchez has already filled out an intake form and has been given a few other forms to fill out in the room with Ms. Struthers. Maggie smiles, reads quickly over the intake form, scanning for anything she would absolutely need to address in this session, and says sympathetically, "There are a few more forms to fill out and go over. And I'd like to talk over any questions you might have about counseling, and tell you a little bit about my background before we begin."

Option One: I've just barely started my second year of graduate school in counseling and you are not only my first Mexican client, you're actually my first real client ever. I've practiced techniques on my fellow graduate students in class, though. But if you don't think I can help you, I can get someone else for you next time. And as you know, we'll be videotaping everything we do, so I'll get some help that way.

Option Two: I'll finish up my graduate studies this coming year, and I hope to work here in the Santa Fe area when I've finished. My practicum supervisor is Dr. Carstens. She is a licensed counselor who teaches and has a small private practice here in town. I see that you signed the form allowing me to videotape our sessions. Dr. Carstens and I will go over the videotapes of our work together, so, it's like you're getting two counselors at once. Do you have any questions about any of that?

All professionals give their clients many different competence-related verbal and nonverbal signals. One of your first "competence accomplishments" should be finding a congruent way to confidently and empathically represent yourself and your background to clients. Accurately representing yourself as a student is an ethical mandate for yourself and for your supervisor.

From the ACA *Code of Ethics*

F.1.b. Counseling supervisors work to ensure that clients are aware of the qualifications of the supervisees who render services to the clients (See A.2.b.).

From the NASW *Code of Ethics*

3.02 (c) Social workers who function as educators or field instructors for students should take reasonable steps to ensure that clients are routinely informed when services are being provided by students.

[handwritten margin note: don't want to decrease hope factor]

You have nothing to apologize for as a graduate student. If you are training in a reputable program, you have had many hours of role-plays, class demonstrations, and instruction in theories and techniques of counseling and psychotherapy, ethics courses, and so on. You are ready to offer helpful basic interventions, assuming you have competent supervision. In addition, remember that in our culture, simply listening with heart, depth, and acceptance to another human being is a great gift and by some accounts, the counselor's most therapeutic activity (L. S. Greenberg, Watson, Elliot, & Bohart, 2001; Lambert & Barley, 2002; J. Sommers-Flanagan & Sommers-Flanagan, 1997). You do not have to be a polished, experienced counselor to offer a healing environment and an ethical professional relationship.

Sometimes texts or supervisors encourage students, when unsure of themselves, to just try something. However, this may not be the wisest course of action, clinically or ethically. *Just trying something* has many potential hazards. It can:

- provoke even greater anxiety in the fledgling mental health professional
- cause client confusion or resistance
- take the process and relationship far off track
- set in motion a pattern of counselor-led initiatives
- be difficult to explain to a supervisor

Therefore, when feeling uncertain, we advise students to breathe deeply, listen fully, offer reflections, and sit quietly in the moment, perhaps reminding themselves of the quote at the beginning of this chapter. If you find this difficult, it is an important topic to explore with a supervisor or your own counselor. You can gain valuable insight into yourself as well as your client if you are attentive in your analysis of first sessions (J. J. Mohr, Gelso, & Hill, 2005). There are many comforting and encouraging nonverbal signals counselors can offer hesitant, anxious, or rambling clients that will help clients feel safe and attended to. This, in turn, will usually allow clients to get more focused and go deeper into the areas needing attention (J. Sommers-Flanagan & Sommers-Flanagan, 2003).

WHEN YOUR SKILLS AND CLIENT NEEDS DO NOT MATCH

There are many dimensions to competence (see Chapter 9). Initially, those training in the helping professions will likely have the repeated experience of feeling they do not know enough, or have enough experience, to be of real help to clients. This is why close, skilled, and caring supervision is such an essential aspect of healthy professional development. There will be clients who present problems or needs that are beyond your skill level and with whom you cannot ethically work. In consultation with your supervisor, you will need to plan how to refer the client to an appropriate professional or setting.

Referring clients to other professional resources is a competency issue in itself. Before you even begin seeing clients, it is wise to know potential referral sources for problem areas that will most likely call for special clinical training. Such areas might include psychotic symptoms, active suicidality, dissociative disorders, and potentially violent clients or situations (B. Welch, 2004). You might generate your own list of such areas—

but more importantly, it is essential to know what lists of referral options exist in your community and/or within your internship site.

Communicating the need to refer an already distressed client is a delicate clinical task. It is difficult for newly minted professionals to admit they are not yet ready to work in certain problem areas. It is even more difficult to frame the need for the referral so that clients do not feel upset, abandoned, or interpret the referral as a message that there is something gravely and distinctively wrong with them.

Besides severity of problem, it is possible that counselors will need to refer a client from a particular cultural background, simply because they lack the necessary multicultural competence and have no way to obtain the close supervision they would need to provide the counseling. Again, this is a challenging process that demands humility and grace from the professional. It must be made clear that this lack of skill or competence is the professional's problem—not an indictment of the client's needs or background.

A final dimension of competency is lack of objectivity, counselor impairment, and/or counselor burn-out. You, and often only you, will know when the particular attributes of a client or problem area touch on a personally scarred, painful, or "hot" area for you, thus compromising your ability to see clearly and work without bias. It is not necessarily unethical to work with a client that pushes buttons, or upsets you because of your life situation or history, but such a choice should be articulated clearly with a supervisor and/or peer consultation group, and you should proceed very cautiously (see the following Case Examples).

Case Example: Samantha and her husband, Ted, waited to have children until Samantha was in her last year of graduate school in Counselor Education. They then began trying to become pregnant, but were not successful. After many months of medical tests and interventions, the couple was told that they were very likely unable to have biological offspring. This was extremely difficult and disappointing news for both of them. Fortunately, Samantha was employed as counselor at a community college counseling center with a large staff and an understanding supervisor. She was able to arrange her caseload so that for a while she was not given any clients for whom an unwanted pregnancy was one of the main issues. "I think I could stay objective, but I'm just not sure," she told her supervisory group. "Ted and I are getting some counseling ourselves, to help us with the grief, and to help us decide what to do. I just need to take care of this area of my life without any more pain or complications than necessary. Do you all think I'm a counseling wimp?"

Of course, her colleagues assured her that in no way did they consider her "a wimp" and, in fact, many told Samantha that they admired her courage and her wisdom in being so open, and thus taking care of herself and any potential clients she might inadvertently harm.

How do you react to Samantha's choice? What areas in your own life could cause you to seek some kind of limit or referral of clients because of similar pain or trauma?

Each of us has our own insecurities about being inadequate, biased, or unprepared to address certain problem areas. Here are some typical, but unethical ways counselors might be prone to react:

- engage in denial, simply ignoring the warning signs, quieting our emotional reactions, and barging ahead ("I'm fine. I can handle this")

- abandon ship early, trying to refer anyone who causes us the slightest discomfort or anxiety ("This client needs a referral to someone who can really help her")

- realize the need to refer, but manage to blame the client rather than take responsibility ourselves ("This client is too crazy for me to work with")

We hope you do not allow yourselves any of these options. Referral can be a professional and ethical choice. It is a clinically demanding process that should be role-played and considered carefully under supervision before enacted. It is especially important to plan how much self-disclosure is appropriate, given the need to take responsibility so that the client does not feel judged or blamed. Related concerns will be covered in more depth in other chapters.

TECHNOLOGY REARS ITS UGLY (BEAUTIFUL?) HEAD

The title of this section may reveal a slight bias on our part, but we *do* realize the enormous potential presented by technology. Ours is an age of nearly inescapable technological options: land lines, cell phones, email, chat rooms, online instruction, instant messaging, mental health self-help web pages, flash drives capable of storing entire libraries, real-time supervision options by a supervisor a half-world away—an incomplete list that we are confident will continue to grow. As we become increasingly accustomed to these communication and (dare we say) relationship options, whole new layers of specific ethical behaviors and concerns will come into focus.

Case Example: Daleep was an international graduate student at a small private college in the Pacific Northwest. He reluctantly came to the student counseling center on the advice of a professor in whom he had confided his great distress: Daleep had been walking home late one night when a group of teenaged boys jumped out of their car, pulled him into the bushes, and beat him unconscious. Fortunately, he was not permanently disabled, but he suffered nightmares, numbness, inability to concentrate, heightened startle response, and emotional lability. His counselor, Roy, was a doctoral intern who had significant training in trauma work. Daleep expressed great relief that counseling was helping. He asked Roy if they could keep in touch over email while Daleep traveled to India during the upcoming 6-week break. He told Roy that his wishes to kill himself or seek revenge had subsided, but he knew that going home was going to be hard, even for a short while.

Roy readily agreed, but after Daleep left his office, he had second thoughts. What if Daleep emailed, but Roy didn't get the email? What if Daleep became acutely suicidal while home? What if Daleep's family read the emails? Roy grabbed the phone and called Daleep, asking him to come back in before leaving the country.

If you were Roy, what would you do? What would you say to Daleep, or arrange with him regarding his request? What problems occurred to you that Roy didn't even think of?

The addition of technological connections and options does not change our core ethical mandates one iota. We are still obligated to safeguard the welfare of our clients. We must work within our areas of competence, preserve confidentiality, avoid interactions with clients that could lead to exploitation or reduce our objectivity, and be guided by the principles and orientations we covered in Chapter 2. However, operationalizing these overarching obligations is an ongoing challenge to our field (Welfel & Heinlen, 2001). Ethics codes are beginning to provide basic guidance (be sure to check the codes of your professional organization for technological applications), but much remains to be answered. Questions to ask yourself before using technology in your counseling practice, supervision, or teaching include:

1. Do I understand enough about this technology to explain its use and potential dangers or failures to those with whom I will use it?
2. Can I be reasonably certain of the competencies and intentions of those involved?
3. Do I have an adequate back-up plan if the technology fails?
4. Can I develop a comprehensive *and* comprehensible informed consent form if I use this technology with clients?

There are also many large research questions still to be explored. For instance, how do internet-assisted counseling outcomes compare to traditional counseling outcomes? What theoretical orientations are most compatible with telephone, email, or other on-line forms of professional contact? How do certain problem areas and/or other client characteristics interact with technological options? A recent study demonstrating efficacy for telephone counseling for depression by David Mohr and colleagues (2005) provides an encouraging example, applicable for both rural and homebound populations. Also, email has similar important clinical applications (Hunt, Shochet, & King, 2005).

The Internet and related technologies hold great promise for adding many options and dimensions to traditional counseling, teaching, and supervision (Harris, VanZandt, & Rees, 1997; Sabella & Booker, 2003; Ybarra & Eaton, 2005). However, before automatically adding a technological component to your professional relationships, you should be very well versed in the basic ethical obligations covered in this book and in your ethics codes. You will then need to use this lens to examine the pitfalls and/or advantages of the technology you are considering.

ENDING WELL

Many years ago, Robert Langs (1980) wrote that the termination of any relationship, especially a counseling relationship, is a significant event in our lives—one that we often underestimate in impact and significance. Langs believed that one of the reasons the importance of relationship termination is underplayed or ignored is that any such ending reminds us of our own mortality. It symbolizes the powerlessness we experience in the face of inevitable endings and death. Whether or not Langs is correct, few would argue with the observation that the dominant White-American culture tends to do endings poorly. We worship eternal youth and have medicalized, sterilized, and sanitized the aging and dying process (Byock, 1997). Ending the counseling relationship well is, therefore a skill that must be developed. It is not an easy task under the best of circumstances, but the true story in Digressions for Deliberation 5.3 is one of a truly accomplished counselor, ending well.

Most counselors won't have to face the enormous challenge Barbara Honeyman faced, contacting an entire slate of clients for a caring farewell, but even ordinary endings are clinically significant events. Counselors who pay attention to the dynamics of ending the professional relationship consciously and compassionately are acting therapeutically at three levels. First, they are providing their client with a good ending to an important relationship. Second, they are modeling the importance of ending other relationships well. And third, they are taking good emotional care of themselves. In the following, we consider each of these.

Helping clients end their work with you on a constructive and conclusive note is your final contribution to the growth and development they hopefully achieved in their work with you. A good ending enhances therapeutic work already done. An inconclusive, abrupt, or unplanned ending fails to provide closure and can undo even some of the good work done earlier. A good ending also increases the likelihood that clients will seek professional assistance again, should the need arise.

At a deeper level, when you help your clients prepare for ending the professional relationship well, and then go through a good ending, you could be contributing to their skill in handling the ending of relationships in other domains in their lives. Most of us have faced some kind of loss or ending that did not go well—a divorce, sudden death, romantic break-up, or friendship altercation that left us with feelings of unfinished business and loose ends. Because most, if not all, counseling relationships have elements of transference (see Chapter 7), and become symbolic of other relationships, the weight of these other unfinished terminations can come to bear on the ending of the counseling relationship. Helping clients explore their patterns and fears related to endings, and then ending well, can be a great parting gift from effective counselors. A well-done ending may act as a corrective emotional experience for clients who previously experienced traumatic or unresolved relationship endings (Epstein & White, 1995).

Finally, for counselors, consultants, supervisors, and professors, saying good-bye and farewell to people is an ongoing and integral part of the job. Such relationships are often intense, emotional, and deep. Students and clients invest a great deal of themselves in the process of seeking graduate education, or seeking counseling, and often this investment is reciprocated by the professionals providing the counseling and/or the education. After repeated deep relationship investments, the letting-go and closure process can cause the one who needs to repeatedly say good-bye to become jaded, numb, or overreactive. Good endings are hard work, but bad endings can quickly contribute to, or be a sign of, burnout (Bakker, Schaufeli, Sixma, Bosveld, & Van Dierendonck, 2000).

What are the elements of a good termination? In our experience, they include the following:

- A good ending is foreshadowed and talked about long before it is time to end.
- A good ending allows time for reminiscence.

Digressions for Deliberation 5.3

When My Counselor Died

by Joyce Jarosz Hannula

I was drawn to Barbara Honeyman for counseling because I had heard she was supportive as well as willing to confront and to ask difficult questions. As our sessions progressed over the course of a year, her inner strength and clear acceptance of herself nurtured a new vision of possibilities. Although our time together could be incredibly challenging, it clarified my understanding of myself and my relationships.

I can still describe in vivid detail the session when she began our conversation with the news that she has been diagnosed with cancer. She asked me how much I wanted to know and if I would like to talk about it. Even though I asked for the details, I knew I was not ready to face the reality of her terminal illness.

Two or three sessions later, completely out of context, I blurted, "Barbara, if someone like you can't beat this, who can?" She looked at me with absolute focus and said quietly, but firmly, "We need to talk about this, Joyce,". . . and she invited me to explore her impending death with her.

We made one final appointment, but Barbara called shortly before the scheduled time. "I had hoped to be able to see you, but I can't," she said. "I have to close my practice." She calmly offered referrals and left me with two observations pertinent to our work together: One lent me continuing strength, and the other prompted me to grow.

The announcement of her death in our local paper invited friends and clients to join the family at the memorial service. There was no doubt in my mind that I would attend. Her family had arranged a service that reflected Barbara's many colorful dimensions. As I glanced at the other mourners, it was clear that many of us were clients—a visible weaving of Barbara's life work. We had come to share our grief and our gratitude. It is now 13 years later and I find that my gratitude has matured. I'm not only thankful for Barbara's work with me, but also for the style, courage, and integrity she modeled as she faced her own death.

- A good ending provides closure.
- A good ending bridges to the future—seeking appropriate continuity in the domains of interest, such as social contact, access to records, and so on.
- A good ending defines the parameters of appropriate contact in the future.
- A good ending allows time for reflecting on any loose ends and time to address them, or acknowledge that they will not be addressed.
- A good ending makes room for the feelings associated with endings, and deliberately marks the ending—sometimes with ritual, sometimes with a firm hand-shake or hug, sometimes with commemorative summaries, pictures, notes, or transitional objects.

- A good ending is a two-way ending so that both parties (or all parties) have a chance to do what they need to do to have closure.

CHAPTER WRAP-UP

Whether technologically assisted or entirely face-to-face in real time in a real place, counseling involves a professional helping relationship. The framework surrounding and supporting this relationship is entirely the responsibility of the professional who is offering the help. A well-constructed, thoughtful framework is integral to the relationship's healing potential and to an ethical practice.

The component parts of the framework include setting, the opportunity for informed consent or refusal, and professional competence, which includes the ability to counsel, to refer, and to bring the helping relationship to a graceful and professional conclusion. As Henry Wadsworth Longfellow said, "Great is the art of beginning, but greater is the art of ending. Many a poem is marred by a superfluous verse" (Longfellow, 1882/2006).

Chapter Six ————————————————————————

CONFIDENTIALITY AND TRUST

> *We are all, in a sense, experts on secrecy. From earliest childhood we feel its mystery and attraction. We know both the power it confers and the burden it imposes. We learn how it can delight, give breathing space, and protect.*
>
> —Sissela Bok

CHAPTER ORIENTATION

A helping relationship has certain professional obligations imbued by society and thought to be necessary to the healing or growth process in mental health and counseling work. Confidentiality is arguably the most vital of these obligations. This chapter informs readers about the centrality and complications of confidentiality in the helping relationship. We cover common expectations associated with professional confidentiality and its limits, and consider special concerns present in working with groups, classrooms, and families.

Ethical record keeping is obviously related to confidentiality. This chapter revisits recent changes in federal law about client records and offers guidance for keeping current in this area. And as always, setting and culture are also essential to consider. Because confidentiality is closely related to professional boundaries, we refer you to the discussion on cultural and rural considerations in the next chapter. Here are the specific areas for consideration:

- the central connection between confidentiality and the therapeutic relationship;
- the limits of confidentiality and how these limits have evolved;
- categories of exceptions to confidentiality, including the protection of self and others, professional communications, and court-related matter;
- technology and the impact of the Internet on confidentiality;
- particular populations, such as children, families, and groups;
- confidentiality concerns with involuntary clients; and everyone's favorite,
- professional record keeping.

CONFIDENTIALITY AND THE THERAPEUTIC RELATIONSHIP

Of all the ethical domains that touch the profession of counseling, perhaps none is more central than confidentiality (J. C. Beck, 1990; Dearing & Maddux, 2005; Denkowski & Denkowski, 1982). As counselors, helpers, therapists, *and* as human beings, we recognize the healing power of a trusting relationship. In fact, without interpersonal trust, it is unlikely humans could live together in any sort of healthy community. The human condition is also replete with trust violations. We have all experienced anguish and anger when friends or family members have broken their word, telling secrets previously entrusted to them. These painful reactions speak to trust and confidentiality's centrality and power.

Harvard professor Sissela Bok (2002) has written extensively about the societal and interpersonal dimensions of trust. We should not confuse trust with absolute confidentiality. Think about what causes you to trust someone. Trusting relationships include honesty, fulfillment of obligation, and demonstrated interest in each other's welfare and best interests.

Professional Dimensions of Confidentiality

Confidentiality entails a certain amount of complexity for those who have professional roles in peoples' lives. One study, comparing the most common ethical dilemmas reported by mental health professionals across seven different nations found that confidentiality topped the list for practitioners (Slack & Wassenaar, 1999). Expert and clinically sensitive handling of confidentiality is much more than simply keeping secrets. Professionals have a fiduciary responsibility toward those who seek their services. They need to be discrete and invested in the public and their clients' best interests—which includes keeping interactions and records private and protected. Although this expectation of fidelity spans many professions, it may be the most challenging and intricate for mental health professionals. This probably accounts for the careful coverage confidentiality receives in most ethics codes.

ACA *Code of Ethics*

Section B Introduction

> Counselors recognize that trust is a cornerstone of the counseling relationship. Counselors aspire to earn the trust of clients by creating an ongoing partnership, establishing and upholding appropriate boundaries, and maintaining confidentiality. Counselors communicate the parameters of confidentiality in a culturally competent manner.

Section B.1.c. Respect for Confidentiality

> Counselors do not share confidential information without client consent or without sound legal or ethical justification.

APA *Ethical Principles*

4.01 Maintaining Confidentiality

Psychologists have a primary obligation and take reasonable precautions to protect confidential information obtained through or stored in any medium, recognizing that the extent and limits of confidentiality may be regulated by law or established by institutional rules or professional or scientific relationship.

NASW *Code of Ethics*

1.07 (c) Privacy and Confidentiality

Social workers should protect the confidentiality of all information obtained in the course of professional service, except for compelling professional reasons. The general expectation that social workers will keep information confidential does not apply when disclosure is necessary to prevent serious, foreseeable, and imminent harm to a client or other identifiable person. In all instances, social workers should disclose the least amount of confidential information necessary to achieve the desired purpose; only information that is directly relevant to the purpose for which the disclosure is made should be revealed.

AMHCA *Code of Ethics*

Principle 3

Mental health counselors have a primary obligation to safeguard information about individuals obtained in the course of practice, teaching, or research. Personal information is communicated to others only with the person's written consent or in those circumstances where there is clear and imminent danger to the client, to others, or to society. Disclosure of counseling information is restricted to what is necessary, relevant, and verifiable.

ASCA *Ethical Standards*

Preamble

Each person has the right to privacy and thereby the right to expect the counselor-student relationship to comply with all laws, policies, and ethical standards pertaining to confidentiality in the school setting.

Confidentiality in professional helping relationships is neither absolute nor without controversy. In professional counseling, there are pressures working both for and against confidentiality from many sides. Besides your immediate client or clients, there are family members, agency expectations, administrators, concerned teachers, society, law enforcement officers, and insurance carriers, all with a stake in what you keep confidential and what you reveal.

Misunderstandings can arise on many fronts. On one side of the issue, there are those who assume that anything they tell a professional will be confidential, whether they are clients, consultants, professional associates, parents, teachers, or simply acquaintances. It's not unusual to have the experience of chatting with someone in a social setting who says something like, "Since you're a counselor, I know I can tell you about my daughter's medication problems and you'll keep it to yourself." Of course, this may or may not be true. It is wise to develop comfortable ways to remind people that mental health professionals are obliged to keep confidentiality when in a *professional* helping relationship, but not necessarily in other relationships. Otherwise, you may begin feeling like a repository for endless amounts of information with little certainty about what you can and cannot share.

On the other side, many people in our culture assume they have the right to know information that has been shared in a counseling relationship. Parents, teachers, probation officers, physicians, police officers, spouses, and others with concerns or curiosities may be surprised or even offended when a counselor refuses to divulge client information to them. Some may even have an established, legal right to know certain aspects of your work with a given client. For example, a probation officer may have made an arrangement with her parolee that includes having the professional verify not only attendance, but also some of the substance of the counseling sessions. Colleagues or supervisors might ask about a particularly difficult client's progress. Parents may ask to be kept apprised of their child's progress. Insurance companies may require that you send copies of counseling notes to help them make a determination about continuation of benefits. Teachers may ask to be informed about the home life of an obviously sad or angry student. Which of these requests do you comply with? Which is legitimate? How do you determine an ethical course? We hope by the end of this chapter, you will have satisfactory answers to these questions.

Why Confidentiality?

There are three overarching and related sources for the power and importance of confidentiality in the counseling relationship:

- stigma
- moral obligation and modeling
- efficacy and healing

Stigma.   In their discussion about the origins of confidentiality, Remley and Herlihy (2005) point out that the profession of counseling has divergent roots, some of which link us to ancient stigmas associated with serious mental illness. Beliefs that those suffering from schizophrenia were possessed by the devil, as well as the overemphasis by Freud and others on all things sexual or aggressive, have contributed to these stigmatizations (Freud, 1958). Historically, there has been a shameful cloud hovering over psychiatry and psychotherapy. Unfortunately, the stigma has not entirely disappeared. Clients may still fear being seen as "crazy" if they seek any kind of counseling, or may expect to discuss embarrassing or taboo material during counseling (Farber, Berano, & Capobianco, 2004). In addition, seeking help carries a stigma in many cultures because it is seen as a failure of families or churches to take care of their own. Seeking counseling might involve a loss of face, or cause the client's family or community a sense of shame (Cuellar & Paniagua, 2000; Richards & Bergin, 2000).

Regardless of cultural, religious, or familial background, seeking help from a counselor or therapist might also seem weak or shameful to clients themselves (Frank & Frank, 1991). Prospective clients sometimes struggle with notions that they should have been able to solve their problems by themselves. They might worry about what others think or assume about them. They might be concerned that seeking counseling will affect their work or home lives, their future promotions, or their chances at running for public office.

When stigma is a factor, clients want and need confidentiality not only to cover the content of information shared, but also the professional relationship itself. In such cases, separate and private waiting rooms and entry areas are of great value, although privacy can be protected in other ways as well. Of course, clients who wish for this level of confidentiality might not be concerned about stigma. They might be naturally private people who do not wish for others to know even very positive things about their private lives.

Pause for Reflection

Some time ago, a graduate student dared to take a very provocative stance. "Acting like confidentiality is so essential sends the wrong message about human problems and about seeking counseling or other kinds of help," she said. "Colluding with clients to keep their problems 'secret' reinforces the notion that having problems is bad and that clients themselves are to blame. We should help clients be proud that they are seeking help, instead of pretending we don't even know them in public." What do you think about her stance? Do you see merit in her argument?

Moral obligation and modeling.   As discussed previously, many moral philosophers believe that fidelity and trust are paramount for a morally correct professional relationship. Behaving professionally is synonymous with discretion and with keeping one's word. By joining the counseling profession, in a broad sense, you are agreeing to live up to these high moral expectations (Starr, 1982). Failing to do so can harm both clients and the stature of the profession. Gossiping is not a particularly admirable practice for anyone, but professionals who gossip or discuss thinly disguised clinical work for entertainment or self-aggrandizement are behaving neither wisely nor ethically.

Related to the moral obligation of discretion is the notion of modeling in the therapeutic relationship. The counseling relationship, while unique, shares similarities with other intimate relationships. Many have written of the counseling process as a type of reparenting or corrective emotional experience (Kohut, 1984; Paivio & Greenberg, 1995; Rogers, 1959). While you may not agree with this analogy, there are undoubtedly reparative aspects to a healthy counseling relationship. The counselor is in a position of caring authority and has the opportunity to behave in ways that are respectful, honest, and collaborative. Not only does this provide a healing environment, it gives clients a prototype for future relationships (L. S. Benjamin, 2003; Teyber, 1997). It gives them a vision of what they might expect in healthy relationships with others, as well as how they might choose to behave in future relationships (Glasser, 2000; Rodman Aronson & Schaler Bucholz, 2001).

Efficacy and healing.   Although not universally accepted, nor always substantiated by research, there is a broadly held conviction that confidentiality is an important component of counseling efficacy (J. C. Beck, 1990). Pope and Vasquez (1998) use a surgical analogy:

> In its reliance on trust as fundamental, therapy is similar to surgery. Surgery patients allow themselves to be physically opened up in the hope that their condition will improve. They must trust that surgeons will not take advantage of their vulnerable state to cause harm or exploit. Similarly, therapy patients undergo a process of psychological opening up in the hope that their condition will improve. (p. 41)

This quote graphically expresses the assumption that the therapeutic relationship will contain private interactions and deep sharing of sensitive information in the healing process. The potential for growth and healing is linked to sharing information that one would not readily share in other relationships. Such sharing creates significant psychological vulnerability. Therefore, the potential for harm resulting from mishandling this information, or breaking the trust, is also increased.

THE LIMITS OF CONFIDENTIALITY AND THEIR EVOLUTION

As alluded to previously, confidentiality is not absolute in the counseling relationship. Over time, society has come to insist that certain information be shared for the welfare of clients, counselors, and others who might be affected or endangered. Further, practicalities, policies, and issues of accountability also influence the level of confidentiality one can assure clients. The exact nature of what must be shared and what must not be shared varies from state to state, and has changed over the past 20 years as a result of various court rulings. The now-famous court case involving Tatiana Tarasoff is a good example (Quattrocchi & Schopp, 2005).

The essence of the *Tarasoff* case is this: A young man sought counseling at his college counseling center. He told his counselor of plans to kill a young woman, later identified as Tatianna Tarasoff. The counselor believed there was real danger in these threats, and contacted the campus police to have the client assessed at a mental facility. The client was assessed and judged to be rational. He promised he would not harm Ms. Tarasoff, who was currently out of the country. When Ms. Tarasoff returned, the client did, indeed, kill her. Her parents sued the college and, though dismissed in a lower court, the California Supreme Court ruled that the counselor had not only a duty to contact the authorities, but also a duty to warn the intended victim *directly*. This case was heard in California between 1974 and 1976. The findings reflect California state law, and will not necessarily apply in your state (Meyers, 1991; Quattrocchi & Schopp, 2005). For example, in Texas and a few other states, contacting the intended victim would not be your duty, nor would it be considered appropriate. Mental health professionals in these states are authorized to contact only medical and law enforcement personnel (Bernstein & Hartsell, 2004). We will discuss the broader issues related to this case in the following sections. We mention it here as a cautionary tale about variations over time and locale in legalities related to confidentiality.

CATEGORIES OF EXCEPTIONS TO CONFIDENTIALITY

Although they necessarily overlap, we offer general domains to consider as you develop your understanding of the limits of confidentiality:

- protecting self and others;
- communicating with other professionals;
- billing and office procedures; and
- court-related requests.

To help with the anxiety this area sometimes generates, we have included clinical reflections with each category, and will point out areas you will need to research through collegial input, supervision, and correct legal and policy information for your own region and setting. No matter what your professional setting, you will want to develop a very clear confidentiality statement and clinically sensitive ways to explain the limits of confidentiality to clients. See Applications 6.1 how you might describe one of the exceptions to confidentiality.

Protection of Self and Others

Counselors hear the darker secrets of the heart and soul. They sometimes stand in as society's confessors (Doherty, 1995). Our profession, along with other related professions, has even been referred to as the secular priesthood (McDonald, 2003). Mental

---

Applications 6.1

Describing an Exception to Confidentiality

There is an art to describing many of the exceptions to confidentiality. For instance, in the exception created by consulting with supervisors or colleagues (discussed later in this chapter), your language and presentation can be crafted to help clients see the positive possibilities, rather than causing them to focus on your inexperience or the sense of being exposed to too many people. Here is a sample of what you might say:

> I want you to know that I am in a supervision group with other professionals. We talk about our work, and different kinds of problem areas and counseling possibilities. Sometimes I will talk about some of the people I'm working with to get ideas and to make sure I'm thinking of all the possible angles I should be. I don't mention names, and I don't tell the group anything especially unique about any of my clients. But it's really helpful to get different professional views and ideas. That way, you get the benefit of other perspectives, and I stay current in my field. Is it okay with you for me to occasionally ask my colleagues how I can best work with you?

health professionals create a space where clients can work out their worst fears, most shameful moments, their most dreadful desires, and their worst betrayals. It is of utmost importance to be very clear with clients at the outset regarding what you must legally disclose to others. This is a part of the informed consent process and is articulated clearly in the various ethics codes.

Sorting out fantasy, threat, and the law.   Students are sometimes surprised to realize that the helping professions are not extensions of law enforcement. If your clients reveal past illegal behaviors, in most instances, you must still maintain confidentiality. Some time ago, a doctoral intern had a client who told her about his incredible guilt and angst related to a murder he had committed 10 years previously. The intern and her supervisor were understandably shaken by this admission, but were able to work together so that the intern could provide the client with the kind of safe, caring environment necessary to work through this horrendous past event.

Even current or planned illegal behaviors are *not* reportable if they are vague or not endangering anyone directly. However, in some states, law enforcement officers can legally require you to release counseling records if they are investigating a specific suspect in a specific crime (Glosoff, Herlihy, & Spence, 2000). Please note, however, that you must simply comply if legal authorities request your records. These laws neither mandate nor permit counselors to initiate a report.

Professional helpers often hear of illegal and/or immoral behaviors, and most experience some degree of indignation, anger, or perhaps even disgust. These reactions are normal, understandable, and emotionally taxing. Unaddressed, they can lead to boundary breaking or burnout. Counselors need to find ways to resolve these reactions without breaking confidentiality. As a mental health professional, your duty is to provide a safe, nonjudgmental environment, offering assistance with personal problem-solving that may facilitate the emotional growth and healing necessary for moral development. If you cannot provide such an environment in a given situation, seek consultation and supervision to enable a smooth referral or resolution. If you find you cannot provide a relatively safe, nonjudgmental therapeutic relationship more generally, then you may need to change clientele, setting, or profession.

Pause for Reflection

Obeying the law and doing our duty to society are bedrock moral imperatives for many of us. It is troubling—even offensive—to listen to reports of tax evasion, drug experimentation, acts of cruelty or violence toward humans or pets, plans to hide resources from siblings or spouses, sexual affairs, and so on. What kinds of "bad" or illegal behaviors will be the hardest for you to hear about? What kinds of behaviors have you engaged in that you would never want anyone to know about?

Case Example: Al, a practitioner at a mental health clinic, was seeing Jane, a very attractive 18-year-old woman who was finishing her senior year in high school. Jane had sought counseling on her own, and was paying a sliding fee out of her own money. A few months before, Jane had begun volunteering at a news agency and had begun an affair with Tom, a married, 38-year-old man who was quite well known in the region.

Jane reported enjoying the sex a great deal, and enjoyed Tom's stories of how her body compared favorably to other interns with whom he had had sex. Tom told Jane she was a sexually gifted young woman, and was encouraging her to consider joining a local group of highly paid prostitutes as a way of earning college money. Jane's counselor, Al, was enraged and deeply distressed. He had daughters close to Jane's age and desperately wanted to find a way to protect Jane from the influence of Tom. Al sought supervision from a trusted female colleague. He knew that Jane needed a neutral, safe environment to sort out her emotions and choices and was struggling to provide this for her. He admitted that he had fantasies of finding ways to expose Tom and ruin Tom's career. The supervision helped Al examine his reactions so that he could preserve a caring, nonjudgmental relationship with Jane as she sorted out her emotions and life choices.

In many states, mental health professionals are required to take protective action if they believe a client intends *imminent* harm to self or others. As the ruling in the *Tarasoff* case discussed previously suggests, when a client intends to harm someone else, the counselor may need to do more than inform legal authorities. This requirement has been referred to as *duty to warn*, although a more current and accurate term is *duty to protect* (Quattrocchi & Schopp, 2005). The exact actions required vary from state to state. In some states, contacting the authorities is enough. In others, the professional must also contact the intended victim(s). In yet other states, there is no expectation for mental health professionals to accurately assess dangerousness and take action. This is one of the many excellent reasons to be in touch with your state licensing board and to be an active member of your state and national professional organizations.

It is very difficult to accurately predict dangerousness. Research indicates that while mental health professionals may be somewhat better at predicting dangerousness than chance, they often overpredict (Otto, 2000). Well-developed clinical interviewing skills should include the basics of assessing dangerousness (J. Sommers-Flanagan & Sommers-Flanagan, 2003). In addition, consultation with an attorney, your malpractice insurance carrier, and/or colleagues should be part of your decision-making process if you are considering reporting a client or warning an intended victim. Consider the following sobering quote:

> There is no way to tell whether psychotherapists, following *Tarasoff*, have ever saved a potential victim from injury, but it is clear that at least two psychotherapists, ordered to testify over objections and claims of privilege, helped prosecutors convict an ex-patient of first-degree murder and contributed to sentencing him to penalty of death. (Meyers, 1991, p. 27, as cited in Welfel, 2006)

Pause for Reflection

How many times have you muttered empty threats about slashing someone's tires, smacking someone in the nose, or wishing harm on someone else? Because of recent tragic events, such as the school shootings and global terrorist activities, our society's tolerance for such venting is at an all-time low. The signs at the airport clearly warn us "Talking about bombs is NOT a joking matter." Schools have tried to enforce zero-tolerance for violent threats. Yet, words are not actions. Fantasies are not realities. Expressing outrage, pain, and fantasies of revenge may be an important part of regaining perspective and reasserting cognitive control after being abused, bullied, betrayed, or humiliated by someone (Beale & Scott, 2001). As mental health professionals, we have to find ways to create safe space for venting, while also discerning when the threat is so real that we must take action. This is a balancing act made much safer by consistent contact with a skilled consultation group.

The angry client threatening to harm or kill someone presents different challenges than the sad or desperate client considering suicide—yet our duty is to try and prevent harm or loss of life in both cases. Working with suicidal clients is stressful, and it requires significant clinical sensitivity and skill (Welch, 2004). Assessing suicidality is a basic skill that all mental health professionals should possess and should fine-tune on a regular basis (J. Sommers-Flanagan & Sommers-Flanagan, 2003; see Chapter 8). States vary in their legal requirements for actions that must be taken if a client appears at risk for committing suicide.

Most mental health professionals do not have admission privileges allowing them to directly hospitalize a client. Therefore, they must contact the appropriate authorities as part of the process of keeping a client safe. Bernstein and Hartsell (2004) recommend that you routinely obtain client permission to contact specific family members or friends in the event that you believe the client is a danger to self or others. For an excellent summary of the complexities and current thinking on these related issues, read the article *Tarasaurus Rex: A Standard of Care That Could Not Adapt,* by Michael Quattrocchi and Robert Schopp (2005).

AIDS and assisted suicide: Modern challenges.　　Duty to protect and the obligation to report intended harm to self or others can take on interesting moral dimensions in certain modern societal and medical situations. Clients with HIV or AIDS have presented an ethical challenge in the domain of duty to warn. The American Counseling Association (ACA) took the lead in 1995, guiding ethical decision-making in cases wherein clients with deadly communicable diseases reveal that they are endangering partners with their behavior. Such guidance for making difficult choices in this area is now present in other professional codes as well, though not currently as clearly presented as ACA. The guidance is compassionate and nondirective. The counselor is not *mandated* to warn an unaware partner, but can choose to do so if it is determined that the situation warrants such a choice. In contrast, the NASW code forbids disclosure to a partner unless mandated by state or federal law.

Until quite recently, counselors, therapists, and social workers were all required by ethics codes to report any and all intended suicides if the threat appeared to be real and imminent. As society has begun to wrestle more openly with the deep and difficult concerns surrounding assisted suicide and end-of-life choices, certain codes have developed ethical guidance that is less absolute. No doubt counselors and other professionals working with terminally ill clients have chosen not to report clients who were grappling with the possibility of ending their own lives, but in doing so, these counselors were taking legal and ethical risks. In Chapter 2, we wrote of Joseph Fletcher's (1966) demanding ethical mandate—*in this place, at this time, with this set of needs, what is the most selflessly loving action I can take? I have the conscience and intelligence to figure that out.*

The loving action is the highest ethical action I can enact. End-of-life counseling is an excellent, if troubling, example of the arduous, soul-level work that helpers must sometimes do when seeking the ethical way.

As we noted in Chapter 2, from a deontological (Kantian) perspective, suicide is never a moral option. However, some contemporary utilitarian philosophers take the position that suicide and euthanasia have a moral place in society (Singer, 1993). Further, the questions surrounding adequate palliative care are hotly debated by medical and bioethicists. Many contend that if the pain is managed well it would alleviate at least some of the suicidal motivations experienced by the terminally ill (Byock, 1997).

Pause for Reflection

Our clients may need to use their counseling time to work out decisions we would never consider ourselves. Suicide, or assisted suicide, is a highly emotionally charged subject for most of us. Until recently, mental health professionals have been required, legally and ethically, to side with life, regardless of the circumstances. We can now ethically make other choices, although state laws will continue to vary. When, if ever, would you kill yourself? Can you identify circumstances that make suicide an acceptable option for others? You will give yourself and future clients a great clinical gift if you work through your reactions and stances now, before being faced with this challenge directly.

Case Example: Susan's mother was dying of cancer. Susan was a nurse, and she knew both her craft and her mother very well. One day Susan asked her counselor, Lonnie, a pointed hypothetical question: "I'm not saying this is the case, but I was just wondering if, at some point, my mother asked me to help her take an overdose of her pain medication so she could die on her own terms, and I needed to talk with you about that to sort it out in my own heart, would you have to call the police or something?" Lonnie had listened carefully to Susan over the many weeks of counseling, and had anticipated this question. "No, Susan," Lonnie said. "I have thought about your situation, and I wondered if you might face that kind of request. I don't have to tell anyone. You can use this time to sort out your own thoughts and emotions."

Reporting child and elder abuse.   The laws in most states are fairly consistent and require reporting in one harm-related area: Most helping professionals must report suspected instances of unreported child or elder neglect or abuse, whether sexual or physical. As a society, we have decided that protecting vulnerable individuals who are under the control of others and cannot act to protect themselves overrides the client's right to confidentiality. Reporting such abuse is difficult for at least two reasons. First, there are significant ramifications for the therapeutic relationship when a trusted professional reports abuse. This is true whether the client is the abuse victim, witness, or perpetrator (Levine & Doueck, 1995).

A second reason reporting can be difficult is that initiating the report does not guarantee safety, behavioral change, or a positive outcome. Most child and family welfare systems are overworked, foster care is in short supply, and children and elders can be further traumatized by what happens as a result of the report (Shin, 2005). Of course, regardless of these issues, you must still obey the law and report the abuse. As concerned citizens, we must also continue to work toward a society in which all children and elders are safe and well cared for, and as counselors, we must do what we can to mitigate the psychological damage done by the failings of the system (Leslie et al., 2005).

A complication to this ethical and legal mandate is the fact that abuse and neglect are not exact, quantifiably measurable acts. Determining if abuse or neglect has actually occurred is not the counselor's job (Bryant & Milsom, 2005). State laws usually require the reporting of *suspected* abuse or neglect, and leave it to professionals hired by the state to investigate the veracity of the suspicion. However, because of the serious disruption such reporting causes in any helping relationship, most counselors weigh their suspicions very carefully before acting.

While the counselor cannot control or completely eradicate potential negative impacts of reporting, there are actions you can take that might lessen the damage and even increase the likelihood of a positive outcome. If at all possible, consistent with the ethical codes, we encourage counselors to make the reporting call in collaboration with the client.

When an adult has admitted to child abuse, the scenario (in abbreviated form) might be something like this:

Counselor: I know it is hard for you to talk about your temper, James. It sounds like you really feel awful about hitting Sherry so hard last night when she spilled that paint. But you might remember from our discussions, and the paperwork when we first started working together, that I have to report instances of child abuse, if they haven't been reported.

James: What? No way. I don't think that's abuse. I hit her too hard, and I lost it for a while. But she fell, too. I don't think the gash will need stitches. It's just . . .

Counselor: James, I can't determine how bad the injury is. I just know that I have to report this. It's the law. As a professional, I have to make a report if I have any reason to suspect that child abuse has occurred. I also think it would be better if you and I make the call together. I know you're trying to be a good parent, and if you talk with the social worker yourself, you can explain things in your own words, which might help the process along. But either way, this has to be reported.

With a child who reports being abused, or appears to be abused, the scenario might be quite different.

Counselor: Kerry, I am very sorry to hear that your mommy hurt your arms and legs so much last night. That must have been very scary and awful for you. Your mommy probably feels bad about it, and she needs some help to stop hurting you. It isn't okay for this to happen to you, and I need to call some people who will help.

Kerry: I don't want anyone to know about it but you. My mommy will be mad at me.

Counselor: I know that, Kerry. I want to help you, and I'm really glad you told me because it isn't okay to be afraid and hurt. And you're right, your mommy might be upset, but we still have to call and see if there are some ways to keep you safe and help your mommy.

Kerry: Will they take me away? Will my mommy go to jail?

Counselor: I don't know for sure. I will do everything I can to help you through this, but we have to do something to try and make things better. I'm really sorry. Would you like to stay in the office with me while I call the people I have to call? You can ask them questions, too, if you want to.

It is also possible in most states to make hypothetical calls to ascertain if a given set of circumstances is reportable. If you are uncertain, it is wise to make sure you *need* to report before actually doing so, since the consequences of breaking confidentiality can be so damaging.

Case Example: Eighth-grader, Nina, stopped in to talk with her school counselor, Mr. Winston. She was distressed because her crazy father had exposed himself to three neighborhood children by standing in the picture window naked, masturbating. Nina told Mr. Winston that her father had been injured in a car wreck last year, and wasn't right in the head anymore. Nina's mother was out of town because of a family emergency. Mr. Winston sympathized with Nina, and let her pour out her embarrassment and anger. The bell rang, and as Nina rushed away, her parting words were, "Please don't tell anyone about this. It's so embarrassing. It helps to talk, though. My dad doesn't really mean to be so weird. He just can't control himself."

Mr. Winston decided he should get some help deciding what to do. He was worried about Nina, and her father's actions. Without identifying Nina, he told his principal the story, and the principal told Mr. Winston that this should be reported to the child and family services. Mr. Winston complied.

Even though the source of the call was not revealed to Nina, when the child and family protective services social worker interviewed her, she knew instantly who had "ratted her out." She stopped by Mr. Winston's office and told him in no uncertain terms what she thought of him, of teachers, social workers, and "all the rest of the phony, lying, butt-in, assholes in the world."

Communication with Office Staff and Other Professionals

State laws and agency policies vary regarding sharing case notes and other information with other professionals. In some states, you can legally share pertinent information with colleagues in the same agency, or even across agencies, on a need-to-know basis, without first seeking client permission (Bernstein & Hartsell, 2004). In other states, you need a signed release of information form before disclosing anything to anyone. You need to do the research about these laws and policies in your particular state and work setting, and then include this in your informed consent forms and discussions.

Often, records are seen by supervisors or office staff. Clients have the right to know if case notes and files might be viewed by others. In some situations, this may seem self-evident, but it is better to mention it as a matter of course, rather than trust that clients or students make this assumption. It is also necessary to store your records in a locked filing system, and not ever leave identifying information lying around on your desk or in public view so that personal information is not on display for passers-by or janitorial staff. Both FERPA (Family Education Rights and Privacy Act) and HIPAA regulations make proper records storage not only an ethical issue, but a legal one as well (Stone, 2005d).

As students and/or newly graduated professionals, you will need to be in supervision, and clients have a right to be informed of this. As you mature and develop, we hope you will form peer consultation and professional support groups. While you probably will not talk about every client, this is another customary break in confidentiality that should be noted in your informed consent forms. In some situations, it is wise to actually provide the names of the other professionals in your group, so that clients can let you know if there are reasons to *not* share any information about them with these colleagues. The ACA code indicates that clients do have the right to be made aware of the composition of any supervision groups.

Case Example: Miriam was newly hired at a community mental health center. Kim, her clinical supervisor, also saw clients for therapy. The informed consent forms informed clients that Miriam would receive in-house supervision, and Miriam talked with clients about this fact as well. This was done even though in Miriam's state, the law allowed for professional counselors to exchange information with other professionals on a need-to-know basis. Miriam was assigned to see Sam, an angry 17-year-old boy who was on probation for a number of minor property-damage offenses. He quizzed Miriam thoroughly about confidentiality. He wanted to know exactly who she might talk with and what she might share about him. His main concern was that his parents and his probation officer not be told things he might say about his friends or girlfriend. Miriam assured Sam that unless it was a matter of life and death, or a case of unreported sexual or physical abuse of a minor or elderly person, she would not need to disclose any specifics to anyone. She did mention, however, that she would be talking with her supervisor about her work with Sam. Sam didn't seem to mind this fact.

As it happened, unbeknownst to Sam, his parents were seeing Miriam's supervisor, Kim, for couple's counseling. One of their main concerns was—you guessed it—Sam, and his relationships with friends and his girlfriend. Miriam and Kim discovered this overlap in a supervision session in which Miriam had begun to tell Kim about Sam's first couple of sessions. What do you see as the ethical concerns in this scenario? How do you think they should be addressed?

Communication with Funding Sources or Third Party Payers

As insurance companies, managed care companies, and public funding sources struggle with the ever more thinly stretched medical dollar, demands for counselor accountability have grown. The number of counseling sessions a client can receive is often based on diagnosis and progress toward appropriate goals. This necessitates much more detailed communication between the counselor and the funding source than in times past, and may even include a requirement to send weekly counseling session notes to the company. We have colleagues who have found these requirements so invasive they have

========= **Digressions for Deliberation 6.1** =========

"Accidental" Breaches of Confidentiality

From a Professional Ethics Listserv: I have had some negative experiences with particular cases with Medicaid HMOs, but a worse scenario was described by a student in one of my classes several years ago. By day, she worked at a managed care insurance company and when we discussed confidentiality, she described what happened when information came into the company. "Everybody loved the boob jobs and psychotherapy notes." Apparently the staff used to send around photographs that were used to document the operation. In addition particularly "juicy" therapy notes that were used to document psychotherapy were also photocopied and passed around by the staff. Even more horrifying was that although she'd expressed discomfort with what her peers were doing, she had no idea about the issues of confidentiality until she'd been exposed to the information in my class. Needless to say, we had a lively class discussion about these issues!

refused to work with certain companies. See Digressions for Deliberation 6.1 and you will understand why.

Most counselors adjust to insurance and managed care demands and have found ways to inform and protect clients in a manner that meets basic ethical and clinical standards. We will discuss this area further in the following section on records. While you may not be able to develop your informed consent forms to specifically describe all the permutations of what various third party payers require, you can include a statement such as the following: *Depending on your insurance coverage or other sources of funding, I may need to disclose information about our work together. I will keep you informed of these requirements and we can talk over the best way to handle this.*

Depositions, Subpoenas, and Court Orders

We live in what some have called a litigious era. There are at least three reasons you might find yourself or your records in the courtroom. The first is by far the more common: Clients are often in distressing legal entanglements, such domestic violence problems, divorce settlements and custody arrangements, injury-related suits, and so on. Your work with a given client might be assumed to bolster one side or the other, and thus, you might find yourself with a subpoena or court order to produce your records or testify in person. You could also be asked to participate in a deposition. Here are definitions of these terms:

Deposition: A meeting that usually takes place in an attorney's office. The purpose of a deposition is so attorney(s) can try to discover evidence that might later be used at trial. A deposition might also be used to preserve testimony that will later be introduced during the trial. Those asked to participate are sworn in by a court reporter, and the proceedings are recorded. There is no judge present, and the attorney(s) control the proceedings (Bernstein & Hartsell, 2004).

Subpoena: A legal demand to appear and produce testimony for the court. Subpoenas can be issued by the clerk of the court, at the request of attorneys on either side. They are not reviewed for their legal relevance. A *subpoena duces tecum* is a demand to appear in court and bring along records. Your records can also be subpoenaed separately.

Court Order: A legal demand to appear in court, usually the result of a hearing evaluating the merits of requiring such an appearance. The order is issued by a judge.

In general, you should seek legal and supervisory advice before agreeing to participate in a deposition or complying with a subpoena, because it is most likely you should not readily comply. In fact, the ACA ethics code is clear on this point. You need to get a judge's ruling before testifying or producing records. This brings us to another important legal term, client privilege. *Client privilege* is a legal right that clients have with certain professional relationships. State and federal laws vary on which professional relationships have privilege. In 2000, Glosoff, Herlihy, and Spence (2000) reported that licensed counselors were included in the privileged communications statutes in 44 states. Client privilege is granted in state legal statutes. It provides clients with the right to privacy in their interactions with designated professionals. Privilege is the right of the *client,* not the mental health professional, so clients can waive privilege, even if the professional might wish otherwise (Shuman & Foote, 1999).

Be sure to investigate state and federal statutes concerning privilege, confidentiality, and privacy in your state; and if you move, remember there are significant state-by-state differences. Even if you don't move, these are areas that change depending on case law and legislation, so you need to develop a habit of checking these matters routinely. Continuing education lectures and workshops also help to keep current—but be careful: Acting in accordance with educational information is not the same as seeking legal advice. You, and you alone, will be held responsible for any actions you take based on educational materials, whereas if you seek an attorney's counsel, the attorney is professionally directly responsible for the advice given (Bernstein & Hartsell, 2004).

While it occurs relatively infrequently, a second reason you might face our judicial system is a claim of malpractice against you. We cover this possibility in the epilogue. We sincerely hope this is something you never have to face, as it can be a traumatic and grueling experience. Such claims can be for good reasons, or have no merit whatsoever. Either way, they must be faced and answered. When clients bring forward a claim of malpractice, or unethical behavior, they legally give up certain rights to confidentiality, as you have the right to defend yourself. Should this occur, you will be extremely glad if you followed our advice and are part of a trusted collegial consultation group.

The third reason you might be in court would be to serve as an expert witness (Bernstein & Hartsell, 2004). Professionals who have developed special expertise in various areas of forensic concern might be hired to provide their judgments about particular matters in a given case, or you might be court ordered to testify if you have expert information pertinent to the case. In any event, professional demeanor is essential, and you should give yourself plenty of time to adequately prepare. Bernstein and Hartsell (2004) offer the following helpful hints for testifying in court:

- Tell the truth.
- Testify from your own personal knowledge or observation, unless asked otherwise.

Digressions for Deliberation 6.2

One Therapist's Story

From early in my practice, I found I enjoyed occasional forensic work. I liked being of help when there were difficult cases of child sexual abuse, questions of terminating parental rights, and so on. My circle of professional friends included many attorneys, and I testified as an expert witness once or twice a year. I also did a fair number of custody evaluations, sometimes with a partner, and sometimes alone. Gradually, I became known as someone willing to take the really contentious, high-profile family break-ups. It was hard work, but I felt like I was able to work diligently to find the best possible solutions, always with the children's best interests foremost in my mind.

For over 10 years, I never had a single ethical claim filed against me, even though my work often made parents upset and angry with me. Then came the year from hell. Four different claims were filed with our state ethics board, and I was informed I was being sued for malpractice. To my own surprise, I was devastated, even though I was certain each of the claims would eventually be overturned. I knew in my heart and mind that I had not acted unethically or unprofessionally. And I was right. Two and a half years later, it was all cleared. That was 2½ years of legal fees, insulting ethics board meetings, copying and recopying paperwork, proving and reproving what I had and had not done. It was exhausting, demoralizing, and infuriating. It significantly changed my practice, and nearly drove me from the profession. Therapists are drawn to the field because they want to help needy, mixed-up people. We forget that sometimes, these are also vindictive, angry, and sometimes severely disturbed folks who will turn on us for trying to help. I am grateful that I found a very competent attorney and had adequate malpractice insurance. But looking back, I realize that if I had not had a close circle of fellow mental health professionals who knew and affirmed my work, I would have given up and changed professions.

- Listen to the question.
- Answer only the question asked of you; if you do not understand it, ask that the question be rephrased.
- If you don't know the answer, say so.
- Don't exceed your level of competence, experience, or training and qualify your testimony when necessary.
- Avoid being specific about dates, times, and empirical statistics unless you personally recorded them and are certain they are correct.
- Be prepared and never testify without reviewing your records and any prior depositions you have given in the case. (pp. 170–172)

Most counselors find that legal interactions or requests for records provoke significant anxiety. The more prepared you are, the easier it will be. Remember, you cannot ignore them entirely, and you have an ethical and legal obligation to protect your client's confidentiality as much as you possibly can. Of course, when you prepare informed consent forms, you do not need to spell out every detail of the possible ways you may be asked by our legal system to break confidentiality. Simply note that in the event of a court order to reveal information, you may need to break confidentiality by testifying or releasing your records.

Summarizing the Limits and Exceptions

In Applications 6.2, we have prepared a list of possible exceptions to confidentiality. This is not a complete list because the rules vary from state to state and from agency to agency. In the spirit of empowerment and informed consent, we encourage you to develop a written document that adequately and humanely describes these possibilities in a way that informs but does not frighten or overwhelm your clients. Remember: *Informed consent is the most obvious respectful and legal exception to client confidentiality.* If you construct your forms well, and take the time to build an informed foundation with your clients, your confidentiality risks and anxieties will be greatly reduced.

TECHNOLOGY AND THE INTERNET

In recent years confidentiality issues began to interact with technology with the advent of the telegraph and have proceeded to grow more complex with each new layer of technologically assisted communication. The telephone is a great example. Our grandparents enhanced their social lives by listening in on other people's conversations on "party lines," which, for those of you too young to know, has nothing to do with political affiliation. More recently, cell phones, answering machines, and fax machines have been added, along with computers, and then the Internet not far behind. With each addition, the issues have grown exponentially more complex.

=== **Applications 6.2** ===

Possible General Exceptions to Confidentiality

- your client's stated or written request to release information or records
- *unreported* instances of child or elder abuse, whether physical, emotional, or sexual
- the need to inform insurance or funding sources
- imminent and serious suicidal or homicidal threats
- laws or policies that require parental notification
- court-ordered release of records or testimony
- legal action the client has chosen to engage in, against you or others
- supervision and professional consultation groups
- office personnel who handle records and requests for services
- use of Internet for communication, billing, or records transmission (see the section "Technology and the Internet" in this chapter)

To state the obvious, answering machines and fax machines receive information you send in settings over which you have little to no control. Therefore, before sending information in this manner, you must alert clients that you are going to do so, and obtain their permission. Further, you must take every precaution possible to ensure that the information reaches its intended recipient without also reaching the eyes and/or ears of other people.

Clients may have little choice but to use their insurance benefits to cover their counseling costs, and you may not have control over the manner in which funding sources receive diagnostic and progress information. However, you can talk this over carefully with clients, and you can certainly take great care in the preparation of your paperwork. For many reasons, learning to write factual, respectful, and circumspect case notes is an essential part of your ethical and clinical education.

Billing and accountability to funding sources is not the only aspect of professional practice affected by technology. The Internet has expanded interpersonal communication options in ways that still astonish many of us. Searching the Internet itself we found the following quotes (at http://en.thinkexist.com).

> *Advances in computer technology and the Internet have changed the way America works, learns, and communicates. The Internet has become an integral part of America's economic, political, and social life.*
>
> —Bill Clinton

> *The Internet is the first thing that humanity has built that humanity doesn't understand, the largest experiment in anarchy that we have ever had.*
>
> —Eric Schmidt

Together, these quotes sum up our caution to you—the Internet has drastically changed most aspects of our lives. We do not yet fully grasp the significance, risks, and potential this resource represents.

While the functioning and reach of computers and the Internet may stretch our understanding, precautions for confidentiality are comfortably within the realm of common sense. Whether you write your case notes by hand and store them in a locked drawer, or use the latest voice technology to dictate them straight into your networked computer, it is still your responsibility to ensure confidentiality and to inform clients fully of your practices. Here are precautions we offer today. As technology advances, you will need to create your own list, depending on technology tools you choose to use.

If you do case notes on a computer: (a) Make sure others cannot enter your worksite, (b) change your password often, (c) watch for signs that your worksite has been visited, (d) back up your files on a thumb drive (aka: flash drive) daily (using two methods to back up records would be even more prudent), and (e) purchase high quality virus protection and update it regularly.

If you contact clients via email: (a) Include this fact in your informed consent, (b) consider carefully the words you write, as you simply cannot control their destiny, and (c) once your words float into cyberspace, assume they never cease to exist. The ACA Code of Ethics is especially clear in its guidance. Read Section A.12: Technological Applications, but also, stay alert to changes, as this is a rapidly expanding area of concern.

PARTICULAR POPULATIONS AND CONFIDENTIALITY CONCERNS

Protecting client confidentiality is a general ethical mandate. Protecting the confidentiality of particular vulnerable populations requires special attention.

Children and Adolescents

We have often claimed that working with young people has similarities to working across cultures (J. Sommers-Flanagan & Sommers-Flanagan, 1997, 2004a). Adults forget what it felt like to be told when to get up, when to go to school, what to eat, what to wear, and even when we could go to the bathroom—but this is the norm for most children. As children grow and develop, they are usually given more choice and control over these day-to-day decisions on a gradual basis. In counseling, privacy and confidentiality can be especially important to children and adolescents who have little control in other parts of their lives.

Our laws generally favor the rights of parents over the rights of children, so it is often necessary for counselors to seek informed parental or guardian consent before entering into a counseling relationship with children (Koocher & Keith-Spiegel, 1990). This does not mean you have to agree to tell parents everything their children disclose. In fact, it is wise to develop an informed consent policy statement *and* process for parents that explain what you will and will not disclose to them. Young people deserve the same confidentiality considerations that adults have, and most of the rights and exceptions are the same. However, ongoing awareness of adolescent culture and issues is essential in determining when/if to break confidentiality (J. R. Sullivan, Ramirez, Rae, Razo, & George, 2002).

The ideal situation, clinically and ethically, is to have an initial meeting with parents and the young client—all present. The goal is for everyone to come to an open agreement as to how confidentiality will be handled. This gives the therapist an opportunity to educate both parents and young clients about confidentiality and the important role of trust and autonomy in the counseling process. See our example in Applications 6.3.

As mentioned in Chapter 5, adolescents can legally seek mental health assistance on their own for certain problem areas. This presents interesting confidentiality challenges. Even though young people may have the right to seek mental health help, they might not have the means to do so. Accessing their parent's health insurance will most certainly alert parents to the fact that their child is seeking counseling. Obtaining transportation, explaining the time away, and many other obstacles might make it difficult for young people to obtain help without others knowing they are doing so. Before you guarantee young clients the privacy they are seeking, explore these difficulties with them so they have a chance to consider how realistic privacy might be.

Pause for Reflection

Agreeing to counsel a young person without parental awareness or consent adds a layer to your therapeutic relationship. Working with children is laden with counter-transference potential even under the best of circumstances (B. G. Richardson, 2001).

Caring professionals can be sorely tempted to allow their rescue fantasies to bloom, imagining themselves to be much better for the child than the child's parents. On the other hand, some might also find themselves feeling tempted to punish or discipline young people because the usual power differential between counselor and client is magnified. Either way, without a parent involved in or even aware of the counseling relationship, these nurturing or punitive parental urges should be monitored very closely.

Applications 6.3

Sample Confidentiality Policy Statement

Dear Parent,

   When working with young people, it is essential to be clear about confidentiality. Confidentiality is very important in counseling. It is just as important for your child as it is for adults. Therefore, my policy is to keep what your child talks about confidential. I won't disclose what we talk about without your child's permission—even to you! There are certain exceptions, which we will talk over. They are on page __.

   By signing this form, you are indicating your understanding and agreement with this policy.

Confidentiality Concerns in Families, Couples, and Groups

Any time you have more than one person in the room, the parameters of confidentiality shift. The counselor, as a trained professional, can be expected to keep even the most shocking or endearing or inflammatory material private. The other persons in the room cannot. This has clinical, ethical, and legal ramifications. Legally, privilege extends only to a client-counselor relationship. Information shared in a larger context may not be considered privileged communication. Ethically, all clients deserve to have the limits of family, couple, or group confidentiality carefully explained through a thoughtful informed consent process. And clinically, the skilled professional will find ways to help individuals calibrate their self-disclosures so that they do not feel overexposed.

Families and Couples.   People in romantic or familial relationships have webs of connection that extend far beyond the counseling room and therefore working with couples or families presents unique confidentiality concerns. We will return to this area in more depth in Chapter 12, but it deserves mention here as well. Sometimes, the couples or families themselves are the defined *client,* but at other times, family members act as consultants to the counseling process with a loved one. A partner or family member might telephone the counselor and share solicited or unsolicited information, or they might come to a counseling session for a particular reason. This does *not* make this family member your client. Be sure to be clear about what you will and will not keep confidential.

Case Example: Dale, a 17-year-old openly lesbian woman, was seeing Ms. Landon for counseling. Dale's parents were paying for the counseling, and had signed an informed consent form indicating their willingness for Dale's counseling to be completely confidential. Dale's mother, Bernice, called Ms. Landon and said, "I am so happy with your work with Dale. She's much happier, and more self-confident. But I want to tell you something in confidence. She has a little crush on you. But don't tell her I told you that, okay? I just didn't want you to be caught off guard. And also, I hope you talk to her about her drinking. I'm worried about her getting drunk so often. I know the kids these days . . ."

At this point, Ms. Landon pulled herself together and said, "Bernice, I have to stop you for a minute. I know you love your daughter very much, and are concerned about her. And that's great. However, it's Dale who is my client, and so when other people tell me things about her, I have to decide myself if it is important for me to tell her. I can't necessarily keep things you tell me confidential. Does that make sense to you?"

Bernice sounded a little hurt. Ms. Landon decided the best course of action would be to offer to meet with Dale and Bernice together, if Dale agreed. She believed she could help them talk about these issues without either one feeling betrayed.

How would you have solved this problem? Can you think of other ideas and/or problems with Ms. Landon's idea?

Groups.   Working with groups entails many confidentiality related challenges. The most obvious is the fact that group facilitators cannot mandate or ensure that all participants will uphold commitments to confidentiality. When individual members disclose personal information in a group setting, other members may choose to share that information outside of group. When the group session ends, the group leader or counselor has no control over whether other individual members violate confidentiality.

The Association for Specialists in Group Work "recognizes the commitment of its members to the Code of Ethics and Standards of Practice" of ACA (ASGW, 1998, p. 1). However, it also provides "Best Practice Guidelines" for its members (ASGW, 1998). The ASGW Best Practice Guidelines state:

> Group Workers define confidentiality and its limits (for example, legal and ethical exceptions and expectations; waivers implicit with treatment plans, documentation, and insurance usage). Group Workers have the responsibility to inform all group participants of the need for confidentiality, potential consequences of breaching confidentiality, and that legal privilege does not apply to group discussions (unless provided by state statute). (p. 2)

Similarly, the American Group Psychotherapy Association has ethical guidelines for its multidisciplinary membership. Interestingly, the AGPA emphasizes that group therapists obtain agreements from patients or clients regarding confidentiality. The AGPA Guidelines for Ethics state: "The group shall agree that the patient/client as well as the psychotherapist shall protect the identity of its members" (AGPA, 2002, p. 1).

Groups for children or minors present an expanded array of confidentiality issues. Most prominent is the fact that children, more than adults, seem disinclined to maintain confidentiality. For example, it is not unusual for children to inadvertently or intentionally break confidentiality almost immediately after group ends. Additionally, ethical group therapists who work with children and adolescents keep in mind that they are usually simultaneously working with many constituents, including parents, teachers and school administrators, and probation officers.

When it comes to managing confidentiality during group therapy, the bottom line is the old tried-and-true guideline of informed consent. In all cases, group workers are encouraged to develop and use written informed consent procedures that, in essence, tell prospective clients the rules of the group therapy before group therapy is initiated. This bottom line is true for both adult and child or adolescent populations. Ethical group therapists do not proceed with group formation and work without a clear informed consent process.

Mandated or Involuntary Clients

Confidentiality is challenging when clients are voluntarily seeking counseling or mental health services, but it is even more so if they are attending sessions involuntarily. Mandated counseling is most commonly initiated through legal proceedings, but also occurs somewhat frequently in school settings. The key to managing confidentiality with mandated clients or students is, once again, a clear and consistent informed consent procedure—one that includes not only the client, but also the party in charge of monitoring the counseling process.

For example, if you are working with a court-referred man and his probation officer contacts you to inquire about your client's progress, you will want to have clarified in advance with your client and the probation officer how you handle such requests. The trick is to balance the business obligation you have to the probation officer (who relies on you to provide therapeutic services for his or her caseload) with the ethical obligations you have with your client. In most cases, probation officers will trust you to report about client attendance and to make general statements regarding progress, but this agreement should be in writing, and in advance. Otherwise, the probation officer may decide to press you to provide extensive personal information about the client. Then, when the probation officer calls you and asks if your client has violated probation by consuming alcoholic beverages, you will be able to note an earlier agreement that does not require or allow you to provide such information. Even when working with mandated clients, you are functioning as a counselor, not as an additional probation officer. Your informed consent should spell out the unique limits of confidentiality inherent with mandated clients, such as your responsibility to contact the referral source should the client miss a scheduled appointment.

PROFESSIONAL RECORD KEEPING

Although the task is unlikely to be anyone's preferred way to spend time, counselors cannot *not* keep records. It is now a basic standard of care, and failure to keep records could be grounds for malpractice. In fact, there are entire books written just about record keeping for mental health professionals (Wiger, 2005). Record keeping includes much more than the hastily scribbled case note. Your professional records might include your schedule book; signed informed consent forms, other intake forms, your treatment plan, and referral notes or information you gathered about the client; a progress note written after each session; a termination note or plan; any written correspondence with other professionals, family members, or your client; and a case summary.

Helping professionals keep records for a number of reasons. Each reason contributes to the overall picture of ethical, professional, and legally defensible record-keeping practices. We discuss each in the following paragraphs.

- Competence and Efficacy: Professionals might like to believe they will remember all the important details a client shares with them, including relevant history, counseling goals, and how things paused and/or eventually ended. But from the perspective of our advanced ages, we have one thing to say to this belief: Fat chance. Conducting caring, mindful counseling of any kind requires sensitive note taking.
- Client Protection: Clients expect counselors to remember what they've shared, and to be able to access this material.
- Counselor Protection: Professional documentation is both a standard of care, and the counselor's proof of treatment interactions. As the old saying goes, if it isn't written down, it didn't happen.

As we have mentioned previously, HIPAA has a few things to say about the care and maintenance of medical records. You ignore these guidelines at your own peril. But that's not all there is to good mental health record-keeping practices. All codes urge that records be respectful, securely stored, and available to clients. There are ethical and clinical implications in record keeping that you should attend to throughout your career. Keep the following in mind.

- Your records are an expression of your care and concern for your clients. They should have a professional, but kind, tone. They should be written so that you would not feel defensive or apologetic if clients asked to read what you wrote.
- Your records are to be kept confidential. If you have someone who files or types for you, this person should be trained in appropriate confidentiality practices. Further, your files should not be accessible to cleaning staff or other office personnel.
- Your records are your best defense if challenged with malpractice or other unethical conduct.
- Your records serve to guide your work. You cannot possibly keep all the goals, plans, and details in mind. You need to learn to write notes that contribute to the therapeutic process you've undertaken with your clients.
- Your records need to last a long time. Just how long is a matter of particular ethics codes, state licensure policies, agency policies, and the original purpose of the professional relationship. Write your notes legibly in ink on good paper, or type them, or store them safely electronically, with a state-of-the-art backup system.
- Your records matter to others. You need to have a plan for how people could obtain their records in the event of your sudden death or disability.
- Your records could become public, usually because of part of a legal process or challenge. This means that, as you write your notes, you should write them in ways that would be viewed as respectful to your client and to yourself from outside viewpoints.

CHAPTER WRAP-UP

Confidentiality is a burden and a gift. Students and clients with whom you work may be entrusting you with their deepest and darkest secrets. There will be times in your career when you feel a temptation to inappropriately share details of what you have heard during therapy sessions with someone close to you, with a class you are teaching, or with another client. In each of these cases, it would be an ethical betrayal to share information that might identify the person without having an official release of information, signed by the client.

Maintaining confidentiality requires a particular mindset and personal discipline. No one can blame you for feeling the temptation to violate confidentiality. However, if the enormity or enticing nature of the client's confidential material begins to overwhelm your desire to maintain confidentiality, you should talk about this with your professional colleagues and/or supervisor. Sometimes it can be too much to be alone with your clients' secrets and you may need professional support.

Chapter Seven

BOUNDARIES, ROLES, AND LIMITS

Dibs suddenly stood up. "No!" he shouted. "Dibs no go out of here. Dibs no go home. Not never!"

"I know you don't want to go, Dibs. But you and I only have one hour every week to spend together here in this playroom. And when that hour is over, no matter how you feel about it, no matter how I feel about it, no matter how anybody feels about it, it is over for that day and we both leave the playroom."

—Virginia Axline, *Dibs: In search of self*

CHAPTER ORIENTATION

Taking on a professional helping role in someone's life has immediate responsibilities *and* implications that far outlast the actual professional relationship. In this chapter, we invite you to consider practical, clinical, professional, and personal perspectives on the roles and boundaries that professionals must orchestrate in their service to clients. The potential for subtle or blatant abuse of helping relationships is considerable. We hope that examining the dynamics from every angle possible will at least reduce the risks of inadvertent harm. This chapter is all about boundaries.

Even if we lived in one nice, discrete sphere labeled *Personal* and traveled to a completely different sphere labeled *Professional* for work, boundaries would be challenging because we would be bringing our whole selves back and forth. But of course, our spheres are not discrete. Our lives are much more complex, interconnected, and fluid than that. The many challenging rural and cultural boundary implications cannot be lightly dismissed either, and deserve a bit of specific scrutiny. Specifically, in this chapter you will have the opportunity to consider:

- the definitions and functions of roles and boundaries in human relationships;
- the many reasons boundaries are absolutely central to ethical practice;
- the contributing dynamics of transference and countertransference;
- client responses to boundary setting;
- the realities and concerns about multiple roles;
- ways to deconstruct the generic term *multiple roles* to determine a wise course of action;

- gift giving and receiving, self-disclosure, and considerations about touch;
- methods for assessing benefit and harm;
- rural and community concerns;
- the dynamics and realities of sexual attraction.

INTRODUCTION TO ROLES, BOUNDARIES, AND RELATIONSHIP RULES

In exchanges between humans, there are implicit and explicit rules for interaction that maintain the fabric of culture and the integrity of each individual. We begin learning these relationship rules at birth, and they continue to guide our interactions throughout our lives.

Relationship rules create boundaries within and around all human relationships. Often, we only become consciously aware of these boundaries when they are violated. These boundary rules include the "proper" amount of interpersonal space for various types of interactions (business, professional, service, sales, romantic, familial). They include expectations for verbal styles and output, based on such factors as gender, power, age, and relationship (e.g., Tannen, 1990; e.g., Young-Eisendrath, 1993). They also include rules about dress, touch, food consumption, appropriate work and recreation, sleeping arrangements, and probably thousands of other aspects of human society, including the boundaries between "the personal" and "the professional" (Pipes, Holstein, & Aguiree, 2005).

These rules and resulting boundaries have obligations as well as privileges associated with them (Kitchener, 2000). There are cultural differences in the role expectations (Marcussen & Piatt, 2005), but regardless of these differences, the roles carry weighty expectations. All human relationships or interactions involve risk. You might place your trust in a painter who ultimately fails to listen and paints your kitchen the wrong shade of lime green or orange. You might have welcomed a neighbor's pet into your yard, only to find the pet loves to dig in your precious flowerbeds. Even the briefest encounters have implicit or explicit boundaries and rules, which if broken, can be damaging or even disastrous. For example, we literally trust our lives to others operating motor vehicles every time we drive or even walk along a roadside. We trust mail-order pharmacies to send us the right medications, in the right dosage. Some of these rules have the weight of law behind them, but others do not. Either way, we trust other people to obey the rules and laws as we interact with them, and if the trust is broken, there are consequences (Kavathatzopoulos, 2005). When we fail to live up to the obligations—or violate the privileges—at the very least, there is discomfort and confusion. At the worst, there is pain, broken relationships, lawsuits, and other collateral damage.

In Chapter 1, we talked about the social origins of professionalism. Professionals are expected to perform their duties *objectively* and with *client welfare* as their highest concern. It is a widely held assumption that certain personal relationships will, almost by definition, compromise professional objectivity. Familial and sexual relationships, as well as long-term or deep friendships, have many role expectations that come into direct conflict with roles that demand objectivity and equal treatment.

Pause for Reflection

Close personal and familial relationships give our lives meaning and connection. These relationships are where we hope to find shelter, loyalty, compassion, and ready forgiveness. In his poem, The Death of the Hired Man, *Robert Frost (Latham, 1979) wrote, "Home is where, when you have to go there, they have to take you in" (p. 38). How do you imagine your professional life intersecting with your personal life? Are you likely to seek friendships in your workplace? Romantic partners? What concerns do you experience when coworkers are also friends or lovers? How do you create and maintain boundaries that keep your home and your relationships safe and healthy?*

Maintaining healthy boundaries around personal and professional relationships is an important component of burnout prevention as well as professional fidelity. Although they may offer the biggest challenges, personal and familial roles are not the only roles with expectations that might conflict with professional role demands. As an individual, you have many associations with other people in your life. By definition, each of these relationships has role expectations, boundaries, and interests—and many will have competing demands on your allegiance, time, and energy.

WHY ALL THE FUSS ABOUT BOUNDARIES AND RELATIONSHIPS?

As you become a mental health or helping professional, this new role will influence your consideration of other potential roles in your life. Some of these considerations may surprise you. Some may seem overly protective or misguided whereas some may simply seem like good common sense. In most forms of counseling, boundary concerns are central because the trusting professional relationship *itself* is part of the healing process (Gelso & Hayes, 1998; Rogers, 1958). In this sense, a counseling relationship is both professional and very intimate.

Any intimate relationship has emotional risk. When the rules of interaction are broken in our closest relationships, the damage can be painful and extensive. Even small or unintended failures can take significant time and energy to repair. If the rules are extensive and/or repeatedly broken, chances increase that the relationship will be permanently altered or will end.

Sometimes intimate relationships are enhanced when the parties in the relationships have multiple roles in each other's lives. Romantic partners or friends often find their relationships improved if both members are interested in similar hobbies, share membership in the same faith community, or become active in supporting a similar political cause. Parents can sometimes improve relationships with children by coaching the soccer team, leading the scout troop, or being a classroom parent. Of course, intimate relationships can also be complicated or harmed by overlapping roles. The role expectations could run counter to each other, or disappointment or failure in one set of roles could affect the other relationship. If your mom is your soccer coach, and as a good mom she knows how much you want to play and improve, but as a soccer coach she knows you aren't good enough to be a starter, there will be tension in both relationships.

As we noted in the introduction, it might be easier if our personal lives and our professional lives never intersected—but that is rarely the case. Some might even argue that the complexities of our boundary intersections keep life interesting. Regardless, we would argue that large quantities of awareness and integrity are necessary to manage boundaries between the personal and the professional. For instance, when two or more mental health professionals are also in close personal or familial relationships, issues such as client confidentiality need to be addressed carefully with all stakeholders, including clients. It is not uncommon for mental health practitioners to be married, or to have a practice that includes a sibling or parent. The public nature of professional life raises boundary issues for those involved, those affected, and those observing (see Digressions for Deliberation 7.1 for a case in point).

DISTINCTIVE ASPECTS OF PROFESSIONAL HELPING RELATIONSHIPS

Counseling relationships have dimensions and dynamics that make them unlike any other personal or professional relationship. Because of this, counselors have especially significant fidelity responsibilities. We list some of the main differences in the following paragraphs:

- Counseling relationships have aptly been described as *one way intimacies* (Shirley Emerson, 1995). Significant relationship risks are incurred by clients as they bare their souls, their needs, or their foibles while being dependent on the counselor to honor the trust. Professionals do *not* engage in reciprocal depth of self-disclosure. Any self-disclosure should be done in the service of the helping relationship, with the client's best interest as a guide.
- Just as the intimacies are one way (client to professional), the *ethical boundary responsibilities* are also one way (professional to client). As Bernstein and Hartsell (2000) note, "It is unethical for a therapist to become involved in a dual relationship with the client, but the client can violate boundaries with impunity" (p. 62).
- There is a *power differential* in the helping relationship. The client is seeking help from a professional who is assumed to have knowledge and skills. The therapist comes to know the client's fears and weaknesses. The combination of professional knowledge and personal knowledge make the therapist potentially very powerful in the client's life (Cummings, 2000).
- Professional helping relationships are *resource dependent.* Clients cannot simply have as much time as they might like with their counselors. Managed care, sheer numbers of students, insurance rules, agency policies, and other financial practicalities define and limit the quantity and quality of the therapy relationship (Michels, 2001).
- Helping relationships are *outcomes driven.* Even if finances are no concern, both the number and length of sessions are determined by the counselor's best judgment and accepted professional practices (e.g., Stricklin-Parker & Schneider, 2005).

In addition to these overt dimensions that make professional counseling relationships unique, there are other powerful dynamics that operate at the unconscious level and

---

Digressions for Deliberation 7.1

The Authors' Boundary Challenges

For less observant readers, it may come as a surprise to learn that the authors of this text are married. We have worked together as writers, professors, researchers, psychological evaluators, and counselors. A generation ago, due to nepotism laws, some of these shared roles would not have been legally possible in some states and, though strides are being made on this front (Foster, 1993), they are still the source of occasional suspicion and awkwardness. What if there is a divisive issue in a faculty meeting and a close vote is expected? Will we be seen as voting independently or as an automatic voting block? What if a student offends one of us or performs very poorly in one of our courses? Will that student worry about the effects not only on one of us, but on the other as well? What if a student needs to complain about being treated unfairly by one of us? Will we always leap to each other's defense?

In our clinical work, clients who know we are married sometimes assume we talk about them to each other. In public, they might approach us and begin talking about issues and concerns they raised in a counseling session with one of us. This sort of behavior was initially quite surprising.

We've found that there are ethical practices we can use to prevent or mitigate the potential harm our spousal relationship might have on students, colleagues, and clients. For instance, we are explicit in our *informed consent process* about the fact that we do not ordinarily discuss our professional work with each other. We explain that if we believe such discussion would be helpful, we will talk it over with our client first. In classes with new students, we make a point to note that we are married, and work together, and give students permission to talk about that, either in class, with us directly, or with another faculty person, should it pose any problems for them. And our colleagues . . . ? Faculty alliances form over issues of great import, such as resource allocations, and slightly lesser import, such as who should make the coffee. We disagree as often as we agree, which is a comfort to those worried about a voting block—but perhaps less of a comfort to those who are more conflict avoidant.

Finally, we've discovered that the multiple-roles impact is a two-way street. We have to make sure we also take steps to keep the professional demands we share from taking a destructive toll on our personal lives.

---

contribute to boundary concerns. These two related concepts, transference and countertransference, are explained next.

Transference

Sigmund Freud (Freud, 1949) first described, and thus got naming privileges for, the transference phenomenon. Transference occurs when clients project unconscious material onto their therapist and into the professional relationship—usually related to unfinished business with early childhood caretakers and authority figures. Harry Stack Sullivan's concept of parataxic distortion (H. S. Sullivan, 1953) is a similar concept, but is not limited to the therapeutic relationship. Parataxic distortion occurs when our perceptions of others are distorted by our past, our own needs, and/or our unconscious fantasies. We then relate to these others, not on the basis of who they are, but on our projections of who they are.

Certain approaches in counseling utilize this projective phenomenon directly by allowing the transference to develop and then helping the client see the projective and inaccurate quality of the transferential beliefs. Psychoanalysts and others who work therapeutically with transference have extensive training and have sought their own analytic therapy as well (J. Sommers-Flanagan & Sommers-Flanagan, 2004b). Not every mental health professional will directly work with transference within the therapeutic relationship, but we believe that to some extent, transference is operative in most helping relationships. Transference also has significant emotional weight. Therefore, clients will not only assume many things about you and how you behave, but they will also likely have strong feelings about these assumptions. Contact outside the professional relationship can add unnecessary, confusing, or even harmful dimensions to clinical work and the transference process. Consider the case of Lin and Ginny.

Case Example: Lin, a 40-something counselor in a university counseling center, was seeing an attractive, athletic young woman named Ginny. Ginny was insightful and eager to work out her conflicted relationship with her mother, which she believed was contributing to her struggles with body image and mild eating disordered behaviors. Ginny loved her counseling and made it clear that she admired Lin and her work. Although Lin's approach in her work with Ginny included cognitive behavioral strategies, Lin was well aware of the transference dimensions in her therapeutic relationship with Ginny. Unbeknownst to either of them, both Lin and Ginny had signed up for a campus recreation class for beginning tennis. It was a small class, with members often paired to work on their skills. Fortunately, Lin was not paired with Ginny the first day, but both were keenly aware of the other. Lin knew this would be an issue for Ginny, so she took some time with a colleague to talk over the best course of action. Together, they went over the options:

1. Lin could continue the tennis class and conduct herself as if she did not know Ginny from any other context. She could limit contact with Ginny as much as possible, and try to get over her own self-consciousness of being in a tennis class with a young, athletically able client who would likely be closely watching Lin's attempts to learn tennis. In this option, she would simply allow Ginny to talk about the tennis class if she chose to.

2. Similar to the first option, Lin could stay in the class, but consciously use the class interactions to further Ginny's work on her body image and relationship with her mother.

3. Lin could drop the tennis class for now and simply tell Ginny nothing. If Ginny brought it up, Lin could indicate that she had found the tennis class didn't fit in her schedule, or life, right then.

4. Lin could drop the tennis class and talk with Ginny about the decision. Lin could explain to Ginny that the class would be available later, and that because her time with Ginny was limited and very important, she (Lin) didn't want to complicate things by the extra contact.

You may have a variety of reactions to this scenario. We'll refer back to it later in the chapter, but in the meantime, put yourself in Lin's shoes. What do you imagine yourself wanting to do? What about if you were Ginny?

Of course, transference and/or parataxic distortions are constantly in flux, acting and reacting in the context of dynamic interpersonal relationships. The antiquated notion that the counselor somehow stays objective and neutral in this process has been displaced by an awareness that counseling techniques and relationships affect both the counselor and the client in a mutually influential set of interactions (Renik, 1993). Therefore, we must look at the other side of the coin.

Countertransference

In the thirteenth century, the Sufi poet, Rumi wrote, "Many of the faults you see in others, dear reader, are your own nature reflected in them. As the Prophet said, the faithful are mirrors to one another" (Helminski, 2000, p.18). In the narrowest sense, countertransference is an unconscious reaction on the part of the professional to the unconscious material transferred onto the helper by the client (Freud, 1966). More broadly, countertransference refers to the process by which we project *our* unconscious unfinished business onto our clients (L. S. Brown, 2001). Sometimes this is in reaction to our clients' transferential materials, but sometimes, it happens just because they directly trigger unconscious reactions, or (to use sophisticated clinical language) *push our hidden buttons.* Even more broadly, countertransference is sometime defined as any reaction the counselor has toward the client, or a supervisor (Dass-Brailsford, 2003). As you may have experienced, some clients will be much harder to care about, work with, and to respect than others. For no obvious reason, you might feel angry, protective, overly affiliative, or sexually aroused when working with certain clients.

Countertransference-based emotions may impair your objectivity—your determination to be fair and treat all of your clients with the same respect. When strong emotions have been triggered, a very common human reaction is to react impulsively. What would this acting out look like in the counseling world? It might involve thinly disguised story telling about the client's amazing or disgusting life details, or talking to colleagues in greater detail or length about the client than you usually do. It could also involve "accidentally" double-scheduling, being late to sessions, going over time, cutting sessions short, hasty referring, "innocent" flirting, or early termination. And if left unaddressed, countertransference might lead to boundary breaks that cause further loss of objectivity, and harm.

Digressions for Deliberation 7.2

Counselors as Projective Targets—A Protective Image

In our teaching, we take the stance that without Rogers' core conditions of congruence, empathy, and nonjudgmental positive regard in the counseling relationship (Rogers, 1957), chances for therapeutic change are very slim (J. Sommers-Flanagan & Sommers-Flanagan, 2003). Students wonder aloud about how any professional can work authentically and caringly with racist or homophobic clients, or child abusers, murderers, or pedophiles. Peace activists worry that they could not work with pro-war clients. Atheists, with people of various faiths, hunters with vegetarians. We acknowledge that into almost everyone's life will come a few clients with whom they simply cannot work (Mehlman & Glickauf-Hughes, 1994), but assure students they will be amazed at the magic of counseling; astounded at how often they will find within themselves empathy, compassion, and positive regard for clients very different than themselves.

Clients will not always be congruent, empathic, and/or nonjudgmental in return. In fact, sometimes they will be angry, accusing, mocking, malicious, insulting, flirtatious, whiney, blaming, and otherwise quite unpleasant. We offer our students an image for handling the intense emotional energy that can fly around the room during sessions, warning them that sometimes, clients aim flaming arrows at them with precision born of desperation and finely developed defenses.

This is the image: Deep inside you, there is a warm, empathic beating heart and a keen, insightful mind. Your professional skills and talents provide you with an impenetrable shield over these vital organs. This shield allows empathy and wisdom to flow out, but does not allow mortally wounding arrows in. The shield has a thick layer of soft, downy material—similar to a huge feather quilt or that new impact-absorbing material developed by NASA. You can catch anything that comes at you without fear of mortal emotional wounding. You don't have to judge, counter attack, or seek revenge. You have control of your voice, your words, your facial expressions—all can remain compassionate and reflective. Even when directly attacked, you have protective coverings that allow you to relax and see the pain behind the attack. You understand that you are *standing in* for life's injustices, disappointments, and cruelty. You can be a safe container, offering patience and thoughtful, cautious interpretations that gently hold up the mirror.

Hopefully, you will take our advice from Chapter 5, and have a very well-developed informed consent process that addresses boundaries and potential nonprofessional contact. Explaining boundaries and roles can be challenging. We provide an example in Application 7.1. However, even the perfect paragraph would not allay all the transferential assumptions clients have about your behaviors, or free you from your own countertransferential impulses. Clarity is essential, and keeping your word once you have shared your policies is also essential—and sometimes difficult to do.

Client Indignation or Relief

Defining and keeping boundaries will often have an impact on clients emotionally. It is natural that clients will like and care about their counselors. Some will hope for special favors, or want to become friends or even lovers (Heyward, 1994). We have had adolescent clients ask how we would feel about adopting them. This positive regard and wish for closeness could be considered positive transference, but that may not be the only way to think about it. Instead of being unconscious, it might be a conscious recognition that the therapist is an accepting, caring person with great listening skills and a nice office. Who wouldn't want such a friend or lover? Who wouldn't fantasize about what a great parent this kind person would be?

This urge for closeness with one's counselor—whether driven by unconscious needs and fantasies, or a more conscious response to being listened to and cared for—is a vulnerable emotional reaction to the helping process. In response to this vulnerability, the ethical professional must find wise and gentle ways to explain these necessary professional boundaries so that clients do not feel embarrassed, judged, or rejected. Boundary breaking *and* keeping both can elicit strong client reactions. There are popular press books that detail the pain and anger of damaging boundary breaks in helping relationships (Strean, 1993). There are also books that express deep disdain and disappointment in counselors who would *not* break boundaries that the client longed to have broken (Heyward, 1994).

Of course, not all clients long for special treatment, friendship, or other connections to their counselor. In fact, many would find the thought of a personal connection or relationship with their counselor or therapist very threatening or unappealing. They want their counselor to be a safe confidant, interacting in strictly professional ways and staying out of their personal lives. They want their personal materials and interactions to stay private and contained. These clients are overtly relieved when assured that their counselors understands boundaries and will thus be trustworthy in this way (Epstein, 1994).

Whether they receive the information with relief or indignation, your clients deserve to know your boundary-keeping practices. Your informed consent process should include talking about boundaries and ethical concerns regarding nonprofessional interactions. We discuss this in the next section.

ETHICS CODES AND TERMS

Boundaries and roles have been addressed in various ways in the helping profession's ethics codes. Earlier ethics writers and codes referred to the ethical concerns of *dual roles* but, recognizing our increasingly complex and interconnected world, the terminology has morphed to *multiple roles*. Because of the complexities involved in defining and keeping professional boundaries, it is not surprising that when mental health professionals are asked to name the most difficult ethical concerns they face, they often name *dual* or *multiple roles* (K. Pope & V. A. Vetter, 1992).

The term *multiple roles* refers to an individual having two or more types of relationships, either simultaneously or sequentially, in another person's life. As noted previously, any kind of relationship between humans has role and boundary expectations, so if you have more than one type of relationship with someone, you will also have more than one set of role expectations. These everyday difficulties are not necessarily ethical problems. They become ethical concerns when one of the roles is a professional counseling role.

Herlihy and Corey (1997) write, "Multiple relationship issues exist throughout our profession and affect virtually all counselors, regardless of their work setting or the client population they serve. . . . No professional remains untouched by the potential difficulties inherent in dual or multiple relationships" (p. 1). Further, most of us realize that no amount of rule making will ensure client safety. As Lazarus (2005) writes:

> There are therapists who display poor social judgment, disordered thinking, and impaired reality testing. Some are sociopathic or have narcissistic or borderline personalities. But in my opinion, many of these unscrupulous practitioners will not be cowed or deterred by facing longer and more stringent rules and regulations. What we need are far more careful selection criteria so that we weed out these people before they enter into our graduate schools and training programs. (p. 26)

Codes of ethics for many helping professions directly address multiple relationships, cautioning against most and forbidding a few.

NASW *Code of Ethic*

1.06 Conflicts of Interest

(c) Social workers should not engage in dual or multiple relationships with clients or former clients in which there is a risk of exploitation or potential harm to the client. In instances when dual or multiple relationships are unavoidable, social workers should take steps to protect clients and are responsible for setting clear, appropriate, and culturally sensitive boundaries. (Dual or multiple relationships occur when social workers relate to clients in more than one relationship, whether professional, social, or business. Dual or multiple relationships can occur simultaneously or consecutively.)

APA *Ethical Principles*

3.05 Multiple Relationships:

(a) A multiple relationship occurs when a psychologist is in a professional role with a person and (1) at the same time is in another role with the same person, (2) at the same time is in a relationship with a person closely associated with or related to the person with whom the psychologist has the professional relationship, or (3) promises to enter into another relationship in the future with the person or a person closely associated with or related to the person. A psychologist refrains from entering into a multiple relationship if the multiple relationship could reasonably be expected to impair the psychologist's objectivity, competence, or effectiveness in performing his or her functions as a psychologist, or otherwise risks exploitation or harm to the person with whom the professional relationship exists. Multiple relationships that would not reasonably be expected to cause impairment or risk exploitation or harm are not unethical.

(b) If a psychologist finds that, due to unforeseen factors, a potentially harmful multiple relationship has arisen, the psychologist takes reasonable steps to resolve it with due regard for the best interests of the affected person and maximal compliance with the Ethics Code.

(c) When psychologists are required by law, institutional policy, or extraordinary circumstances to serve in more than one role in judicial or administrative proceedings, at the outset they clarify role expectations and the extent of confidentiality and thereafter as changes occur. (See also Standards 3.04, Avoiding Harm, and 3.07, Third-Party Requests for Services.)

3.06 Conflict of Interest: Psychologists refrain from taking on a professional role when personal, scientific, professional, legal, financial, or other interests or relationships could reasonably be expected to (1) impair their objectivity, competence, or effectiveness in performing their functions as psychologists or (2) expose the person or organization with whom the professional relationship exists to harm or exploitation.

3.08 Exploitative Relationships: Psychologists do not exploit persons over whom they have supervisory, evaluative, or other authority such as clients/patients, students, supervisees, research participants, and employees.

Interestingly, in ACA's most recent code the terms *multiple roles* and *dual roles* have been eliminated. After explicitly forbidding counselors, supervisors, and counselor educators certain roles in client or student lives, the code then states that nonprofessional relationships with clients, former clients, their romantic partners, or their family members should be avoided, except when the resulting interaction is potentially beneficial to the client. The wording of this portion of the code for counselors is provided in the following code example. It reflects a new way to approach the problems of boundaries and multiple relationships.

ACA *Code of Ethics*

A.5.d Potentially Beneficial Interactions

When a counselor-client nonprofessional interaction with a client or former client may be potentially beneficial to the client or former client, the counselor must document in case records, prior to the interaction (when feasible), the rationale for such an interaction, the potential benefit, and anticipated consequences for the client or former client and other individuals significantly involved with the client or former client. Such interactions should be initiated with appropriate client consent. Where unintentional harm occurs to the client or former client, or to an individual significantly involved with the client or former client, due to the nonprofessional interaction, the counselor must show evidence of an attempt to remedy such harm. Examples of potentially beneficial interactions include, but are not limited to attending a formal ceremony (e.g., a wedding/commitment ceremony or graduation); purchasing a service or product provided by a client or former client (excepting unrestricted bartering); hospital visits to an ill family member; mutual membership in a professional association, organization, or community.

This wording places the evaluative burden on the professional who might be considering "nonprofessional interactions" or roles in addition to the counseling role. No guidance is given for multiple relationships that might be neutral or unavoidable, and no mention is made of counselors who might have an additional *professional* role in a client's life. There is certainly cause for concern when a counselor is considering two professional relationships with a client, such as being a client's teacher, coauthor, or employer. Later, the code specifically addresses the potential dual role of being someone's evaluator and counselor, counselor educator and counselor, and/or clinical supervisor and counselor.

As is often the case with new ideas, the wording is a bit awkward and there are processes and questions that go unaddressed. Consider the preceding case example of Ginny and Lin. The ACA code indicates that counselors should avoid nonprofessional interactions except when the interaction is potentially beneficial to the client, but the code says nothing about the relative costs to the counselor or how to assess the potential benefits and harms. Perhaps one could argue that Ginny might have benefited from seeing Lin struggling to learn to play tennis. However, one could also argue that Ginny did not need the distraction. The extra transference-related issues might be too much to process in short term work. If Lin postponed her class, she is not making a huge sacrifice. But what if the campus was a small one and clients seemed to be everywhere, thus limiting the campus opportunities the small counseling center employees could take advantage of?

Ethics codes offer rules and guidance, but we will never be able to fully or rigidly codify the nuanced clinical and ethical dimensions of boundary concerns. This area of ethical behavior will require your attention throughout your professional life, and there will be many attempts to articulate ethical guidelines. We hope this chapter will at least raise the questions clearly and offer sound suggestions for practices that reflect the spirit of this latest guidance in the ACA code.

BOUNDARIES, ROLES, TIMING, AND INFORMED CONSENT

Basic explanations about boundaries should be provided during the first meeting with clients. Both in writing and in conversation, counselors need to explain the nature of the professional relationship and the primacy of this professional responsibility. We provide a sample paragraph in Applications 7.1, but settings and expectations vary, and professionals have unique ways of expressing this information.

In addition to differing demands due to settings and professional orientation, there will be variations in boundary discussions due to the unique attributes of individual clients. If your new client is a well-known public figure, teaches in a school where your children attend, conducts the symphony in which your wife plays violin, or sold you your last car, these boundary overlaps should be discussed.

The ACA ethics code injunction about nonprofessional contact with clients underscores the fact that informed consent is an ongoing process throughout the professional relationship. There are potential overlapping roles and boundaries before, during, and after counseling. Each point of concern is discussed in the following paragraphs.

Applications 7.1

Example of Relationship-Boundary Explanation

As my client, your welfare is my main concern. Our therapeutic relationship is primary—which means that I will not become your friend or enter into any other kind of relationship with you while we are working together, or after we have finished working together. We might see each other at social events, or at local businesses. You can decide if you want to say hello. I will treat our relationship as confidential, so I'll let you decide if you want to act like we know each other or not, and we can discuss any outside contact that happens, any time you like.

Boundary Overlaps that Predate the Professional Relationship

As you develop professional helping skills, your friends, family, romantic partners, and even grocery store clerks may suddenly decide you are just the person to talk with about deep, troubling private concerns. It is not an unusual assumption on their parts: people might date a massage therapist hoping for some great back rubs, or rejoice that their favorite cousin is studying medicine so their mysterious ailments can be healed. You are ethically free to share the professional knowledge you acquire in graduate school. You are also free to use your finely honed listening skills to enhance your personal relationships. However, you are not ethically free to begin professional counseling relationships with family, friends, colleagues, or business partners. In extreme circumstances, such a choice might be justifiable, but it would require extensive consultation and documentation. This distinction between sharing knowledge or listening well and professional counseling may seem confusing. Here are some examples to illustrate the difference.

- You might have a friend who reveals to you that she is in an abusive intimate relationship. As her friend, you can tell her what you have learned about such relationships. You can support her, listen to her, advocate for her, and investigate referrals and other possible resources. As you do these things, you make it clear to her that you are her friend, not her counselor, therapist, or social worker. You would not be able to have the professional objectivity necessary for a counseling relationship. Even if you could somehow muster that kind of boundary, and you became your friend's counselor, your friendship would be forever altered.

- Your spouse's business partner confides in you that she is deeply depressed. As she describes her symptoms, you are fairly certain she meets the criteria for major depression. You can express your concern and offer to help her locate a skilled mental health professional. But even if she insists you are the only person she could possibly trust, you would be on ethically shaky ground to take her as a client. Your obligation, should you agree to see her, would be first to her—not to your wife or her business concerns. What if her depression was so severe she was a business liability? What if she had thoughts of sabotaging the business? Would you warn your spouse? The entanglements could be damaging to everyone. And in the worst case scenario, if this client was disappointed in your work with her, she would have grounds for a malpractice case, because your choice to see her in the first place would not be considered the usual standard of care (see Chapter 3).

The caution around taking clients with whom you have a preexisting relationship is not unconditional. To be absolutely certain, counselors could refuse to see anyone they had ever known or heard of, and refuse to see anyone related to anyone they had ever known or heard of. But in the real world, this is neither practical nor reasonable. Factors such as the extent of importance and intimacy of the preexisting relationship, the future trajectory of the preexisting relationship, and the nature of the client's need(s) must all be considered and weighed against the loss of objectivity and the potential harm to the preexisting relationship, as well as to the proposed professional relationship (Gottlieb, 1993).

Case Example: Franklin, a 56-year-old Vietnam veteran, is a licensed professional counselor working in private practice. His girlfriend, Amy, has a son, Jacob, who returned from combat in Iraq shaken, bitter, and changed. Amy wants Franklin to meet with Jacob a few times to talk over how he's doing. She knows that Franklin will be balanced, but also, that Franklin will level with Jacob about the psychological aftermath of combat. She trusts Franklin, and believes he would be the perfect counselor for Jacob. Amy also knows that Franklin runs an open-ended support group for military personnel returning from duty, as well as their family members. She wants to attend the group with Jacob. Jacob is lukewarm about the idea, at best. Amy asks Franklin to talk with Jacob, and convince him to come in for just a little bit of counseling.

What should Franklin consider in this complex request? He loves Amy, and would want to be of help to any of her family members. He doesn't know Jacob well, but he has a deep loyalty to returning veterans, and he knows he has the knowledge and skills necessary to help Jacob, should Jacob want help (Burham, 2004). Franklin also knows that Jacob is likely facing a long road toward the integration and healing necessary after combat trauma.

Franklin is aware that there are other resources besides him available to Jacob, but he is worried that Amy will be disappointed if he doesn't agree to see Jacob for counseling. It might seem to her that Franklin is denying Jacob something Franklin has, and Jacob needs. He is also worried that Jacob will refuse to pursue any other kind of help.

After consulting with a colleague, Franklin's solution was this: He talked to Amy about his professional ethics, and why there were ethical boundary concerns in her request. He then offered to take Jacob out for dinner, to reach out to him as a fellow veteran, and to do his best to connect Jacob with skilled help. He also decided that since the group he offered was open-ended, free of charge, the only such group in town, and conducted as a support group, he would let Amy decide for herself if she, or if she and Jacob, might want to attend. He did tell Amy that should she decide to attend, he would introduce her as his girlfriend, and Jacob as her son.

Boundary Overlaps During the Professional Relationship

After beginning work with a client, it is not at all unusual to find that your life overlaps with your clients' lives in ways you had not predicted. As the Case Example of Lin and Ginny illustrated, you and your client might find yourselves both beginning something new. You might also discover that you know the same people, attend the same church, or have other connections that predate your professional relationship. Finally, you might find that your counseling relationship itself has generated potential nonprofessional contact. Each of these deserves informed consent airtime.

Beginning something new.   Beginning something new together can be unsettling for client and professional alike. Starting lessons, joining a club, attending a class, going on a retreat, doing volunteer work—the potential list is endless. At the very least, these new shared environments should be discussed and explored *at the professional's initiative.* Most likely, when possible, it will be best for the therapist to postpone or minimize involvement in the new environment. However, that is not always the case—or even possible. It depends on the size of the new group, the level of direct contact, the level of intimacy required in the new endeavor, and both parties' level of self-consciousness about the contact and the new activity.

Current overlapping connections.   In the most careful and thorough intake process, it is not possible to unearth all possible overlapping relationships that *might* exist between mental health professionals and new clients. Even in large urban areas, the chances of people knowing the same people or belonging to the same organizations is surprisingly high. Discovering connections you did not know you had with clients can present interesting challenges. These connections might come to light in the overlapping setting, or in the context of the material your client is sharing.

Here are some quotes from real-life situations:

—*"Oh, guess what," says your client. "It turns out my husband is your husband's supervisor at work. Isn't that something?"*

—*"Well, Hell-ll-o," says your wide-eyed client as you exit the shower. "I didn't know you belonged to this athletic club."*

—*"I saw you at Red Robin last week," says your client. "It looked like you were with Cheryl. Are you two dating? She's my cousin's best friend. And I can tell you all about her."*

Each of these declarations calls for careful, professional attention. The counselor needs to reassure the client that confidentiality boundaries will hold, and explore the feelings associated with these connections. It is possible to consult with your client, or with colleagues or supervisors, as to how to minimize the contact and uncomfortable sense of exposure that might come with these overlapping boundaries.

Counseling-related nonprofessional interactions.   As the ACA code notes, there are interactions that might stretch or extend the professional relationship boundaries (R. Sommers-Flanagan, Elliott, & Sommers-Flanagan, 1998). The code explains the need to process and obtain informed consent for these interactions ahead of time and to only consider them if they are potentially beneficial to the client. The examples given suggest a humane extension of relationship, such as hospital visits, or attending meaningful ceremonies in the lives of clients.

These types of nonprofessional interactions may seem harmless and simple, but there are ethical and clinical ramifications to consider. When clients ask their counselors to attend weddings, visit them in the hospital, or come to their championship tennis match, they are asking for time, connection, and special attention. These are life activities usually attended by friends and family. Professional helpers are neither. The careful deliberation called for in the ACA code necessitates taking time to respond, and involving the client in thinking about the meaning of the request and how the potential outcomes might feel. There is no easy or correct response, other than careful and interactive consideration (Glass, 2003).

Memberships in professional and community organizations are also potential nonprofessional interactions. It is hard to imagine how the professional helper's membership in a church, political party, or professional organization would be directly beneficial to the client. On the other hand, such multiple roles likely pose little to no harm to the client, if properly acknowledged and considered.

Postprofessional Relationship Boundary Considerations

There are many factors to consider in postcounseling or posttherapy relationships. Transference dynamics and all the other unique attributes of the professional relationship argue against such later relationships, or at least offer grounds for caution. We will discuss sexual relationships in later paragraphs, but other than sexual relationships, the codes do not directly prohibit postcounseling friendships, teaching, or business relationships. However, in our opinion, and that of others (T. Remley & Herlihy, 2005), counselors should not readily engage in postcounseling relationships. Here are several reasons:

- The good work done in counseling can be damaged by later friendships that reveal shortcomings in the counselor or have other relational things go wrong (Kitchener, 2000).
- Clients may need to return to counseling, and may much prefer to see the same counselor. If the counselor has become a friend, this option would not be ethical (Vasquez, 1991).
- The power differential, and the responsibilities associated with it, never really ends, even though therapy ends. In a recent study, the vast majority of mental health

professionals surveyed indicated they believed in client perpetuity, or "Once a client, always a client" (Lamb, Catanzaro, & Moorman, 2004).

• Professionals who entertain the idea of postcounseling relationships with clients may unconsciously treat clients differently, depending on their potential as later friends or business associates.

PRACTICES AND TECHNIQUES WITH BOUNDARY IMPLICATIONS

Your theoretical orientation, setting, and the type of therapy or helping techniques you use will define a large portion of your counseling boundaries (Glass, 2003; J. Sommers-Flanagan & Sommers-Flanagan, 2004b). Your usual and customary practices should be well defined and available to clients in your paperwork. In general, treat clients equally, and when you decide to extend or change one of your customary practices, document your therapeutic reasons for doing so. This creates your own standard of practice, and a set of boundaries that define your work. There are, however, certain practices and/or techniques that fall in boundary gray areas (Glass, 2003), and should be carefully considered. We discuss some of these in the following paragraphs.

Gift Giving and Receiving

One potential interaction that has boundary challenges within many professional relationships is that of gift giving. More commonly, counselors must address gifts offered by clients, but occasionally, counselors will experience an urge to give clients a gift. Either direction, the gift and the urge must be consciously considered and usually processed with the client (Smolar, 2002). Many mental health professionals avoid this potential problem by stating in their intake paperwork and/or informed consent process that they cannot accept gifts. Clients may or may not pay attention to this statement, but if they bring a gift, the counselor can gently remind them of the policy.

Some counselors accept small gifts. The usual monetary cutoff suggested is $10.00, which comes from research done in the late 1980s (Borys & Pope, 1989). Perhaps, allowing for inflation, that figure could now be $20.00. The point is that some professionals are comfortable accepting small gifts from clients and it would be difficult to prove that, as a general practice, this harms clients. What might be more important to consider is the nature and meaning of the gift (Smolar, 2002). While not expensive, two long-stemmed red roses probably carry a different message than a jar of homemade jelly. The meaning behind each gift needs to be explored in the context of the therapeutic relationship.

Large gifts are more problematic. In the research previously cited, 90% of the respondents thought that accepting gifts valued at $50.00 or more was ethically questionable (Borys & Pope, 1989). This consensus underscores the significance of this seemingly simple human ritual—gift giving. Accepting a large gift has the following ethical ramifications:

• The gift could be a wonderful, tasteful gift you enjoy a great deal. This could lead to a slight loss of objectivity. Despite yourself, you might find yourself favoring the gift-giving client over others, or worrying more about upsetting or offending the gift-giving client than doing good work.

- The gift could be odd, offensive, or something you cannot use. This could lead to either dishonest behavior on your part, as you assure your client you like and appreciate the gift, or to hurt feelings if you reject it or fail to use it.
- The client could expect you to display the gift. This could easily interfere with your office décor, and could lead to issues in confidentiality if you were asked where you got the gift.
- The gift could involve travel or attending an event. This creates a quasi-social relationship, should your client plan to attend with you, or something social that connects you and your client in future conversations.
- If things take a difficult turn in your counseling relationship, the client might request you give back the gift or reimburse the costs.

Given the complexities and future potential temptations, it is easier to have a consistent no-gift policy. However, it may certainly be ethical to accept small gifts, especially when refusing to do so would harm your therapeutic relationship, and in fact, the process can provide opportunities for insight and growth (Hahn, 1998). Deciding when and/or if to accept a gift requires clinical wisdom and maturity. It is a great topic for ongoing discussions with colleagues and supervisors.

Children present a special challenge in the gift-giving arena. The gifts they offer are often small, homemade, and very meaningful. It is possible to develop practices that allow for these gifts to be received and honored. Counselors might explain to children that they display gifts and artwork for one month, sort of like museums do. At the end of the month, the child can have the gift or artwork back, or the counselor will put it away in a special place, so that there is room for other "displays." Counselors can also explain that they do not tell other people who did the art or gave the gift because some people like to have their counseling stay private. This type of solution will vary, depending on setting, theoretical orientation, school or agency policies, and your own personality and comfort levels.

Sometimes, mental health practitioners will feel a need or wish to give their clients gifts. If invited to a ceremonial event in the client's life, or if a young client makes the counselor acutely aware of an upcoming birthday, the pull can be quite strong. One concern in choosing to give a small gift, or sending a card, is the insinuated intimacy, or special status, of the client. Gift giving by counselors is not a common practice, so it is a boundary extension, or break, in usual practices. When working with children and teens, set a policy ahead of time for how to handle the inevitable requests to buy fruit, cookies, trinkets, and other fundraising items.

Another concern in gift giving is the break in impartiality. Are you willing to give gifts to all clients in similar circumstances? As we mentioned in Chapter 2, impartiality is an important dimension in certain moral philosophies (Rachels, 1986). For instance, from a deontological perspective, you might consider it your duty to be fair and impartial. From a consequentialist perspective, you would need to consider your actions in terms of the greatest good for the greatest number.

The complexities of gift giving and the culturally varied meanings provide an example of how ethical concerns and clinical concerns are so deeply interrelated. Even if you ultimately decide you cannot accept a gift offered by a client, there are many possible issues to explore together as part of the therapeutic relationship.

Deepening Diversity 7.1

Gift Giving and Culture

Gift giving has culturally imbued meanings to consider. For many American Indian tribes, gifts are given as a sign of honor, and the act of giving is a sacred privilege (Herring, 1996). There are gifting ceremonies that involve many rituals and expectations for both the gift givers and the gift receivers. In Asian cultures, gifts can signal respect and express gratitude (Cuellar & Paniagua, 2000). Increased understanding and important clinical work can be accomplished as the cultural meaning of gifts is explored with clients. Obviously, gift giving and receiving from both professional and cultural viewpoints offers significant food for thought.

Families, as mini-cultures, have gift-giving rituals that may date back to cultural practices so old that the family no longer even realizes the connection. Consider the role of gifts in your family and community. What occasions call for gifts? What is being expressed? Are gifts valued for their monetary worth? Their symbolic message? Do the gifts involve services, homemade items, or other personalized attributes? What happens if a gift is rejected or unappreciated?

Self-Disclosure

Self-disclosure is an expected social interaction in the dominant culture in the United States. Sometimes, new counselors have a difficult time calibrating self-disclosure. It can feel imbalanced or unfair to listen as a client discloses, but then to offer few disclosures in return. Beginning professional helpers often experience an urge to tell their clients about similar life experiences, reactions, or common tastes, such as favorite teams or local restaurants. Even more difficult are direct questions from an inquisitive or intrusive client. The ability to respond with grace and sensitivity to personal questions, while at the same time not necessarily answering them, is an important skill to develop (A. Benjamin, 1981).

Certainly, you can choose to answer certain personal questions, but just like gift giving, exploring the client's urge to ask such questions might hold rich clinical material. A rule to keep in mind when asked questions is explore first, then answer if appropriate (J. Sommers-Flanagan & Sommers-Flanagan, 1989). On some occasions, it is acceptable to answer the questions first and then explore afterward, if needed. A basic rule of thumb for self-disclosure is that it should always be in the service of the client. In other words, in the context of a professional relationship, self-disclosure is a professional activity that could seem quite personal to a client, and ultimately create confusion about boundaries (Pipes, Holstein, & Aguiree, 2005).

Case Example: Melodee was an intern working with a socially anxious young man named Will. During his third session, Will talked about how he longed for the courage to ask out someone as nice as Melodee. He paused, looked down, rubbed his hands on his pants, blushed, and said, "I guess you're probably married, huh? I bet you married someone good looking. Someone smart? Am I right?"

Melodee felt a rush of gratitude for the role-plays that had prepared her for such an emotionally charged direct question.

"Will," she said. "I can tell that it took real courage for you to ask me that. And I take it as a compliment, too. Could you talk just a little bit about how you got the courage to bring this up and to give me that nice compliment?"

Will looked a little confused, but smiled. "Yeah. I can talk about that, but are you going to answer me?"

Melodee smiled too. "Sure, I will, but let's talk about the question first, if that's okay. The work we're both here to do is for you. It's a lot more important to figure out where that courage came from so you can use it again soon. If we get distracted talking about my personal life, we may lose this chance."

Self-disclosure also has cultural variation in efficacy and appropriateness (Kim et al., 2003; Simi & Mahalik, 1997). In certain American Indian tribes, silence signals respect. However, self-disclosure, especially when it provides common ground, can help increase trust and connection (D. Wetsit, personal communication, November, 1993).

Considerations about Touch

Touching, like gift giving, can seem deceptively simple and innocent. Most of us distinguish between *nonerotic touch* (handshakes, pats on the arm, comforting hugs) and *erotic touch* (sensual hugs, stroking, and kisses intended to communicate sexual interest or cause sexual arousal). Or at least we think we do. But touch is not something that can easily be dichotomized. Lovers know that even the slightest brush of arm to arm can be arousing. Trusted family members or close friends can engage in full-body hugs, pats to the fanny, farewell kisses, and other forms of intimate touch that carry no sexual content for either party. And in the event of a big win, team players practically maul each other—lots of emotion but, at least to the observing sports fan, little erotic intention. To further complicate things, nonerotic touch can become erotic in certain circumstances, and touch intended to be erotic can fall far short of its goal in others. Examples of this from your own lives might make for a lively class discussion. Ask your professor to take the lead in this self-disclosure.

Rather than attempting to define touch as either erotic or nonerotic, it is probably more accurate to think of touch as a powerful form of communication with comfort and erotic potential. Touch patterns and rules are also gendered. In our culture, touch also carries nonverbal signals of power and hierarchy. Women tend to touch in order to offer comfort, and men in order to signal power (Woods, 2004).

ASSESSING POTENTIAL BENEFIT AND HARM

Mental health professionals have long been charged with assessing potential harm to clients when boundary extensions, breaks, or multiple roles are being considered. The new ACA wording changes the focus to an assessment of potential benefit—but in reality, both harm and benefit must be considered. This consideration must take into account the counselor as well as the client. Karen Kitchener (2000) offered guidance for assessing the potential harm in overlapping roles. She noted that the differences in obligations and expectations between roles can cause clients confusion, misunderstanding, and even anger. As the potential for conflicts of interest increases, so does the potential for difficulties. Professionals can be tempted to place their own needs ahead of the client's needs.

More recently, in the article entitled *Managing risk when contemplating multiple relationships,* Younggren and Gottlieb (2004) offer the following questions to consider:

1. Is entering into a relationship in addition to the professional one necessary, or should I avoid it?
2. Can the dual relationship potentially cause harm to the patient?
3. If harm seems unlikely or avoidable, would the additional relationship prove beneficial?
4. Is there a risk that the dual relationship could disrupt the therapeutic relationship?
5. Can I evaluate this matter objectively? (pp. 256–57)

It is not possible to numerically quantify the harm or benefit to assess when counselors consider engaging in multiple roles or nonprofessional interactions with their clients. Gottlieb (1993) presented a decision-making model that included three aspects of the relationship: the amount of power or personal influence involved in the relationship, the duration expected in the relationship, and whether the proposed professional relationship would likely terminate conclusively or intermittently (with the client perhaps needing to return for additional assistance over time). As you face multiple role decisions, we suggest using a dimensional approach. We describe such an approach in Applications 7.2. By actually filling in the quadrant and assigning relative values to the differing dimensions, you can more closely examine the potentials.

It may seem self-serving or even unethical to consider professional benefit and harm in relation to client benefit or harm. However, to be effective and compassionate professionals, all kinds of helpers need to take care of themselves, and do not make decisions that put themselves or their families in awkward or dangerous situations. If they did, ultimately, the welfare of their clients would be in jeopardy. This is why self-care is closely related to providing ethical client care, especially in rural areas, with the demands discussed in the following section (Nickel, 2004).

There is a range of views on what constitutes a counseling relationship boundary violation. Some writers and practitioners believe the profession itself has become overly rigid about boundaries, arguing that artificial barricades between professionals and clients can impede or even harm therapeutic relationship connections (Fay, 2002; Lazarus & Zur, 2002). For example, Lazarus has long argued that activities such as playing tennis or having dinner with a client can have therapeutic benefit, and that occasional human connections such as catching a ride will not necessarily do any harm (Lazarus, 1994).

Generally, theories of counseling or psychotherapy that emphasize longer and deeper treatment protocols have tighter, more rigid boundaries. This is partly due to the im-

=== **Applications 7.2** ===

Analyzing Multiple Roles or Nonprofessional Interactions

Create a four-square grid, similar to the one pictured. Within your grid, list all possible outcomes that might result from the role or interaction under consideration. Place every outcome you can think of in the appropriate box, and assign each one a rating of *neutral, slightly,* or *very.* Then give each entry a second rating of *not likely to happen, slightly likely to happen,* or *very likely to happen.* If your answer to Younggren and Gottlieb's question number 5 (can I evaluate this objectively?) is no or even maybe, then involve a supervisor or colleague in this process from the onset.

Outcomes with Potential Client Harm (Rate each as to how likely it is to occur) (Rate each with how damaging it might be)	Outcomes with Potential Client Benefit (Rate each as to how likely it is to occur) (Rate each with how damaging it might be)

Outcomes with Potential Harm to
   the Professional
(Rate each as to how likely it is to occur)
(Rate each with how damaging it might be)
	Outcomes with Potential Professional
	   Benefit
	(Rate each as to how likely it is to occur)
	(Rate each with how damaging it might be)

For practice, with classmates or on your own, try using this system to consider the following:

1. Chan is contemplating providing counseling to a teenage boy, Milo, who plays on his son, Ben's, soccer team. The parents have heard about Chan's great work with underachieving teen boys, and they very much want Chan to see their son. Milo and Ben know each other, but are not good friends. There are 18 boys on the team. This is Milo's second year, but Ben's third. Both families live in the suburbs of a town of 100,000, with similar cultural backgrounds.

2. Tamika is working with 38-year-old Shari who is suffering from anxiety and mild depression. During the time she is working with Tamika, Shari's mother was killed in a tragic car wreck. Although the funeral was small and private, Shari's mother was an active member of many community organizations, so there is going to be a memorial service. Shari asks Tamika if she would like to attend. Tamika lives in an Asian neighborhood, married to a man from China. Shari is African-American.

portance of working with transference in longer-term work and partly because of deeper and more personal disclosures associated with long-term therapy (Glass, 2003). On the other hand, counselors working primarily with children might approach boundaries with a slightly looser frame (J. Sommers-Flanagan & Sommers-Flanagan, 1997; Thompson & Rudolph, 2000). And remember, human relationship boundaries of all sorts are culturally determined. Therefore, culture will play a central role in the subjective experiences of clients and professionals.

LITTLE COMMUNITIES, BIG BOUNDARIES?

In little towns, lives roll along so close to one another; loves and hates beat about, their wings almost touching.

—Willa Cather

No chapter on boundaries would be complete (especially by authors residing in Montana, who've lived in upstate New York, and have colleagues in tiny towns in Mississippi, Pennsylvania, Iowa, and the Dakotas) without considering the important dynamics of smaller, more intimate communities. Although small towns and rural communities are sometimes romanticized in literature and the media, they are just as often maligned for their damaging limits. The Reverend Vernon C. Mcgee once said, "Man made the city, God made the country, but the devil made the small town" (2004, p. 48).

The realities of rural America are that depression, alcoholism, cancer, heart disease, diabetes, and arthritis all occur at higher rates in rural communities than in urban communities (Thurston-Hicks, Paine, & Hollifield, 1998; Wagenfeld, Murray, Mohatt, & DeBruyn, 1997). The need for competent mental health counseling services is acute, and the problems inherent in rural work, whether ongoing or emergent, are complex (Jackson & Cook, 1999). Simply maintaining confidentiality becomes nearly impossible when everyone in town knows who is parked outside the counseling office, the cashiers at the bank know the people writing the checks to pay the fees, office staff are related to the clients, and so on. A number of studies have indicated that those working with rural patients and clients believe that these clients worry about confidentiality and privacy, and are less likely to talk openly about all areas of their lives (Ullom-Minnich & Kallail, 1993; Teddy D. Warner et al., 2005).

Of course, confidentiality isn't the only ethical issue. Multiple relationships between counselors and their clients are inevitable, as are overlapping relationships that involve family members of counselors and clients. An ethical indictment of all multiple roles is unrealistic and harmful to all concerned (Brownlee, 1996). In one small study, rural and frontier professionals expressed a clear need for ethical training specifically tailored to nonurban settings (Roberts, Warner, & Hammond, 2005).

Case Example: While working with a 15-year-old boy, I (JSF) found myself with several rural boundary related decisions. The two most memorable were, (a) the fact that the boy went to the same school as my daughter, and (b) the boy's need to have a comforting adult accompany him to three stressful court hearings. Although other professionals could have made different decisions about these boundary issues, I chose to handle them in the following ways:

1. I informed the boy that my daughter attended his school and assured him that I did not talk to her about my clients. I explained to him that he could make his own choices about having contact with her at school or during social activities after

school. I told him that I specifically did not want to hear about anything she might say or do at school or during social activities outside school.

2. I told the boy that if he wanted me to, I would attend the court hearings as a support person, if he informed me of the day and time at least 1 week in advance.

Besides rural communities, there are other forms of small, connected communities of people, such as the gay/lesbian/transgendered/bisexual community (Kessler & Waehler, 2005), military bases, spiritual or religious communities, athletes, academics, and cultural enclaves. Membership in these communities can actually increase trust among the members (Lazarus, 2005; Robinson, 2003) when they interact professionally, but the roles and boundary negotiations require extra professional attention and care. Professional helpers who share membership in small communities with their clients have more complex boundary considerations than those who do not share such memberships. Unidimensional declarations such as "client welfare trumps all other considerations" must be widened and contextualized, but not ignored. Of course, client welfare must always be considered, but by using the grid previously depicted in this chapter, it might be possible to work out a satisfactory balance between client needs and professional contingencies. For example, the ideal situation might be for your client, who happens to be the only pediatrician in town, *not* to meet or offer medical care to your child. However, assuming your child needs this care and there are no realistic alternatives, you can work clinically to reduce potential discomfort for your client while not necessarily being unethical in seeking medical care for your child.

ROMANCE, SEX, LOVE, AND LUST

> We have grown weary preaching that sex with clients, former clients, and any person in a close relationship with a client is prohibited. There is not a therapist in the country that does not know this ethical restriction, yet it still happens with alarming frequency. (Bernstein & Hartsell, 2000, p. 115)

We share the weariness expressed in the previous quote. When is it appropriate to consider a sexual relationship with a client? (Fill in the blank:) _____

We hope you can fill in the blank accurately. But what if the client is a virgin, who is dying, and wants to experience sex just once, and only trusts you? But what if you have fallen in love? But what if this is the first person you have ever, ever felt this way about? But what if you are willing to give up your career and become a baker? But what if you terminate the relationship, and then he/she is not your client? Maybe you can think of other "but what ifs." The answer remains the same. Never. It is never ethically permissible, by any codes, in any helping relationships, to initiate or participate in a romantic or sexual relationship with a current client.

ACA *Code of Ethics*

A.5.a. Current Clients

Sexual or romantic counselor-client interactions or relationships with current clients, their romantic partners, or their family members are prohibited.

NASW *Code of Ethics*

1.09 Sexual Relationships

Social worker should under no circumstances engage in sexual activities or sexual contact with current clients, whether such contact is consensual or forced.

Social workers should not engage in sexual activities or sexual contact with clients' relatives or other individuals with whom clients maintain a close personal relationship when there is a risk of exploitation or potential harm to the client.

APA *Ethical Principles*

10.05 Sexual Intimacies with Current Therapy Clients/Patients

Psychologists do not engage in sexual intimacies with current therapy clients/patients.

10.06 Sexual Intimacies with Relatives or Significant Others of Current Therapy Clients/ Patients

Psychologists do not engage in sexual intimacies with individuals they know to be close relatives, guardians, or significant others of current clients/patients. Psychologists do not terminate therapy to circumvent this standard.

Unfortunately, this code clarity and unanimity does not mean such interactions are rare. Various self-report studies, dating from 1977 to 1995, indicate that approximately 7% of male mental health professionals and 1.6% of female mental health professionals admitted to having sexual relations with current or former clients (T. Remley & Herlihy, 2005).

Why do we have these mandates? All the cautions we offered in the previous portion of this chapter regarding multiple relationships are magnified a hundredfold when sexual attraction and arousal are part of the equation. This multiple role has enormous potential for client harm. The following list details the categories of client damage. The list was summarized by Karen Kitchener (2000) from the work of Ken Pope (1988).

- Clients experience ambivalence about the professional. They feel attached and afraid of losing the counselor, but also have feelings of rage and other negative feelings.
- Clients experience guilt. They worry that they are somehow responsible.
- Clients feel empty, isolated, and estranged from others. They feel unworthy of other relationships.
- Clients experience confusion about their sexuality, which may lead to other abusive or traumatic sexual encounters.
- Clients have an impaired ability to trust. Their counselor violated their trust at a most vulnerable time.
- Clients experience difficulty sorting out boundaries. They lose clarity about their own needs and their own role in intimate relationships.
- Clients become depressed and/or emotionally volatile and labile due to being overwhelmed by the situation.
- Clients report suppressing their rage at being victimized.

- Clients report increased suicidal and self-destructive feelings.
- Clients have symptoms such as flashbacks, nightmares, and unbidden images in their minds.

The power differential is immutable and cannot be wished away, defined away, or diminished. The professional is *always* the party responsible for keeping this boundary absolutely intact. The harm done by sexual relations with clients often extends beyond the client to other family members as well. Unbelievable as it may seem, marriage therapists on occasion choose to begin an affair with one member of the couple they are seeing. Understandably, the other member sometimes pursues legal action (Alexander v. The Superior Court of Los Angeles, 2002; Stevenson v. Johnson 32 Va. Cir. 157, 1993).

With laws and practices so firmly established, choosing to become involved sexually with a client also has enormous potential for harm to the professional. Criminal charges (Bernstein & Hartsell, 2004), financial ruin from civil suits (Jorgenson, 1995), and the loss of one's career are all very real possibilities for the professional who engages in sexual contact with a client.

Given the clarity of this edict, and the obvious potential harm, why does this ethical violation continue to occur? Of course, this cannot be answered definitively. However, the pioneering and ongoing research by Ken Pope (1990b) and colleagues has helped paint a picture of the circumstances and rationalizations that are related to this offense. These include therapists who use intimidation or threats, who exploit extremely needy clients, or who allow their own wishes and needs to dominate. There are still counselors who claim that having sex with a client is a valid part of the treatment, or that it is permissible to have sex with the client between sessions, or out of the office setting (Somer & Saadon, 1999).

Some sexually offending mental health professionals are burned-out, lonely, isolated, and/or inadequate (Shirley Emerson & Markos, 1996; D. S. Smith & Fitzpatrick, 1995). Others have serious antisocial or narcissistic personality disorders, with general feelings of entitlement and little to no empathy for their victims (Scheoner & Gonsiorek, 1988). However, there are also offenders who are naïve or badly trained. They typically engage in other forms of boundary violations, such as hugging, social contact, or inappropriate and excessive self-disclosure before slipping into full-blown sexual relationships (Lamb & Catanzaro, 1998). Kaplan (2001) notes that a number of studies suggest that a significant number of therapists who have sexual relationships are white, male, private practitioners who are either divorced or going through a divorce.

Ignorance of ethics and/or of one's own sexual being and needs are not excuses for sexual misconduct. Education and overall character development play an important part in humans achieving healthy sexual lives and making mature sexual decisions (Krebs & Denton, 2005). Often, graduate students in the helping professions do not find sex terribly easy to discuss. However, graduate school is an excellent time to learn more about human sexuality and your own areas of ignorance, fear, need, vulnerability, and longing. People often seek counseling because of disappointments in intimate relationships. They may need to tell you about these disappointments, and their needs, fears, or fantasies. The more you know about sex and yourself as a sexual being, the less likely you will be to react with embarrassment, shyness, curiosity, or indignation. More importantly, the less likely you might be to act out sexually with a client—thus avoiding a potentially disastrous mistake for all involved.

The professional helping relationship itself has many potentially erotic aspects. Being listened to attentively and caringly *and* listening deeply to another can elicit intense feelings of connection. For some, the power differential itself might play a role in erotic attraction. There are plenty of famous sayings about the attractiveness of forbidden fruit, and Hollywood seems unable to resist producing movies with the main theme revolving around the seductive client, the seductive counselor, or the inevitability of their "love."

Clients can be intriguing, beguiling, vulnerable, seductive, incredibly erotic creatures. Professionals are human beings. They will, on occasion, be sexually attracted to a client. This is not unethical. It is simply human. It's what they *do* when they notice the attraction that is of ethical concern. We offer the following suggestions for ethically handling sexual attraction.

- Do not panic. You can sort this out with clinical and ethical wisdom.
- Do not tell your client you are attracted to him/her.
- Call supervisors and/or colleagues and seek their input right away. Do not reveal the identity of your client. Describe your client and your work enough to get a sense of the client's diagnostic categories, needs, and role in the attraction you are experiencing. Discuss how reciprocal you think the attraction is, and how long it has been there.
- Do an inventory of your own intimacy and sexual needs. Is this a signal that you've not been attending to this area of your life? If you are in a committed romantic relationship, it may be time for some serious talking, or other forms of relationship enhancement or repair.
- With supervision, decide if you can safely continue to see the client while you do the consulting or counseling work you need to do. If the attraction does not seem to be growing, or out of control, focus on rejuvenating existing mutual relationships, and take care of yourself in other ways. You may not need to refer the client. You may be able to work through this set of feelings with the help of supervision, collegial support, and/or therapy.
- If you cannot continue to see the client due to continued sexual attraction, review the case very carefully with a supervisor, and come up with a plan for referring the client that will cause the least possible damage. At the very *most,* reveal to the client only that you have some personal needs and must refer some of your clients so that you can attend to these needs. Do not burden your client with any more detail than this.
- If you transfer or refer the client, do not allow or seek any further contact.
- In your own counseling, or in other effective venues, do the extremely important work you need to do to understand how this attraction happened.

SEX BEFORE OR AFTER?

After firmly establishing the notion that sexual interactions with current clients should be forbidden, professional ethics codes began wrestling with questions surrounding the time of active counseling. Could a mental health professional ever ethically treat an ex-lover? Would it be permissible to date a former client? If so, exactly how former should the client be? Students often find it surprising that every step of the way in this intimacy-restricting aspect of ethical codes, the limits have been hotly debated and protested.

At present, most codes prohibit counseling someone with whom you have had a sexual relationship. It is far too likely that objectivity will be impossible to achieve. Also, most codes strongly discourage sexual relationships with former clients, and forbid it for a certain number of years. APA lists 2 years; the Canadian Counselling Association, 3; and the ACA code changed from a 2 year prohibition to 5 years in the latest edition. The NASW code states "Social workers do not engage in sexual activities or sexual contact with former clients because of the potential for harm to the client."

There is consensus among the writers of codes that sex with former clients is highly questionable, and must be scrutinized very closely for any possible exploitation, coercion, or manipulation. Though infrequent, there are court cases wherein counselors who became sexually involved with former clients were sued for negligence *by* the former client when the relationship went bad (Ludka v. O'Brien-Brick 1995 Wisc. App. 1670, 1995).

Pause for Reflection

Sexual attraction is a biologically based phenomenon over which we arguably have little control. Sexual activity among humans, on the other hand, is a highly ritualized, meaning-imbued, culturally regulated interaction. How do you anticipate your own values, needs, hopes, and fears to influence you when clients express sexual attraction to you? When you experience sexual attraction to a client?

CHAPTER WRAP-UP

African-American poet, Gwendolyn Brooks, wrote "We are each other's harvest; we are each other's business; we are each other's magnitude and bond" (G. Brooks, 1970, p. 19). The roles we have in each other's lives, and the borders we create around those roles, are central to our most basic senses of meaning and safety. In one of my clinical settings, I (RSF) interviewed a very disturbed young mother and her 4-year-old daughter, each with the same first, middle, and last name. "Sometimes, I don't know if she's hungry or I'm hungry," the mom said. "So I bake a cake."

The human dance between dependence and independence, between enmeshed and disengaged, is a fascinating, complicated dance. Human boundaries vary based on culture, community, age, and individual style. This chapter covered how they vary based on the definition of the relationship. Professional counseling, consulting, teaching, helping, or supervising relationships have inherent power differentials and, therefore, the professional has boundary-keeping responsibilities of great consequence and complexity.

Chapter Eight

ASSESSMENT, EVALUATION, TESTING: PEERING THROUGH THE RIGHT LENSES

Traditional scientific method has always been at the very best, 20-20 hindsight. It's good for seeing where you've been. It's good for testing the truth of what you think you know, but it can't tell you where you ought to go.
— Robert M. Pirsig, *Zen and the Art of Motorcycle Maintenance*

CHAPTER ORIENTATION

While we are grateful for our colleagues who love assessment and research, we admit that this chapter and the next focus on topics less likely to rank as your favorites within the helping professions. Nonetheless, ethical professional helpers must always be astute observers and must have responsible ways to assess what they observe. They must constantly entertain hypotheses about client problems—their source, accurate descriptions, and appropriate interventions. Helping professionals in school, agency, and independent settings must be able to understand diagnostic nomenclature and the implications of a wide range of assessment and test results. Counseling and mental health professionals from most disciplines engage in at least some formal assessment processes. None of these tasks are without controversy, and all require advanced training and critical thinking skills. As professionals, we must continually face the personal, political, and social implications of testing and evaluation.

Counselors work in settings that may utilize educational, vocational, and psychological assessment strategies and instruments to make decisions about students and clients. There are many ethical considerations to ponder about assessment, including competence, diversity and culture, client and student welfare, instrumentation, and even concepts of "normal." This chapter provides you with the ABCs and XYZs of ethical assessment while taking you along a tour of assessment issues beginning with informal assessment procedures and experiences, moving to clinical interviewing as an assessment strategy, then to formal psychological and educational testing, and finally ending with psychiatric diagnosis. In this chapter, you will specifically focus on:

- the basics and nature of the assessment process;
- technical and ethical concerns in assessment;
- how one engages in informal assessment;
- the use of clinical interviewing;
- testing and other forms of formal evaluation; and
- the method and purposes of mental health diagnostic systems.

THE ROOTS AND NATURE OF ASSESSMENT

Like all sentient life forms, humans assess their environment, companions, and enemies as part of basic survival strategies (Wright, 1994). Research on human sensory systems has shown that the urge to classify, stereotype, and evaluate is hard-wired in our species. This means assessment is unavoidable and ubiquitous.

Over the centuries, human strategies for assessment have become more abstract and systemized. In the latter 1800s, Sir Francis Galton, an Englishman, began systematically evaluating individual differences in sensory acuity, motor skills, and reaction time. His aim was to determine stable human differences that might predict individual potential. Galton's efforts were both scientific and political; like many individuals interested in power and control, he sought to identify more and less capable humans with an eventual goal of improving human potential through selective breeding (Winston, 2004). This historical note, and the fact that Galton's work comprises the roots of intelligence testing, should make it clear why assessment procedures should always be paired with ethical principles. Mahoney (2005) provides us with another reason for emphasizing ethics when conducting assessments:

> The testing industry has been one of the most pernicious influences on psychology ever since Darwin's cousin (Francis Galton [Gillham, 2001]) began secretly counting the yawns of his dinner companions. Standardized tests are standardly stupid, but there are big bucks in them. (p. 354)

Despite Mahoney's obvious distaste for formal testing, assessment remains at the heart of contemporary decision making and is a central activity among many mental health professionals. Currently, various formal and informal assessment procedures are used to make serious, life-altering decisions. The list includes which schools get funding, who goes to which college, who gets to play on which teams, who gets to perform in which musical group, who gets jobs, who gets government aid for a disability, which medications are prescribed, who gets paroled, who gets special-education instruction, who gets custody of the children, and who gets to join organizations who have an actual cutoff for membership IQ scores—just to name a few.

Clients seek mental health assistance for a nearly endless list of human concerns. Take a minute and fill in the box in Applications 8.1.

═══ Applications 8.1 ═══

Reasons People Seek Counseling

In the following spaces, list all the reasons you imagine people might seek assistance from school counselors, psychologists, family counselors or therapists,
mental health counselors, social workers, or any other helping professionals.

_____

_____

_____

_____

_____

_____

Now look back at your list and think about how you might assess the concerns you listed. Would you assess the severity of the presenting concerns?
Would you ask family members to provide collateral information? Would you
assess strengths and potential for change? Would you assess social and familial
support and financial resources? Would you screen for an addiction? How would
you evaluate for attachment problems? What other areas might warrant some
kind of formal or informal assessment?

THE ABCs OF ETHICAL ASSESSMENT

Most helping professions have lengthy sections within their ethics codes to help practitioners maintain high ethical standards when conducting assessments. These standards
represent basic principles of ethical assessment and are summarized generally in
Applications 8.2.

Although the assessment ethics statements in the professional codes provide a foundation for clinical practice, there are additional concepts and principles to which ethical professionals should attend.

Assessment Requires Judgment

The word *assessment* implies judgment. Assessment is intimately and historically linked
to the judgment of whether a given individual is normal, abnormal, superior, inferior,
intellectually gifted, intellectually impaired, better, worse, and so on (Binet & Henri,
1896; Galton, 1879).

To many caring helping professionals, using formal and informal assessment procedures with clients is paradoxical, especially given that person-centered theory and recent empirical research emphasize the importance of a nonjudgmental relationship.
Despite reservations about assessment, professionals must be capable of rendering

---

Applications 8.2

Ten Questions for Ethical Assessment

1. Is the assessment procedure or instrument I am using within my scope of practice?
2. Do I have adequate education and training to competently administer a given test or procedure?
3. When using an assessment procedure, am I doing so with the client's informed consent, providing an adequate explanation, and using it in a collaborative manner?
4. Am I selecting the appropriate instrument or procedure to answer the assessment question I (and the client) want to answer?
5. Am I selecting instruments or procedures with standardization or normative data that justify its use with culturally diverse, disabled, or gifted clients?
6. If I use technology in the administration, scoring, or interpretation of test data, am I adhering to the appropriate protocol and using technology within my range of competence?
7. If I use standardized assessment instruments, am I administering, scoring, and interpreting them as intended?
8. Am I providing my clients with an adequate and clear explanation of their assessment results?
9. Are the procedures I'm using for diagnosis and assessment consistent with my training and background and do they represent acceptable standards of practice?
10. Am I keeping all test and interview data secure and releasing it only to individuals who are adequately trained to interpret assessment data?

---

informed judgments about themselves, their theories and interventions, and their client's progress.

The Assessment Continuum

Assessment occurs along a continuum from informal to formal. Informal assessment procedures include intuitive processes, observation, unstructured interviewing, work samples, expressive art or movement, some projective techniques, and other less structured and generally unscored approaches. These procedures are usually nonstandardized, meaning they do not have rigorous and consistent administration procedures and do not have normative data with which to compare client scores.

The purpose of informal assessment is to provide practitioners with information that leads to hypotheses, and sometimes to build rapport (J. Sommers-Flanagan & Sommers-Flanagan, 1997). Due to their nature, informal assessment procedures are more vulnerable to professional projection and bias than more structured and standardized approaches (D. Campbell & Fiske, 1959; Groth-Marnat, 2003). Without the structure or protection of more standardized procedures and comparison samples (norms), mental health professionals may inappropriately project their own issues onto the client—seeing the client only through the counselor's biased perspective.

Practitioner as Instrument

In the professional helping relationship, as the professional, you are the primary assessment instrument. Even in cases where counselors or other mental health professionals employ standardized testing materials, it is still the mental health professional who chooses the instrument, scores and interprets the data obtained, and applies the knowledge to the counseling situation. This implies that professionals must calibrate themselves, much as chemists calibrate instruments they use for studying elements.

Calibrating yourself involves knowing yourself and taking care of yourself. This is yet another reason why it is good practice for mental health professionals to seek counseling. If you do not know yourself well, you risk evaluating your clients inaccurately due to your own biases, needs, or burnout. The following humorous case example is a concrete sort of analogy for how counselors' "stuff" can distort their view of client or student problems.

Case Example: It is an unfortunate truth that some counselors are forced to practice in small offices without windows, a scene especially common among school counselors. Small, poorly ventilated offices can be problematic.

Myles, a 26-year-old school counselor, was well liked by his middle school students. Occasionally, his students were so comfortable talking with him in his small office, they would lean back in the recliner and slip off their shoes. One day, as soon as a young man leaned back and took off his tennis shoes, Myles followed suit. Moments later, the room filled with a very bad odor. Ever alert for a chance to help students understand the importance of hygiene in social relationships, Myles kindly but firmly said, "Billy, I think maybe your feet have a bit of an odor today!" Billy looked defiant. He sniffed at his shoes and shot back, "Un-uh. Might be YOU, buddy." Unfortunately, after a brief investigation, Myles discovered it was, in fact, his own shoes that smelled. He offered Billy an apology, reassuring himself that modeling how to handle chagrin was also helpful for middle schoolers.

Pause for Reflection

Can you identify other ways in which your own conscious or unconscious biases, values, or "smelly shoes" might cause you to experience your client inaccurately? For instance, what if you have strong biases for or against tattoos or body piercing? Could those biases, if unexamined, cause you to make judgments about young (or old) clients in ways that are blatantly inaccurate? Discuss this issue with your classmates when you get an opportunity.

Informed Consent and Confidentiality

Clients have a right to know about the tests and assessments you use and why you use them. They deserve to know, in layperson's language, about the test's reliability, validity, and limitations. They need to understand how the test results might affect their lives. They very much need to know that in mental health no test score or pattern of results provides a final, definitive answer, but rather contributes a small piece of the puzzle. And finally, they need to know the results of the test and who might have access to these results. Concerns related to assessment and informed consent are covered thoroughly in both the APA and the NASW codes of ethics. The ACA Code provides a nice description of what professional helpers should tell their clients about assessment procedures.

ACA *Code of Ethics*

E.3.a Prior to assessment, counselors explain the nature and purposes of assessment and the specific use of results by potential recipients. The explanation will be given in the language of the client (or another legally authorized person on behalf of the client), unless an explicit exception has been agreed upon in advance. Counselors consider the client's personal or cultural context, the level of the clients' understanding of the results, and the impact of the results on the client.

Providing sensitive, positive, and accurate explanations of test and assessment results is a mature clinical skill, as the following Case Example illustrates.

Case Example: Samir was a counselor in a youth detention facility. He had extensive training in administering and interpreting many achievement and psychological measures. Cooper was a 16-year-old boy with a record of arrests for shoplifting, possession of illegal drugs and drug paraphernalia, and assault. Cooper had lived as a ward of the state, in foster care, since he was 4. While in the facility, Cooper got into a serious altercation with two other boys, resulting in Cooper getting knocked unconscious. Following this incident, Cooper began having seizures, and sometimes, during conversations, seemed to lose touch with reality. His hygiene deteriorated, and he became withdrawn and even more irritable than he had been before the fight. The seizures were successfully managed medically. Samir was asked to give Cooper some rather routine testing to determine his learning needs and potential. Cooper was cooperative and mildly interested in the process, and told Samir he wanted to know the results.

After scoring the instruments, Samir was surprised to find that Cooper's scores indicated a sharp decline in intellectual functioning, as compared to earlier group scores from his school. In addition, Cooper had endorsed a number of items that suggested magical thinking and odd or bizarre ideation. Imagine the clinical and ethical concerns Samir would consider before meeting with Cooper and his guardian to go over the test results. What further testing might be appropriate? With what other professionals might Samir consult?

In rare cases, there may be an ethical justification to temporarily withhold assessment results for the client's welfare. However, the entire realm of testing and assessment requires attention to many ethical and clinical dimensions. Read through the code examples, but also be sure to read the entire sections of the codes as they address assessment and the welfare of our clients.

ACA *Code of Ethics*

E.1.b. Client Welfare

Counselors do not misuse assessment results and interpretations, and they take reasonable steps to prevent others from misusing the information these techniques provide. They respect the client's right to know the results, the interpretations made, and the bases for counselor's conclusions and recommendations. . . .

E.3.b. Recipients of Results

Counselors consider the examinee's welfare, explicit understandings, and prior agreements in determining who receives the assessment results. Counselors include accurate and appropriate interpretations with any release of individual or group assessment results.

APA *Ethical Principles*

9.04 Release of Test Data

. . . Psychologists may refrain from releasing test data to protect a client/patient or others from substantial harm or misuse or misrepresentation of the data or the test, recognizing that in many instances release of confidential information under these circumstances is regulated by law.

NASW *Code of Ethics*

5.02 Evaluation and Research

(d) Social workers engaged in evaluation or research should carefully consider possible consequences and should follow guidelines developed for the protection of evaluation and research participants. Appropriate institutional review boards should be consulted.

(e) Social workers engaged in evaluation or research should obtain voluntary and written informed consent from participants, when appropriate, without any implied or actual deprivation or penalty for refusal to participate; without undue inducement to participate; and with due regard for participants' well-being, privacy, and dignity. Informed consent should include information about the nature, extent, and duration of the participation requested and disclosure of the risks and benefits of participation in the research.

When withholding test data or results from clients, counselors must be prepared to fully explain their decision, as this would not be usual and customary practice.

Confidentiality can be confusing in certain testing situations. Findings from any kind of counseling or psychological evaluation are to be handled with the same care as any other clinical information. In many cases, evaluative information is sought by someone other than the client. Teachers, parents, parole officers, physicians, and others might believe they deserve to know assessment results. It is essential that practitioners engage in a careful informed consent process and obtain signed release of information forms that specifically allow the results and report to be shared with those who need or are seeking the information. Further, assessors must learn to interpret and explain testing results in ways that are clear and culturally sensitive.

Multi-Method, Multi-Source Assessment

Many assessment methods are available to mental health professionals. However, depending on the assessment question, it could be inappropriate and marginally ethical for a professional to base his or her conclusions on any single assessment method or procedure. Using two or more assessment methods that differ in the way they obtain information represents best practice.

There are four common traditional assessment methods or modalities that mental health professionals employ (Groth-Marnat, 2003). These include:

- Objective Measures (e.g., Beck Depression Inventory, Minnesota Multiphasic Personality Inventory [MMPI])
- Projective (aka: Generative) Measures (Roberts Apperception Test, Rorschach Inkblots)
- Clinical Interview (Unstructured interview, Schedule for Affective Disorders and Schizophrenia)
- Performance-Based Measures (Wechsler Intellectual Scales for Children, Scholastic Aptitude Test)

Assessment procedures can also be categorized on the basis of who provides the information. This is commonly referred to as the *source* of assessment information. Typical assessment sources include:

- Self (the client himself or herself)
- Intimate others (parent, neighbor, or peer)
- Professional (counselor, psychiatrist, psychologist, teacher, social worker)

The multi-method, multi-source assessment concept is important to ethical assessment practice because of the fact that overall assessment validity and reliability is increased when data are obtained via more than one modality and more than one source (D. Campbell & Fiske, 1959; J. Sommers-Flanagan & Sommers-Flanagan, 1998). For example, if a mental health provider is evaluating a young client for depression, the evaluation is more definitive and informative if the provider uses (a) a client self-rating scale, such as the Children's Depression Scale (e.g., Patton & Burnett, 1993), (b) an instrument completed by a parent or teacher or both, (c) a clinical interview, and (d) a projective measure, such as the Roberts Apperception Test or Draw-A-Person test. This multi-method, multi-source assessment procedure is advantageous, but also problematic when you vary the measures and sources and they each suggest different results.

INFORMAL ASSESSMENT

Informal assessment skills are used at the beginning, throughout the middle, and at the end of counseling. The purpose of all assessment procedures, including informal assessment, is to facilitate the delivery of effective, ethical, and clinically sophisticated interventions and interpersonal assistance (Hodges, 2004).

Two examples of informal assessment techniques are described in the following subsections. Many other informal strategies are available to mental health professionals, including work samples, interpersonal simulations, and nondirective interviewing (Groth-Marnat, 2003).

Observational Strategies

Direct observation of clients or students is a fundamental assessment procedure. Obviously, when clients walk into your office, you observe their behavior—the way they walk, the sound of their voice, their choice of attire, how they introduce themselves, and more. Consider for a moment, what behavioral signals you typically scan for when initially meeting people? Will you use the same signals to assess your clients?

Many school psychologists and school counselors go to classrooms and employ direct observational procedures. These procedures may be more or less formal. For example, a school counselor may casually drop in on a class to see how a student with anger problems is faring on that particular day. In contrast, the same school counselor might employ a very formal behavioral coding system to rate and classify the student's behavior (Pelham, Fabiano, & Massetti, 2005). Most professionals consider more formal observational assessment procedures to be more reliable and valid (and therefore ethical) than informal approaches—but informal approaches also serve a purpose (J. Sommers-Flanagan & Sommers-Flanagan, 1997). The important issue for ethical professionals to keep in mind is the purpose of the observational procedure. If the observations are to be used to document the student's off-task behavior, then a more formal procedure is warranted. However, if the school counselor is functioning as the student's "anger coach" or advocate, then an informal observation can deepen the counselor's understanding of the student's behavior and improve the treatment alliance (Belsler, 1999).

Using Art and Drawings in Assessment

Human figure drawings have often been criticized as having little reliability and validity. In fact, these approaches, including the Draw-A-Person, Kinetic Family Drawing, and House-Tree-Person drawings, are in such scientific disregard, a case can be made that professionals who rely on drawings as a core assessment strategy are behaving unethically (Bekhit, Thomas, & Jolley, 2005). For example, it is completely inappropriate for a counselor to conclude that a child who draws sexual genitalia on a human figure has been sexually molested. Assessing is much more complex than that (Cook et al., 2005). Similarly, students who draw tombstones may or may not be thinking about suicide.

On the other hand, such drawings can be used to generate hypotheses about a client's potential problems or to simultaneously gather information while establishing rapport. While it would be inappropriate to come to a single conclusion on the basis of a drawing, it also would be unethical to ignore the significance of a drawing with a tombstone inscribed *R.I.P.* that included the student's name and date of death. This example illustrates how important it is to carefully weigh all assessment information obtained, regardless of whether it was obtained through standardized, reliable, and valid instrumentation.

CLINICAL INTERVIEWING

As with most assessment approaches, some professionals embrace and others reject clinical interviewing as an assessment tool. Nonetheless, we believe that clinical interviewing is the single most common form of assessment for counselors and mental health professionals (J. Sommers-Flanagan & Sommers-Flanagan, 2003). However, perhaps due to this ambivalence, interviewing is only rarely mentioned in ethics codes. Several samples of where and how it is mentioned are offered in the following code example.

APA *Ethical Principles*

9.02 Use of Assessments

    (a) Psychologists administer, adapt, score, interpret, or use assessment techniques, *interviews,* tests, or instruments in the manner and for purposes that are appropriate in light of the research on or evidence of the usefulness and proper application of the techniques (italics added).

ACA *Code of Ethics*

E.5. Diagnosis of Mental Disorders

    a. Proper Diagnosis

        Counselors take special care to provide proper diagnosis of mental disorders. Assessment techniques (including personal *interview*) used to determine client care (e.g., locus of treatment, type of treatment, or recommended follow-up) are carefully selected and appropriately used (italics added).

AMHCA *Code of Ethics*

I. Principle 3

    Mental health counselors who ask that an individual reveal personal information in the course of *interviewing,* testing, or evaluation, or allow such information to be divulged, do so only after making certain that the person or authorized representative is fully aware of the purposes of the *interview,* testing, or evaluation and of the ways in which the information will be used (italics added).

Clinical interviews are flexible assessment procedures that can be used for many purposes (J. Sommers-Flanagan & Sommers-Flanagan, 2003). As with any assessment, to determine whether a clinical interview is the right assessment tool, it is crucial to identify the purpose of the assessment. If your goal is to evaluate your client within one of the following domains, a clinical interview is your likely first (but not necessarily only) step:

- suicide
- dangerousness
- mental status evaluation (assessing current mental state)
- psychiatric diagnosis

Each of the preceding areas may also be evaluated using alternative assessment strategies. As we stressed previously, the best practice is to use more than one assessment modality and/or source. This is especially the case when assessing a condition as critical as suicide or dangerousness.

In recent years a case has been made within the literature for establishing minimum standards for mental health professionals who conduct suicide and dangerousness assessments, and some have even advocated that dangerousness predictions be made only with actuarial methods, rather than clinical assessments. For an analysis and rebuttal, see Thomas Litwack's (2001) article in this area.

Although a questionnaire may sometimes be used to supplement a clinical interview, a suicide assessment interview (aka: suicide risk assessment) is essential. To meet usual and customary practice standards, suicide assessments should include:

- risk factor assessment/analysis
- assessment of suicidal thoughts
- assessment of suicidal plans
- assessment of client self-control
- assessment of client suicide intent (assessment of client's reasons to live or die)

To become an ethical practitioner, training in suicide and dangerousness assessment is required. If these content areas are not included in your graduate training please seek supplementary training to insure you have basic assessment skills in these critical areas.

ASSESSMENT AND SCIENCE

Assessment and evaluation procedures draw from the basic scientific method of inquiry and require ongoing self-discipline and honest scrutiny. The oft-quoted statement "It is possible to make the same mistake for 20 years and call it rich clinical experience" should give even the most science avoidant among us motivation to attend to the basics. Consider the following excerpt from the book *Why People Believe Weird Things.*

> A sizable literature exists on the scientific method, but there is little consensus among authors. This does not mean that scientists do not know what they are doing. Doing and explaining may be two different things. However, scientists agree that the following elements are involved in thinking scientifically:
>
> *Induction:* Forming a hypothesis by drawing general conclusions from existing data.
>
> *Deduction:* Making specific predictions based on the hypotheses.

Observation: Gathering data, driven by hypotheses that tell us what to look for in nature.

Verification: Testing the predictions against further observations to confirm or falsify the initial hypotheses.

Science, of course, is not this rigid; and no scientist consciously goes through "steps." The process is a constant interaction of making observations, drawing conclusions, making predictions, and checking them against evidence. (Shermer, 1997, p. 19)

The professional mental health world is filled with many assessment instruments purporting to measure pathologies, achievement, career suitability, self-efficacy and esteem, personality inclinations, intelligence(s), conflict styles, learning disabilities, and so on. It is vital that professionals learn basic statistical methodologies to enable them to read about and understand the validity and reliability of any instrument they might choose or be required to use or interpret. Excessive, incompetent, inappropriate, and/or illegal uses of these instruments are all ethical dangers for mental health professionals.

Besides initial assessments, and assessments that might supplement the counseling process, counseling assessment should also include consciously evaluating progress toward the client's goals. Such assessment can occur formally or informally. For example, ongoing assessment might include weekly or monthly administration of the Beck Depression Inventory or the Outcome Questionnaire-45 (A. T. Beck, Ward, Mendelson, Mock, & Erbaugh, 1961). It might include assessing career interests, attachment styles, or conflict management styles that are of help to you or your client. Or it might simply involve asking clients about their perceptions of progress being made.

Counseling assessment can also mean checking in with *yourself* as you work with clients. Counseling is an interactive, relationship-based activity. As the counselor, you are not only listening, you are mirroring things back, reacting to your client, and sorting out your reactions—all simultaneously. Noticing how a client affects you is an important part of ongoing assessment of the counseling process for several reasons. Such introspection provides valuable diagnostic information, helps you maintain awareness of countertransference reactions, and assists you in avoiding burnout. Because this form of assessment is so directly related to issues of counseling competence and accountability, we discuss this issue further in Chapter 9.

TESTING

Without a doubt, test administration is every helper's favorite professional activity. Testing always enhances the therapeutic relationship. Testing is a fair, universally accurate, and entertaining activity, well received by students and clients from any culture. Thus tests, above any other input, should be the guide for making life's most crucial decisions. *Okay. Now that we hopefully have your eyebrows elevated and your defenses activated, we will start this section over!*

Many settings require the administration and interpretation of specific tests as part of serving a particular clientele. School, career, mental heath, and rehabilitation counselors administer and interpret tests in the areas of careers, academic achievement, work-related skills or limitations, personality, and home and social environment. Historically, psychologists have led the way in mental measurement, intelligence testing, and assessing psychopathology. They generally receive more training in the construction, administration, scoring, and interpretation of psychological tests.

Pause for Reflection

To be in graduate school, it is likely you faced many forms of standardized testing, most recently the Graduate Record Examination. Perhaps you, or those you love, have also been tested for marital compatibility, disability services, or chemical dependency or addiction. How fair do you believe these tests to be? How accurate? Did these tests assess what mattered? Could you have been better prepared to take the test or better informed about the process? Keep your answers in mind as you consider the ethical components of testing.

Although it seems obvious, we need to remember that tests measure what is of value to the creator of the test. As Susan Fiske stated (Hackney, 2005),

> In a personality course, I realized that you could always tell a test-inventor's favored end of every personality dimension. There was always a healthy, better way to be, and usually it was identified with the (male) researcher's own perspective. I started thinking about how the researchers' perspectives informed how they framed, labeled, and studied the problem. (p. 196)

Fiske's observation is also true for test writers' beliefs about intelligence and achievement, although of course, researchers and test writers make efforts to create fair and valid instruments. Both creators and users of tests have an ethical obligation to make sure tests are as valid as possible, and test scores are used only in ways that have been empirically supported.

Many tests have been shown to be notoriously racially and culturally biased (Spengler, 1998; D. W. Sue & Sue, 2003). There are very few tests that include mechanisms for systematically accommodating for a test taker who is taking the test in a second or third language.

A comprehensive list of ethical competencies for testing is available from the National Fair Access Coalition on Testing, which is affiliated with the National Board for Certified Counselors. Their comprehensive list is well worth reviewing. Take a look at it on their website at http://www.fairaccess.org/code_of_ethics.htm.

Despite concerns, cautions, and guidelines, tests often provide useful and sometimes extremely important data, especially when combined with other modalities and sources of information. A single test score should never provide the only definitive information upon which an important life decision is based.

Professionals who are responsible for testing and assessment in schools, rehabilitation settings, or in career advisement settings may be asked to administer tests to large groups of people. The same basic ethics apply. Any kind of test administration must be done with clinical awareness, knowledge of the test reliabilities and validities, and awareness of how the test scores will be applied in the client's life.

FORMAL EVALUATIONS

Turf wars are ongoing in the mental health professions. Usually, when turf wars erupt, they include heated arguments about professional competence. We should note the obvious fact that financial issues (aka: the profit motive) underlie many turf issues.

In recent years psychologists have begun moving into traditional psychiatric turf with efforts to obtain prescription privileges (Long, 2005). Naturally, some psychiatrists are unhappy about the entry of psychologists into their professional domain. Similarly, master's level counseling and/or social work coursework has increasingly included the administration and interpretation of various psychological tests.

Psychological Evaluations

One area where the psychology-counseling assessment turf war continues is regarding qualifications necessary to administer, interpret, and integrate the standardized assessment instruments commonly used for various psychological evaluations. These evaluations are used to assess general psychological functioning, necessity of hospitalization, termination of parental rights, adequacy for employment, disability determination (for purposes of disability benefits), capacity to stand trial, and differential diagnosis, to name a few.

These formal evaluations are used to make decisions of enormous import in people's lives. They require extensive training and skill to be done thoroughly, professionally, and with as much fairness and justice as humans can attain. Besides an extensive clinical interview, instruments commonly used for general psychological evaluations include, but are not limited to, some mix of the following:

- MMPI-II
- Millon Multiaxial Clinical Inventory II
- Rorschach Inkblots
- Thematic Apperception Test
- Incomplete Sentences
- Draw-A-Person
- WAIS-III or WISC-III

In addition to general psychological evaluations, neuropsychological evaluations include a different range of tests and are designed to identify client cognitive, intellectual, and/or neurological deficits. Even further, some professionals focus their training and practice on providing specific forensic or custody/parenting evaluations (Lally, 2003; see also Digressions for Deliberation 8.2).

Psychiatrists, social workers, and counselors are increasingly seeking the additional training they might need to conduct extensive psychological evaluations. For example, some psychiatrists have begun using computer automated MMPI interpretative programs to supplement their psychiatric evaluations and some social workers and counselors have obtained the necessary training to provide custody evaluations. Because of both training concerns and turf concerns, psychologists often make strong objections to allied professionals who try to conduct psychological evaluations—some of these objections even involve ethics complaints. Of course, in cases where *any* mental health professionals have not adequately trained themselves to conduct psychological evaluations, the complaints might be justified. Consider this quote:

> Being able to document substantial course work, supervised training, and extensive experience in a given area of testing such as neuropsychological assessment of geriatric populations, intelligence testing of young children, or personality testing of adults *helps* a professional to establish competence in that area of testing. . . . But beyond this evidence of competence, one must also be able to demonstrate understanding of measurement, validation, and research. (K. Pope & Vasquez, 1998, p. 145; italics added)

Certainly, it is clear that conducting formal evaluations requires significant coursework and supervised experience, regardless of the evaluator's academic background. Expert evaluation draws on discrete test administration and interpretation skills as well as clinical interviewing skills and a propensity for "connecting the dots" or putting disparate pieces together to paint a cogent, helpful snapshot—a snapshot relevant to the original referral question. This is why many professionals obtain specific postdoctoral training to prepare themselves to conduct ethical evaluations. Even for the fully trained evaluator, a very common area of ethics complaints is psychological evaluations in general and child custody evaluations in particular. The risks associated with poorly conducted custody evaluations or mediation work can hardly be overstated. There are significant risks for parents, children, and the professional (N. Johnson, Sacuzzon, & Koen, 2005).

Social, Learning, Career, and Need-Based Evaluations

School psychologists, school counselors, career counselors, and rehabilitation counselors all commonly have assessment, testing, and evaluation duties. Some of these evaluations are conducted to ascertain student or client eligibility for government assistance or intervention in the form of special programs or services. Therefore, the professional skills necessary to choose, administer, and interpret the results of the various tests, rating scales, and other assessments are important. These skills have a test-specific dimension and a dimension that involves a general understanding of statistics, test construction, and testing theory.

Any comprehensive evaluation should be tailored to a specific question that can reasonably be addressed. Sometimes, the initial questions, while compelling, are not answerable. Some questions have multifaceted and complex answers—which even a thorough evaluation will not completely answer. The wise professional assessor defines and narrows the question and seeks to understand what information will be helpful to the person asking the questions.

DIAGNOSIS AND THE *DSM* SYSTEM

While Ambrose Bierce (1911/1998) once defined diagnosis as a physician's forecast of the disease by the patient's pulse and purse, Webster's Dictionary (Woolf, 1973) defines

Custody Evaluation Burnout

Early in our careers, after obtaining the appropriate training and supervision, we provided what was then called "child custody evaluations" for divorcing families in the midst of child custody disputes. These cases were usually referred by attorneys or judges, and they were physically and emotionally draining enterprises for everyone involved. As a part of the evaluation process, we did home and school visits, clinical interviews with all parties, and parent-child observations. We also obtained collateral information, administered and interpreted parenting scales, psychological tests, and other instruments as needed. The resulting reports were usually between 20 and 30 pages.

We usually knew we had struck the right balance when everyone was mildly unhappy with our recommendations. There is often great pain when family systems come apart, and no easy answer exists regarding the children's best interests (R. Sommers-Flanagan, Elander, & Sommers-Flanagan, 2000).

During these evaluations we witnessed and heard about stunningly horrid human behaviors—babies stripped down to their diapers before being "transferred" to the other parent, children being bribed to spy or tattle on the other parent, children being asked to become the missing parent, children punished for speaking of the other parent, and parents using their children for financial gain, emotional support, or revenge. We also evaluated families where there was little malice, but painful, unsolvable dilemmas—parents who for financial or personal reasons needed to live thousands of miles from each other, attempting to find fair and reasonable ways to stretch their children across that expanse.

After one particularly brutal and crazy evaluation, we decided we were finished. This activity was no longer worth the emotional cost. We decided our next calling was to move "upstream" and try to work with parent education, early mediation, and the courts to prevent divorcing families from sinking into perpetual and child-damaging conflict. Even after we declared our child custody evaluation days over, attorneys would often call requesting our services. To admit our burnout, we started responding to these requests by telling attorneys that if we did another evaluation, we would have to charge a million dollars because we would need about that much therapy afterward. So far no one has offered to pay us our new fee, but we happily work, for a very small fee, with parents who want to constructively work on their parenting plans and challenges.

Fortunately, our state laws changed and there is less demand for such extensive, definitive evaluations. However, there are still intractable parenting battles, and we are grateful that we have dedicated, well-trained colleagues from various professional backgrounds willing to try and find fair, child-centered solutions. Unfortunately, we are also aware of practitioners who are not trained, not well-supervised, and yet willing to put themselves forward as professional evaluators. We recommend that anyone considering the child custody evaluation market read and follow the APA Guidelines for Child Custody Evaluations (1994), or check other sources such as the *Summary of the Practice Parameters for Child Custody Evaluation* by the American Academy of Child and Adolescent Psychiatry available at http://www.aacap.org/clinical/parameters/summaries/CUSTDY~1.HTM.

diagnosis as "(1) to recognize (as a disease) by signs and symptoms; (2) to analyze the cause or nature of (the problem)" (p. 349). We offer these definitions to help you distinguish between evaluation, testing, assessment, and diagnosis. Diagnosis is problem or pathology driven. It is an activity that requires describing and counting symptoms and arriving at a label that will then explain the symptoms and dictate treatment. Although part and parcel of the medical model, diagnosing is not limited to medicine. It is also used in the auto, appliance, and technology repair professions. It comes from an orientation that something is wrong. This wrong dimension must be located, described, and fixed. If it cannot be fixed, then at least the symptoms must be addressed and eased.

To assign a diagnosis, virtually all mental health providers use the American Psychiatric Association's *Diagnostic and Statistical Manual,* now in its fourth edition (American Psychiatric Association, 2000). Although an effort is made to address social and cultural factors, the *DSM* system is essentially a disease-based medical model that still fails to fully account for cultural and social influences in human distress (Paniagua, 2001). It was designed, conceived, and is updated primarily by psychiatrists and reflects an orientation toward identifying psychiatric disorders that can be efficiently treated via psychiatric means.

The *DSM* system is also a nonetiological diagnostic system. This means that in contrast to most medical diagnosis, psychiatric diagnosis is simply a descriptive system without any implications for underlying etiological (causal) conditions. Therefore, when diagnosing human mental functioning, mental health professionals are assigning a label for a cluster of personal, ideational, and/or social difficulties. They are not necessarily insinuating the cause of the difficulties. A person might meet the criteria for Major Depression for many different reasons, such as physical injury or disease, psychological trauma, existential angst, or loss of a loved one. All of these can contribute to a change in the way our brain functions, which can result in depressive symptoms.

Because of its ubiquitous influence, mental health professionals should be familiar with contemporary *DSM* diagnostic criteria and most should be qualified and able to use it professionally and accurately. *DSM* labels offer compact summaries about a person's symptoms and distress, and thus provide a language for communicating across professions and orientations.

THE PURPOSE OF DIAGNOSIS

According to most texts and professional journals, the traditional purpose of psychiatric diagnosis is at least threefold.

1. To provide efficient communication among professionals.
2. To facilitate empirical research in psychopathology.
3. To assist in the formulation of appropriate treatment (Sadler, 2002).

Somewhat more cynically, some professionals contend that the primary purpose of diagnosis is to obtain insurance reimbursement (Braun & Cox, 2005; Sadler, 2002). Although we admit there are many problems associated with clinical diagnosis using the *DSM* system, it is the dominant nomenclature in all mental health and related fields.

Diagnosing comes with a particularly sharp ethical quandary on which many of us are impaled. Similar to the universal ban on sex with clients, all ethics texts admonish mental health professionals to refrain from over or under diagnosing. Of course, the motive for overdiagnosing is most likely financial reimbursement. In our ethics course, students make a video or DVD dealing with a current ethical issue. One of our top 10 all-time favorites was a short drama that used a game show format. Volunteers displayed various levels of psychological distress while the professional contestants hit a bell when they were ready to render their diagnostic verdict. The title of this creative ethical production says it all: It was "Diagnosing for Dollars." Overdiagnosing your clients' distress to make sure they qualify for insurance or Medicaid coverage of their counseling has a sobering name: insurance fraud. And it is not only unethical, it is also illegal (Braun & Cox, 2005).

Case Example: Casey is a well-trained counselor in her mid-50s. She has been in private practice for over 20 years. In her practice, she specializes in working with couples—a part of her practice that she truly loves. Unfortunately, most insurance providers do not reimburse mental health professionals for couple or marital therapy. Consequently, when couples come to Casey for counseling, she is forced into a practical and ethical dilemma, which she generally describes to her clients:

"As you may know, your insurance company does not cover couples counseling and so we have three choices. First, we can decide not to submit our sessions for insurance reimbursement and you can just pay me $90 per session. Second, we can decide which one of you would like a diagnosis—either of you could probably meet the criteria for Adjustment Disorder with Mixed Anxiety and Depression, which is a very benign disorder without any specific symptoms. Then, what I would do is to submit the insurance billing under one of your names for individual counseling and your insurance company would probably pay me 50% of my fee after your deductible is met and then you would pay me the rest. Third, we could decide to skip the couples counseling and I could meet with one of you individually."

In almost every case, when offered these options, Casey's clients choose option number two; one of them is then diagnosed and the insurance company reimburses Casey and the clients get to spend less money for their counseling. However, the big question in this case and others like it is whether or not Casey's practice is ethical and/or legal? What do you think?

Overdiagnosis is a widely recognized problem, but deliberate underdiagnosing occurs as well. Motives for underdiagnosis include preserving your client's public image, protecting your client from hospitalization, reluctance to use psychiatric labels, discomfort with the concomitant explanation to the client that such diagnosis might require, or fear that your client will later be unable to get health insurance. Some of these may be worthy motives. However, deliberate underdiagnosis is paramount to telling a lie. From a deontological perspective, this damages the professional culture. It is better to refrain from using diagnosis completely, relying instead on direct payments from clients, than to be dishonest about your client's psychiatric condition.

Case Example: Carmen has a private counseling practice. She is working with a young Asian Indian graduate student named Suveni, whose husband recently died in a motor vehicle accident. Based on an initial clinical interview, it is clear that Suveni meets the *DSM-IV-TR* diagnostic criteria for Major Depression, and probably was struggling with depression long before the accident. However, Suveni is from a prominent family in her country of origin, and anticipates a public spotlight in her life. Her parents are very disapproving of her even seeking counseling. Suveni's father, a physician, contacts Carmen via email and instructs her to diagnose Suveni with Adjustment Reaction so his insurance will cover the sessions. He is very clear that he does not believe his daughter is depressed, and therefore, should not be diagnosed with anything other than Adjustment Reaction. Pretend you're the colleague that Carmen has decided to consult with. How would you respond? What would you tell her to do?

THE XYZs OF ETHICAL ASSESSMENT

This chapter has already raised daunting ethical concerns in assessment. Nevertheless, we have a few more important comments for you to consider.

Be Mindful of Issues in Technology and Setting

Sometimes it all seems so simple. After all, by just perusing the *APA Monitor* or *Counseling Today,* you can order automated testing software that can simplify your life. It is possible to obtain a wide variety of psychological tests, personality tests, interest inventories, and achievement tests online or in computerized formats. First and foremost, you must have training and supervision before using a new assessment instrument. With adequate supervision and careful limits on interpretation, sometimes adding a new test or instrument to sort out a complex question is warranted. Overall, you should know the statistical properties of the test, such as the norming procedures, test-retest reliability, factorial purity of scales and subscales, and culturally appropriate use.

Second, while computer administration is efficient, it is important to remember the limits and pitfalls of technology—including potential computer malfunction, accidental posting of results in nonconfidential ways, and nonstandardized test-settings. Testing environment has been shown to significantly influence outcome (Groth-Marnat, 2003). Test conditions should be as similar as possible to the conditions in which the test was normed. It is not ethical to allow students or clients to take tests or assessment instruments in an unsupervised setting unless that is the intended use of the instrument. In cases where the outcome matters a great deal, the temptation to consult, or use someone else's answers, could be too great for many test takers.

Use the Least Severe Diagnostic Label

Morrison (1994) recommends that, when in doubt, mental health professionals assign the least severe diagnostic label to their clients. We strongly agree with this principle. For example, although it is currently quite popular to assign a Bipolar Disorder diagnosis to children, we recommend using less severe labels, as long as those labels adequately account for the presenting symptoms. In many cases, instead of Bipolar Disorder, many young clients should be diagnosed as having Attention-Deficit/Hyperactivity Disorder or in some cases, where the child is concurrently experiencing familial stress and disruption, a more appropriate and less severe diagnostic label might include Adjustment Disorder With Mixed Anxiety and Depression, or even a V Code (American Psychiatric Association, 2000). Unfortunately, there is evidence that some mental health practitioners illegally assign more severe diagnostic labels, primarily to assure third party payment by managed care companies (Braun & Cox, 2005).

what are the effects of a diagnosis?

Recognize That All Assessment Procedures Are Flawed

There is no such thing as a perfect assessment instrument. In scientific terms, there is no instrument with a reliability coefficient of $r = 1.0$ and no instrument that is always a valid measure or predictor of human behavior. The inherent problems that exist within all assessment procedures are exacerbated when practitioners use the procedures inappropriately. Inappropriate uses include:

- not following standardized test administration procedures
- giving clients guidance or too many clues on how to take the test
- using a procedure with an individual who is not in the normative group on which the test was normed (e.g., giving an adult intelligence test to a child)
- using a procedure that is known to be culturally biased with a client from the non-dominant culture
- using a procedure normed on native English speakers with an individual who speaks English as a second language

Overall, all informal and formal assessment results should be questioned—especially when standardized procedures are not used. See Deepening Diversity 8.1 for a view from our Brasilian colleague.

Honoring Client Perspectives

Ethical assessment procedures involve clients throughout the assessment process. This means that practitioners should administer and interpret tests and other assessments in a collaborative manner. For example, when conducting an assessment interview, interviewers should clearly tell the client the purpose of the interview. Additionally, after the interview assessment (or any other assessment procedure) is over, the therapist needs to openly share the results with the client by articulating the results and then asking the client questions like, "Does this seem to fit for you?" The purpose of this checking-in process is to honor the client's perspective.

Be Attentive to Diversity Issues and Potential Misuse

Inaccurate and sometimes unconscionable conclusions have been drawn about people from diverse backgrounds based on their performances on culturally biased tests

=== **Deepening Diversity 8.1** ===

Diversity Testing Concerns

by Dr. Aida Hutz

As we all know, there are a number of concerns about how psychological assessment instruments have been used with individuals who belong to diverse ethnocultural groups (i.e., those who do not identify as White, middle-class, European-Americans). My background has made me particularly sensitive to some of these issues. I am a Brasilian woman who has lived in the United States for more than a decade, and I'm a mental health professional and counselor educator who teaches a mental health assessment course. Throughout the entire testing and assessment process, there are several issues to consider related to (a) building rapport with a client, (b) test construction and selection, and (c) interpretation and implications of the assessment results.

First, consider rapport building with clients. It is crucial for mental health professionals to be aware, at both cognitive and experiential levels, that one's relationship with a client will reflect the racial dynamics present in the larger society (D. W. Sue & Sue, 2003). Therefore, a trusting and genuine relationship between White counselors and ethnocultural minority clients can only develop if counselors are committed to doing their own psychological work to uncover their racial and ethnocultural biases. If minority clients can sense their White counselors have embarked on this journey, there is a greater likelihood for honest self-disclosure, cooperation, and lessened anxiety about the assessment process.

Next, consider test construction and selection. It is important for mental health professionals to be knowledgeable about basic psychometrics (e.g., issues related to test reliability, validity, and normative sample). A test must be appropriate for the test taker! Often individuals who belong to ethnocultural groups other than White European-American are not well-represented within the normative samples (Paniagua, 2001). As a result, even measures with well-established psychometric properties may not have appropriate validity when used with diverse populations. Tests are culturally loaded with values and norms of the culture from which it was created (D. W. Sue & Sue, 2003). Most often, tests are developed by White, middle-class, European-Americans.

Linguistic factors are also important. For example, when assessing clients for whom English is not their first language, using a translated version of an instrument (if available) might seem like a great option. However, the essence or meaning of what an instrument purports to measure can be lost or changed through translation. Thus, prior to using or interpreting translated instruments, mental health professionals need to make sure appropriate measures were taken to retain test validity.

Finally, when interpreting results and making recommendations, we need to keep in mind that counseling is generally *etic* in its application. That is, it does

---

Deepening Diversity 8.1 (continued)

not identify cultural influences that affect personality formation, career choice, education, and manifestation of behavior disorders (Bernal & Castro, 1994). This carries on to the testing situation where normality is defined as behaviors that occur most frequently in the population whereas abnormality is defined as behaviors occurring least often. Individuals with a strong ethnocultural orientation will not fall within the *normal* range of a distribution based on White, European-American, middle-class attitudes, values, and behaviors. Unfortunately, mental health professionals often interpret these ethnocultural departures from the norm as deviant and pathological. Consequently, *objective* psychological inventories can often assess deviance of ethnoculturally diverse clients as pathological. Therefore, as mental health professionals we need to know about racial, ethnocultural, and linguistic differences that help shape both our and our clients' worldviews.

Prior to making recommendations that can deeply impact the lives of clients and their families, mental health professionals must ask themselves questions such as: (a) Have I began the process of acknowledging my own racial and ethnocultural biases? (b) Do I understand basic psychometric concepts to the extent that I am able to discern if an instrument is appropriate for use with an ethnoculturally diverse client? and (c) Do I know enough about specific cultural beliefs, traditions, and practices other than my own, in order to distinguish deviance from difference?

(Paniagua, 2001). These conclusions have harmed individuals and entire cultural groups, influenced public policy, and furthered damaging and inaccurate stereotypes. The global history of mental health testing and diagnosis suggests that such practices can also be used for political purposes.

Who gets to decide what's normal? The influence of popular media can hardly be underestimated as it perpetuates narrow stereotypes of maleness, femaleness, blackness, whiteness, and so on. It tells us what is meaningful and what is mundane. It elevates, as normal, patterns of interacting and ways of being that do not even exist in the real world (R. Sommers-Flanagan, Sommers-Flanagan, & Davis, 1993). Consider this quote in light of ethical concerns about psychological testing. It is from an interesting book entitled *The Tyranny of the Normal* (Donley & Buckley, 1996).

> Our ability to normalize people is already far ahead of our thinking about who decides what is normal and abnormal, who decides whether normalizing someone is the best thing to do, who has the authority or the right to make any of the possible changes, and last but not least, who is going to pay for it. (p. XIV)

Pause for Reflection

Some have argued that we all carry, with unconscious terror, the secret of our own "abnormalities." We have an acute need to distance ourselves from these craziness and uglinesses—so we pathologize, marginalize, and are frightened by anyone differ-ent than we are. The fear leads to hatred. The hatred leads to justified aggression—sanctions, surgeries, diagnoses, forced medications . . . A compassionate response to the confusion and pain of deformities, mental illness, or other abnormalities might be liberating for both persons involved in the encounter. Your thoughts?

CHAPTER WRAP-UP

In this chapter, we considered the generic concept of assessment and then divided it into three somewhat distinct areas: formal evaluation, testing, and diagnosis. All of these activities ultimately call for a kind of judgment that causes unease among some mental health professionals. We have sympathy for this unease, and suspect it has multiple causes. One such cause is our growing constructivist awareness that human beings are not reducible to test scores, evaluative conclusions, or diagnoses. Though the following quote requires a few (in fact, perhaps quite a few) read throughs, it is worth it. It captures so aptly this human irreducibility. Explaining her claim that humans must be consid-ered through their "irreducible *scrappiness,*" Barbara Herrnstein Smith (1988) writes:

> I wish to suggest with this term not only that the elements that interact to constitute our motives and behavior are incomplete and heterogeneous, like scraps of things, but also ("scrap" being a slang term for fight) that they are mutually conflicting or at least always potentially at odds. That is, the relations among what we call our "actions," "knowledge," "beliefs," "goals," and "interests" consist of continuous interactions among various struc-tures, mechanisms, traces, impulses, and tendencies that are not necessarily ("naturally" or otherwise) consistent, coordinated, or synchronized and are therefore always *more or less* inconsistent, out of phase, discordant, and conflictual. It must be added, however, that although these interactions obey no "rule" and have no "reason" they do *nevertheless* operate reliably enough under recurrent conditions to permit their more or less coherent description through various modes of reflexive (that is, self-descriptive) analysis and also yield local resolutions and provisional stabilities that, for longer or shorter periods of time, are good enough to keep us—and thus *them,* the interactions—going. It is out of these scrappy (heterogeneous) elements and the local resolutions and provisional stabilities that we (and from various perspectives, others) construct our various versions of our various "selves" and, as necessary, explain or justify our actions, goals, and beliefs. (p. 148)

In addition to, or in part because of, human irreducibility, mental health profession-als are also uneasy about testing because of the skills required for and the consequences attached to the world of testing and evaluation. Both have significant ethical weight, which we have covered in this chapter, and in some ways, will cover further in Chapter 9.

Chapter Nine

COMPETENCE, ACCOUNTABILITY, AND RESEARCH: HOW WE KNOW WHAT WE SHOULD KNOW

Only two possible escapes can save us from the organized mayhem of our dark potentialities—the side that has given us crusades, witch hunts, enslavement, and holocausts. Moral decency provides one necessary ingredient, but not nearly enough. The second foundation must come from the rational side of our mentality. For, unless we rigorously use human reason both to discover and acknowledge nature's factuality, and to follow the logical implications for efficacious human actions that such knowledge entails, we will lose out to the frightening forces of irrationality, romanticism, uncompromising "true" belief, and the apparent resulting inevitability of mob action.

—Stephen Jay Gould

CHAPTER ORIENTATION

Similar to the previous chapter, this chapter covers unsettling and sometimes unpopular material. Who decides what a professional credential means? How do you know when you are qualified and when you are not? How do you justify the use of some kind of strategy or technique if no one has done any outcome research on it? And how do you know if the "outcome research" has been conducted in a responsible, scientific, and value-neutral manner that ensures it is replicable? Students have many justified concerns about how to begin practicum, how to assess what they are capable of doing, and when to consider themselves trained *enough* in a given theory, technique, or specialty. This anxiety parallels many concerns in the helping professions. Competence in a multicultural, resource-deficient society includes knowing how to assess ourselves, and our impact on clients, students, and others who receive our assistance. Competence also includes knowing how to evaluate the research of others, as well as how to conduct our own ethical and relevant research.

In this chapter, you will have the opportunity to specifically consider the following:

- the definition of competence in our field;
- how one might define the minimal boundaries of competence through education and training, professional credentials, and experience;
- ongoing competence and the role of self-assessment, including accountability and research evidence;

- the contribution of evidence-based practice principles;
- core ethical concerns in research and publication, including essential concerns with multicultural and vulnerable populations;
- research and the importance of informed consent; and
- ethical concerns in research design, funding, and topics.

COMPETENCE: YOU'LL KNOW IT WHEN YOU SEE IT?

Similar to pornography, it is difficult to define competence—though hopefully, the similarities stop there. This difficulty is present for a number of reasons. Competence can be objectively defined by degrees or credentials, or subjectively experienced as a feeling of confidence in a given technique or problem area. Competency includes consideration of knowledge, skills, attitudes, and values (Rodolfa, et al., 2005). Competence can also be related to treatment outcomes. In the mental health field, multiple factors contribute to positive treatment interventions and outcomes (Lambert & Bergin,1994; Mahoney, 1991; Westen, Novotny, & Thompson-Brenner, 2004).

This chapter covers the ethics of professional competence in both applied counseling settings and in research related to our field. To begin, we define the baseline components of professional competence. Second, we focus on one of the most challenging areas for mental health practitioners, multicultural competency. Third, because mental health professionals are increasingly urged to engage in counseling practices that are based on rigorous research methodologies (ACA, 2005, p. 9), we review literature on counseling and psychotherapy treatment outcomes; and finally, we discuss concerns related to conducting ethical and relevant research.

DEFINING THE MINIMAL BOUNDARIES OF COMPETENCE

Ethics codes define the boundaries of competence by education, training, supervised experience, state and national professional credentials, and appropriate professional experience. The ACA and APA ethics codes statements related to competence follow.

ACA *Code of Ethics*

C.2.a. Boundaries of Competence

> Counselors practice only within the boundaries of their competence, based on their education, training, supervised experience, state and national professional credentials, and appropriate professional experience.

NASW *Code of Ethics*

1.04 Competence

> (a) Social workers should provide services and represent themselves as competent only within the boundaries of their education, training, license, certifica-

tion, consultation received, supervised experience, or other relevant professional experience.

APA *Ethical Principles*

2.01 Boundaries of Competence

(a) Psychologists provide services, teach, and conduct research with populations and in areas only within the boundaries of their competence, based on their education, training, supervised experience, consultation, study, or professional experience.

Education and Training

The education and training gold standard in counseling, social work, and psychology is the completion of a master's or doctoral degree from an accredited university. Ideally, the professional training program within the university is accredited by the appropriate professional accrediting body, which insures a nationally accepted level of curricular depth and currency.

Supervised Experience

Most mental health professionals receive oversight and clinical supervision from a licensed provider both during and after academic training. Many academic training programs, in compliance with their accrediting bodies, require that their students receive a specified ratio of qualified clinical supervision for direct mental health service provided. The purpose of clinical supervision is at least two-fold: (a) to protect the consumer; and (b) to help students in training achieve competence (Haynes, et al., 2003). The specific nature and practice of clinical supervision as related to ethics is covered in Chapter 13.

State and National Professional Credentials

Specific professional credentialing options are available through state and national mental health organizations. These credentialing options go beyond simple membership in a professional organization. Almost every state in the United States has licensing laws governing the practice of school counseling, mental health counseling, clinical social work, family counseling, addictions counseling, and clinical or counseling psychology. In contrast with the aspirational nature of professional ethical codes, state licensing laws constitute minimal standards for practicing within a particular mental health profession.

Most states require a combination of academic training, supervised experience (e.g., 3,000 hours post-master's, 5,000 hours postdoctorate), and a passing score on a licensing exam. State licensing requirements serve as a means of consumer protection. In most cases, a state license is necessary to obtain third party reimbursements from private insurance or government sources. When mental practitioners do not abide by state licensing laws, the state may suspend or revoke the professional license. Most states mandate continuing professional education to maintain a professional license.

Appropriate Professional Experience

Although disconcerting, the truth is that once credentialed, school counselors and mental health professionals can choose to work with any client they wish and provide just about any treatment they want. This is one place where the distinction between ethical guidelines and state licensing becomes obvious. Based on the ethics codes, it is inappropriate for new (or old) mental health professionals to provide any kind of services without adequate training and experience. In contrast, state licensing boards and national certification programs rarely monitor closely enough to know whether a professional has overstepped competence boundaries. However, if the licensing or credentialing board receives significant complaints about a particular practitioner's competence, and an inquiry supports the complaint, then the practitioner's license or certification may be suspended or revoked.

Pause for Reflection

In an agency or school setting with limited resources and limitless human need, can you image giving in to the pressure to stretch, to do things you were never trained to do, just because the need is so great and there are few, if any, other options? If you decide to eventually open an independent counseling practice, do you think you might succumb to seeing whatever clients are referred to you, regardless of whether you have adequate professional preparation?

SPECIALTIES, SPECIALIZATION, AND COMPETENCE

The divisions in professional organizations such as ACA and APA reflect the amazing diversity of interests within the profession. At what point does an interest become a specialty? What defines a *specialty* in counseling or psychotherapy and what distinguishes a specialty from an entirely different profession? These are not easy questions to answer.

For master's level counseling specialties, the National Board for Certified Counselors (http://www.nbcc.org/) provides a general, nationally recognized credential (National Certified Counselor), and specialty designation in School Counseling (NCSC), Clinical Mental Health Counselor (CCMHC), and Addictions Counseling (MAC).

For master's level social workers, the NASW offers an entry-level credential, the Qualified Clinical Social Worker (QCSW). The organization also offers an advanced credential, Diplomate in Clinical Social Work (DCSW). There are also specialty designations for youth and family, health care, addictions, case management, and school social work at the master's level.

For doctoral level counseling and clinical psychologists, the American Board of Professional Psychology (ABPP) http://www.abpp.org/abpp_certification_specialties.htm provides official specialty designation in the following areas: child and adolescent, clinical, clinical health, clinical neuropsychology, cognitive-behavioral, counseling, family, forensic, group, organizational and business, psychoanalysis, rehabilitation, and school psychology. On their website, a specialty is defined as "a defined area in the practice of psychology that connotes specialty competency acquired through an organized sequence of formal education, training, and experience." They further note, "Specialties, by definition, are advanced levels of practice that include doctoral and post-doctoral preparation."

Thoughtful and well-respected researchers, faculty, and scholars differ in their opinions about appropriate definitions and representations of specialization. For instance, should counseling be considered a generalist profession, with specialties added by certification, or should states license counselors in different domains separately (Remley & Herlihy, 2005;Remley, 1995)? Or, because states license psychologists simply as *psychologists,* is it ethical to advertise as a "Licensed Clinical Psychologist" or "Licensed Forensic Psychologist" when the test and the license are simply for psychologists (P. Davis, 2005)?

Most would agree that the proliferation of flimsy or bogus certifications confuses or deceives the public and can harm professional identities among mental health providers. It is essential that you investigate certification bodies thoroughly, and not yield to the temptation to bolster your professional standing or identity by adding simplistic or meaningless certifications to your professional credentials. Research is limited in this area, but some studies suggest that credentials themselves do not play a large role in either attracting clients or in client perceptions of helpfulness (Kim, et al., 2003; Farberman, 1997). It may well be that increasing the number of letters following your name, or adding words to your professional description, can cause public confusion (even derision), rather than increased credibility.

Clinical and philosophical differences and the distinct needs of particular populations or problem areas generate motivation for specialization. Market forces and jealously guarded professional designations also contribute to the controversies in this area. As is true in many domains of life, obtaining credentials does not guarantee authentic competence, but specialization clearly requires additional training and supervision.

ONGOING COMPETENCE AND SELF-ASSESSMENT

Look back on your list in Chapter 8, from Applications 8.1: Reasons People Seek Counseling. How would you know if you had the competence to help with the concerns you listed? What kind of self-assessments would you make to determine your competence? The following is a checklist of factors that contribute to competence:

- training, educational, and skill-based readiness—This includes specific coursework, workshops, degrees or certifications, supervised applied experiences, and outside readings the professional may have completed to prepare to work in a certain area.
- access to skilled, specialized supervision—This has to do with the professional's ability to locate a willing and available supervisor who has worked in the methodologies or problem-areas of interest (e.g., Bidell, 2005). The Internet makes long-

---

Applications 9.1

Cross-Cultural Competencies and Objectives

Cross-cultural competencies have many important dimensions. These have been thoughtfully detailed in a guide developed by the Association for Multicultural Counseling and Development and are available at http://www.amcd-aca.org/. The overarching areas of concern include:

- professional awareness of our own cultural values and biases
- professional awareness of our client's cultural heritage and worldview
- professional skill in implementing culturally appropriate intervention strategies (American Counseling Association, 2002)

---

distance supervision a distinct possibility for mental health professionals working in remote areas or in clinical areas that are new, unusual, or especially complicated.

- potential for personal issues to block efficacy—This requires introspection and consultation with trusted colleagues. For instance, a counselor with a recent tragic loss might need to consider screening referrals with issues that would painfully intersect with the loss, or a social worker with a marriage coming apart may need to abstain from couples work. As we covered in Chapter 4, impairment and/or burnout are both ongoing concerns in the helping professions.

- multicultural competence—This is a large and important factor to consider that requires professional self-awareness, knowledge acquisition, and skills training. Refer to Applications 9.1 for an overview of cross-cultural competencies, provided by ACA. Also, refer to the comprehensive article on multicultural education, training, research, practice, and organizational change provided by the APA (2003).

Take time to consider the multicultural competencies mentioned in Applications 9.1, and consider the dynamics described in the following case example.

Case Example: Rasheed, an African-American professional counselor, was employed at a community mental health center. A local physician referred Steve, a 30-year-old Caucasian graduate student, because of recurrent depressive symptoms.

After Rasheed went over the informed consent forms, Steve said somewhat aggressively, "I need to tell you something about myself. I'm what you would probably consider Texan White Trash. I was raised in a trailer park in West Texas. My parents hated Black people and blamed everything that went wrong in their lives on 'niggers.' I grew to hate my parents. When I was 9, I was sexually abused by my uncle and after that, I decided I would do everything and anything I could to get away from my family. That's why I moved here 12 years ago, and I haven't had much contact with them since."

Rasheed nodded. Steve took a breath and continued in a more subdued tone. "But my dad has cancer and my sister keeps calling me, saying that he wants to see me and that I've got to come back home to visit. I'm struggling to face the fact that I should go back and say good-bye to my father before he dies. And the weird thing about this is that now I've come to see you and you seem fine and all that, but your job is to help me go back and be with my father who spent his life hating Blacks. Are you okay with that?"

What are your thoughts and reactions to this case? Does it bring up personal issues for you? If you were in Rasheed's position, would you feel competent to work with Steve? What if Steve discovered that he harbored negative attitudes toward African Americans? Would that make a difference in your response to this scenario?

Of course, expectations of multicultural competence extend to persons with different sexual orientations, religious views, and different ability levels. These competencies must also extend to teachers, supervisors, and researchers. Rhoda Olkin (2004) writes:

> Culturally-competent research includes an awareness that there is a split in the ways we conceptualize disability. In an older, more medically oriented model, the emphasis is on disability and accommodation. The disability is the defining feature of the person in question, and this serves to distance the person from the helper, the researcher, etc. . . . A more current and client-centered model, the emphasis is less on disability and more on strengths and wellness. In this model, the disabled person is incorporated into the community at large, or included directly in designing and implementing research. (p. 332)

COMPETENCE, ACCOUNTABILITY, AND RESEARCH EVIDENCE

Thus far, the history of mental health counseling and psychotherapy has been characterized by four *forces*. In chronological order, these include:

- psychoanalysis
- behaviorism
- existential-humanism
- multiculturalism

Although some have idealistically argued that the fifth force should be social justice, political and economic tensions in our culture are pulling in another direction. In reality, a candidate that seems to be elbowing its way into position for the fifth force is *accountability*. Rainer (1996) states: "We have entered into an age of accountability for the provision of psychotherapy services to individuals and their intimate systems" (p. 159); and Bartley and colleagues (2003) add, "Counselor educators are faced with the challenge of preparing new counselors for employment in practices where evidence-based interventions is becoming standard of care . . . the standards set forth by EBR should drive how counselor educators should train mental health and school counselors" (pp. 3–4).

Several different terms are used to discuss the accountability movement, including: (a) empirically supported (or validated) treatments (Procedures, 1995); (b) best practices (Shelton & James, 2005); and (c) evidence-based practice (Myers & Harper, 2004; Nemec, 2004). The term *best practices* has primarily been used within school and school counseling settings, while *empirically supported treatments* (ESTs) and *evidence-based practice* (EBP) have been used within research and academic psychology and counseling.

The accountability movement has implications that are both practical and ethical. In the next section, we provide a brief history of counseling and psychotherapy outcomes research because such research helps contextualize the accountability movement. Later in the chapter, we also cover accountability issues related to school counseling.

COUNSELING AND PSYCHOTHERAPY OUTCOMES RESEARCH

In the late 1970s, researchers essentially declared that all forms of psychotherapy are generally effective (Luborsky, Singer, & Luborsky, 1975; Smith & Glass, 1977; Smith, Glass, & Miller, 1980). Despite this declaration many individuals, both within and outside the mental health professions, continue to question the efficacy of counseling and psychotherapy (Masson, 1988; Smail, 1984). As Rainer (1996) notes:

> The paradigm of the health care environment has shifted to a "cost effective" focus. Mental health professionals—both researchers and clinicians—are now called on to demonstrate the full value of psychotherapy when it is applied to commonly encountered crises in life. (p. 159)

Essentially, mental health professionals want to make money providing professional services, while insurance companies and other third party payers want to reduce the amount of money they pay for health services in general and mental health services in particular (typically referred to as "cost containment"). Consequently, there has been a strong move among academics and mental health professionals to "prove" or establish the validity of various psychotherapeutic treatment approaches. This mentality is probably best captured in the movement within clinical psychology originally referred to as *empirically validated treatments* (Procedures, 1995).

A list of empirically validated treatments was originally compiled by APA's Division 12 Task Force on Promotion and Dissemination of Psychological Procedures (1995). This group, born from "social, economic, and political exigency" (Deegear & Lawson, 2003, p. 271), originally established a list of 18 "empirically validated treatments" based primarily on the Food and Drug Administrations procedures for determining medication as safe and effective (Beutler, 1998).

Not surprisingly, the list stirred up a significant controversy. Most of the 18 treatments included were behavioral or cognitive behavioral and many popular approaches to counseling were excluded. Naturally, advocates and practitioners of excluded approaches were unhappy (Silverman, 1996; Bohart, O'Hara, & Leitner, 1998; Garfield, 1998). See Digressions for Deliberation 9.1 for an interesting memory about professional preferences and counseling.

The reaction to the initial empirically validated treatment list inspired at least two significant changes to the task force's approach. First, the phrase *empirically validated treatments* was replaced with *empirically supported treatments* (ESTs). Second, additional treatments were added to the original list. These modifications did not satisfy those who view the procedures and logic associated with identifying ESTs to be flawed. Many concerns have surfaced in the literature, including the omission of preventative or developmental interventions, such as career counseling (Wampold, Lichtenberg, &

===== **Digressions for Deliberation 9.1** =====

Who Do Behavioral Scientists Seek When They Need Counseling?

In 1982, I (JSF) attended an Association for the Advancement of Behavior Therapy (AABT) conference, where I saw impressive presentations by Michael Mahoney, Joseph Wolpe, and other prominent behaviorists. But perhaps the presentation that impressed me the most was by Marvin Goldfried, coauthor of the authoritative text on behavior therapy at that time (Goldfried & Davison, 1976). I can't recall his exact words, but his meaning was clear. Dr. Goldfried speculated about why so many staunch behaviorists, himself included, chose to go to nonbehavioral clinicians when seeking psychotherapy. He spoke about the emotional power of moving from one chair to another in Gestalt therapy, and wondered aloud about why he and his empirically minded colleagues would choose to get therapy from nonempirically oriented clinicians.

Gilroy, Carroll, and Murra (2002) surveyed 1,000 members of the Counseling Psychology division of the American Psychological Association (Division 17) about their own experiences with clinical depression and treatment. One hundred sixty-seven of 425 respondents reported obtaining therapy for their depressive symptoms from therapists with the following theoretical orientations:

- psychodynamic (40%)
- gestalt, systems, and other (19%)
- eclectic (18%)
- cognitive-behavioral (12%)
- humanistic (existential/feminist; 11%)

Twenty years after Goldfried's disclosure at AABT, it still appears that when seeking counseling for themselves, counselors do not necessarily seek empirically focused orientations. These findings are particularly surprising given the fact that scientific research on cognitive-behavioral treatment efficacy for depressive symptoms is so robust.

I have one last recollection about Dr. Goldfried's musings. He said something like, "One reason for this is that we're capable of doing behavior therapy on ourselves, so when we're in distress, it makes sense to seek help from someone who will help us look at ourselves and our issues from a different perspective." His statement makes me wonder whether psychodynamically oriented therapists seek behavior therapy more often than psychodynamic therapy. This would make an excellent inquiry.

Waehler, 2005), the fact that the ESTs are validated on single-diagnosis clients under experimental conditions, rather than in clinical practices (Westen, Novotny, & Thompson-Brenner, 2004), and the fact that the therapy relationship is ignored (Norcross, 2002).

Some fear that managed care organizations may misuse EST research findings to control practice in the real world, denying payment to anyone but those who agree to use manualized treatments that some feel cause counselors to feel more like technicians

(Garfield, 1998; Silverman, 1996; Westen, Novotny, & Thompson-Brenner, 2005). Further, equating the use of ESTs and other outcome-based treatments with competence insinuates a narrowing and simplification of a complex professional duty. The preceding concerns are serious, and obviously, ethical mental health practitioners must define efficacy and professional competence more broadly than the empirically supported treatments approach.

ACA *Code of Ethics*

C.6.e. Scientific Bases for Treatment Modalities

Counselors use techniques/procedures/modalities that are grounded in theory and/or have an empirical or scientific foundation. Counselors who do not must define the techniques/procedures as "unproven" or "developing" and explain the potential risks and ethical considerations of using such techniques/procedures and take steps to protect clients from possible harm.

APA *Ethical Principles*

2. Competence

2.04 Bases for Scientific and Professional Judgments

Psychologists' work is based upon established scientific and professional knowledge of the discipline.

NASW *Code of Ethics*

4.01 Competence

(c) Social workers should base practice on recognized knowledge, including empirically based knowledge, relevant to social work and social work ethics.

Although the ACA and APA codes emphasize "scientific" foundations for therapy interventions, they also recognize that practitioners can maintain an ethical practice as long as their approaches are based on established theory/professional knowledge. However, there is no denying the importance of understanding and using scientific data to guide mental health treatment. For example, consider this statement:

Because of research on ESTs, we know, for example, that exposure-based treatments can be very useful for a substantial subset of patients with Posttraumatic Stress Disorder (PTSD) and Panic Disorder. Given that these are two very troubling disorders with enormous consequences for life satisfaction, the refinement of exposure-based techniques for these disorders represents a tremendous accomplishment, about which every clinician should know. (Westen, Novotny, & Thompson-Brenner, 2005, p. 427)

As noted earlier, the problem is that we do not yet have consensus about the interactive roles of techniques, common factors, multiple diagnoses, prevention, early intervention, and education (Frank & Frank, 1991). Staying informed is ethically essential as our field continues to grapple with the broader concepts and complications

---

Digressions for Deliberation 9.2

Child and Adolescent Treatment that Works (or Not)

The following commentary is from a review of *Psychotherapy for Children and Adolescents: Evidence-Based Treatments and Case Examples,* by Dr. Weisz, a prolific writer, researcher, and proponent of ESTs. This review appeared in the *American Journal of Psychiatry,* written by Lawrence Hartmann, M.D (2005).

Dr. Harmann notes, "A young or relatively naïve reader" might actually mistake the book for a general text about positive or "good" approaches to child and adolescent treatment. He then lists the issues that this "neat and accurate" book has left out regarding real-life child and adolescent treatment:

> It avoids biological psychiatry. It nearly wholly avoids not only dynamic psychiatry and the unconscious but also meanings, psychological understanding of feelings, relationships, conflicts, defenses, anger, pain, shame, guilt, and self-deception. It has a rather narrow view of human adaptation. It has nearly nothing to say about the nature of the therapist, and the patient's relationship with him or her. It says little about the difficulties of listening, to oneself and to others. It nearly wholly avoids the family. It nearly wholly avoids social psychiatry: society, culture, race, class, prejudice, poverty, ethnicity, schools, religions, public economic institutions and arrangements, etc. It tends to avoid development. It accepts 6 months as an adequate follow-up in child studies. It tends to avoid causality. It nearly wholly avoids prevention. It avoids severe illness, such as autism, pervasive developmental disorder, schizophrenia, bipolar disorder, severe depression, and major substance abuse. It evades intelligence, learning disorders, psychosomatic disorders, parental illness or absence or death, other lack of good enough parenting, neurological and other physical illness, divorce, many problems with sex and aggression, abuse and neglect, loss, trauma, and posttraumatic stress disorder. (p. 1231)

Hartmann's list should not be viewed simply as a criticism of Weisz's generally excellent and well-regarded work, but rather an acknowledgment of the complexities involved in helping. We hope the list will inspire you to keep reading, studying, and getting supervision so that you can competently offer services to children, adolescents, and their families. The list certainly illustrates why providing good counseling and psychotherapy for young people is so challenging.

---

of evidence-based counseling and accountability. See Digressions for Deliberation 9.2 for an example.

SEARCHING FOR COMPROMISE: EVIDENCE-BASED PRACTICE PRINCIPLES

After reading about the power and flaws associated with empirically supported treatments, we are left with an ethical quandary. Do ethical mental health professionals jump on the "empirical" bandwagon and obtain training only in empirically supported, manual-based treatments? Or, do ethical counselors focus on the flaws within the empirically supported treatment movement and ignore the growing mandate for manualized best practices?

As usual, the ethical answer lies somewhere in the middle—in a place where we value the logic of empirical research and the added information provided by personal experience. In the next sections we identify and describe key components of an evidence-based practice for mental health professionals and for school counselors.

Evidence-Based Mental Health Practice

Sexton and Liddle (2001) describe three components of an evidence-based mental health practice. These components include: "(a) Using the general trends from meta-analyses and critical review studies that identify broad trends relevant for practice; (b) identifying specific protocols that offer direct and specific guidance for intervening with specific clients in specific settings; and (c) measuring outcomes on a local level to continually inform the clinician's practice" (p. 388).

Using the general trends.   There are many sources of general empirical trends in mental health practice. In an article titled "Empirically Based Decision Making in Clinical Practice," Beutler (2000) identified eight optimal treatment principles. The following list is based on Beutler's principles [with our additional comments in brackets]. Because these principles are general and because they are so good, it is helpful to read them at least twice.

- Therapeutic change is greatest when therapists are skillful and provide trust, acceptance, acknowledgment, collaboration, and respect for the client within an environment that both supports risk and provides maximal safety. [This principle is based on decades of research that supports the central function of a therapeutic alliance in positive treatment outcome (Rogers, 1957; Norcross, 2002).]
- Therapeutic change is most likely when the counseling procedures do not evoke client resistance. [Research on motivational interviewing has been especially informative regarding the fact that therapist confrontation is likely to evoke resistance and interferes with positive treatment outcomes (Miller & Rollnick, 2002).]
- Therapeutic change is most likely when clients are exposed to objects or targets of behavioral and emotional avoidance. [This principle articulates the efficacy of exposure treatments, which have been documented since Mary Cover Jones's early experiments (Jones, 1924) and Joseph Wolpe's publication of *Psychotherapy by Reciprocal Inhibition* (Wolpe, 1958).]
- Therapeutic change is greatest when clients are stimulated to emotional arousal in a safe environment until problematic responses diminish or extinguish. [Again, this refers to the behavior therapy exposure and extinction paradigm, but also might be explained by the psychoanalytically oriented corrective emotional experience (Alexander & French, 1946).]
- Therapeutic change is most likely if the initial focus of change efforts is to build new skills and alter disruptive symptoms [Clients often do best when they immediately begin learning new skills, often within the context of behavioral response

prevention (Foa, Rothbaum, & Furr, 2003). Immediate skill-building seems to facilitate initial hope and motivation (Frank & Frank, 1991).]

- Therapeutic change is greatest when the relative balance of interventions either favors the use of skill building and symptom removal procedures among clients who externalize or favors the use of insight and relationship-focused procedures among clients who internalize. [This differential treatment principle speaks to the fact that some clients seem to need more concrete interventions, while others thrive with more abstract, relationship-based interventions (Linehan, 1993; Ackerman, Benjamin, Beutler, Gelso, Goldfried, Hill, et al., 2001).]

- Therapeutic change is greatest when the directiveness of the intervention is either inversely correspondent with clients' current resistance or authoritatively prescribes a continuation of the symptomatic behavior. [When clients are not resistant, then very directive interventions can be successful; when they are resistant, less directive interventions are warranted; and sometimes paradoxical strategies are effective when resistance is high (Shoham-Salomon & Rosenthal, 1987).]

- The likelihood of therapeutic change is greatest when clients' emotional stress is moderate, neither being excessively high nor excessively low. [Similar to the transtheoretical change model, this principle suggests there is an optimal time for effective therapy to occur (Prochaska & DiClemente, 1982).]

Identifying specific protocols.   Sexton and Liddle (2001) stated: "broad and general findings do not help practitioners know exactly which interventions program to apply to which client" (p. 389), which is why it is recommended that practitioners explore more specific protocols. The good news (and perhaps the bad news as well) is that there is no shortage of specific protocols, manual-based therapies, and evidence-based strategies available to therapists (see Applications 9.2 for information about how to identify specific evidence-based or empirically supported treatment protocols).

Measuring outcomes.   As research-oriented standards continue to be integrated into mental health professional ethics codes, there will be additional pressure for individual practitioners to become "local clinical scientist[s]" (Sexton & Liddle, 2001, p. 390). To address this pressure, Sexton and Liddle recommend that mental health counselors begin using measures of client progress with standardized instruments related to specific problem areas.

To further specify best practices in mental health counseling, the ACA recently established a Practice Research Network (Bradley, Sexton, & Smith, 2005). Practice Research Networks (PRNs) are collaborative groups of health care or mental health care providers who work to collect data on a range of service delivery and outcomes issues. The advantage of establishing PRNs is that they help bridge the gap between service providers and clinical research.

Evidence-Based School Counseling Practice

Professional school counselors have begun a strong push toward accountability. This push includes the establishment of the Center for School Counseling Outcome Research

=== **Applications 9.2** ===

Resource Information on Specific
Evidence-Based Treatment Protocols

The information available on evidence-based treatments is voluminous and confusing. The original listing of empirically validated treatments from the APA Division 12 Task Force is difficult to obtain online. An updated list, published in 1998, is available at http://home.comcast.net/~dave.combs/valther.pdf. The updated list includes 16 "well established" treatments and 55 "probably efficacious" treatments (Chambless, Baker, Baucom, Beutler, Calhoun, Crits-Cristoph, et al., 1998).

The Center for School Counseling Outcome Research (CSCOR) is online at http://www.umass.edu/schoolcounseling/services.htm. This site publishes quarterly research briefs that highlight important contributions to the school counseling outcomes research. You can also sign up for a listserv and access other resources.

The Society of Clinical Psychology also has a website with information about empirically supported treatments at http://www.apa.org/divisions/div12/rev_est/.

At http://www.effectivechildtherapy.com/ you can read about evidence-based treatments for children and adolescents.

(CSCOR) at the University of Massachusetts. The following quote is from their website at http://www.umass.edu/schoolcounseling/ : "CSCOR is dedicated to improving the practice of school counseling by developing the research base that is necessary for responsible and effective practice" (Carey, 2000).

Research on school counseling programs and intervention efficacy has been summarized in several articles, book chapters, and online at CSCOR's website. Similar to the ACA-PRN established for mental health counseling, many counselor educators and school counselors are advocating increased collaborative, action research (Rowell, 2005). However, at this point, empirical research on school counseling is limited, so the following statements should be considered as hypotheses about school counseling efficacy, rather than firm conclusions.

- Prevention programs in school settings are moderately effective. For example, there are data indicating that the Peacebuilders program and Second Step reduce school violence and interpersonal aggression in elementary schools (Flannery, Vazsonyi, Liau, Guo, Powell, Atha, et al., 2003).

- Counseling programs in school settings are moderately to very effective. Research on school counseling programs generally show that individual counseling within schools has moderate to strong effect sizes (Whiston, 2003).

- School counseling interventions appear more effective during elementary and secondary years (Prout & Prout, 1998). Counseling for middle-school students has shown fewer clear, positive results (Whiston, Sexton, & Lasoff, 1998).

- Programs for low-achieving students tend to be more effective when students participate voluntarily (Wilson, 1986).

- The research findings are mixed with regard to whether it is more effective when students receive group versus individual counseling. Generally, group counseling for elementary-school students has more empirical support than group work with high-school students (Whiston, 2003).

- There is no clear empirical support for classroom guidance activities, although there are some results suggesting that programs focusing on self-esteem in elementary-school children may help improve academic achievement (Whiston et al., 1998).

- Research on career guidance and counseling services is generally positive and especially positive when the career guidance is delivered in a one-on-one setting (Whiston et al., 1998).

- There is only minimal support for the effectiveness of school peer mediation programs (Gerber & Terry-Day, 1999).

- The benefit of parent training and family counseling is well-established, although family counseling is generally outside the role of school counselors (Henggeler, 2003).

- When functioning as consultants, the research suggests that a direct, problem-solving approach is most effective (Zins, 1993).

Outcomes Research on Divergent Minority Groups

As the field of mental health has matured, so has the interest and willingness to evaluate what forms of counseling or related interventions are effective for members of minority groups (Atkinson, Bui, & Mori, 2001). There is clear evidence that one size or form of therapy is not equally effective for different cultural groups. Stanley Sue (1998) has translated this fact into a multicultural competency that he refers to as "Dynamic sizing." Ethical and effective multicultural counselors need to remember that even individuals within a common cultural group may respond differently to the same counselor intervention; the effectiveness of one size or form of therapy often may not generalize within a specific cultural group and certainly may not generalize across cultures.

When outcomes research focuses on ethnic and cultural variables, the results are often complex. For example, some studies have shown that ethnic matching (matching professional and client on the basis of ethnic origin) facilitates positive treatment outcomes (Jerrel, 1995), while other studies suggest ethnic matching has little effect (Maramba, & Hall, 2002). For example, in a recent study of 1,946 child and adolescent community mental health center clients, ethnic matching showed no significance (after controlling for seven important variables), except in cases of African-American youth (Gamst, Dana, Der-Karabetian, & Kramer, 2004).

Ethical practitioners will recognize the general cultural limitations of treatment outcomes research. Olkin (2004) noted that these limitations are true not only for clients from different races, but also for clients with disabilities. She stated: "People with disabilities are less likely than those without disabilities to be included as research participants, as many aspects of research design may be barriers to participation" (2004,

p. 332). To help include disabled clients in treatment research protocols, Olkin recommends that researchers: (a) remove their pathologizing manner of looking at the disabled, (b) make material available in alternate formats, (c) do effective outreach to the disabled community, and (d) when appropriate, specify disability groups (pp. 336–38).

Future treatment outcomes research should make efforts to isolate variables in addition to disability. These variables might include client age, sex, poverty conditions, and other factors that could mediate or moderate treatment efficacy. For example, some research reviews on treatments for older adults suggest that supportive psychotherapy groups may be as effective (or even more so) in treating anxiety than standard cognitive-behavioral treatment protocols (Myers & Harper, 2004). The ethical professional should treat all clients as individuals while remaining informed about specific research that might guide treatment selection and the counseling process.

ETHICAL CONCERNS IN RESEARCH AND PUBLICATION

As can be seen in earlier sections in this chapter, such research is a complicated endeavor that calls into question very basic ethical concerns. How do we more efficiently and effectively help people? What, exactly, should be defined as *help*? The more general fields of experimental, social, and developmental psychology include inquiry into many aspects of human functioning. Professionals in counseling or related applied areas are often more directly interested in conducting research that contributes to our understanding of how to facilitate positive change in our clients (Remley & Herlihy, 2005).

Pause for Reflection

The classic question, "How do you know what you think you know?" is apropos about here (Anchin, 2005). Humans are notoriously stubborn about their preferred ways of knowing, yet able to assume a meta-perspective that allows them to question what they've assumed to be true. What "truths" have you changed your mind about? What research findings do you trust or distrust?

Most of the APA's and ACA's research and publication ethical principles can be boiled down to a few basic "Commandments." They include:

- Do not lie (when reporting results, assigning authorship, communication with IRB, or directly to participants, unless deception is justified in advance).
- Do not cheat (no plagiarism, no publishing the same data twice, no fudging or massaging the data).
- Do not steal (someone else's work or ideas, grant money, or information from participants without their consent).
- Do not have sex (with research participants or research assistants).
- Do not exploit (student researchers, assistants, vulnerable or culturally diverse participants, or funding sources).

- Do not break trust (by failing to obtain informed consent, or letting anyone have access to the participants' identities unless permission was obtained in advance).
- Do not lose focus (by allowing conflicts of interest to bias your research or relationships).

As suggested from the preceding list, ethical researchers strive to protect vulnerable or subordinate participants from feeling coerced, through financial, educational, or relational means. However, at an aspirational level, the ethics of research go much deeper (Olkin, 2004; Warner & Roberts, 2004) and cover a much broader range of concerns (Anchin, 2005).

Research with Multicultural and Vulnerable Populations

Historically, medical, pharmaceutical, and psychological researchers have taken advantage of vulnerable populations that were not able to initiate an informed refusal process. These populations have included prison inmates, low income individuals/families, children, and minority groups. With regard to research with children, Stiffman and Brown (2005) state:

> Children's vulnerability is greater than that of adults, because their lack of competence may lead to involuntary or nonvoluntary assent. In addition, the adult consenting may not necessarily have the child's best interests at heart. In the case of institutionalized children or children who are in state custody, the legal consenting guardian may be far from the ideal protective caregiver. Research has an unfortunate history of abusing or exploiting children as research participants. (p. 2)

Another complicated and vulnerable group of people are the survivors of trauma, crisis, and/or disaster (Collogon, Tuma, Dolan-Sewell, Borja, & Fleishman, 2004). While there is a pressing need to evaluate interventions, people who have endured life-threatening circumstances or immense losses may not be in a position to give authentic informed consent to serve as research participants.

The past omission and/or mistreatment of nondominant or dependent populations has understandably contributed to the reluctance of minority populations to embrace participating in research. The horrific examples that surfaced in the Nuremberg trials, or the gross and malicious negligence evidenced in the Tuskegee research has proven there are substantial reasons for this reluctance (Shavers, Lynch, & Bermeister, 2000).

Overburdened researchers may sometimes be tempted to give up or minimize the importance of including valid diverse points of view in their work. For the reasons previously noted, and because there are simply fewer possible participants in these groups, it isn't easy to do the work necessary for responsible inclusion. However, neither the deontologists nor the utilitarians (not to mention the feminists) would let researchers off the ethical hook just because inclusion is difficult. We all suffer diminished access to accuracy and richness when parts of the human family are silenced, ignored, exploited, or oppressed. Charmaine Williams (2005) writes:

From a deontological perspective, including racial and ethnic diversity in research samples responds to a moral expectation of fairness. . . . From a utilitarian perspective, the ethical appropriateness of including racial and ethnic diversity in research samples is determined by an analysis of the good that it confers to study participants and society as a whole. (p. 511)

As a partial response to omissions and participant exploitation, obtaining the correct informed consent for research has become much more complex proposition, detailed in the next section.

Research and Informed Consent

In codes addressing the ethics of research and publication, the subsection on informed consent is the longest and most detailed. Informed consent for research participation has become a complex legal and ethical process governed by institutional review boards (IRBs) designed to protect the rights of research participants *and* protect the institution from research-related litigation. Unfortunately, it appears that the complexity may, at times, work against the actual intent of empowering research participants to make knowledgeable choices or to remember the basics of their consent (Mann, 1994). In medical research, Chilean Professor, M. Kottow (2004) notes the ongoing struggle to preserve and advance the autonomy of all, noting "Autonomy is also eroded when subjects receive placebos or insufficient treatment," or are denied the benefits of the research, or endure "other unacceptable conditions offered to destitute populations on the presumption that poverty and lack of education entail the inability to exercise autonomy and make decision" (p. 565).

Most university or hospital IRBs will have a specific list of informed consent items that must be included in research participant informed consent forms. The following checklist represents an integration of the concerns present in the APA, ACA, and NASW ethical codes; most institutional forms are likely to require very similar content. Researchers should include the following items in their informed consent forms for research participants:

1. The purpose of the research, expected duration, and procedures.
2. Participant right to decline or withdraw from participation at any time without penalty.
3. Foreseeable consequences of declining or withdrawing.
4. Potential risks, discomfort, or adverse effects that may be associated with participation.
5. Potential research participation benefits.
6. Limits of confidentiality.
7. Incentives for participation, including possible financial compensation.
8. Whom to contact with questions about the research protocol.
9. Identification of any experimental procedures.
10. Services that will or will not be available to the control group (if utilized).
11. How participants will be assigned to treatment and/or control groups.

12. Available alternative treatments available if the individual does not want to participate.

13. Specific information about recordings of the participant that may be obtained and retained.

14. Potential expenses associated with the research, including whether payment will be sought from a third party payer (e.g., Medicaid, private insurance).

15. When and how debriefing from the experiment will be provided.

16. The format and potential target audiences for the dissemination of research findings.

This list may seem overwhelming, but it not only serves to protect participants, it actually helps researchers think through the meaning, plausibility, and value of their research ideas.

Pause for Reflection

Again, we find ourselves wrestling with how to encode morality. Just as we mulled over in Chapter 3, does a code or set of rules really engender or enforce morality? Are researchers more ethical now (assuming they are) because of the rules, or because of an awareness of the painful outcomes of atrocious, morally bereft research? By including the information in Applications 9.3, have we achieved the spirit of informed consent?

At the global level, there are many reasons for attention to the ethics of research across cultures. The complexities of obtaining meaningful informed consent vastly increase across cultural and language barriers, and the issues of appropriate design and competent interpretation of findings are also highly salient (Christakis, 1992).

Ethics in Qualitative, Quantitative, and Mixed Designs

Because quantitative research methods have provided the dominant paradigm for inquiry in the behavioral sciences for so long, the general ethical concerns discussed in this chapter are most directly related to these methods. In addition, issues such as the cost of assignment to a waiting list control, rather than the treatment group, unwarranted deception, placebo washout practices, and the issues of statistical significance as opposed to clinical significance are all important to consider in advanced research courses.

There is an inescapable and central relationship between the researcher, the research method(s), and the research question. Just as "method for method's sake" is questionable (Holloway & Todres, 2003, p. 346), so to is the abdication of responsible method choice.

Ethical Concerns with Funding and Findings

Over the past two decades, external funding has become a significant budget line item for most universities, both public and private. In some cases, there is no doubt but that

===== Applications 9.3 =====

Guidance from a Qualitative Researcher

by Cathy Jenni

Qualitative approaches have appeal to researchers seeking knowledge about marginalized groups, unique experiences, and deeper understanding of complex or ambiguous situations (Haverkamp, 2005). Qualitative research designs feature discovery. In qualitative models, knowledge emerges "up" from the everyday lives of particular people (Giorgi, 1986). The magnetic pull of qualitative work, because it feels honest and trustworthy, can blind researchers to the singular ethical challenges inherent primarily in the intimacy between the subject, researcher, and consumer of qualitative work.

Qualitative approaches are diverse, but all generate unique ethical dilemmas. Confidentiality is inevitably partial (Christians, 2000). Both danger to self or others and previously unreported abuse come to mind. But confidentiality is also compromised by the distinctiveness of certain subjects (first generation Hmong college graduates are an example). The depth of verbal or written material contains details that may reveal identity. I once supervised a doctoral dissertation in which a small phrase used by a subject about her spouse, a distant acquaintance of mine, immediately told me the exact identity of the subject and her husband. Direct quotes from subjects are frequent in published studies. Dissertations may contain entire interviews or other material. Disguising identifying information is standard, but what is identifying may be known only when a reader recognizes it. Disguised information can also compromise research design because subject characteristics are central to the findings (Haverkamp, 2005). Qualitative researchers have a penchant for researching socially stigmatizing situations or people, such as prison inmates, women who are HIV-positive, or married men who are bisexually active. There can be grave consequences when confidentiality is compromised.

Informed consent offers ambiguities as well. Though the qualitative researcher will attempt to identify foreseeable events that may occur as a result of the subject's participation, because qualitative work is focused on discovery, what is to be discovered is not specifically known in advance. Discovery can take subjects where they did not expect to go (Fine, Weis, Weseen, & Wong, 2000). Though it is standard to inform subjects that they may withdraw from a study at any time, the power differential between subject and researcher may leave this option in the background for both (Haverkamp, 2005). Material that emerges may be disturbing and subjects may require referral to sources of assistance. The subject's participation in data gathering may lead to changes in perceptions of important relationships or life situations. Whether this is helpful or harmful in the long run, the subject could not consent in advance. Subjects will likely speak about others who have not consented to the research as well. While any research is an "intervention," the depth and intimacy that characterizes

---

Applications 9.3 (continued)

qualitative approaches may influence subjects powerfully, with unknown future consequences.

Competence is an ongoing concern. Researchers may not have received substantial training in qualitative approaches. Qualitative research has its own rigorous standards and procedures (Creswell, 2003) and these can be poorly understood or invisible. In some studies qualitative data analysis is neither systematic nor accomplished according to a preestablished, well-founded plan. Even the philosophical foundations of qualitative work differ from the quantitative, and misunderstanding can lead to the imposition of quantitative language and standards on qualitative approaches. The resulting design may produce compromised results. Such research can have harmful effects on the very individuals who graciously revealed the intimate details of their lives. Qualitative work requires that researchers conceptualize their relationships with subjects as calling for continuous attention to emergent, potential harm. This means resolute alertness to each subject's well-being and safety before, during, and after the research is analyzed, reported, and applied.

---

the "tail" (external funding) has begun to wag the "dog" (university systems). For example, you might want to gather some information on the amount of research and corporate money obtained by your college or university on an annual basis.

The David Healy case illustrates the power of finances over ethics. In 1997, before age 50, Healy, a psychiatrist in Wales, established himself as a major psychiatric historian. Soon afterward, however, he conducted a research study wherein several "normal" college students became acutely suicidal after taking the antidepressant sertraline (Zoloft; Healy, Langmaack, & Savage, 1999). Consequently, he began researching and speaking about the fact that not only Zoloft, but also other antidepressants, like Prozac, produce suicidal impulses in a significant minority of individuals. In 2001, just after having been offered a prestigious position at the University of Toronto, Dr. Healy gave a public lecture about Prozac's contributions to suicidality. Shortly thereafter, the University of Toronto rescinded its job offer. Later, Healy sued and the University of Toronto settled the case out of court. The implied bottom line: pharmaceutical influence kept Dr. Healy out of Toronto—even after he had started furnishing his office (D. Healy, personal communication, April 2001).

Research Topics: Choosing Wisely

Significant time and resources are absorbed by behavioral science research. "Poor quality of research design, poor quality of data analysis, and poor quality of reporting of research findings all lessen the ethical justification of any type of research project" (Rosenthal, 1994, p. 128). Research competence is clearly essential to conduct ethically sound research. Further, clinical sensitivity and a willingness to explore the costs and risks in relation to each other are an ethical mandate.

Research consultation and/or research teams are helpful sources of support and guidance when troubleshooting a research design for ethical concerns and scientific merit (Rosenthal & Rosnow, 1991). Unfortunately, the realities of time and resource constraints sometimes limit this kind of research deliberation.

CHAPTER WRAP-UP

Competence is a basic expectation of all professionals. Professionals have to hold this expectation in tension with the knowledge that we are all, by necessity and hopefully by choice, lifelong learners. While we may consider ourselves competent at any given time, there is always room to grow, to add new skills, to become better, wiser, and more capable. Competence is assessed many ways. Do you have the right degrees? Training? Licenses or credentials? Have you passed the right exams? Have you obtained enough supervised experience? Are you able to demonstrate the effectiveness of what you do? These are all questions that competent professionals ask themselves as they develop.

Understanding research methods and outcomes is directly related to both clinical and research competence. Ethical concerns in research have both a pragmatic set of rules and guidelines, and a rich, deep ocean of ethical points to ponder—leading to some of the most basic questions humans ask themselves: How do I know what I know? On whose authority will I accept knowledge to be accurate? In what ways do my answers to those first two questions limit my grasp of the world?

SECTION THREE

SPECIFIC SPECIALTIES AND PROFESSIONAL IDENTITIES

Chapter Ten

COUNSELING IN THE SCHOOLS

By John Sommers-Flanagan, Nancy Bodenhorn,
and Rita Sommers-Flanagan

> *Birdfoot's Grampa*
> *The old man*
> *must have stopped our car*
> *two dozen times to climb out*
> *and gather into his hands*
> *the small toads blinded*
> *by our lights and leaping,*
> *live drops of rain.*
> *The rain was falling,*
> *a mist about his white hair*
> *and I kept saying*
> *you can't save them all*
> *accept it, get back in*
> *we've got places to go.*
> *But, leathery hands full*
> *of wet brown life*
> *knee deep in the summer*
> *roadside grass,*
> *he just smiled and said*
> they have places to go to
> too.
>
> —Joseph Burchac

CHAPTER ORIENTATION

As one of the largest and most distinct specialties in the counseling field, professional school counselors find themselves knee deep in challenging predicaments. First and foremost, school counselors work for the well-being and welfare of their vulnerable and sometimes "blinded by the lights" charges—the students. Although this is the ethical school counselor's primary focus, concurrently, school counselors also serve teachers, principals, parents, and the community, all of whom sometimes view themselves as the school counselor's number one priority. In addition, schools are generally governed by superintendents and school boards. The local community, as well as state and federal laws, all exert influence over issues such as school safety, academic success of students, sex education, and teen pregnancy. This chapter examines the complex and competing ethical demands that school counselors are likely to experience. Throughout the chapter we emphasize the role, nature, and behaviors associated with ethical school counseling.

Specifically, in this chapter you will consider the following:

- the professional nature and identity of school counseling, including history and trends;
- particular ethical challenges in school counseling;
- the role and function of the professional school counselor;
- confidentiality and the reasons it can be so complicated;
- sexual abuse and harassment concerns;
- informed consent approaches for students and parents;
- legal issues and concerns;
- multiple roles and relationships—how to recognize and juggle them;
- hot areas—sex, drugs, pregnancy, eating disorders, and suicide;
- career and college guidance;
- doing ethical group work; and
- a school-specific ethical decision-making model.

PROFESSIONAL SCHOOL COUNSELING

Over the past 100 years or so, our educational systems have undergone nearly constant change and evolution. The helping and guiding functions associated with professional school counseling have changed correspondingly. Because professional identity informs ethical behavior so directly, we begin this chapter with a short historical overview.

The History

Young people have probably always received informal advice, guidance, and counseling from people outside their homes. For example, educators, supervisors, bosses, and mentors have often sought to educate children about nonacademic subjects, such as health, emotional regulation and well-being, social skills, study skills, and making positive personal and career choices.

Like many important advances in human history, the foundations of modern counseling (lifespan developmental focus, advocacy, and wellness) came together thanks to a serendipitous combination of forces. By the late 1800s, vocational guidance was an idea that had come of age in the United States. Historians note George A. Merrill's vocational education efforts in California, Jesse B. Davis's role as an educational and vocational counselor for high school students in Detroit, and of course, Frank Parsons' influential work in Boston (Zunker, 2002).

Parsons' contributions usually get significant attention, perhaps due to his many accomplishments, his social justice and feminist writings, and his connection with Pauline Agassiz Shaw (1841–1917). The wealthy Agassiz Shaw devoted her life to supporting education for all. In Boston, she opened the first kindergarten in 1877. By 1883, she was supporting 31 Boston-area kindergartens and had founded day nurseries that later became settlement houses (Lazerson, 1971). In the meantime, she also supported a weekly suffrage newspaper and raised five children. In 1901, she established the Civic Service House in Boston to provide educational opportunities for immigrants and young persons seeking work (G. Nichols, 2005). Frank Parsons became director of one of the Civic Service House programs called the Breadwinner's Institute (Zunker, 2002).

This opportunity appeared to spur Parsons on. He organized what was called the Bureau of Vocational Guidance, which was used to train young men to be counselors and managers for YMCA's schools, colleges, and businesses. As a forerunner of the scientist-practitioner, Parsons presented a report that described systematic guidance procedures used to counsel 80 men and women who used the bureau for help. Frank Parsons died 4 months later, on September 26, 1908. His book, *Choosing a Vocation* (Parsons, 1909), was published posthumously. Some years later, the School Committee of Boston created a counselor certification program, later adopted by Harvard University as the first college-based counselor education program (J. J. Schmidt, 2003). In a similar act, the superintendent of Boston schools designated 100 elementary and secondary teachers to become vocational counselors, which became known as the Boston Plan. Within a few years, school systems across the country followed suit.

Although state certification of school counselors began in 1924 and the American School Counselor Association (ASCA) was founded in 1953, there were few professional school counselors in American schools until the late 1950s. Russia's launching of Sputnik in 1957 provided quite a wake-up call as national pride tinged with a bit of fear appears to have stimulated a proliferation of high school counselors in the United States. Soon after Sputnik, the U.S. government responded, in part, with the promotion of professional school counseling through the National Defense Education Act (NDEA), passed in 1958. Shortly afterwards, James B. Conant (1959), in his popular book, *The American High School Today,* recommended the employment of one full-time school counselor for every 200–300 high-school students. In 1964, NDEA was extended to elementary schools (Baker & Gerler, 2004).

The Transformations

The school counseling profession has undergone a series of significant shifts in emphasis and orientation. Early on, school guidance was a directive approach that advocated goal-setting, overcoming obstacles, and career satisfaction. In the 1940s, due to Carl Rogers and the influence of humanism in education, school counseling activities broadened to include mental health counseling consultation and service coordination. Then, in the 1960s, 70s, and 80s, graduate training in school counseling emphasized developmental school counseling—focusing on how school counselors might facilitate child and adolescent development through school counseling programming. Most recently, there has been another strong movement among school counselors to professionalize and transform the identity and duties associated with school counseling. These changes were stimulated in the 1990s by 10 Dewitt Wallace-Readers Digest Fund grants awarded

Table 10.1   The Transformed School Counselor Role

Old Model	Transformed Model
Mental health focus	Academic and student achievement focus
Provides service, one-on-one counseling, and small group counseling	Leading, planning, and developing programs
Involvement primarily with students	Involvement with students, parents, teachers, community, community agencies, etc.
Little or no accountability	Full accountability for student success and effectiveness data

Summarized and adapted from B. Erford (Ed.), 2003. *Transforming the School Counseling Profession,* p. 6.

to counselor education programs throughout the United States and are perhaps best captured by the publication of *The National Standards for School Counseling Programs* (C. Campbell & Dahir, 1997) and *The ASCA National Model* (ASCA, 2003). The "National Standards" and the "National Model" as they are now called, provide guidelines for the content and delivery of school counseling programs. Rather than continuing to emphasize its links to the counseling field in general, school counselors are now being recast as educational leaders with roles and functions much different than traditional mental health counseling. The changes that began in the 1990s include placing less emphasis on individual mental health assistance and expertise, and more on systemic involvement and the academic success of all students.

Erford (2003), and the authors in his edited text titled *Transforming the School Counseling Profession* provide an extensive table outlining how school counseling is being transformed. This text and concept of professional renewal parallels the Education Trust Transforming School Counseling Initiative (TSCI) aimed at impacting the preparation of future school counselors. Table 10.1 includes some dichotomies or differences between the "old" school counseling model and the new "transformed" school counseling model (see Table 10.1).

Pause for Reflection

Some school counselors believe their freedom and/or creativity has been diminished by these transformations listed. In addition, the transformations have been linked to an increased use of the word professional. *Some professional school counselors are reluctant to refer to themselves as such in front of other (professional) colleagues for fear of seeming arrogant. What are your reactions to these concerns? Do you think of school counseling as more or less distinct from other specializations or forms of professional counseling?*

As noted, the evolution of school counseling is a historical phenomenon influenced by many forces and factors. This latest rendition of school counselor identity transforms school counselors into educational leaders who advocate, coordinate, and facilitate the academic success of all students. In fact, the emphasis is much less on the individual school counselor and much more on delivery of a school counseling program that is consistent with the national standards.

Another factor that has undoubtedly influenced school counseling transformation is the progressive infusion of mental health personnel and social workers into the schools. Funded by federal, state, and local initiatives and grants, many schools now have mental health professionals housed within their walls. In such cases, school counselors are viewed as educational leaders who collaborate, refer, and support service delivery. The result is that more often school counselors are less likely to meet individually with students for personal counseling. Instead, especially in situations where there are substantial and complex mental health issues, school counselors collaborate with mental health counselors and social workers who work more directly with students and outreach to families who need more systemic and systematic intervention and case management.

At this point, you may be wondering how all these professional identity issues are related to school counselor ethics. Generally, professional identity drives professional role and function and therefore guides professional ethics. However, because school counseling professional identity is, in reality, in the midst of transformation even as we write, it's critical for school counselors to clearly define their professional identity, role, and responsibilities within their individual school. This professional definition process will require school counselors to consistently and effectively communicate with school administrators, teachers, mental health professionals, and school social workers in an effort to clearly carve out their roles and responsibilities within each individual school.

WHY ARE SCHOOL COUNSELING ETHICS SO CHALLENGING?

In our opinion, the ethical challenges inherent in professional school counseling are as constant and difficult to deal with as those of any counseling specialties—and more so than most. This is because of the sheer number of ethical dilemmas that school counselors face on a daily basis. Kitchener (2000) defined ethical dilemmas as, "problems for which no choice seems completely satisfactory, since there are good, but contradictory reasons to take conflicting and incompatible courses of action" (p.2). When a school counselor colleague read Kitchener's definition of an ethical dilemma, she responded, "Welcome to my life" (N. Bishop, Personal communication, February, 2005). The following case example provides one of literally thousands of scenarios that school counselors will be faced with in their careers.

Case Example: Sara recently graduated with her master's degree in school counseling and was hired as a high school counselor at a medium-sized school. During her first week on the job, Sara was happy to discover that the students were eager to stop by and talk. In fact it seemed like students were literally lining up at her door to grab a few minutes of her time. One day, toward the end of the blur of her first week, a 15-year-old sophomore girl named Angie popped into her office and before Angie even got comfortably seated, she blurted out that her older brother, Andrew, had decided to try Meth. She wanted to know if Sara would try and get him to change his mind. As Angie talks, Sara begins to worry that Andrew might even have the Meth with him at school, but Angie doesn't say so directly. She just asked Sara what she would have to do if someone had something illegal in a locker. The big questions on Sara's mind centered around how to proceed, how to handle the instant trust issues, who to consult, and why she didn't prepare to be an elementary counselor instead!

If you were the counselor in this case example, to what source(s) of information would you turn to guide your behavior? ASCA's recently revised ethics code? Quick emails to your school counseling professor, and/or your fellow students from graduate school? Would you locate the other school counselors in your school, or your principal? Maybe you would first consider your own emotional reactions and values, and even wish you could take a minute to call your mom.

Of course, the correct answer is "all of the above" and more (with the possible exception of your mother). The best guide to ethical behavior comes from both your professional codes and from fellow school counselors. After all, if someone (for instance, an attorney for Andrew's parent) begins questioning your decisions, your best defense will be that you followed your professional code, your school's stated policies, and the relevant laws.

A School Is a School Is a School . . .

Obviously, school counselors are school employees—a reality that influences the school counselor's role and function, and illustrates the inseparability of context in professional practice. School counseling identity and ethical responsibilities must be viewed within the school framework.

Although public and private schools in the United States serve many functions in the lives of our youth, their overt purpose is to provide education to students. Consistent with this, the American School Counselor Association (ASCA) has endorsed academic success as the primary purpose of a modern professional school counseling program. Their website states: "Professional school counselors implement a comprehensive school counseling program that promotes and enhances student achievement. . . . Incorporating leadership, advocacy and collaboration, professional school counselors promote equity and access to opportunities and rigorous educational experiences for all students" (ASCA, 2005).

School policy and public laws.   Ethics, law, and policy interact in interesting ways for school counselors.

- Like all mental health professionals, school counselors are mandated reporters of suspected child abuse, including physical, emotional, and sexual abuse as well as neglect (Bryant & Milsom, 2005).
- The Family Educational Rights and Privacy Act (FERPA) mandates the parties to whom student educational records can be released.
- In addition to the general Duty to Protect discussed in Chapter 6, many school systems have policies and procedures in place for threats to individuals or the school building.
- School systems, reflecting the community and school board culture, may also have policies related to disclosures of drug or alcohol use, or issues related to sexual activity or pregnancy.

Main Dish: Education—Side Dishes: Optional?

For those of you who've never studied the history of education in the United States, we recommend reading at least an article or two. It is a fascinating and contentious history—one laden with conflicting values and beliefs still at odds today. Are publicly funded schools a dangerous extension of the government? An unfair burden to taxpayers? Or are they a vehicle to ensure justice and equality in our pluralistic society? Is there such a thing as too much education? Other nations predate the United States in providing public education, but this provision began early in our history as well (J. A. Johnson, Musial, Hall, Gollnick, & Dupuis, 2004). The fact that schools do more than *educate* has also long been acknowledged. In 1886, writing about the value of early education in *The Journal of Education,* Angelina Brooks (1886) wrote:

> In the first 7 or 8 years of a child's life, it will probably be settled whether he is to be swayed by superstition or intelligence, whether he is to live terrorized by fear or buoyed up by hope and courage. (as cited in Lazerson, 1971, p. 118)

Schools provide peer groups; sports teams; musical, artistic, and dramatic instruction; role-models; food; ideas; facts; apprenticeships; bad examples; good examples; challenges; and betrayals. Schools serve a central role in moral and social development. Our current K–12 system takes in 4- and 5-year-old children and 13 years later, releases into society 17- and 18-year-old young adults. What does it mean to produce educated citizens? What factors are most salient for school counselors charged with helping students achieve their individual best? What role does moral and emotional development play for you and your students? Are you Aristotelian in your approach, helping students discover their unique gifts and skills, and striving toward moral excellence? Or perhaps feminist, as you work from within a relationship frame to help students understand and resist certain forms of hierarchical limitations in their vision of themselves? While doing your duties as a professional school counselor, consider these deeper ethical questions of role and function—of both education and school counseling. And then we hope you will find ways to contribute your informed and thoughtful voice to this cultural conversation.

As you begin your job search, be sure to ask and read about these policies to make certain your values are basically consistent with what you read. As you know from Chapter 4, working in settings that violate the professional's basic values can lead to early burnout.

Distinctions between teaching and school counseling.   If the role and function of school counselors began and ended with academic success for all students, then school counselors would be indistinguishable from teachers and would not require a separate professional identification or their own ethical standards of practice. While there are certainly similarities, teaching and counseling have underlying professional values that

Applications 10.1

Managing Confidentiality in Schools: Scenarios and Solutions from Practicing School Counselors

Pointers from an Elementary Counselor:

For the most part, the teachers and parents are the ones who make the referral or ask me to speak to the student. They then believe they have a right to any information that is revealed. Since I do work with such young children, the idea of confidentiality is incomprehensible to some of the adults. Usually, I tell them that of course I will let them know if the child expresses anything that I think they need to know. I tell the child if there is something that I feel I need to share that I would like to share that particular information, tell the child exactly what I would say, and ask if that would be okay. I then share the information that the child has given me the okay for.

An Example from a High School Counselor:

A student mentions that she might be pregnant. My employment contract stipulates that I must notify parents in the event of a pregnancy. From previous dealings with her parents, I have seen a very rigid and harsh parenting style. I worry about her safety and whether she would be kicked out of the house. Further, she is an excellent student and a disruption like this could ruin her chances of being admitted to the selective schools she has applied to. Lastly, I do not want to cause any unnecessary trouble and stress for a situation that is already very difficult. However, I have school policy and legal statutes to follow. I know that I cannot get involved in overt discussions about pregnancy, as the mention of "abortion" can be grounds for dismissal.

The operative word here is that she *might* be pregnant. At this point, I might recommend that she get a pregnancy test, and then get re-tested to insure the results are accurate. She might want to be screened for STDs as well. I would instruct her NOT to tell me the results of those tests, but to instead tell the school nurse, who has a different set of disclosure laws than I do. The nurse can provide more information to the student without worry about it being perceived as "values clarification," and so on. At that point, the school nurse can talk candidly with her about her options.

I would be in contact with the nurse to make sure she/he has followed up on it. If the parents need to be notified (because the student intends to maintain the pregnancy), I would have a discussion with the student and the nurse, and together we would devise a plan to notify the student's parents. If the student was not pregnant, I would not notify the parents about my meetings with the student. And if the student was pregnant but terminated it, I would not know about it and would not have to notify anyone.

======= **Applications 10.1 (continued)** =======

Recommendations for Handling Curious Teachers from Various Practitioners:

- Educate staff frequently (i.e., not only when an issue arises) as to the importance of confidentiality for a trusting relationship between the school counselor and the students. Keep a copy of your ethical code available for teachers to see.
- Reassure teachers that you need to maintain confidentiality to serve the best interest of this child and to maintain the trust of all the other children in the school. Let them know that if you were to learn something really critical, you would do your best to have the child share the information or give you permission to share the information.
- Remember that teachers have no legal basis to request information. (Please note that this is a tip for you as a counselor, we aren't suggesting that you use this as a verbal rationale with your teacher colleagues.)
- When appropriate and approved by the child, share information with teachers that will help them support the child. Use standard counseling process to establish this as a consultation—ask the child what information can be shared, starting with minimal information; offer to facilitate a three-way conference with you, the teacher, and the child so that everyone knows what is being said; or practice a role-play if the child wishes to tell the teacher on his or her own.

sometimes clash. Perhaps the biggest values clash occurs with regard to confidentiality. For teachers, communication is fluid and ongoing. They talk to each other between classes, in the teacher's lounge, and before and after school. These conversations are generally open and constructive, with teachers sharing ideas, frustrations, and stories about their students (J. S. Peterson, Goodman, Keller, & McCauley, 2004). In some cases, such conversations about students and families can become destructive or simply deteriorate into gossip.

Isolation?

In contrast, school counselors are ethically bound to uphold students' rights to confidentiality—which we will discuss in some detail in the next section (Glosoff & Pate, 2002). Unfortunately, if school counselors attempt to maintain confidentiality when in conversation with teachers, they may be seen as uncooperative or as "not a team player." This perception can adversely affect the teacher-counselor relationship, especially when teachers do not understand why the school counselor refuses to tell them potentially important information that might contribute to academic success (Clark & Amatea, 2004).

Another reason the teaching/counseling distinctions present challenges to school counselors is this: Often, but certainly not always, school counselors have teaching backgrounds (ASCA, 2003). Our personal and professional backgrounds naturally influence the ways we view and enact new layers of professional identity. For counselors who have teaching backgrounds, making the identity transition is sometimes difficult. They naturally want to teach and to identify with teachers and their struggles.

For counselors who do not have a teaching background, the challenges may include fitting in, understanding both the overt and subtle dynamics of our educational systems, and finding a comfortable professional connection to administrators, teachers, and other school personnel (Clark & Amatea, 2004; J. S. Peterson et al., 2004; J. Schmidt, 2005).

Additionally, most elementary school counselors, and to a lesser extent secondary school counselors, spend much of their time in classroom guidance lessons, which can look and feel very much like teaching. Indeed, one of the authors of this chapter (NB) used to answer the inevitable question of "Oh, what do you teach?" after telling people that I worked in a K–12 school with the response "I teach life, I am a counselor." While that response is a bit glib, it does reflect the overlaps between the two roles.

Working with minors.   Working with minors is rarely easy and straightforward, principally because there are many constituencies with strong and vested interests in the well-being of our youth. In particular, when school counselors work with minor students their professional responsibilities automatically extend beyond the student and include parents, teachers, and school administrators (and to some extent, especially within public school settings, the community and the government). In addition, like other school personnel, school counselors assume, by default, the role of "In Loco Parentis" (meaning they take on a parental role in the absence of parental presence); students within schools are the legal responsibility of school personnel including the school counselor (Stone, 2005b). This responsibility is even more pronounced when school counselors are employed in a residential school (Stone, 2004).

Minors, by definition, are a vulnerable population that could potentially be manipulated or abused by adults. This is particularly true with elementary- and middle-school students, partly because younger students are generally not viewed as competent to make decisions in their own best interests. Even high-school students are often viewed as lacking the competence needed to make significant life decisions.

Pause for Reflection

As you contemplate working with minors, what sorts of decisions do you envision them as competent to make? For example, are middle-school students competent to make their own decisions about how much soda pop to purchase out of school vending machines? Do elementary students need adult guidance to help them protect themselves from strangers? Can high-school students be expected to responsibly handle the burden of going to school on an open campus, where they can come and go over lunch and during breaks from class? How much supervision do elementary-, middle-, and high-school students need when there is a school-sponsored party or dance? Do students of all ages need a dress code?

Multiple school counseling competencies: Counseling, coordination, consultation, and classroom guidance.   The multiple competencies and relationships inherent in the professional create additional ethical challenges for school counselors. School counseling programs can be built on a variety of models, but they all incorporate the roles of counseling coordination, consultation, and classroom guidance (ASCA, 2005). Increasingly, responsibilities of evaluation and advocacy are also incorporated (Hatch, 2005). Each of these responsibilities individually presents ethical challenges, but the combination can present even more. Not only can the school counselor interact directly with a student in different capacities (i.e., individual counseling, group counseling, classroom guidance, observing in the hallway or elsewhere on school grounds, writing a college recommendation), the interaction can simultaneously be indirect through consultation with teachers or other staff, and coordination of services provided by other agencies as well. School counselors may serve between 300 and 600 students (national average currently is 478), and serve those students in multiple capacities.

Because of the large caseloads and the general community expectations that schools focus on academic success, most school counselors do not provide long-term therapy. Some school counseling models even discourage individual counseling sessions because of concerns about serving all students equally. This is arguably an ethical dilemma and decision in itself.

Managing relationships with a wide variety of school professionals.   When placed in a school counseling internship, many graduate students in school counseling are surprised at the vast variety of professionals squeezed into the school setting. There are, of course, teachers, parents, and administrators present in the building, but there are also resource teachers, school psychologists, school nurses, school social workers, school resource (police) officers, and many other professionals providing services to students.

School psychologists and school social workers often work together to provide academic, personal-social, and career support services to students. School psychologists generally focus on assessments for academic and special-education purposes, while school social workers usually provide sociological or systems assessments for child study proceedings and work with families to secure appropriate federal and state social, medical, and financial services. However, when school emergencies arise, typically school counselors, psychologists, and social workers are together on the front lines providing essential trauma or grief counseling.

The Role and Function of the Professional School Counselor

"The professional school counselor is a certified/licensed educator trained in school counseling with unique qualifications and skills to address all students' academic, personal/social and career development needs" (ASCA, 2005). Based on the National Standards, professional school counselors are committed to facilitating student development in three primary areas. These include:

- Academic Development: Facilitation of the skills, attitudes, and knowledge related to learning throughout the lifespan.
- Career Development: Facilitation of the skills, attitudes, and knowledge that enables students to successfully transition from school to career.
- Personal/Social Development: Facilitation of the knowledge, attitudes, and interpersonal skills to: help students understand and respect self and others; make

decision, set goals, and take necessary action to achieve goals; and, understand safety and survival skills (ASCA, 2003).

General Guidelines for School Counselors

The American School Counselor Association (ASCA) revised its Ethical Standards for School Counselors in 2004. You can find the website for these standards in Applications 3.1 in Chapter Three. As is the case with most ethical codes, ASCA's standards have aspirational components, and are helpful in a general sense, but purposefully do not provide professional school counselors with definitive "commandments" on many issues. As Carolyn Stone, chair of ASCA's ethics committee, has written: "As frustrating as it may be for counselors caught in a conundrum, there is always room for interpretation in each situation" (Stone, 2005b, p. 2). Stone and others in the school counseling profession consider legal and ethical issues to be ultimately contextual (Baker & Gerler, 2004; T. P. J. Remley, Hermann, & Huey, 2003).

Despite the general nature, there are a number of clear and important messages provided in the code. Before we dive more deeply into frequent and perplexing ethical and legal dilemmas facing school counselors, we provide you with a brief summary of the most clear and direct mandates derived from the ASCA code.

As a school counselor, you:

- Have a primary obligation to _all_ students. This means that you are committed to treating all students with respect and dignity and providing all students with equal access to school counseling services.
- Make an extra effort to provide information and support to students who have historically been shortchanged or ignored in the larger educational context.
- Optimize and understand the limitations of educational choices.
- Do not impose your personal values onto students.
- Provide informed consent to students, parents, and others who partake in your services.
- May disclose confidential information in the following specific circumstances:
  ✓ when you believe there is a clear and imminent danger to the student or others
  ✓ when legal requirements demand that you reveal confidential information
  ✓ when a student has a communicable and fatal disease and has an identifiable partner and the student has refused to notify his or her partner of the danger
- Balance the confidentiality obligation to your students with the legal rights of parents/guardians.
- Avoid dual relationships that might jeopardize your objectivity and/or counseling relationship.
- Collaborate with and provide appropriate referrals to outside resources that support students and families.
- Practice personal wellness and self-care to optimize effectiveness.
- Seek continuing education for yourself and become involved in professional groups to enhance your functioning.

Pause for Reflection

What is your reaction to these clear and direct ethical mandates for school counselors? Are there any specific mandates that seem especially difficult from your perspective? Overall, do the preceding mandates feel too restrictive or too permissive to you? As you review these mandates, how would you summarize their main message in one sentence?

CONFIDENTIALITY: A COMMON CONUNDRUM

In a recent study conducted with school counselors in Virginia, confidentiality of personal disclosures was ranked most often as one of the top three common and challenging dilemmas experienced (Bodenhorn, in press). This is consistent with the larger population of counselors and psychologists. Each year, both the American Counseling Association and the American Psychological Association publish the numbers of consultation calls received. Questions about handling difficult issues with confidentiality consistently top those lists as well.

At the core of many confidentiality concerns in the schools is the need to balance student and parent rights, and to determine how much information is appropriate to share with colleagues who presumably also have the best interest of the student at heart.

ASCA *Code of Ethics for School Counselors*

Section A.2.g

. . . the professional school counselor recognizes his/her primary obligation for confidentiality is to the student but balances that obligation with an understanding of the legal and inherent rights of parents/guardians to be the guiding voice in their children's lives.

School counselors constantly balance the student's need for a confidential, safe relationship, and the understanding and belief that the family is (or should be) the primary source of support for children (Bodenhorn, 2005). Parental rights to information is a gray area legally, with a general tendency toward parental rights lessening as student age increases.

Despite the fact that the ASCA and ACA ethical codes do not make clear confidentiality distinctions between the two settings, in practice, confidentiality within a school setting is generally less strict than it is within a mental health setting. The school setting is regulated by school board or community policy. This means that when school counselors violate state/local statutes or school board policy, they are breaking the law (Stone, 2004). Consider the following case example.

Case Example: One day, Sophie, a talkative 8-year-old second grader, came to school with bruises on both cheeks. Shortly after the first bell, her teacher sent her to see Mr. Clyde, the school counselor. Mr. Clyde noticed that Sophie was unusually quiet. After spending some time together drawing pictures, he commented to Sophie that the bruises on her cheeks look like finger marks. She looked down, began crying, and said that her dad squeezed her cheeks over and over last night because she wouldn't "shut up."

Mr. Clyde knew that he needed to make a report to his state child protective services (CPS) division. Breaking confidentiality in this situation is required for both school and mental health professionals. Legally, he didn't have a choice about whether to report the child abuse and in his case, needed to do so immediately (within 24 hours). However, in Mr. Clyde's school, school policy mandated that all staff inform the principal before contacting CPS. Therefore, regardless of whether Sophie wanted the principal to know about her situation, Mr. Clyde knew he had to follow the school's protocol and inform his principal that he was going to be contacting CPS. If he had failed to do so and the child protective investigative officer arrived to interview Sophie, surprising the principal, Mr. Clyde would have most likely been reprimanded.

Another complication in confidentiality practice in schools is that often, a school counselor learns confidential information outside of a confidential relationship. Consider the following possibilities:

- A sixth-grade girl (Leslie) comes to talk with you, she is upset that her friend (Amy), another sixth-grade girl, has reported that she (Amy) had sex with one of the high-school boys. To whom do you owe confidentiality? When Leslie's parents come in concerned because something is disturbing their daughter and they know she has talked with you, is this Leslie's confidence, or Amy's confidence?

- In your office with the door open, a few students are talking about a recent rape threat made to some girls in the school. One of the boys relates that he was raped when he was in the first grade. In a meeting with the parents, you verify that this is indeed true. Not a confidential setting, but certainly confidential information, and potentially important in understanding some of his acting-out behavior and identification as *emotionally disturbed.* Can this information be shared in a child study team meeting with the special-education teachers who are working with him?

- A senior student is arrested for assault, which occurred at a party attended by many students. You learn about the arrest and the extent of the assault, which was very brutal, from other students, who tell you in the hallway. The student does not communicate any of the information with you directly. The parent drops off a college application. What information do you include?

Each of these situations involves confidential information learned in a nonconfidential setting. School counselors are frequently responsible for information of this nature. From an aspirational point of view, school counselors are advised to consider information confidential regardless of the source, but must always consider policy, safety, ethics, and law when deciding how to handle this type of information.

Sexual Abuse

Addressing sexual abuse is one of the more straightforward ethical issues that school counselors face (Bryant & Milsom, 2005). Specifically, if you suspect, based on reasonable information obtained from a child, that sexual abuse has occurred, then you are mandated to report the abuse and must do so soon after obtaining the information. This is true even if the student does not want you to make the report or says it has already been dealt with.

One possible exception to automatic sexual abuse reporting occurs when one parent in a divorce or dual-home situation "informs" you that the other parent is sexually abusing the child, but you have no direct evidence from the child. In such cases parents may be trying to manipulate the school counselor into making a child abuse report. If you suspect this is the case and the sexual abuse information comes only from a parent with a possible underlying motive, then you should simply encourage the parent to make the report himself or herself, rather than becoming involved in this contentious situation.

Sexual Harassment

"School counselors are required by law to report sexual harassment to school officials" (Stone, 2005b, p. 218). In addition, according to Title IX, schools can be legally liable for damages if they fail to stop student-to-student sexual harassment. These factors, on top of the professional responsibility of establishing a safe and comfortable environment for all students, means that school counselors have to be vigilant about responding to situations involving sexual harassment. Honoring the confidentiality of the victim while ensuring that perpetrators are disciplined and required to stop their behavior can be challenging, and usually requires the trust of the disciplining administrator (Stone, 2000).

Sexual harassment can take many forms. Recently, harassment via the Internet has become increasingly common (Barak, 2005). Harassment of gay and lesbian youth is often, but not always, considered sexual harassment (McFarland & Dupuis, 2001). And adult-on-student sexual harassment is a phenomenon that, like sexual relations between mental health professionals and their clients, persists at a puzzling high rate (Timmerman, 2003). In each of these cases it is the school counselor's responsibility to report the harassment while protecting the student's confidence.

FERPA, Records, and Sole Possession Records

According to The Family Education Rights and Privacy Act (FERPA), records made by counselors are exempt from educational records when they are kept only in the possession of the person who wrote the record, and are not accessible to any other person except someone who is a temporary substitute for the maker of the record (U.S. Department of Education, 1973).

Case Example: Ms. Terry, an elementary-school counselor, has been seeing Katie (a fifth grader) off and on for 6 months, working on social skills and study habits. Katie's mom is aware of this work. She calls and requests a copy of the "case notes" on Katie for her pediatrician. She believes Katie might need medication, and wants the notes as evidence. How should Ms. Terry handle this call? Is she legally or ethically required to provide the notes?

This is the sort of case that can create stress and conflict for school counselors, especially if they are unaware of the distinction within FERPA between case notes or sole possession notes and educational records. Overall, parents have complete access to their child's educational records. However, as described previously, FERPA allows school counselors to have sole possession records outside student educational records.

To answer the questions posed, school counselors should proceed carefully and collaboratively when parents request student records. The bottom line, of course, is that the school counselor's sole possession notes are private and do not need to be shared. They are, by definition, owned by the school counselor. However, FERPA also emphasizes that sole possession notes are very narrowly defined, and must:

- only serve as a memory aid
- not be accessible or shared in either verbal or written form
- be a private note created solely by the individual possessing it
- include only observations and professional opinions

The big danger in the case of sole possession notes is that if the content of these notes are shared with other school personnel (e.g., at an IEP meeting), then they automatically become part of the educational record—and then the parent can claim complete access.

Further, although FERPA legally defines who can have access to educational records, questions remain as to whether sole possession notes kept by a school counselor are considered part of a student's educational record. Until a legal case is brought and tried, this will remain a question (and we are not recommending that you become the subject of solving this question!). Many school counselors also wonder how long they should keep their notes. At this point, clear guidelines for how long to keep notes are not available. Standard practice is to generally purge sole possession notes when students transition out of the school, but essentially school counselors can probably purge their notes at their discretion. One exception to this rule is that school counselors should not purge their notes after a subpoena has been issued (Stone, 2004).

In practice, many school counselors do not keep notes about their counseling sessions or have widely varying practices (Merlone, 2005). Ethically, if not keeping notes diminishes performance and results, this practice needs to be examined. School counselors need to be involved in practices that improve their performance. Notes that include only facts and behaviors, rather than hypotheses and emotional impressions, are helpful and considered safer if accessed by others (Stone, 2005b).

INFORMED CONSENT(S): AN INCREASINGLY IMPORTANT PRACTICE

The most common type of informed consent in schools is a general statement about services and programs offered with an accompanying "opt-out" form that parents can sign and return if they want their children excused from the school counseling program. Most states mandate that such a form is offered to parents. The information included is usually quite general, and might not serve the full ethical intent of informed consent.

With and For Students

The general ethical expectation for informed consent is that students will have the information they need to make a decision as to whether you are a person who they want to work with and confide in. The information a student should have in order to make an informed decision would include, at minimum, the limitations to confidentiality as indicated by law and school policy, the limitations of the counseling relationship (if you are required to refer after a certain number of sessions or in case of a particular disclosure, the student should know that initially and *before* the disclosure occurs), how you hope or expect to handle any multiple relationship issues as you interact in situations outside of your office, and whether there are any alternatives that would not be considered within counseling (i.e., dropping out of school, abortion).

Typically, school counselors disclose student information to parents and school officials for more reasons than mental health counselors might. Consequently, school counselor should include all these exceptions to confidentiality within the student informed consent process. For example, if the school has a policy that all students in possession of drug paraphernalia on school property are reported to law enforcement, then this should be included in the informed consent.

In contrast to other counselors who work with minors, school counselors are often able to provide a limited amount of counseling to students without parental consent. This is partly due to the fact that counseling sometimes occurs, as suggested previously, as a function of incidental or informal contact between counselor and student. Of course, providing counseling without parental consent (whether incidental or intentional) is a tricky and complex practice and is not without opposition—especially from parents who consider counseling an unacceptable activity within schools. Consequently, for school counselors, it is essential to completely understand your school district policy on providing counseling services without parental consent. Typically, school counselors are able to provide two or three individual sessions to students before parental notification and permission is required (Glosoff & Pate, 2002). However, obtaining the informed consent of the student remains essential.

For Parents

The general expectation for informed consent for parents is that parents will have the information they need to make a decision to allow and/or encourage their children to work with you. In addition to the issues indicated previously, you should specifically clarify with parents what your policy and their expectations are regarding sharing information with the parents. Both children and parents should be aware of these limitations and policies as a student considers joining a group or talking with you individually. As discussed previously and illustrated through examples, sometimes school counselors have individual meetings with students without prior approval from parents (Glosoff & Pate, 2002). However, T. Davis (2005) recommends obtaining parental consent: "It seems reasonable that seeking parental consent and student compliance with counseling would be the best in terms of potential efficacy of counseling services and embracing the notion of building collaborative relationships" (p. 36).

LEGAL CONCERNS

Being served with a subpoena is one of the more stressful or even frightening experiences any counselor might face. While not a common occurrence, it is wise to be mentally and professionally prepared for such an event.

Subpoenas and Testifying

As we explained in Chapter 6, a subpoena is a legal demand to appear and produce testimony for the court. All school counselors should know how to respond to a subpoena (Stone, 2004, 2005c):

1. Inform your principal and determine whether or not your school or school district has a specific policy for you to follow when school staff is served with a subpoena. If there is a policy, work closely with your principal and make sure you follow the policy to the letter. If your school or school district does not have a policy, consider the following actions.

2. Contact your school board and see if there is a designated attorney in the school board's employ. If so, ask the attorney if he or she can request a motion to quash. A motion to quash is exactly what it sounds like. If the motion is successful, you will not have to show up in court and testify.

   a. You can go to the attorney who subpoenaed you and ask them to make a motion to quash (or the other parent's attorney).

   b. You can ask the judge to take notes to chamber and determine what's relevant.

   c. You can turn to the judge and ask to be excused (based on the fact that you're the only person the student can trust).

   d. Testify if necessary.

3. There are specific ways to talk with parents and attorneys to make it less likely you will be subpoenaed. Pointing out that you are not an evaluator, and cannot make assessment-based recommendations often helps.

4. Regardless of your personal position about child custody, it is generally inappropriate and unethical for school counselors to testify and give custody recommendations in child custody cases. This is because most mental health professionals follow the ethical guidelines that recommendations cannot be made unless a complete evaluation process was provided. If you are ever asked to provide custody-related recommendations in court, you should simply turn to the judge and say something like, "I am unable to ethically provide such recommendations because I haven't objectively evaluated both parents." If you continue to be pressed, you may be required to provide your professional "observations," but you should never provide professional recommendations. Professional observations might consist of witnessing one parent being late or failing to pick up a child after school, a parent hitting a child, the child's poor hygiene or physical state, and so on.

Depending upon your judgment and your informed consent protocol, if testifying in court, you may or may not decide to provide specific statements the child made to you in the course of counseling.

Negligence

Negligence is a legal term meaning that a particular duty expected from the school or counselor was not delivered and some harm or injury was experienced directly related to the expectation not being fulfilled. The components of negligence include:

- you owe a duty to the student/parent
- you breach the duty owed
- the student/parent/guardian suffers an injury
- there is legal causation between the breached duty and the "injury"

Negligence suits are very rare, as proving both explicit expectation and direct harm are challenging. In one case that was eventually settled out of court (Sain v. Cedar Rapids Community School District, 2001) the student claimed to have received wrong information about course requirements for NCAA scholarships. In this situation, the student had initially been awarded a scholarship, which was not valid until after the graduation transcripts were evaluated, which was the basis of the direct harm claim. The student claimed the counselor had agreed to place him in a new English class with the assurance that the course would be approved by the NCAA clearinghouse. However, the course was not included on the NCAA request that year, so it was not approved. This was the basis for the duty expectation claim in the lawsuit. School counselors should be careful about providing accurate information, and publicize information as formally and publicly as possible to avoid the potential of appearance of negligence.

Despite the recent Iowa case of Sain v. Cedar Rapids (Sain v. Cedar Rapids Community School District, 2001), generally school counselors are considered immune from negligence unless they engage in egregious behavior. Specifically, Alexander and Alexander have asserted that the rule prevails that the state and its agencies (including schools), as well as the state's agents, officers, or employees, will be generally considered immune from tort liability, while engaged in school functions (K. Alexander & Alexander, 2005).

MULTIPLE RELATIONSHIPS: MANY HATS, ONE SCHOOL

Similar to counselors in small communities, school counselors cannot escape having multiple relationships, both with students and with their colleagues. Managing them well and professionally is necessary to avoid ethical conflicts.

With Students

As indicated earlier in the chapter, school counselors interact with students in a variety of situations, both in school and in the community. Many schools encourage all staff, including counselors, to sponsor clubs or coach sports. While offering these programs can be supportive to student growth, sponsoring or coaching also creates a significant and complicated dual role with students.

School counselors who live in the same community in which they work may interact with students in social or religious settings, may be friends with their students' parents, or have children of the same age who interact with their students. School counselors need to be vigilant about their roles, responsibilities, and boundaries in all of these settings to avoid ethical conflicts. According to a survey conducted in Virginia, middle-school counselors may experience more frequent and more challenging dual relationships with their students than counselors at other academic levels (Bodenhorn, in press).

With Colleagues

School counselors are in a unique position of needing to retain some separation from their colleagues (especially regarding confidentiality) while simultaneously pursuing collaborative and cooperative relationships. Elementary-school counselors, who usually are the only counselor in the building, are more likely to report experiencing dual relationships with their colleagues. Even if the counseling staff is a large one, school counselors work closely with faculty and administrators in situations involving high levels of trust, and friendships are bound to develop. As friendships develop, the boundaries are even harder to maintain. The ASCA code indicates that care should be taken to avoid any relationships with school personnel that might intrude into or have a negative impact on the counselor/student relationship. This infringement may be difficult to predict and difficult to avoid when working in collaboration with colleagues.

Managing Consultation Relationships

The ethical dilemmas that arise in consultation are likely to revolve around confidentiality and the sharing of information. Whenever appropriate, school counselors are advised to let students know when consultation is being sought, and what information might be shared. Legal requirements need to be fulfilled in sharing educational records with consultants outside of the school system, meaning that parents of minor students need to sign a release for information to be shared. Ideally, the school counselor and an external counselor would receive permission from students and parents to consult so that the school can be supportive of the treatment plans and consistency can be maintained between the home and school environments.

Most often, school counselors will function as a consultant for teachers and parents. When doing so, a collaborative consultation model is recommended to assure that teachers and parents do not feel in a one-down relationship with school counselors. Ethical dilemmas will emerge more often when school counselors consider themselves as authoritarian experts whose goal is to *teach* teachers and parents (Stone & Dahir, 2006) rather than work collaboratively with them toward a constructive solution to the presenting concerns.

Assessment and Accountability

Just when you thought it couldn't get any more complicated—new to the ASCA ethical code is a section indicating that the professional school counselors assess the effectiveness of their programs across the domains of academic, career, and personal/social development. School counselors are to use objective accountability measures in this effort (Bartley, Biles, Low, Nakazawa-Hewitt, & Windish, 2003). We hope the content in both Chapters 8 and 9 will help you sort out the dynamics in this edict.

In an odd way, this task creates yet another set of roles for certain school counselors, as they become assessors of their impact on the overall performance and well-being of the students in the school. School counselors need to be able to explain and prove that their program is making a difference to the students in the school. Recently, a number of accountability resources for school counselors have been published (S. Johnson, Johnson, & Downs, 2006; Stone & Dahir, 2004).

HOT COUNSELING TOPICS AND CONCERNS

School counselors may have many legitimate reasons to complain about their jobs— but boredom would not be among them. Young people face a myriad of temptations, challenges, and freedoms that would have been unheard of in other generations.

Counseling in the Event of an Unwanted Pregnancy

Counselors in all settings need to examine their personal beliefs and values about sexual activity among young people, unwanted pregnancies, and abortion. School counselors have additional issues to consider, including the age and maturity level of the student, parent rights, state laws, and school policies. As Fischer and Sorenson (1996) stated:

> If an immature, emotionally fragile young girl procures an abortion with the help of a counselor, under circumstances where reasonably competent counselors would have notified the parents or would have advised against the abortion, liability for psychological or physical suffering may follow. (p. 60)

It is difficult for anyone to objectively provide counseling related to sex, pregnancy, and abortion. Most of us have deeply personal feelings and values in these areas, and are thus in danger of attempting to influence the young person in question. The ASCA ethical code is clear about the need for school counselors to keep their personal values out of the counseling process. However, students can often "read" the counselor's nonverbal cues to ascertain where the counselor stands on sexual activity, pregnancy, and abortion. Stone (2005b) describes how hard it can be to keep one's values out of such counseling areas:

> The counselor who is vehemently opposed may not voice his or her opposition to abortion, but values are revealed in voice tone, a raised eyebrow at certain junctures in the counseling session, a heavy sigh, a diverted glance—all of which inadvertently impose the counselor's values on a vulnerable student. (p. 196)

Overall, it is particularly vital for you to know your options, policies, and personal beliefs before a student brings a sex, pregnancy, or abortion issue to you. In the absence of a school policy that forbids discussion of abortion, school counselors can discuss the topic and options with students. However, they should avoid being involved with referring or arranging for medical care (Stone, 2002). Of course, the school counselor should let the student take the lead in identifying the pros and cons of informing parents and others, seeking abortion, or planning for childbirth.

Dangerous Behaviors: Sex, Drugs, Eating Disorders, and More

The ASCA ethical code indicates that school counselors break confidentiality in situations that present clear and imminent danger to the counselor, the student, or others. Unfortunately, imminent is not clearly defined. Some may consider any drug involvement as imminently dangerous, others only inhalant or intravenous use, and still others may consider only the threat of a suicidal overdose to be imminently dangerous. Consider this possibility: During a brief meeting with Matthew, a 13-year-old eighth grader, he reveals that he sometimes smokes marijuana on the weekends. Consider the following questions: Do you have a legal obligation to inform Matthew's parents? Do you have an ethical obligation to inform Matthew's parents?

At a recent ethics workshop one school counselor indicated he would report Matthew for his occasional recreational marijuana use, but all other counselors present felt recreational marijuana use (off school grounds) was not an imminent danger and therefore should not compromise confidentiality. This suggests that reporting recreational marijuana would not be standard practice. Therefore, to justify breaking confidentiality in this sort of case, automatic disclosure of recreational drug use should be included on the school counselor's informed consent form. The ASCA ethical guidelines echo this sentiment.

ASCA *Ethical Standards for School Counselors*

A.2. Confidentiality

      f. [The professional school counselor] protects the confidentiality of information received in the counseling relationships specified by federal and state laws, *written policies* and applicable ethical standards. Such information is only to be revealed to others with *the informed consent of the student,* consistent with the counselor's ethical obligation (italics added).

To take Matthew's case a bit further, consider what your ethical obligations would be if Matthew is using methamphetamines instead of pot? The same school counselors at the recent workshop uniformly agreed that methamphetamine use should be reported to parents and possibly to child protective services if the parents were also suspected of using around their children or of supplying their children with methamphetamines. This illustrates the range of reactions to student drug use. It is clear that if your personal values about drug use are affecting your judgment, you may inappropriately break confidentiality without adequate justification—which is another good reason to consult with colleagues when dealing with this complex issue.

Pause for Reflection

Value discussions about legal and illegal mood-altering substances evoke strong reactions from most people in our culture. Your own experiences and choices obviously will play a role in your considerations about dangerousness and parental rights to know. Consider the following questions: What if you found out that Matthew's parents were providing the pot? What if you were personal friends of Matthew's parents?

Repeat these considerations, only have the drugs of choice be whisky, then meth, and then psychedelic mushrooms.

In some unusual cases students may show drugs or drug paraphernalia to their school counselors. Based solely on the ethics codes there is no mandate for school counselors to break confidentiality and make a report in such cases. However, most schools have clear policies about how the discovery of drugs or paraphernalia is handled on school property. Typically, the drugs/paraphernalia are confiscated and the student turned over to law enforcement. Additionally, many schools have established zero-tolerance policies regarding threats and weapons in schools. If a student writes or verbalizes a threat indicating danger to others, the student is removed from the school for a period of time.

Because these procedures are not consistent with ethical guidelines about confidentiality, we recommend students be apprised of school policy about drug possession in your warm, student-friendly informed consent forms. Being expected to "narc" on students can be upsetting to school counselors. One way to reduce the stress is making sure students understand what the counselor is mandated to report.

Eating disorders and self-mutilation are distressing concerns present in many middle and high school-aged children. Similar to the drug use example, counselors may have different views regarding when these issues should be considered imminently dangerous. For both clinical and legal reasons, it is wise to include parents as early as possible in these situations (Froeschle & Moyer, 2004; Stone, 2005a), but cutting behaviors are not the same as suicide attempts, and though alarming if continued over some years, eating disorders are not automatically lethal.

Case Example: Ms. Chung was a school counselor and cheerleader adviser in a large high school. Mica, a sophomore cheerleader, had clearly dropped a large amount of weight over a 2-month period. At cheering practice, Ms. Chung noticed that Mica was drinking large amounts of diet soda. Her lycra exercise outfit was growing increasingly baggy, and Mica looked awful. The other girls were initially impressed, but then began telling Mica to eat something, and occasionally would make fun of her behind her back. Ms. Chung decided to talk directly with Mica. Of course, Mica denied having any problems. Ms. Chung asked Mica how she would feel about Ms. Chung calling her parents, and to her surprise, Mica said, "Whatever."

Ms. Chung spoke with Mica's mother, who insisted that Ms. Chung was overreacting. She asked Ms. Chung to leave Mica alone. Ms. Chung told Mica's mother that she was not sure she could leave Mica alone, as the problem seemed quite serious. Ms. Chung consulted with her principal, and together, they decided the situation might warrant a call to child protective services. What do you think? How would you handle this? Can you think of other options that might be available to Ms. Chung if her objective is first and foremost the welfare of Mica?

Although some may disagree, Stone (2005b) considers an eating disorder to be an imminent danger and recommends telling the parent(s). She notes that the trouble or complaint caused by acting protectively is less trouble than the possible negative outcome of cardiac arrest. Of course, school counselors should be familiar with the actual diagnostic categories and criteria before assuming such a risk exists with a given student. Many forms of eating disturbances are clearly not lethal and do not warrant parent involvement—especially against the adolescent's wishes. Again, the ASCA ethical guidelines are very helpful in this area.

ASCA *Ethical Standards for School Counselors*

A.7. Danger to Self or Others

The professional school counselor:

a. Informs parents/guardians or appropriate authorities when the student's condition indicates a clear and imminent danger to the student or others. This is to be done after careful deliberation and, where possible, after consultation with other counseling professionals.

b. Will attempt to minimize threat to a student and may choose to 1) inform the student of actions to be taken, 2) involve the student in a three-way communication with parents/guardians when breaching confidentiality, or 3) allow the student to have input as to how and to whom the breach will be made.

Given the increase in self-mutilation incidences among adolescents, there also may be specific school policy to guide how school counselors respond to this complex problem. Some writers have emphasized that students with eating disorders or other potentially lethal behavioral problems are not capable of making sound decisions regarding their health or well-being (Bardick et al., 2004). In such cases, the school counselor may need to contact the student's parents with or without the student's permission. However, it is very likely to be much better clinically and ethically if the school counselor makes it clear to the student that this contact is going to be made.

Suicidal Threats or Behaviors

Statements or threats of suicide are clearly in the domain of danger to self and need to be responded to quickly. Your school may have a clear policy or protocol for handling suicidal statements or threats and if so, you should follow the policy. It is also both comforting and good practice to involve another professional in the assessment, if at all possible. Even if you are reasonably sure that the student is not going to carry out an earlier threat, you are advised and warranted to inform parents (or a legal guardian) about the threat and concern. If parents are dismissive or uncooperative, you may need to refer to child protective services or a local hospital. Some schools have adopted policies requiring an assessment with a mental health counselor or psychologist before the student may return to school (Capuzzi, 2002). If your school does not have such a policy, you may want to consider this option.

CAREER COUNSELING AND COLLEGE GUIDANCE

In both career and college counseling, counselors need to monitor their own biases and beliefs to ensure that students have equitable options and information. Similar to the diversity issues mentioned earlier, and consistent with the requirements of No Child Left Behind, school counselors should be aware if there are achievement gaps or differential college attendance rates among their students. Usually, these differences are found in gender or ethnicity. Achievement gaps may include testing scores, enrollment in college preparatory courses, or enrollment in advanced science or mathematics courses. If these gaps exist, they are intertwined with the equity of career counseling and should be examined. School counselors have an ethical obligation to serve the academic needs and interests of all students.

High-school counselors are frequently asked to provide recommendations for college applications. This can present a variety of challenges. Based on large student loads, counselors may be asked to write letters of recommendation for students whom they do not know well and may not feel able to articulate the student's best qualities. Honesty is the best policy here; college admissions personnel are aware of the realities of school counseling and if they are told that the counselor feels a bit limited in his or her knowledge, more emphasis will be placed on a teacher recommendation.

Another challenge with recommendation writing is the pressure to write glowing letters about students who the counselor may not believe are entirely deserving of such accolades. No counselor wants to risk feeling responsible for a student not being accepted to college, even if the counselor believes that it may not be the best college for that student. Consequently, in practice school counselors may end up omitting information to avoid discussing a student's problems. For example, if a student has been involved in cheating, usual and customary practice may be to specifically avoid including any information about the student's integrity. Many school counselors struggle with this dilemma and the resolution is often a compromise between potential legal liability and ethical principles.

DIVERSITY ISSUES

The ASCA ethical code indicates that "the professional school counselor affirms the diversity of students, staff, and families," which includes aspects of ethnicity, gender, sexual orientation, religion, and economic status, among others. Multicultural counseling competence skills (see Chapter 9) include being aware of our own beliefs and biases regarding issues of cultural identity. School counselors need to be both self-aware and vigilant about the environment of the school and how diverse populations are affected systemically (Hobson & Kanitz, 1996; Holcomb-McCoy, 2004).

It is difficult for school counselors to move toward multicultural competency without adequate education, training, and experience. For example, a recent survey of 209 school counselors indicated that school counselors who had taken a multicultural counseling course rated themselves as more multiculturally competent than those who had not taken such a course (Holcomb-McCoy, 2005b). There are additional crucial diversity

=== **Deepening Diversity 10.1** ===

Exporting A Good Thing?

While we believe there are dangers in the wholesale exportation of professions that are as culturally determined as school counseling, this is a trend we have observed in the past few years. There are programs being sponsored by institutions in the United States that train entire cohorts of graduate students from other countries to be school counselors back in their countries of origin. Often, the entire notion of a school counselor is relatively new to the country of origin's educational system. Rather than developing from within that culture's educational and mental health practices, these new professionals are bringing in practices and worldviews that originated in a sometimes vastly different culture.

International scholars and researchers have written of a concern they've dubbed "colonization of the mind" (Chiang, Lu, & Wear, 2005; Lal, 1997). More insidious than political or physical colonization, colonization of the mind refers to the uncritical exportation or adoption of Western ways of valuing, thinking, believing, and acting. Thus, people in other cultures begin to view themselves through words, concepts, values, or even diagnoses developed far outside their own cultures or worldviews. Ironically, if the imported notions contain implicit racist or culturally biased views (which they most certainly do), then those adopting these new views may actually degrade or pathologize their own customary ways of being.

Of course, on the other side of this issue is the fact that many good ideas and new practices develop in one part of the world and are adopted globally as they prove their worth. We hope Western-style school counseling falls more on the latter side of this concern, but we also believe the dangers are there, and are best considered openly.

issues that school counselors should seek to address when implementing a comprehensive school counseling program. These issues include ethnic or culture matching, empowerment, and development of culturally specific counseling skills (Bailey, 2005; Holcomb-McCoy, 2005a; S. Sue, 1998).

Overall, ethical school counselors integrate diversity and alternative cultural values into every professional school counseling domain. For example, in a recent study on diversity within career counseling, Lowe (2005) found that Asian-American college students rated their career counselors as more culturally competent when they expressed a collectivist value orientation.

WORKING ETHICALLY WITH GROUPS IN SCHOOLS

Group work in any setting can present ethical challenges, and these are further complicated by the school setting. Maintaining confidentiality is expected, but cannot be guaranteed, and this of course needs to be clarified at the first session. Group consis-

=== **Applications 10.2** ===

Abbreviated Version of Carolyn Bishop Stone's Ethical Decision-Making Model

- How do your emotions define this problem? What is your initial reaction? File this initial reaction for later reference.
- Look at the facts. Separate the hearsay from facts. There is lots of information and it's hard to tell what's true and what's not. Judges may ask: Why did you ignore the rumors?
- Apply ethical codes and the law (child abuse is one of the only black and whites).
- Consider the chronological and developmental levels.
- Consider the setting, parental rights, and minor's rights. Court cases suggest that we must consider children differently because of their:
  - Peculiar vulnerability
  - Decision-making limits
  - Parental rights (Parents have absolute rights to their children's records)
- Consult, consult, consult.
- Apply the moral principles (Kitchener)
  - Autonomy, independence
  - Beneficence
  - Justice (treat equals equally, but unequals, unequally); just because one person needs CPR doesn't mean we should give it to everyone
  - Nonmaleficence
  - Fidelity (are you being loyal to the child or loyal to yourself?)
- Potential courses of action (ask yourself: would you take the same advice yourself?); test of justice; and test of publicity.
- Consult again.
- Implement the course of action (see Stone, 2005b, p. 16–19).

tency, involvement, and efficacy are challenged by absenteeism and some reluctance of teachers to allow students to leave their classes. Group counseling has been found to be especially effective with elementary students (Prout & Prout, 1998; Whiston & Sexton, 1998), so hopefully school counselors can use the results of previous research to advocate for continued use of groups in the school setting. Consider this possibility: You have been asked to develop a small group for disruptive fourth-grade students. Eight students are referred from teachers. The principal decides to add two more very aggressive boys. You start a group, but it turns into a terrible mess and failure. What ethical concerns occur to you in this scenario?

ASCA codes are similar to other ethical guidelines for group work. The ethical school counselor should screen prospective group members and take precautions to make sure members are not at risk for physical and psychological harm resulting from membership in or interaction within the group. Based on the ASCA guidelines, you are behaving unethically if you do not appropriately screen potential group members prior to initiating a group. Additionally, it is standard practice in most school districts to obtain parental permission prior to initiating a group. The Association for Specialists in Group Work (ASGW) recommends this practice as well: "Group workers obtain the appropriate consent forms for work with minors and other dependent group members" (ASGW, 1998). The ASCA code also states that you should notify parents/guardians and staff of group participation if you believe it to be appropriate and if doing so is consistent with school board policy or practice.

AN ETHICAL DECISION-MAKING MODEL FOR SCHOOL COUNSELORS

In Chapter 3, we provided examples of general decision-making models. The model in Application 10.2, while similar to the others in many ways, includes components specific to school counseling.

CHAPTER WRAP-UP

The professional identity of the modern school counselor is complex and ever-evolving. The numbers of students, teachers, and parents needing consultation, advocacy, psychoeducational interventions, guidance, and a compassionate, attentive ear are staggering. Boundary concerns, multiple roles, multicultural considerations, confidentiality challenges, and the many competencies required conspire together to make school counseling ethics a lively, daily adventure. School counselors can have significant positive impact on many people's lives. This requires the ability to balance time and attention, as well as a keen sense of awareness of the sometimes competing ethical principles of beneficence, nonmaleficence, autonomy, justice, and fidelity.

Chapter Eleven

PSYCHOTHERAPY, MENTAL HEALTH COUNSELING, AND CAREER COUNSELING

Where am I going? And why am I at the base of this mountain fighting to see the top? Is it the climb that's important? Or the summit? Can it be both? Or something else? Perhaps it's how we go down from the hill that counts. Or is it in simply endouring that we find the strength and purpose we seek?

—Ron Jones, *The Acorn People*

CHAPTER ORIENTATION

The provision of clinical and counseling psychological services grew out of the academic discipline of psychology, emerging in the mid-20th century. The provision of mental health counseling, as a designated master's level specialty in graduate counseling and social work programs, is one of the newer forms of modern counseling, complete with turf wars and identity struggles. In contrast, career counseling is as old as any form of modern counseling. Lurking underneath its staid presence as the historical matriarch of counseling, there are many exciting modern potential and relevant ethical concerns. In this chapter, we consider the particular ethical demands inherent in providing mental health and career counseling, either as specialties, or in the context of more general counseling practices.

The activity of mental health counseling generally refers to the establishment of a therapeutic relationship between a professional and a client, or a set of clients. The intent of the relationship is for the professional to assist the client(s) in alleviating emotional distress, changing disturbing behaviors, or enhancing the client's development in a specific area. A variety of mental health professionals are paid to provide this assistance in a number of ways and in a number of settings—each with its own particular ethical concerns and challenges. These challenges include payment structure, insurance, managed care, Medicaid billing, record keeping, expected levels of expertise, and setting constraints.

In this chapter, we will specifically focus on:

- the historical context of psychotherapy mental health counseling;
- distinguishing and common features among the professions, including views of the nature of health and distress, education, terminology distinctions in the field, and professional organizations;

- issues in agency and independent practice such as
  - fees, insurance, and managed care;
  - self-pay issues and problems;
  - confidentiality with other professionals;
  - competence and supervision; and
  - professional representation.
- the ethical challenges in career counseling.

MENTAL HEALTH COUNSELING: ROOTS AND DIRECTIONS

Mental health counseling, once a minor component of the larger counseling, psychology, and social work worlds, is now a central and defining force in these professions' identities. There are undoubtedly many political, professional, and social reasons for this shift. For instance, because mental health counseling developed from within the general counseling profession, some authors date the origins of mental health counseling all the way back to the first efforts to influence education, career and vocational planning, and in a sense, wellness (see Chapter 10 for the inspiring story about the work of Pauline Agassiz Shaw and Frank Parsons). Although it happened earlier in the century, psychology experienced the same shift in emphasis as interest grew in not only studying people, but also in helping them directly through psychotherapy and related applied activities. Social workers, too, have clinical mental health counseling options within their training programs that have grown more popular over the years.

The theories, research, and accepted mental health practices used by counselors, psychiatrists, psychologists, and social workers date back to different pioneers and eras in our culture's history. For instance, psychologists who provide counseling and/or psychotherapy often see the work of Sigmund Freud as a central figure in their history, even though he was a medical doctor, not a psychologist. In contrast, others claim the provision of applied mental health (clinical or counseling) psychology has its unique roots in the advent of intelligence testing and work with soldiers during World War II. As a specific specialty within ACA, mental health counseling came into being with the formation of the American Mental Health Counseling Association as an ACA affiliate, in 1978 (Pistole, 2004). Mental health work includes counseling, case management, and other professional practices with individual clients, groups, and families.

Similarly, family systems counseling has its own particular forebears, as do couples and group work. These forebears come from various backgrounds, including education, social work, medicine, and psychology.

DISTINGUISHING AND COMMON FEATURES AMONG MENTAL HEALTH PROFESSIONS

As mental health professionals, our squabbles over definition and turf sometime yield the same dismissive attitude reflected in Henry Kissinger's statement about academia, "University politics are vicious precisely because the stakes are so small" (Kissinger,

2005). The stakes never seem small or unimportant to those in the fight, but perspectives shift if one considers the view of those outside the battle.

Although some studies suggest that potential clients are more comfortable with the idea of seeking help from a professional "counselor" rather than a "psychologist" (D. Warner, 1991), in our experience, people seeking help pay relatively little attention to the finer distinctions in background and philosophy among mental health professions. What they want and need is effective, ethical assistance (Farberman, 1997). Of course, distinctions between and among mental health professionals do exist, and quite often they influence the orientation and type of assistance the particular professional practitioner provides. The findings just noted may reflect the fact that psychologists traditionally have been more closely associated with pathology, illness, diagnosis, and the medical model, whereas counselors have been more closely associated with helping "normal" individuals with their common life problems, thus generating less stigma when one is seeking help (D. A. Herman & Hazler, 1999; Jane E. Myers, Sweeney, & Witmer, 2000).

Nature of Human Health and Distress

Any attempt to cleanly delineate the differences between the professions when they provide mental health counseling is doomed to failure. In general, professional counseling claims an orientation toward the promotion of wholeness and healthy human development as a central professional value (Jane E. Myers et al., 2000). Nearly 20 years ago, Hershenson and Power (1987) expressed the belief that mental health counseling did not use the term *clinical* because of an emphasis on building on existing strengths, coping, and wellness rather than seeking to cure an illness. As admirable as this stance may be (or may have been), many counselors currently use the word *clinical* in their title. At the same time, many of the other mental health professions have had members move away from pathologizing, moving toward health and wholeness. For example, in psychology there has been a strong movement toward *positive psychology* over the past decade (Csikszentmihalyi, 2000; L. S. Greenberg, 2002). Many social workers and family counselors and therapists, too, have a strong strength-based orientation (M. P. Nichols, 2004), and entire theoretical orientations embrace this perspective (Cheong, 2001). With professional identity, there can be almost as many within-group differences as there are between-group differences. Consider the comments in Digressions for Deliberation 11.1 to see where you find yourself.

As the use of the term *clinical* has become more common in association with mental health counseling, and with social workers who provide mental health counseling, the distinctions have blurred even further. As noted in Chapter 8, like it or not, mental health counselors from all backgrounds and philosophies are expected to be familiar with and able to use the medical/psychiatric *DSM* system competently, should they be in a setting that requires this use.

Educational Backgrounds

Educational requirements are an obvious technical distinction among the mental health professionals. The mental health counseling identity has been refined by state

Perspectives on Human Functioning and Health

Humans have intricately connected brains, bodies, and—many would argue—spirits (or psyches or personalities or souls). We have both body awareness and psychological awareness. We know when our body hurts, or needs attention, and we know when our moods are bad, our hearts are broken, our relationships are unsatisfying, our motivation is lacking, our potential unfulfilled, or life's meaning has been obscured. In many cultures, when our bodies aren't functioning well or have been injured, we seek physical assistance. However, when our *psyche* isn't functioning properly—we've been hurt, feel stymied, disillusioned, disheartened, down, bereaved, or angry, humans turn to a variety of sources of help.

Increasingly, in the United States, we use the scientific/medical model and apply it to our brain, which is a physical organ assumed to be responsible for our moods, motivation, and ways of seeing the world. Pharmaceutical companies have developed medications that alter our complex brain chemistry, which alters our moods, energy level, and motivational and emotional states. Human mental and intellectual functioning is largely (some would argue completely) determined by our brain chemistry and electrical activity. There are a number of factors that contribute to these chemical and electrical functions.

- There are genetically influenced differences in brain functioning and capacity.
- Humans interact with their environment and these interactions change their brain chemistry and electrical activity. Physical exertion, lovemaking, conversation, learning, practicing a musical instrument, counseling—these all change brain chemistry.
- Like the rest of the human body, brains can be injured or become diseased, infected by viruses, bacteria, or cancer, which then alters the chemistry and electrical potentials.
- Finally, humans can ingest substances that temporarily or permanently alter brain chemistry and electrical activity, through changes in blood-sugar levels or neurotransmitter activity and availability. The substances can be eaten, drunk, injected, applied through the skin, or inhaled.

Humans have used mood-altering drugs for thousands of years, but modern pharmaceutical companies have expanded these options dramatically. We have medications that control many symptoms of psychoses, that can lift depression, and that take the edge off of anxiety, terror, and grief. With medication, we can alter our capacity for attending, we can enhance our ability to sleep, and we can relieve some of the urges behind compulsions, obsessions, mania, and rage. The medications don't yet cure any known mental distress or illness, but they do help manage symptoms. They also have known and unknown short- and long-term side effects, financial costs, and other limitations.

Behaviorists point out "a pill is not a skill"; but sometimes, the pills buy time

Digressions for Deliberation 11.1 (continued)

and provide us the necessary energy to add the missing skill or develop a more adaptive attitude. Changes in skills and attitudes are encoded chemically in our brains, so these, too, change our brain chemistry and perhaps structure.

Humans have also realized for thousands of years that loving relationships, good nutrition, exercise, shelter, and meaningful work all contribute to healthy mental and social functioning. We've known, too, that death, loss, broken relationships, trauma, starvation, and cruelty all take a serious toll on mental and social functioning.

As an alternative to directly altering brain chemistry via drugs, many mental health professionals believe the brain can be altered through insight (Kivlighan, 2002), new ways of thinking (J. S. Beck, 1995) and behaving (Fishman & Franks, 1997), mindfully changing habits (Linehan, 2000), restoring or building new relationships (Moreau, Mufson, Weissman, & Klerman, 1991), or patiently working through the pain and betrayals of life (Duncan & Miller, 2000). The works cited are merely representative—there are far too many clinical and research adherents in each domain to list.

Finally, many professionals and philosophers believe the source of the pain, trauma, or lack of development lies primarily outside the individual, contained instead within social, political, cultural, or institutional structures (Adler, 1964; Worell & Remer, 2003). Rather than helping the individual or family adjust to the way things are, professionals with a sociocultural orientation might work to help individuals see the injustices that cause the pain and loss, hoping to empower clients to take control over their lives. These mental health professionals might work within social systems for change in policies and laws that are destructive or limiting to human potential.

The roots of the various mental health professionals can be seen in the ways we explain and address human psychological suffering. Humans are bio-psycho-social-spiritual creatures of great complexity and potential. There is no single best explanation of human pain, wholeness, or healing. Each orientation offers an important glimpse into this complex picture. We need all the points of view. Where do you stand? What does your point of view contribute? Can you find ways to appreciate other approaches? Do some seem more limited (even useless) or potentially useless or dangerous to you?

---

licensure requirements, national certification requirements, and academic accreditation requirements.

While some states certify or license counselors from programs with less than 60 semester credits of coursework, and less than 3000 hours of supervised practice, CACREP requires these credits and hours for mental health counseling training accreditation. In many states, these requirements are quite similar to other master's level practitioner credentials, such as the clinical master's in social work.

In most cases, clinical and counseling psychologists have doctoral level training—a Ph.D., Psy.D., or an Ed.D.—and can only be licensed *as psychologists* if they have a doctorate from a state-approved institution and acceptable coursework and training. The American Psychological Association only accredits clinical and counseling practitioner programs at the doctoral level. However, sometimes students obtain a master's degree in clinical or counseling psychology and become licensed as a professional counselor because they have a 60 semester credit master's with a state and/or CACREP-approved curriculum. In addition, school psychologists often obtain master's or educational specialist degrees as their terminal degree, but refer to themselves as school psychologists or psychologists.

Clinical social work and psychiatric nursing are also common educational backgrounds for mental health professionals. Training and credentialing requirements vary, but are usually fairly similar in length to CACREP-accredited mental health counseling programs. However, the theoretical orientations and practical training modalities reflect the particular roots of these different disciplines.

Psychiatrists constitute the final large group of mental health professionals with a distinct educational background. Psychiatrists are medical doctors who have 4 years of general medical instruction, followed by at least 3 years of psychiatric residency training. Before the rapid acceleration of pharmaceutical options for altering brain chemistry, psychiatrists commonly engaged in one-on-one, 50-minute-hour psychotherapy sessions with patients. However, currently fewer psychiatrists actually practice psychotherapy. Instead, much of their time is devoted to prescribing and managing medications aimed at alleviating psychiatric symptoms of human malfunctioning and distress. This is both demanding and lucrative work, leaving little time for the traditional psychotherapeutic roles psychiatrists formerly played. Further, learning about the advances in neurology, brain chemistry, and pharmaceutical options leaves little time for the kind of training most counselors and psychologists receive to provide effective and ethical counseling.

Psychiatrists are not the only medical professionals who prescribe psychotropic drugs. Nurse practitioners, physician assistants, internal medicine, family practice, and pediatric physicians commonly prescribe psychopharmaceuticals, and psychologists are rallying in some states to undertake the necessary training and be given prescription privileges as well (Tulkin & Stock, 2004; Wiggins & Wedding, 2004). Further, when a family practice physician takes time to talk with a patient about mind/body connected symptoms, such as stomach pain that may be related to stress or anxiety or low energy related to depression, the patient billing codes may include mental health counseling. This is especially important to know in that many clients have a limit or *cap* on the number of sessions or amount of financial coverage they have for mental health care, and may not realize they have already used some of their coverage by discussing their problems with their physician.

Perhaps unfortunately, the remuneration and prestige associated with the credentials and professional backgrounds previously listed tend to correspond with the competitiveness of admission and the length and depth of training for the types of training—not necessarily with ultimate professional competence or effectiveness. Research has repeatedly shown that counseling or psychotherapy effectiveness is primarily related to the client's personal motivation, strengths, and resources and the development of a positive therapeutic relationship (Frank & Frank, 1991; M. J. Lambert, 1992; M. J. Lambert & Barley, 2002; L. Luborsky, Singer, & Luborsky, 1975). In our observations, the internal politics and turf wars over title, reimbursement, and credentials have less to do with efficacy and caring for people and more to do with money and power. Years ago, Jay Haley, a renowned master's level therapist, shared his thoughts on the differences between psychiatrists, psychologists, social workers, and counselors: "Except for ideology, salary, status, and power the differences are irrelevant" (Haley, 1977, p. 168).

Certainly, there are important concerns regarding competence, ethics, and accurate representation of credentials and skill levels covered in other chapters. However, our earnest belief is this: Every mental health profession contributes important worldviews, identities, and potentially enormously effective work to a world in great need. We are behaving far more ethically, and present a better image to the public, when all counselors and mental health professionals treat each other with professional regard.

Terminology Distinctions

As if the varied orientations and educational backgrounds were not confusing enough, we must also note that our craft, as mental health professionals, has many names— each with distinction, infamy, and baggage. Some of these terms are jealously guarded, with their use legislated in some states. The following list is intended to help define these terms. Please note that these definitions will not travel well. In other countries and regions in the world, the terms are translated differently and have come to have meanings and expectations specific to the given culture and service-provision systems.

Counseling.   We begin with counseling because we believe it is the broadest, least-pathologizing term (Maniar, Curry, Sommers-Flanagan, & Walsh, 2001; J. Sommers-Flanagan & Sommers-Flanagan, 2004b). When people say they are "getting some counseling," this is generally understood to mean they are meeting regularly with a mental health professional to work on psychological growth or psychological distress. The mental health professional is being compensated, either by an agency, the government, or directly by the client. Sometimes, the counseling has a distinct focus, with an added delimiter in the name, such as *pastoral, addiction, couple,* or *rehabilitation* counseling. We address specific ethical issues for these specialties in Chapter 12. In the finer shades of meaning, counseling may be associated with the provision of more direction, advice, or guidance than the other terms in this list (G. Corey, 2005; Corsini & Wedding, 2000; J. Sommers-Flanagan & Sommers-Flanagan, 2004b). It may also connote less of the deep probing of the unconscious that the public may associate with *psychotherapy.*

Therapy.   This term, similar to counseling, is frequently used to refer to counseling or psychotherapy. In fact, some mental health ethics and theories texts simply use the terms *therapy* and *counseling* interchangeably (G. Corey, 2005; J. Sommers-Flanagan & Sommers-Flanagan, 2004b). On the continuum, though, the meaning of therapy begins to move toward intervention by an expert who can fix something that is wrong, broken, or diseased. There is less of a connotation of guidance and more of the application of treatment, which may be why *therapy* is also often used to refer to physical therapy or speech therapy or other forms of direct interventions for problems, injuries, or disabilities. In the provision of mental health work with groups or families, a number of authors make a distinction between group counseling and group therapy, or family counseling versus therapy. Consistent with the move along the continuum toward deeper work, group counseling has been defined as shorter, more focused on day to day problems of living, whereas group therapy is longer and more focused on using the group process to uncover early and unconscious material, seeking characterological change (Furr & Barret, 2000; K. R. Greenberg, 2003; Yalom, 1995). However, this distinction of depth does not seem present between the terms *family counseling* and *family therapy.*

Similarly, school counselors often emphasize that they "do not do therapy," which they see as a more in-depth process best left to mental health counselors. Generally, the term therapy probably came into common usage as a shortened version of psychotherapy.

Psychotherapy.   This term moves further along the continuum. It is understood to be the professional endeavor of providing some kind of treatment or remedy to the psyche—rehabilitating it or curing it of its ills. The term has greater specificity than therapy; when people disclose they are getting psychotherapy, it is unlikely the listener will assume anything other than "the talking cure" (Bankart, 1997). In the United States, professionals who describe themselves as psychotherapists intend to communicate that they use interventions involving depth work, drawing on the theoretical orientations that feature the role of the unconscious more prominently. The professional work is expected to last longer, as well. In these days of managed care, it seems almost unbelievable that books written in the 1980s about brief psychotherapy considered 20 to 30 sessions to be *brief* work (L. Luborsky, 1984; Strupp & Binder, 1984)!

Analysis.   A shortened version of the following term, analysis is a professional endeavor conducted by professionals with a very specific background and training. The term dates back to Sigmund Freud (1957/1910).

Psychoanalysis.   This is a specialized term, which should only be used with individuals who have received formal psychoanalytic training (Spitzform, 2004). The approach has its roots in Freudian psychoanalytic theory, with an emphasis on the power of the unconscious, the importance of transference, and the centrality of interpretation as a technique to help make the unconscious conscious (E. E. Jones, 2000). If someone claims to be a psychoanalyst, they must have received extensive psychoanalytic training.

Like the professions that engage in them, the preceding terms share common ground, and yet have distinctions that are more or less important to the average layperson.

Professional Organizations

One of the largest professional organizations of mental health counselors is the American Mental Health Counseling Association (AMHCA), which began as a division of the ACA. In the mid-1990s, ACA underwent a major reorganization due to pressures brought to bear by AMHCA and other divisions wanting greater autonomy and professional distinction within and/or separate from ACA. This reorganization created a structure that allows AMCHA and other divisions to have members who do not necessarily belong to ACA. Similar to members of the American School Counseling Association (ASCA), AMCHA members can choose to be part of ACA along with their

AMCHA membership or can carry their AMCHA membership separately. There are philosophical as well as financial reasons for these options.

Mental health counselors might also belong to a number of other divisions of ACA, depending on their practices and interests. These divisions provide a wonderful vehicle for connection and professional development along specific lines of interest and expertise. It is also wise to consider membership in state and local professional organizations.

The other professions who provide mental health counseling (e.g., clinical social workers, psychologists, psychotherapists, psychoanalysts, psychiatric nurses) all have at least one professional organization to which they might belong, and many mental health professionals belong to more than one. Although controversial because of APA's stance of "doctoral only practitioners," there is even a specific professional organization for practitioners holding a master's degree in psychology—the North American Association of Masters in Psychology.

ISSUES IN AGENCY AND INDEPENDENT PRACTICE

Most mental health professionals can recall their first meeting with their first client. For some of us, this recollection includes flashbacks commonly associated with Posttraumatic Stress Disorder—but then, some of us may not have had the benefit of all the readiness information in Chapter 5. Like many professional endeavors, the provision of counseling services brings up not only competence-related anxiety, but also the challenging issue of fees and fee payment. This section discusses the ethical ins and outs and ups and downs associated with counseling as a business.

Health Insurance, Managed Care, and Fees

Mental health counseling practice providers, whether in independent practice or working for a community agency, are at least in part paid directly or indirectly by third parties. These third parties include insurance companies, Medicaid, Medicare, special funds set aside for counseling services, such as crime victims' funds, and other sources.

In the 1970s, most mental health funders (aka, third party payers) did not place many demands on agencies and independent practitioners. Although there were limits to the number of sessions and the amount of money a given third party payer would reimburse to agencies and practitioners, reimbursement procedures were generally simple and straightforward: The provider or agency would bill the third party payer (usually an insurance company) and the third party payer, after a modest delay and after the client had fulfilled his or her deductible, would pay the provider a prearranged percent of the bill (see Application 11.1, Understanding Insurance Company Lingo).

Unfortunately, just as mental health counseling was becoming more widely accepted throughout the United States, a number of converging historical events, including the rising cost of healthcare and the publication of *DSM-III,* has led to a movement toward "managed" health care. As Cottone and Tarvydas (2003) note, "About the same time that mental health counseling spread its wings and took flight, it encountered the 'wind shear' of managed care" (p. 261).

Applications 11.1

Understanding Insurance Company Lingo

The following table is designed to help you navigate the often-confusing linguistic world of health care insurance and managed care. Terminology in this area changes rapidly, but this table will give you a starting point.

Term	Definition and Use
Third Party Payer	An entity outside of the therapist-client dyad that pays the professional for his or her therapy services.
Deductible	A specific amount of money that the client (patient) must pay directly to the provider before his or her insurance "kicks in" or begins to reimburse for the professional services. If a client has a $1,000 deductible, it means that he or she is required to pay the first $1,000 of medical costs "out of pocket" (meaning out of his or her own pocket).
Co-payment	The specific amount for a particular professional service that the client/patient is responsible for paying. For example, most insurance packages pay something like "50% of professional fees after deductible," and so if the fee is $90, the insurance pays $45 and the client's co-payment is $45 after his/her deductible is met.
Mental Health Parity	A concept meaning that mental health problems are covered by insurance at the same level as physical health problems. Most or all mental health professional groups advocate or lobby for mental health parity.
Managed Care Organization (MCO)	An organization that manages or controls whether a specific medical or counseling service will qualify for insurance coverage. For example, many managed care companies do not authorize insurance reimbursement or payment for specific diagnoses (e.g., Adjustment Disorder) or procedure (e.g., couple, marriage, or family counseling).
Preferred Provider	Many managed care companies have a preferred provider panel or network. When clients/patients use a "preferred provider" they receive increased insurance coverage or reimbursement. When clients/patients use an "out of network" provider, there is reduced (or no) insurance coverage.
Preexisting Condition	A mental or physical diagnosis that predates enrollment in a particular insurance plan. Sometimes insurance companies refuse to reimburse for services that treat a preexisting condition.
Psychiatric Diagnosis	A diagnosis of a mental disorder generally assigned by an appropriately trained and credentialed provider. To receive insurance reimbursement, a psychiatric diagnosis is required.

Applications 11.1 (continued)

Multi-Axial Diagnosis	A detailed diagnostic system outlined in *DSM*, wherein a client's condition is described on five different axes or domains.
Treatment Summary	A summary of treatment provided. A treatment summary or specific case notes are often requested by managed care companies before they will authorize insurance payments.
National Practitioner Data Bank	A national source of information about individual practitioners or providers. This data bank is often accessed by managed care companies to determine whether a particular provider should be included on their preferred provider list.

Of course, mental health counselors were not the only professionals whose practices were profoundly altered by the advent of managed care and other health insurance cost-containment arrangements. All agencies and professionals in independent or group practices have been greatly affected. Managed care practices raise many fundamental issues, some ethical, some practical, and some emotional. As we describe managed care practices, you will likely understand why there is such a wide range of issues associated with this particular approach to reducing the cost of mental health services.

Although there are variations on the theme, the basic arrangement is this: In order to be paid for medical/psychological services covered by a client's insurance, the professional must be on the approved panel. To be on this panel, providers must sign a contract that specifies arrangements for fees, treatment plans, session limits, and communication procedures. For example, providers may be required to provide the managed care company with case notes or treatment summaries and these notes and summaries and/or requests for additional sessions are reviewed by a case manager. In addition, providers provide evidence of malpractice insurance and are held responsible for continuity of care or appropriate referral, should the benefits run out before the client is "cured."

Both managed care and traditional insurance companies require that a psychiatric diagnosis be given to clients seeking mental health counseling. This is not necessarily true for Employee Assistance Programs, which are defined below. This diagnosis must come from either the *DSM-IV-TR* or the *International Classification of Diseases—10th Edition* (ICD-10) and be within a certain group of reimbursable diagnoses, or clients cannot use their insurance benefits for counseling. As discussed in Chapter 8, those who diagnose are pulled in two opposite directions:

- Giving clients a serious mental disorder diagnosis is a significant step. It will travel with them the rest of their lives, and shape the ways you work and the ways they see themselves. Caution is called for, and a conservative diagnosis is wisest from this perspective.
- Clients and/or their employers pay a great deal for their insurance coverage. They deserve to have it cover their medical and mental health needs. If someone is just on the border of meeting a diagnostic criteria, the counselor may feel a strong pull

toward giving the client the "pathological benefit of the doubt" and diagnosing the disorder in a way that ensures coverage.

Diagnosing is not an exact science, and the gray areas will provide many ethical challenges for mental health professionals.

Diagnostic challenges and session limits are not the only areas of ethical concern with health insurance and billing practices. Often, clients have deductible and co-payment requirements. This means that they must pay, out of pocket, the amount of their deductible before their insurance benefits begin, and then pay some predetermined percent of the actual costs. While it might be tempting to wave the deductible, or allow clients to *not* pay you their co-payment, such a practice is illegal. It is called insurance fraud. You may argue that such a practice benefits clients, and in a way, it does. However, your beneficence may be more safely and legally expressed by complying with laws and ethics codes and instead, providing services to a certain number of those unable to pay each year (see the following aspirational statements from ACA and APA).

ACA *Code of Ethics*

Section A Introduction

Counselors are encouraged to contribute to society by devoting a portion of their professional activity to services for which there is little to no financial return (pro bono publico).

APA *Ethical Principles*

Principle B: Fidelity and Responsibility

. . . Psychologists strive to contribute a portion of their professional time for little or no compensation or personal advantage.

NASW *Code of Ethics*

Section on Principles

Social workers are encouraged to volunteer some portion of their professional skills with no expectation of significant financial return (pro bono service).

Case Example: Nikki Chang, a recently licensed mental health counselor, had a small independent counseling practice. She also had a modest contract to provide counseling at her local battered women's shelter. She never felt she was quite busy enough in her practice, so was motivated to take most referrals. She got a call from a woman named Jan who wanted to come in for counseling. Jan said that Dr. Freeman had referred her because his practice was too full right now. She asked about Nikki's fee.

> **Nikki:** My fee is $70.00 an hour. I usually see people for one session per week. Is that about what you were expecting?
>
> **Jan:** Well, yes. Actually, I think Dr. Freeman charges $80.00. My insurance covers

80%, so he would have gotten about seventy-something. You'll wave my co-payment like he does, won't you? He does that for my neighbor. It's such a nice thing.

Nikki felt her stomach drop. Dr. Freeman was a well-known practitioner. She wanted more referrals from him. Nikki also wanted to work with Jan. She knew if she explained that she simply could not legally wave Jan's co-payment, Jan would be angry, probably look elsewhere for counseling, and maybe even tell her neighbor about it so that it would get back to Dr. Freeman.

Somewhat related to waiving deductibles or co-payments are issues of free first sessions, sliding fees, and bartering. We discuss each in the following paragraphs.

Self-Pay Issues and Problems

Insurances and managed care systems obviously present some ethical quagmires. Unfortunately, having clients simply pay as they go can also be more complicated than it might seem at first.

Free sessions.   Free first sessions can be a very kind and helpful policy, or a manipulative marketing strategy. Luborsky and Crits-Christoph (1998) found that when people are socialized and instructed about therapy, they make better use of it, benefit more quickly, and drop out less. Corey and Corey (2002) advocate a pre-group group to help people understand how group works. Before "starting the clock," giving people a chance to form an impression of you and your work, and offering them time to ask questions and get their bearings is wise clinical practice. You might do this by scheduling extra time at the front end of your first billed session, or you might offer people a chance to come in for a free or reduced-fee half-hour informational session.

However, a free first *real* counseling session raises ethical concerns. If the free session is intended to let clients check out the mental health professional, then clients might end up in the awkward position of "beginning" counseling two or three times, telling their stories and needs over and over again. For many clients, this free time will create a sense of obligation to the professional, thus ensuring they will return. Finally, the laws protecting insurance companies come into play again. You cannot offer free sessions to selected clients. If you have a practice, it must be consistent across clients with insurance and clients without insurance.

Sliding fees.   Sliding fees can be an admirable but somewhat complicated practice. It is ethically and legally permissible to offer clients a sliding-fee scale, but the scale must be consistent. It should be based on multiple considerations, which can include family size, available insurance coverage, income, expenses, and so on. It must be included in your intake information for all clients, and cannot differentiate solely between people who have insurance and people who do not. Sliding fees cannot simply alleviate the co-payment or deductible, as we explained previously. Unfortunately, it is often tempting for clinicians to violate the sliding fee consistency rule. For example:

If your sliding-fee scale allows a client to see you for $30 and his/her insurance pays 50% after a $150 deductible, then your client will pay $30 for the first five sessions and then the insurance company will reimburse you $15 for additional sessions and the client will be responsible for the other $15; as you can see, it would be tempting to charge your usual $75 fee for the first two sessions and then begin sliding your fee after the deductible is met, but doing so is illegal; it is also tempting to have an "inside arrangement" where you charge your client $75, accept $37.50 from the insurance company and then "waive" the copayment, but this is illegal too.

Sliding fees also present the moral problem of trust. Most helping professionals do not want to be in the position of checking up on their clients' finances, so if you have a sliding-fee scale, you will most likely simply trust your clients' accounts of their financial and familial situation. If your client claims a very low income, and then arrives in expensive clothing and driving a far nicer car than you can afford, you might find yourself feeling a bit judgmental, or even a bit abused. This is a hazard of the practice, and one that most who charge sliding fees have learned to work with and live with.

Bartering.   Ethics codes have often prohibited, or nearly prohibited, bartering as a form of payment arrangement. The practice has obvious ethical challenges. If you barter for services, you have an instant new role in your client's life—that of boss or customer. What if you don't like the job your client does mowing your lawn? What if the engine she repairs stops working? If you trade a service that brings your client into your home, or into contact with your family, you have just broken a number of boundaries that are assumed to be in place in the therapeutic relationship. And even more difficult sometimes is the issue of your client's occupation versus yours. Maybe your client gets paid $15.00 an hour to landscape, but you get paid $75.00 for the therapy hour. Will you expect 5 hours of landscaping for 1 hour of therapy? This exchange can have the effect of indirectly devaluing your client's time or work.

If you barter for goods, you are forced to put a monetary value on items that may not have had a clear market value beforehand. How many fresh-baked, whole-wheat loaves of bread are equal to an hour of counseling? What about a lovely piece of pottery or a beautiful painting? Can you find an agreeable price? What if the painting offered isn't appealing to you? You are then in the position of judging your client's work, which can have ramifications in the counseling relationship. No wonder the ethics codes have shied away from bartering (Woody, 1998). However, because some of our American-Indian students have explained to us that the practice of bartering may be more accepted, and in fact, sometimes essential in their cultures (K. McDonald, personal communication, October, 1996), we appreciate that the codes have not banned bartering entirely.

ACA *Code of Ethics*

A.10.d Bartering

Counselors may barter only if the relationship is not exploitive or harmful and does not place the counselor in an unfair advantage, if the client requests it, and if such arrangements are an accepted practice in the community. Counselors consider the cultural implications of bartering and discuss relevant concerns with clients and document such agreements in a clear written contract.

APA *Ethical Principles*

6.05 Barter with Clients/Patients

Barter is the acceptance of goods, services, or other nonmonetary remuneration from clients/patients in return for psychological services. Psychologist may barter only if (1) it is not clinically contraindicated, and (2) the resulting arrangement is not exploitative.

NASW *Code of Ethics*

1.13 Payment for Services

(b) Social workers should avoid accepting goods or services from clients as payment for professional services. Bartering arrangements, particularly involving services, create the potential for conflicts of interest, exploitation, and inappropriate boundaries in social workers' relationships with clients. Social workers should explore and may participate in bartering only in very limited circumstances when it can be demonstrated that such arrangements are an accepted practice among professionals in the local community, considered to be essential for the provision of services, negotiated without coercion, and entered into at the client's initiative and with the client's informed consent. Social workers who accept goods or services from clients as payment for professional services assume the full burden of demonstrating that this arrangement will not be detrimental to the client or the professional relationship.

We would add one last step to the code requirements: seek consultation or supervision if you have decided to enter into a bartering arrangement. If you are bartering across cultures, seek culturally informed supervision or consultation, as you may unwittingly miss an important step in the culturally accepted process.

Pause for Reflection

Insurance changes, billing practices, and the pressing needs of people are weighty matters. In order to be reimbursed for your work, you take on liabilities and diagnostic challenges that complicate a wish to simply provide clients with the best counseling possible. Although mental health professionals joke about vying for the young, ambitious, verbal, intelligent, wealthy, and insightful clients—in other words, the worried well—most drawn to the profession care deeply about people in pain and want to offer effective, therapeutic services to the needy as well as those with resources. What do you anticipate, or already find, to be most troubling about insurance, managed care, and Medicaid systems as they interface with your professional calling to provide effective help?

Confidentiality with Other Professionals

Licensed mental health professionals often work in agencies with other mental health professionals and/or (hopefully) have consultation or supervision groups. They may also have colleagues who are social acquaintances or friends. We discussed this component of confidentiality in Chapter 6 in a general sense, but we want to revisit it specifically with mental health counseling and the specialties in the next chapter. Why are we insisting on this redundancy? The 50-minute-hour therapy relationship has predictable dynamics that make confidentiality in professional interactions something to be especially wise about.

You may wish to review the discussion about transference and countertransference in Chapter 7. Transference might reveal itself in the assumptions clients make about your interactions with other professionals. For instance, some clients may have had parents or caretakers who were overly controlling and/or talkative. These parents may have told their children's secrets to others—teachers, family members, physicians, pastors, and so on. Depending on how this activity was perceived, these clients may assume you will betray or take care of them in similar ways. They may assume everyone in the office, and even people in offices down the hall, know all about them. Conversely, clients may have had parents or caretakers who were especially private, or who completely ignored their children's needs or accomplishments. These clients may have entirely different transferential expectations about how you will or will not share information with other professionals. Your informed consent process will need to be very specific so that people understand with whom you will and will not be sharing information.

Further, in the somewhat likely event that you are in a close business or romantic relationship with another mental health professional, perhaps even married to one, rest assured that clients will make assumptions about what you do or do not share with this person. We are occasionally quite surprised at the assumptions clients make about what we do and do not tell each other about our work with given individuals.

Remember, too, that your own countertransference, or parataxic distortions about clients, could influence the ways you speak about your clients to other professionals. If you find yourself being overly open, chatty, scornful, or dramatic about your work with certain clients, you might want to give the matter some serious thought, and perhaps get consultation or supervision. Clients will have life stories and ways of being that you will find difficult to contain. You may also have colleagues who thrive on hearing about others' clinical work, and make ask for inappropriate information. Neither of these are justifications for breaks in confidentiality.

Case Example: A midlife counselor, Fred, was seeing a man who was in the midst of a horrible divorce. The man was a well-known newspaper editor, and the reasons for the divorce included the client's wife getting in a fistfight with a local attorney, with whom she was having an affair. The police were called, and the whole thing, much inflated and sensationalized, was on the evening news. Fred was at a party with many other mental health professionals. His colleague, Joanne, approached him and began a conversation about this news story, not knowing that this man was Fred's client. Fred dropped his guard for a moment and told Joanne that the news account wasn't entirely accurate, and that the woman in question had a history of physical violence toward men. Joanne gave him a funny look and asked how he would know. Fred felt a rush of embarrassment. He knew he should not have said a word. He could tell that Joanne wanted to know more, but he also knew she would be disappointed in him if he admitted his error.

Competence and Supervision

Most mental health counseling programs have a generalist curriculum that prepares students well in the foundations and basic skills of counseling. However, very few programs have enough time or room in the curriculum to provide extensive coursework in specific clinical areas, such as childhood sexual trauma, couples work, personality disorders, suicidality, bi-polar or obsessive-compulsive disorders, panic attacks, phobias, pedophilias, and so on.

A generalist master's also does not usually provide graduates with advanced skills in using theory-driven or general counseling techniques such as systematic desensitization, hypnosis, psychodrama, cognitive-behavioral homework, dream work, or even advanced group work. Often, practicum and internship sites are able to give students exposure to some, but certainly not all, of these problem areas and intervention strategies. Recent graduates often grapple with the ethical conundrum of knowing just enough to know they should know more.

The requirement to practice competently—which requires experience beyond graduate school—may seem like a double bind. How can you offer competent counseling to teens that cut or burn themselves when you've not worked with this age group or problem area before? The answer lies in two very important practices: informed consent and supervision. In graduate school, or shortly after, we strongly advise you to find a group of colleagues and form a consultation group. There can be great comfort and wisdom in such groups. Further, you will need to find both good overall supervision and supervision that helps you grow and develop your skills in specific problem areas and in the application of specific techniques.

Case Example: Joseph, a newly hired counselor in a group practice, had an intake interview with Naomi, a 14-year-old girl, and her parents, Isaac Rosenthal and Esther Ruben. Isaac explained that Naomi had terrible mood swings, and had recently been staying up all night, cleaning her room and listening to music. They had consulted their family physician, who had diagnosed Naomi with Bipolar I Disorder and had prescribed Abilify. The physician had suggested family counseling, and since Joseph's group practice offered the only sliding fee in town, they had chosen to come there. Joseph had never worked with anyone who had this diagnosis, but he had worked with a large number of families with various problem areas in his internship. Here is how he presented this information to the Rosenthal-Rubin family:

"It is really a good thing that you've come in for counseling as a family. Naomi, obviously your parents care a lot about you and what's happening in your life. I've worked with families facing all sorts of challenges, and I know it's a good thing when families work together. I want to let you know that I haven't had a chance to work with anyone who has a bipolar diagnosis, but I certainly know about the diagnosis, and the struggles that come with it. If we decide to work together, my intention would be to get some consultation and supervisory input from someone who has more knowledge in this particular area. I will also do some specific research and reading on Bipolar Disorder, and on families facing this challenge. I imagine we all have something to learn, and with the technological resources we have nowadays, we can keep up with the latest medical and counseling information out there. How does that seem to you all?"

Developing new specialty skills can be an exciting prospect for mental health professionals, both young and old. It provides new opportunities for skill development and helps keep professional life interesting. As noted in Chapter 9, because our field is constantly evolving, simply maintaining competence in our core areas requires continuing education, so adding competencies or specialties can be challenging.

ACA *Code of Ethics*

C.2.b. New Specialty Areas of Practice

Counselors practice in specialty areas new to them only after appropriate education, training, and supervised experience. While developing skills in new specialty areas, counselors take steps to ensure the competence of their work and to protect others from possible harm.

C.2.f. Continuing Education

Counselors recognize the need for continuing education to acquire and maintain a reasonable level of awareness of current scientific and professional information in their fields of activity. They take steps to maintain competence in the skills they use, are open to new procedures, and keep current with the diverse populations and specific populations with whom they work.

APA *Ethical Principles*

2.03 Maintaining Competence

Psychologists undertake ongoing efforts to develop and maintain their competence.

NASW *Code of Ethics*

1.04 Competence

(b) Social workers should provide services in substantive areas or use intervention techniques or approaches that are new to them only after engaging in appropriate study, training, consultation, and supervision from people who are competent in those interventions or techniques.

(c) When generally recognized standards do not exist with respect to an emerging area of practice, social workers should exercise careful judgment and take responsible steps (including appropriate education, research, training, consultation, and supervision) to ensure the competence of their work and to protect clients from harm.

Even though Chapter 9 covered competence generally, it is an especially salient and important ethical boundary for mental health counselors. In independent practice, there are few, if any, outside observers of your work. The creativity and spontaneity that comes naturally to some counselors must be reserved for settings that are overtly designed for this kind of intervention. We quote one of our favorite supervisors: It is *not okay* to fly by the seat of your pants (P. Bornstein, personal communication, March 10, 1984). The place for the development of new theories and techniques is in the context of experienced practitioners who are situated in a way that allows collegial input, research, and careful analysis of the effects and outcomes associated with the new techniques or strategies. And of course, clients involved should be fully informed of the experimental nature of any treatment.

This admonishment may seem ridiculously obvious in a nice, safe classroom environment, or when read in an ethics text. Sitting stymied or inspired with a vulnerable client who will not know the difference between a theoretically sound, professionally accepted technique and one you just made up on the spot is a different story. Sometimes, you will be tempted to do something provocative or refreshingly new. This is not necessarily forbidden ethically, but to make such an intervention ethical, you need to:

- fully inform your client that the thing you are doing or suggesting is new and has no evidence of effectiveness;
- explain your rationale to your client;
- be able to articulate, to yourself, why you think this intervention would be helpful; and
- be confident that you could fully explain and justify your actions to colleagues or supervisors.

Professional Representation

Mental health counselors are ethically required to practice competently *and* to represent themselves and their skill levels accurately to clients and other professionals. The temptation to represent oneself as specializing in certain areas as a marketing strategy can be quite strong. What amount of training and supervision qualifies someone to claim the specialty? Certain specialties, such as group work, family or couples counseling, or sex therapy, have professional organizations with specific training and supervision requirements beyond a generalist counseling degree. We cover some of these in the next chapter. Clearly, counselors should not represent themselves as specialists simply because of an interest in a certain area. At the very least, claiming a specialty should be preceded by the following:

- advanced study through workshops, classes, books, journals, and continuing education in the area of interest

- role-play of key techniques with willing colleagues or supervisors until you've achieved a sense of ease and can predict the effect of the technique(s)
- supervised work with the problem area of interest by seasoned, professionally recognized experts in the area
- a record of successful outcomes in the problem area

A counseling or psychotherapy practice is a business and so it is natural for mental health professionals and agencies to advertise or otherwise promote themselves to the public. The key ethical issue within this domain is accurate representation. In a free market society, advertising oneself is a basic right. Self-promotion in the media, however, can have mixed results for the field overall. Further, radio and television talk shows often feature those willing to dispense advice and judgments as "Doctors" without actually explaining their professional training or credentials. Of course, this type of activity is in the realm of entertainment, not professional mental health provision, but the public can become understandably confused.

In contrast to statements about professional specialty training and continuing education, ethics codes indicate that misrepresenting professional credentials is unethical.

APA *Ethical Principles*

5. Advertising and Other Public Statements

    5.01(b) Psychologists do not make false, deceptive, or fraudulent statements concerning (1) their training, experiences, or competence; (2) their academic degrees; (3) their credentials; (4) their institutional or association affiliations; (5) their services; (6) the scientific or clinical basis for, or results or degree of success of, their services; (7) their fees; (8) their publications or research findings.

ACA *Code of Ethics*

C.3.a. Accurate Advertising

    When advertising or otherwise representing their services to the public, counselors identify their credentials in an accurate manner that is not false, misleading, deceptive, or fraudulent.

C.3.c. Statements by Others

    Counselors make reasonable efforts to ensure that statements made by others about them or the profession of counseling are accurate.

C.4.d. Implying Doctoral-Level Competence

    Counselors clearly state their highest earned degree in counseling or closely related field. Counselors do not imply doctoral-level competence when only possessing a master's degree in counseling or a related field by referring to themselves as "Dr." in a counseling context when their doctorate is not in the counseling or related field.

NASW *Code of Ethics*

4.06 Misrepresentation

> (c) Social workers should ensure that their representations to clients, agencies, and the public of professional qualifications, credentials, education, competence, affiliations, services provided, or results to be achieved are accurate. Social workers should claim only those relevant professional credentials they actually possess and take steps to correct any inaccuracies or misrepresentations of their credentials by others.

Pause for Reflection

How do you want to represent yourself to the world? Take a few minutes to look carefully at counseling and psychotherapy advertising in telephone books, fliers, newspapers, and Internet sites. What stands out for you? Which forms of advertising seem professional and trustworthy to you? What claims seem questionable?

The bottom line for mental health practitioners is truth in advertising. We are to engage in only *accurate advertising,* which some have observed is nearly an oxymoronic phrase in our culture. Unlike most corporate or retail entrepreneurs, unless you have clear supporting data, you cannot ethically place an advertisement in the newspaper or telephone book (or anywhere) that states, "Guaranteed results." Similarly, ethics codes do not allow practitioners to solicit testimonies about their services, no matter how excellent, from former clients.

As an aside to consider, in our experience in rural communities, too much advertising is sometimes viewed as a sign of desperation, or lack of skill. Word of mouth and referral networks are assumed to be sufficient forms of advertising, and anyone who advertises excessively after getting established might be seen as less than adequate.

ETHICAL CONCERNS IN CAREER COUNSELING

In the counseling world, as a specialty, career counseling is one of the oldest. As a strand of our history, career counseling is a wonderful endorsement of human individuality and the rights of all adults to develop their gifts and passions into meaningful employment. In the excitement of the rapid development of mental health counseling, we may have temporarily forgotten how absolutely central is the place of right vocation in the well-lived life.

The psychologist Abraham Maslow calls spiritual and emotional truancy the Jonah Complex: "The evasion of one's own growth, the setting of low levels of aspiration, the fear of doing what one is capable of doing, voluntary self-crippling, pseudo-stupidity, mock humility" (Levoy, 1997, p. 191).

Cottone and Tarvydas (2003) point out that career counseling played a defining role in establishing the organizational structure of professional counseling, and career counseling led in establishing basic standards for our profession. They write, "The National Career Development Association (NCDA), the primary organization that represents career counseling and development professionals, is the oldest counseling organization in the world and has been defining the profession, its ethics, and standards for almost 90 years" (p. 291). These authors go on to explain the history of struggles over credentialing and levels of professional training required for persons who wish to claim a career-counseling specialty.

As the profession of counseling evolves, it is clear that assisting in career choices, transitions, and development will continue to be part of working positively and holistically with people. Working with employers, employee assistance programs, agencies, and governmental programs will also be specialty avenues for counselors interested in the world of employment. It will probably also be true that paraprofessionals and persons with less overall mental health training will fill some of these positions for the foreseeable future.

Specialty Competencies and Credentials

The NCDA (National Career Development Association, 2005) has established 11 competency areas that are considered the minimum requirements for a career counseling specialty. These requirements are as follows:

1. Knowledge of career development theory.
2. Acquisition of individual and group counseling skills.
3. Acquisition of individual and group assessment skills.
4. Knowledge of information and resources.
5. Skills in program promotion, management, and implementation.
6. Skills in consultation, coaching, and performance improvement.
7. Knowledge and skills for working with diverse clients.
8. Knowledge of supervision skills and theory.
9. Awareness of ethical and legal concerns.
10. Ability to conduct and assess research and evaluate intervention outcomes.
11. Skilled use of available technology.

While there have been many transitions in credentialing, the NCDA now has the Master Career Counselor (MCC) and the Master Career Development Professional (MCDP). Each of these have similar minimal requirements, which include a master's in counseling or closely related field; graduate work in career information, theories, assessment, and development; significant practicum, internship; postdegree supervised experience in the area; letters of recommendation; and ongoing membership in NCDA.

Specific Ethical Concerns and Challenges

Counselors with career specialties face many interesting ethical challenges. As is true with rehabilitation counseling, career specialists are often hired by employers or others with a vested interest in the outcome of the counselor's work with individuals in question.

Values and client rights.   There are many vested interests and pressures that come to bear on people making career decisions. Consider the following publisher's description of the book *Necessary Dreams,* by psychiatrist Anna Fels (2005).

> Despite the huge advances women have made in recent decades, their ambitions are still undermined in subtle ways. Parents, teachers, bosses, and institutions all give less encouragement to women than men, and women still grow up believing that they must defer to men in order be seen as feminine. If their ambition does survive into adulthood, too often those ambitions must be downsized or abandoned to accommodate "wifely" duties of household chores and child care. As a result, women—unlike men—continually have to re-shape their goals and expectations. Yet expressing ambition, pursuing it, and getting recognition for one's accomplishments is critical to identity and happiness. (p. 1)

Career counselors need to make sure they do not allow these pressures to subtly influence the career paths they help people explore.

Informed consent.   Extra care must be taken in the informed consent process, so that clients understand the career counselor's role in their lives. They need to realize that there will be limits to the counselor's advocacy and/or neutrality. This does not mean career counselors are simply extensions of the agency or industry employing them, but it does mean that there are goals, realities, and limits to their work that a generalist counselor might not face.

Confidentiality.   For career counseling, confidentiality is another important concern. The need for career consultation or counseling often arises in the context of life transitions or needs that involve other professionals. Thus, career counselors are commonly part of multidisciplinary teams, and are expected to share information more freely than counselors might in other settings. The amount and type of information shared should be clearly relevant, and shared with the client's welfare paramount. It is all too easy to share more than is necessary in team meetings, simply because it is interesting, or because the team members all seem well-intentioned people who want to know all there is to know about someone. Again, clients should be fully informed *before* you share information about them, and the information should be germane to the stated goals of the professional team.

Competence.   As with any specialty, the question of treatment goals and breadth of service arises. Clients originally come to see a counselor because of a specific goal, need, or problem area, but sometimes, in the context of this work, it becomes clear there are other, possibly related areas of concern. This is an issue of competence, and of course, informed consent. See the following Case Example for a glimpse into how related treatment goals might manifest.

Case Example: Kallen has her M.A. from a counseling program with CACREP-accreditation in the mental health track. She has also obtained her MCC and is a standing member in NCDA. Sara has come for career counseling because she has developed a fear of heights and can no longer climb the ladders necessary for her carpentry job. Her current employer has lost patience with her, and has offered to pay for the counseling. Sara has heard that Kallen is very good at helping women sort out their lives and find new careers.

As it happens, Kallen has done a great deal of reading about specific phobias, attended workshops, and successfully treated clients with panic attacks, claustrophobias, and related problems. While she respects Sara's wish to consider a new career, she also informs Sara that she might be able to help her overcome her fear of heights. Sara agrees, very enthusiastically. What ethical concerns come to mind?

There is nothing inherently unethical about adding or changing counseling goals or techniques in the context of the counseling relationship. The issues to consider are competence and informed consent. If the counselor is trained in areas of concern that arise during the course of work in the specialty area, and/or can obtain competent supervision, then the counselor is well within ethical limits to bring this to the client's attention and engage in a new layer of the informed consent and goal-setting processes.

Of course, we do not know exactly how Sara arranged the payment with her employer. We also do not know if Sara has informed Kallen of the source of payment, or if, at Sara or the employer's request, Kallen has agreed to keep Sara's employer informed. These are all dimensions that would have been included in the informed consent process.

Care must be taken so that the client is aware of the possibilities of adding new goals and directions to the counseling work without feeling pressured to consent. In most cases, the counselor would have both ego investment and financial reasons to hope the client agrees to further counseling. Neutrality is best achieved by counselors who both consciously acknowledge these incentives and do their best to factor them out.

CHAPTER WRAP-UP

This chapter and the next could easily be accused of being redundant with the more general chapters earlier in this text. We plead guilty. Ethical professional conduct has much common ground, with differing emphases and slightly varying contingencies. Because of the ever-emerging distinctions in professional identities, this text has set aside chapters and portions of chapters for specialties and professions that are closely related to the overall provision of professional counseling. Every ethics text tackles these internal divisions and distinctions differently. The provision of mental health counseling and career counseling are distinct specialties with both shared and unique ethical concerns.

Those currently working as mental health counselors face many ethical and practical challenges in today's economy and political climate. As the medical dollar has tightened, independent practice has become ever more challenging—perhaps adding fuel to the age-old turf battles between the helping professions. We have not yet convinced society to create mechanisms that pay collectively for prevention, wellness, and/or early intervention in mental health assistance. Coping with vicissitudes of third party payers while keeping our footing in the great river of human need leaves little time for such societal level dialogues and evolution.

Chapter Twelve

MORE SPECIALTIES: FAMILIES, COUPLES, REHABILITATION, ADDICTIONS, PASTORAL

> *We specialize in the wholly impossible.*
> —Motto of the *National Training School for Girls,* Washington, D.C., c. 1909

CHAPTER ORIENTATION

Through the lenses of four counseling specialties—each with its own professional organizations, training and curriculum requirements, and ethics codes—this chapter continues the examination of counseling specialization. Specialties are often based on some combination of

- the skills necessary to address the particular needs of a certain population (addictions or chemical dependency counseling, rehabilitation counseling, and school counseling might fit loosely in this category); and
- worldviews or philosophies about human nature or behaviors, and the best ways to help (family counseling, pastoral counseling, and strict theory-based counseling, such as behavioral or Jungian, might fit more in this category).

The unique ethical considerations for each specialty are relevant both for those who practice exclusively in the given area, *and* for generalists who may occasionally provide professional services in these specialty areas. In this chapter, we will specifically cover the definitions, origins, professional identity, and ethical concerns of the following:

- couples and family therapy
- rehabilitation counseling
- addictions counseling
- pastoral counseling

We will also consider the activities involved in personal coaching and spiritual direction, contrasting these with the more established specialties.

INTRODUCTION: WHY THESE SPECIALTIES?

As noted in Chapter 9, the relationship between competencies and specialties is multi-faceted. In this chapter, we briefly examine four distinct counseling specialization areas. The four selected are certainly not the only ones we could have chosen. We have organized the chapter in a way that provides a framework, should you wish to "fill in the blanks" regarding other specialty areas. Each specialty covered could have easily filled up an entire chapter or even a book on its own. However, each also shares significant common ground with the overarching principles in ACA, APA, and NASW ethics codes. There are specialties currently growing in popularity, such as sport counseling and conflict mediation, that will likely draw significant attention in years to come.

Specialties require a narrow focus on specific needs or treatment theory and techniques. This sometimes creates an allegiance to the specialty, complete with strong

---

Digressions for Deliberation 12.1

Mulling the Birth of Specialties

In Fiddler on the Roof, Tevye's great love for his daughters compels him to question and transcend some of the traditional Jewish marriage customs. This is no small matter. It involves lyrical soul-searching that includes revisiting his culture's core practices and beliefs about love, procreation, and marriage. He is able to expand his definitions, and thus his approval, for two of his three older daughters; but when Chava, his third eldest, asks his blessing to marry outside the faith, he cannot stretch that far. He cannot give his blessing, and she must marry without it. Tevye declares that Chava is dead to him (Stein, Bock, & Harnick, 1964).

In some ways, specialties in counseling and psychotherapy are like Tevye's daughters. Of course, professional attempts to offer psychological and spiritual help to humans predate Sigmund Freud, but we must admit that the appellation "Father of the Talking Cure" is apt. The deviations and expansions proposed by Freud's first inner circle, especially Alfred Adler and Carl Jung, caused angst and broken relationships similar to those in Tevye's family. The formerly favored "sons" were asked to leave (J. Sommers-Flanagan & Sommers-Flanagan, 2004b). But the ideas these early figures took with them have continued on.

Adler's work certainly contributed to the foundations of cognitive, constructivist, and feminist therapies, and there are many practicing Jungians among us. English novelist, Joyce Cary (Cowley, 1958) noted that our world is always in conflict between new ideas and old allegiances, between new arts and inventions and the old established ways of doing things. Some expansions of the parameters of psychological help have been pushed completely out of the "family" of respected therapies or died infamous deaths (think "orgone box") for various reasons (Rubin, 2003). Others have firmly established themselves as effective, ethical forms of counseling and psychotherapy.

opinions about the best ways to work with people, and the right techniques to use. Not every counseling specialty requires practitioners to be "true believers" but there is always that danger. Unthinking allegiance to any cause or group can be dangerous. Mark Twain (1963) wrote, "When the doctrine of allegiance to party can utterly upend a man's moral constitution and make a temporary fool of him besides, what excuse are you going to offer for preaching it, teaching it, extending it, perpetuating it?" (p. 576).

As discussed in the following section, couple and family mental health professional identity provides a living example of the controversies in specialization. Is couple and family work a profession unto itself? Is it a specialty within counseling, psychology, and/or social work? At this stage, it appears to be both.

COUPLE AND FAMILY THERAPY

In recent history, families and couples in the United States and Canada have come under intense political and media scrutiny. Value "wars" have raged over marriage and family definition and function (Aponte, 2002). Exciting but daunting family choices, such as international adoptions and fertility treatments, have become topics for counseling assistance. Divorce and remarriage rates remain high, and best parenting practices through these family challenges and transitions provide material for countless articles and books (e.g., C. D. Richardson & Rosen, 1999; e.g., R. Sommers-Flanagan, Elander, & Sommers-Flanagan, 2000).

Definition and Origins

Professional attempts to help improve the lives and functioning of families and couples have a rich and fascinating history, too extensive for adequate coverage in this chapter. Similar to other strands of our history as professional counselors, early efforts to help couples and families were psychoeducational and nonpathological in nature (Broderick & Schrader, 1991). Dating back at least to the 1920s, family life educators, social workers, clergy, and other professionals were involved in counseling with couples and family (Gurman & Fraenkel, 2002).

In the 1950s, the Mental Research Institute was founded by Don Jackson. He and colleagues there, such as Virginia Satir and Gregory Bateson, were prolific and influential writers and practitioners who introduced many family- and couple-related concepts still in use today (M. P. Nichols, 2004). Surprisingly, until this time, much of the couples- and family-focused counseling took place with individuals. Jackson and colleagues introduced the notion of "conjoint" therapy, and ushered in an era in which both members of the couple, or all members of the family, were expected to be present for the counseling. The systemic understanding of human behavior became the dominant orientation at this time (T. R. Miller, Scott, & Searight, 1990).

Professionals who work with families and couples come from many theoretical backgrounds and use techniques from these theories, as well as techniques uniquely developed for use with couples or families. Many, if not most, have at least some training in systemic-relational theory (M. P. Nichols, 2004; Cottone & Tarvydas, 2003) and thus are oriented to the systems and relationships among the people they serve (Golden-berg & Goldenberg, 2004). However, the systemic-relational orientation is not the only orientation with which counselors might work with couples or families. There are also counselors working with couples and families who are trained more generally, or who work from behavioral, attachment, or integrative models (Southern, Smith, & Oliver, 2005). Further, in a recent national survey, marriage and family therapists reported that they work more often with individual adults than with couples or families (Northey, 2002).

Professional Identity

There are two major organizations of professionals who work primarily with couples or families: The International Association for Marriage and Family Counseling (IAMFC), which is a division of ACA, and the American Association for Marriage and Family Therapy (AAMFT). The name of a specialty and its professional organizations are important pieces of the specialty's identity. As you know, the definition of family and legal regulations about who can and who cannot get married have become politically loaded topics in our culture. While the name of this specialty has historically included the word *marriage,* many practitioners now use the word *couple* instead. Both professional organizations, while still bearing the word *marriage* in their names, hasten in their mission statements and/or preambles to state that their professional concern extends to any romantically involved couple in any stage of the dating or commitment process, regardless of sexual orientation.

The preamble of the Ethical Codes of the International Association for Marriage and Family Counseling (IAMFC) states:

> Members may specialize in areas such as: premarital counseling, intergenerational counseling, separation and divorce counseling, relocation counseling, custody assessment and implementation, single parenting, stepfamilies, nontraditional family and marriage lifestyles, healthy and dysfunctional family systems, multicultural marriage and family concerns, displaced and homeless families, interfaith and interracial families, and dual career couples. In conducting these professional activities, members commit themselves to protect and advocate for the healthy growth and development of the family as a whole, even as they conscientiously recognize the integrity and diversity of each family and family member's unique needs, situations, status, and condition. (International Association for Marriage and Family Counseling, 2005)

This statement provides a glimpse into the depth and breadth of this specialty. As a distinct track in the CACREP-accreditation process, Marriage and Family Counseling can claim a fairly large area in the counseling world. It is a counseling area that is experiencing significant professional growth and, as such, is undergoing the usual professional identity "growing pains."

The IAMFC began as an affiliate of the ACA in 1989, and is now one of the fastest-growing divisions. The other large professional association in this area, the AAMFT, began in the 1940s, and currently claims to represent the professional interests of approximately 23,000 marriage and family therapists (American Association of Marital and Family Therapists, 2002). Both organizations have similar ethical codes, although as a division, IAMFC points its members to the ACA code as well.

Recently in our state, legislation was introduced (and defeated) that would have created separate licensure for "Marriage and Family Counselors." In most states, this separate credential exists, and the pressure to define couple and family work as separate and distinct from counseling, social work, psychiatry, or psychology will likely continue. We also predict that the skills necessary to address the systemic needs of couples and families will continue to be extremely important to *both* general counseling practitioners and to professionals across the other counseling specialties. As Gurman and Fraenkel (2002) note,

> The breakdown of marriage and other long-term, committed, intimate relationships, whether through divorce or chronic conflict and distress, exacts an enormous cost to public health, and so commands our attention at a societal level. (p. 201)

Specific Ethical Concerns and Challenges

Working with couples and families in distress is a complicated, value-laden, and sometimes threatening undertaking. Although there are many distinctions, there are also similarities between group work and work with couples or families. Counseling simply gets exponentially more complex when the counselor has more than one person literally (or even figuratively) in the room.

Client identification and welfare.   Even though couple and family counselors use different treatment/theoretical orientations, a defining feature is that they are working in a way that affects *both* individuals and a larger relationship unit. Of course, this creates another level of difficulty for treatment and ethical concerns, because each individual must be cared for and attended to as a discrete individual, with individual needs and rights, while the counselor must also attend to the needs of the relational unit.

F. Scott Fitzgerald reportedly said, "The test of a first-rate intelligence is the ability to hold two opposed ideas in the mind at the same time, and still retain the ability to function." Although perhaps not as difficult as holding opposite truths in our brains, family and couple counselors must hold *both* the welfare of each individual and the welfare of the family or couple as a relational entity as primary and sometimes competing ethical responsibilities (R. L. Smith, 1991). Setting clear priorities and therapy ground rules will help practitioners sort through the ethical principles when family welfare and individual welfare are at odds (Stevens et al., 1999).

Pause for Reflection

In our counseling, we have worked with children who have no families. It is a perilous and tragic situation for young people. On the other hand, families can be horrifically abusive and destructive to certain members. Is there ever a time when the welfare of the family is more important than the welfare of an individual member? Can you think of examples when tending to an individual's welfare could be extremely damaging to the family? What does it really mean to have an entire family as your client?

Confidentiality.   The same basic rules and exceptions apply to couple and family work as to general counseling practice. However, there are additional unique characteristics to consider. Mental health professionals vary in their practice regarding confidentiality within the relational unit. If they are working with a family, but occasionally meet with individual members or subsets, they might have one of three possible arrangements. First, they might agree to keep the material from individual or smaller meetings confidential, allowing members to decide to divulge the information or not. Second, they might reserve the right to share information learned in smaller group or individual meetings, based on the counselor's judgment that such sharing would be in the best interest of the family, or stated counseling goals. Third, they might have a policy that they will keep no secrets, and that eventually, all information shared in smaller groups or individually will be shared with the other member of the couple, or the family. These confidentiality arrangements are usually made based on treatment philosophy and theoretical orientation.

Please note that unless carefully spelled out in written form, with the signatures of all affected, the baseline ethic is that you will *not* share information obtained in individual or smaller subgroup meetings with the couple or entire family. To illustrate the importance of this point, we offer this classic scenario:

> Imagine you are working with a couple and the husband asks for an individual session, during which he tells you he is having an affair and that he refuses to stop the affair and does not want to tell his spouse. He explains that he wanted you to know about the affair, but insists that you cannot tell his spouse, because to do so would violate confidentiality.

Obviously, this sort of situation places the professional in a position where his or her work with the couple would be compromised. Couple and family counselors need to be clear about their confidentiality practices verbally and in writing—before they happen to hear a potential secret.

Another unique characteristic of confidentiality in couple and family work is the need to obtain permission from everyone competent to give it before releasing information to outside sources. This is not only time-consuming—it can get quite contentious. Suppose you work with a family in turmoil because of sibling incest. After some time, the parents decide to divorce. One parent wants your records released to her attorney because she believes they will reflect well on her in the upcoming custody battle. The other parent does not want these records released. Being very clear from the beginning regarding this practice is essential.

If your records are subpoenaed or court-ordered, follow the guidelines in Chapter 6. Also, remember that unless you were specifically asked to assess parenting abilities and custodial issues, it is unethical to represent your professional opinion as objective, balanced, or based on assessment of all concerned.

Competence.   There is no question that family and couple counseling requires significant specialized training and perhaps even natural predispositions! Unfortunately, there is also no doubt that many mental health professionals in schools, agencies, pastoral, and independent practices end up working with couples and families, sometimes without enough training and supervised experience.

The ethics codes of both major marriage and family professional organizations speak generally to the issue of competence, but the IAMFC is more specific, pointing the reader to the CACREP Environmental and Specialty Standards for Marriage and Family Counseling/Therapy. These standards specify the educational and experiential backgrounds necessary for working as a marriage and family counselor. The areas of knowledge specified help paint the picture of what any professional working with couples or families should know. These areas include the history of the field, the professional organizations, the contextual and systemic theories and dimensions of couples and family work, specific ethics and professional issues, family interview skills, family life cycle, human sexuality, and social trends and values. Of course, supervised work is also specifically required (CACREP, 2005).

It may not be realistic for everyone working with couples or families to have the training required for the specialization. At the very least, one must seek exposure to the topics listed and obtain knowledgeable supervision over and above generalist counselor training (Warnke, 2001).

The professional's values.   Couple and family work will touch you at your deepest, most basic human levels. None of us grew up in a perfect family, so most likely, we all carry small (or large) reserves of anger, disappointment, and fear of abandonment related to family concerns. Also, very few of us (authors excepted) claim to be in flawless romantic relationships. The countertransference potential in couples and family counseling is endless and therefore, we believe this work requires close supervision and insightful colleagues. In fact, it is an excellent arena for teamwork or doing co-counseling with a colleague, should your environment allow it.

It can be emotionally wrenching to witness people whose malice and wounds are such that loving familial ties are used to hurt and destroy. Of course, it can also be extraordinarily gratifying to offer significant help to a couple or family—being instrumental in an entire family changing its future trajectory for the better. Most likely, these extremes are related not only to human values, but also to our basic instincts for survival. We are born needing familial care to survive, and our species needs successful mating practices to avoid extinction. If teenagers were reading this text, they would roll their eyes right now, shrug, and say, "Duh." Forgive our hyperbole, but if these basics go ignored, the risk of the professional causing damage is high.

These same basic human truths probably account for the political appeal of the term "family values." Our culture is divided over definitions of and values associated with the term *family* because family is such a fundamental unit for human and cultural survival. Helping professionals can all too easily allow negative judgments or ignorance to infuse their work with divorcing couples, single parents, gay or lesbian couples, couples from other cultures, traditional hierarchical marriages, or home-schoolers (e.g., Al-Krenowi & Graham, 2005). This can happen consciously or unconsciously—neither would be ethical (Southern, Smith, & Oliver, 2005).

Pause for Reflection

How would you feel about seeing a marriage counselor who had been divorced? Divorced twice? Never married? If you are a heterosexual, how would you feel about

=== **Deepening Diversity 12.1** ===

Fun Facts about Families

For many decades, family and kinship systems have been the topics of fascinating research for social scientists. We offer the following comments as an invitation to widen your definitions, increase your tolerance, and get in touch with any biases and resistances you may have about family definitions and functioning.

- There are current and historic cultures and religions that permit or endorse multiple wives (Altman, 1993), multiple husbands (Haddix & Gurung, 1999), and other mating, familial relationships.
- The 12 sons of Jacob, who became the heads of the 12 tribes of Israel, were born to 4 different women—2 wives and 2 concubines (Metzger & Murphy, 1994).
- Jesus was born to an unwed teenager. The Prophet Mohammed had 9 or 10 wives, and the Buddah left his wife and child in search of enlightenment (Eliade, 1985).
- Many American-Indian tribes have kinship systems that guide familial responsibilities and communication patterns differently than the dominant cultural patterns. For instance, by custom, Navaho husbands are restricted from seeing or communicating with their mothers-in-law (James, 1920).
- The weight of filial piety is significant for Asian offspring, and the wishes and blessings of ancestors can be deeply influential in the present family functioning (Reese, 2003).
- The identity of offspring and their rightful place in the community can vary radically, depending on many factors including whether the culture is primarily matriarchal or patriarchal (Mazurana & McKay, 2001).
- Estimates vary, but somewhere between 2 and 10 million gay and lesbian parents are raising millions of children in the United States. In addition to facing life in a homophobic, heterosexist society, these families face all the ordinary challenges of other families (Adams, Jaques, & May, 2004).

Cultures and religions define family membership, family duties, and moral or appropriate reproductive patterns in vastly different ways. Governments have a stake in these definitions, as there is power in naming, numbering, regulating, and taxing citizens (J. Scott, 1998).

seeing a gay man for couples counseling? Would it matter if he were in a committed relationship? If you are a lesbian, how would you feel about seeing a straight male for family therapy? What would you want to know ahead of time? Can we put ourselves in our future clients' shoes and sense how very much they need us to not impose our values on their lives, as they struggle to solve romantic and familial problems?

Working with families and couples can be an exhilarating experience. There is enormous need for effective help for families and couples, but such work should be approached with caution. Both specific, well-developed skills and heightened ethical awareness are essential.

REHABILITATION COUNSELING

Rehabilitation counseling generally has a more predefined set of goals and outcomes than most counseling specialties. Rehabilitation counselors work with clients who have disabilities, and their overarching goal is to maximize vocational and/or psychosocial adjustment as it relates to the various disabilities. While this might strike the uninitiated as a narrow professional endeavor, we can assure you, it is anything but narrow or constraining. The life stories, situations, needs, and types of disabilities faced are endlessly varied and challenging.

Definition and Origins

As we've noted throughout this book, one of the main taproots of the history of counseling lies in the early recognition that humans have unique gifts, aptitudes, and callings (Parsons, 1909). As we discussed in Chapter 10, just after the turn of the 20th century, from Boston to San Francisco, men and women like Frank Parsons and Pauline Agassiz Shaw were daring to believe that even immigrants and school drop-outs might benefit from knowing about both themselves and potential vocational opportunities (Baker & Gerler, 2004). As is true of career and school counseling, rehabilitation counseling is a natural extension of the core counseling belief that all humans, despite disadvantages or disabilities, deserve to pursue vocations uniquely suited to each of them.

Social and cultural forces attempting to address the needs of persons with disabilities contributed to Congress passing the National Rehabilitation Act in 1920. Shortly after, the National Rehabilitation Association began serving the needs of people with disabilities, involving such professions as physical, occupational, and speech therapists; job assessors and trainers; instructors for independent living; and of course, rehabilitation counselors (National Rehabilitation Association, 2005). The specialty of rehabilitation counseling came into being in 1958, when both the American Rehabilitation Counseling Association (ARCA)—a division of the ACA—and the National Rehabilitation Counselors Association (NRCA)—a division of the NRA—began (Cottone & Tarvydas, 2003).

Within the APA, Division 22, Rehabilitation Psychology, was established in 1956, as one of the earliest Divisions in APA. Research, clinical applications, and advocacy are all part of the activities of the member of this division.

Professional Identity

With the formation of the Council on Rehabilitation Education (CORE) in 1972, which accredits master's degree programs, and the Commission on Rehabilitation Counselor Certification (CRCC) established in 1973 to certify rehabilitation counselors, rehabilitation counseling has taken giant strides toward professional status in the past 35 years. Additionally, the major rehabilitation organizations were able to agree on a unified code of ethics for rehabilitation counseling practice, which you can view at http://www.crccertification.com/pages/30code.html.

While overall counselor identity is shifting to include more attention to advocacy and social justice, these dimensions have always been part of the rehabilitation counselor's identity. Valuing humans who are "differently abled" and fighting for human potential is a central feature of rehabilitation counseling professional identity.

On their website, ARCA states,

> ACRA is equally interested in eliminating environmental and attitudinal barriers so that more opportunities are available with regard to education, employment, and community activities to people with disabilities. These goals are addressed by ARCA through public education and legislative activities. (American Rehabilitation Counseling Association, 2005)

Specific Ethical Concerns and Challenges

Although the code of professional ethics for rehabilitation counselors has many similarities to the ACA code and related professional codes, there are some unique aspects as well. In addition, from the perspective of having been a rehabilitation counselor (RSF), and maintaining ongoing relationships with rehabilitation colleagues, we are aware of specific and challenging ethical considerations.

Client identification and welfare.   When an ethics code deliberately defines the concept of *client,* (see the following code example), one might assume there is an issue or two at work in the background.

CORE: *Code of Professional Ethics for Rehabilitation Counselors*

A.1.a. Definition of Client.

> The primary obligation of rehabilitation counselors will be to their clients, defined as individuals with disabilities who are receiving services from rehabilitation counselors.

As mentioned in Chapter 1, there are many stakeholders with an interest in the work counselors do. Some of these stakeholders may be actually paying the counseling fees, and may wish for outcomes that are financially advantageous to themselves. In the best of worlds, the best financial outcome would also be the best clinical outcome, but this is not always the case. When rehabilitation counselors begin working with a client, no matter who is paying the bill, the client's welfare must be their primary concern. Like other specialties, rehabilitation counselors and psychologists have had their practices affected by managed care and related funding concerns (Hagglund & Frank, 1996).

Confidentiality and informed consent.   Because rehabilitation counseling is often enacted as part of a team, and because there are often competing financial concerns, rehabilitation counselors must be extremely clear on agency policies, contract obligations, state and federal laws, and professional communication expectations. Clients have the right to fully and completely understand the specific limits of confidentiality. Further, they have the right to know any and all agendas the counselor might have as part of the counseling or evaluation processes.

The *Client Rights* section of the code is necessarily explicit in this domain because of the competing demands on most rehabilitation counselors. It is especially important for

---

Digressions for Deliberation 12.2

A Tribute

The very first client I (RSF) met as a new rehabilitation counselor was a shocking, wonderful, intimidating, amazing 18-year-old woman. She had big, beautiful eyes, a wide smile, a warm, engaging voice, and a sparkling personality. Her head sat sideways on a twisted maze of body parts and protrusions that rested in a kind of heap in her wheelchair. Heather's umbilical cord had been wrapped tightly around many parts of her developing frame, and she was born with a nearly nonfunctional, distorted body. She had been mostly home-schooled, but now that she had her diploma, she was considering college or hunting for a job.

My supervisor had arranged for me to meet Heather in her family home, as traveling was complicated and difficult for her. Her parents chatted amicably with me, as I began trying to grasp how I could be of help to this most unusual human being. It's hard to describe all the emotions that rippled through my body as I rode my bike the ten blocks back to my office. I was keenly aware of and grateful for my health, mobility, and options. I felt shame at my astonishment at Heather's contorted body—a body that would have made Quasimodo seem princely. I felt determined to be of help, to live up to the expectations I had seen dancing in her eyes. And I felt frightened. How could I be of any help, really? How could I argue for resources for someone that limited? How could life be that unfair?

Although Heather was the first client I actually met, I had been reading files all week: car wrecks, job injuries, chronic diseases, birth abnormalities, brain injuries, amputations, paralysis, drug addictions, Schizophrenia. It was too much for me. I was all too aware of the temporary and vulnerable nature of our bodies and minds. I wished I had taken some other kind of job. But with a supportive supervisor and amazingly patient clients, I managed to stay with it.

Heather went to college in her specialized chair, with a note-taker and a cheery attitude. She took a job as a part-time telephone receptionist. To the day of her death from pneumonia, she brought good cheer into the world, inspiring everyone who met her with her expansive humor, deep faith, and incredible courage.

Rehabilitation clients are not all like Heather. They are as varied as the rest of us. Though many are inspiring, some are mired in victimhood. Some are bitter and resistant to change. The tragic losses some endure stand in odd contrast to others with comparatively easy but internally insurmountable problems. Being a rehabilitation counselor taught me how truly interdependent human beings are, each of us with needs—each of us with gifts. And sometimes, the need is the gift.

---

rehabilitation counselors to attend to factors that might temporarily impair client judgment, such as pain, pain medication, or trauma-related mental constriction or avoidance.

Advocacy and empowerment. Ethics codes in counseling areas usually include aspirational statements about advocacy in general terms that allow most of us to take this area less seriously than perhaps we should. Not so with the rehabilitation code. An entire section is devoted to advocacy and accessibility in very specific detail. It is both an inspiration and a challenge. Who among us could not do a better job of accessibility, inclusivity, and an attitude of empowerment?

Just as there is an art to effective counseling, there is an art to advocacy and empowerment. Advocacy can be done in ways that are demeaning, dehumanizing, and actually disempowering. Ethics in photojournalism regarding the use of horrid, compelling photos to shock people into giving money might be an example. And the statement *we should get out there and empower people* seems close to an oxymoron. Empowerment is more about letting go and sharing power, more yin than yang, more joining than leading. Empowerment is about education and inclusion—keeping people connected to community.

A case in point is the repeated research finding that people diagnosed with Schizophrenia have faster recovery rates in developing countries than they do in Western, industrialized countries (Jablensky et al., 1992). Discussing this research, Dr. Daniel Fisher (2005) stated:

> The implications are profound. It shows that schizophrenia is more pronounced and prolonged in industrialized countries. I've started to gather information from developing countries about how they approach treatment and healing. They have a completely opposite approach from Western countries. They're very socially oriented, and they instinctively recognize the importance of keeping people connected to the community. We have ceremonies of segregation and isolation, which is really what our labeling and our hospitalization process is. They have ceremonies of reintegration and connection. (p. 2)

Rehabilitation counselors, in their roles as counselors, team members, case managers, and advocates have much to teach the rest of the counseling world about the power of client advocacy.

An earlier edition of the code of professional ethics for rehabilitation counselors was criticized for omitting any specific mandates for respecting diversity (Middleton et al., 2000), but the current revision clearly addresses this area. One irony of the earlier omission is that arguably, in the case of professional rehabilitation work, some of the diversity-embracing behaviors were largely in place before any code *told* professionals to respect diversity. Another irony is that a field like rehabilitation, which is constantly facing the costs of marginalization, stigma, and stereotypes, could omit an overt ethical statement calling for respect for diversity from its code.

A phenomenon that seems true across various minority groups is that minority groups are not necessarily informed about or tolerant of the needs of other minority groups. Friedrich Nietzsche (1982/1895) claimed that challenges and difficulties that do not destroy us make us stronger. However, the truth is much more multidimensional than that. It may be simplistic to point this out, but oppression, scarcity, disempowerment, and abuse do not enhance empathy or global sensitivity.

ADDICTIONS COUNSELING

Very few human difficulties have generated as much controversy over the millennia as addictions. Perhaps this is because the substance or activity to which the addict is addicted provides moments of comfort, pleasure, arousal, distraction, interesting altered states of consciousness, and/or relief—so at best, the desire to stop partaking is ambivalent. Or perhaps it is because efforts to obtain the substance or engage in the activity take away time, resources, and energy usually devoted to relating to and caring for others—so the cost of the addiction spreads to spouse, family, and the community. Addictions have always generated moral concern, and sometimes, moral condemnation. Because many addictive substances and activities are only addictive for a subset of the population, the addiction appears to be a moral failing rather than a physical or psychological addiction.

Addictions create not only controversy, but great costs as well. The United States Center for Disease Control reports that over 400,000 citizens die every year from nicotine-related health problems and the World Health Organization estimates that internationally, there are five million deaths (United States Center for Disease Control, 1994). The Institute for Health Policy at Brandeis reports that there are over 100,000 alcohol-related deaths in the United States each year. Alcohol and drug abuse costs the American economy an estimated $276 billion per year in lost productivity, health care expenditures, crime, motor vehicle crashes, and other conditions. Just for comparison, untreated addiction is more expensive than heart disease, diabetes, and cancer combined (*Substance Abuse: The Nation's Number One Health Problem,* 2001). The long and contentious history of addictions, the toll taken on family and society, and the psychological, moral, and biological substrates of the addiction make this a particularly challenging counseling specialty.

Definition and Origins

Addictions counselors work to help people control, overcome, or begin recovery from addictive behaviors that harm themselves, their families, and the community. Just as there are political and moral skirmishes over the definition of *family,* there are also ongoing debates over the definition of *addiction* and the substances or activities that might be *addictive.* There are also differences in opinion regarding when the use of a substance or activity crosses the line and becomes abuse, and at what point the abuse becomes a dependency. Symptoms of abuse include physical, legal, relational, and work problems resulting from the use or activity. Symptoms of dependence are more pervasive, including tolerance (needing more and more of the substance or activity), unsuccessful attempts to curb or stop the use or activity, and the continued presence of the symptoms of abuse (Pidcock & Polansky, 2001).

Professional attempts to help people cope with their addictions or regain control over their lives date back to at least 1913, when Courtenay Baylor became the first recovering alcoholic to be paid as an alcoholism therapist (White, 2004). However, long before that, the addictions field embraced the notion of the *wounded healer.* Sometimes, this concept is intended to refer to the more general truth that all humans are imperfect, and must let their imperfections and struggles inform their efforts to offer help or healing. In the addictions world, it refers more specifically to the notion that experiencing and overcoming (or recovering from) an addiction increases one's ability to understand and offer healing help to other addicts. The wounded healer tradition dates back to abstinence-based, Native American revitalization movements in the 18th century. It continues through the 19th century recovery activists and early 20th century lay alcoholism therapists, and is certainly present in current models of addiction counseling (White, 2000).

Besides adherence to the wounded healer model, addictions counseling has historically struggled with rigid and sometimes conflicting beliefs about treatment modalities and what is necessary for recovery. Differences surface over the necessity of abstinence (Marlatt, 1998) and the need for readiness to change (W. R. Miller & Rollnick, 2002).

Professional Identity

Broadly defined, an addictions specialty should prepare the counselor to work with all forms of addictions—including substance addictions; eating or exercise addictions; shopping, stealing, or gambling addictions; and sexual addictions. There may be a common bio-psycho-social substrate in these addictions, but at present, it would be unrealistic to expect any single counselor to have the extensive knowledge necessary to treat addicts in all of these areas. Each area requires significant biological, clinical, and "street" knowledge.

ACA has an affiliate group, the International Association of Addictions and Offender Counselors (IAAOC) and states have certification or licensure requirements for addictions counseling. Because of the huge contributions made by the self-help groups in this area, especially Alcoholics Anonymous, there is significant overlap between lay involvement and professional involvement in recovery. A colleague of ours captured a prevailing belief when he said, "You don't have to have been an alcoholic to help people recover from an addiction to alcohol . . . but it helps!" (S. Kerr, personal communication, September, 2005).

White (2004) writes that there are four defining premises of addiction counseling that historically separate the addiction counselor from other helping roles. Paraphrased, they are:

1. The addiction constitutes a primary disorder rather than a superficial symptom of other underlying problems.
2. The multiple life problems experienced by addicted individuals can be resolved only within the framework of recovery initiation and maintenance.
3. Many individuals with biological vulnerability, high severity, comorbidity, and few internal, familial, or social supports are unable to achieve stable recovery without professional assistance.
4. Professional assistance is best provided by individuals with special knowledge and expertise in facilitating the physical, psychological, socio-cultural, and often spiritual journey from addiction to recovery. (p. 43)

Specific Ethical Concerns and Challenges

Mental health professionals who add addictions specialty training will be primarily accountable to their general professional ethics codes. There are state-by-state codes of conduct associated with various certifications, as well as a code for members of the National Association of Alcohol and Drug Abuse Counselors (NAADAC). This organization began in 1972 to represent the interests and concerns of substance abuse counselors. Since then, NAADAC has evolved in focus, and reflects the increasing number of tobacco, gambling, and other addiction professionals who are active in prevention, intervention, treatment, and education (http://naadac.org/).

Competence.   The history of addictions treatment is unique in that the first professional qualification required for becoming a helper was that of being a recovering addict. Requirements for medical, chemical, and psychological knowledge have been slowly added, so that states have moved from requiring 2-year degrees to 4-year degrees, usually with significant and specific coursework and supervised experience. Of course, most counselors who want to practice addictions counseling will have their master's degree and then need to seek additional training and supervision.

Counselors in the addictions field will find themselves elbow-to-elbow with addictions helpers who have far fewer credentials, degrees, or years of training. As long as these helpers are meeting state or institutional requirements, and staying within the limits of their job description, it is important to put aside any academic pride and realize how much everyone in the addictions field can learn from each other. Mutual support and respect is important for professional growth, and sometimes, professional survival.

Although treating the actual addiction requires specialization, Pidcock and Polansky (2001) argue that substance abuse often leads to behaviors that mimic many of the major mental disorders. Therefore, assessment for addictions should be a regular part of the generalist intake or diagnostic interview (e.g. Teitelbaum & Carey, 2000). Researchers have investigated the use of Web-based assessments, finding these compared favorably with paper and pencil assessments (E. T. Miller et al., 2002). Researcher and clinician, Bryan Cochran, adds "because of the separation between 'addictions' and 'mental health' programs, dually diagnosed clients often get passed back and forth between programs without receiving the necessary treatment for either problem. Ethics in this area involves being competent in assessing for mental health and substance abuse issues, being knowledgeable about both addictions and mental health treatment, and not abandoning clients by referring them for outside treatment without follow-up" (B. Cochran, personal communication, November, 2, 2005).

The professional's values.   Being a recovering addict is no longer a prerequisite for being an effective addictions counselor, but because of the ubiquitous presence of addiction in our culture, anyone considering working with addictions has significant personal values work to do. Some form of addictive behavior has touched almost everyone's life so most of us have personal experiences with and reactions to addictions. Shame, anger, and fear are common emotions associated with family members of addicts.

Burnout rates for addictions counselors are notoriously high (McGuire & Cottone, 2003). This may be related to many factors: the high relapse rate, with sometimes tragic outcomes; the manipulative behaviors associated with addicts; the struggle over resources sufficient to cover the costs of the work; and/or the high level of addicted clients with coexisting disorders (Pidcock & Polansky, 2001). It could also be related to our own personal unfinished psychological work around addictions and a resulting inability to get the professional distance necessary to thrive.

The intense and primary emotions associated with addictions have provided Hollywood with plenty of compelling material over the years. Movies such as *When a Man Loves a Woman,* (Mandoki, 1994), *Traffic* (Soderbergh, 2000), or *Drugstore Cowboy* (Van Sant, 1989) might help you contemplate and work within the complexities of addictions and addictions counseling.

In terms of self-care as it relates to client care, counselors who have relapsed into addictive behaviors are obviously endangering their clients, and should stop doing addictions work until they are able to stabilize in recovery again. At a more subtle level, we've had colleagues whose addictions counseling work led them to discontinue any use of alcohol, or any involvement with gambling, simply out of respect for their clients. The casual use of the substance or social activity no longer felt right to them. We are not advocating this particular outcome; we are merely noting that it isn't an uncommon choice.

Finally, language can be a powerful indicator of political leanings, education, and group membership. This is especially true in addictions work. The terms a person uses (e.g., *addict* versus *user*) denotes a set of beliefs about individuals with substance use disorders. Both careful management of your own word choices and critical thinking about your own beliefs and biases are essential to ethical work in addiction.

Confidentiality and multiple role concerns.   Because of the self-help roots and ongoing wounded-healer models in addictions work, addictions counselors sometimes end up in recovery groups alongside their clients. Or their clients make more assumptions of commonality than the usual client. The same professional rules for confidentiality hold

---

=== **Deepening Diversity 12.2** ===

Addictive Stereotype?

Consider the following observations:

- The movie *Boyz in the Hood* (Singleton, 1991) has a working premise that society colludes with drug pushers to keep African-American youth addicted, and thus disempowered.
- The stereotypic "drunken Indian" has come to be a most offensive racial slur to many American Indians.

These are just two examples of the many ways race, culture, and addictions interact. We may think we are immune to such simplistic stereotypes and associations, but our culture is steeped in such linkages. Which race sips dry martinis? Which gender orders blender drinks with sweet liqueurs? Which races are biologically predisposed to alcoholism? Which athletes chew tobacco? Which cultures smoke more pot? As you mentally answer these questions, it is likely that you also note some level of belief in them. What age or socioeconomic group smokes the most cigarettes? Why have these behaviors and/or associations come to signal gender, racial, and cultural messages? Do the associations then perpetuate themselves and add to the burden of one trying to resist or quit the addictive substance or behavior?

The legality or illegality of the addictive substance or activity also contributes to our stereotypes and moral judgments. Gambling, nicotine, and alcohol are all legal in many forms. Other drugs, such as marijuana, cocaine, heroin, and methamphetamine, are not. Our level of moral concern is likely influenced by legal views and implications as well as actual levels of damage done to individuals and society by engaging in these activities or using these substances.

for addictions counselors. If you happen to be in a group with a client, you cannot reveal anything about your counseling relationship. Further, this dual role may be most uncomfortable for you, your client, or both. Even though you might be a recovering person with needs of your own, it is your responsibility to minimize the impact of the dual role and/or make adjustments for the sake of your client's welfare.

Addictions counseling is a specialty with long roots, wide application, and significant import in our culture. It is unlikely that counselors will work with many people untouched by some form of addiction in their families, friends, or in themselves. Therefore, an awareness of the basic truths and implications of addictions is necessary for all mental health professionals.

PASTORAL COUNSELING

In some cultures, it is unusual or even forbidden to seek mental health counseling outside one's faith. The increasing availability of mental health professionals trained in credentialed programs from diverse cultural and religious backgrounds makes it more likely that a Mormon, Muslim, Jewish, Lutheran, or Buddhist person might find a counselor with a similar faith or philosophical background. This, however, is not necessarily what is meant by pastoral counseling. In the following paragraphs, we discuss this specialty and its unique ethical dimensions.

Pause for Reflection

Where does the brain leave off and the mind begin? Where does the mind become soul? Is biology destiny? Do humans have choices that are neither determined by our biological processes nor our environment? If so, what is the substance of these choices? If not, how can we hold humans accountable for their actions? What is the role of religion and/or spirituality in human functioning and health? As soon as you or your classmates answer these questions definitively, be sure to get in touch with us. We've been wondering about these things for a long time.

Definition and Origins

Pastoral counseling is counseling that assists clients with their problems within the primary context of their faith and faith communities, drawing from both the professional training and the faith system of the counselor. Burcke (2001) writes:

Pastoral counseling, also called "pastoral psychotherapy," grows out of an approach to pastoral care that U.S. Protestantism developed in the first quarter of the twentieth century. This approach taught pastors to listen to the people they counseled, rather than just delivering a message from the faith's teachings. Today, many pastoral counselors devote themselves to the private practice of pastoral psychotherapy, marriage and family counseling, or some combination. (p. 7)

It is important to distinguish between pastoral counseling and the kind of occasional counseling a pastor does. Pastoral counseling has all the trappings of mental health counseling, usually including appointments, 50-minute hours, an ethics code, an agreed-upon fee, informed consent, and so on. Pastoral counselors often view their work as both a profession and a calling, similar to, but also distinct from clergy.

Professional Identity

There are at least two national/international organizations for pastoral counseling: The American Association of Pastoral Counseling (AAPC), and the International Association of Pastoral Counselors (IAPC). Both have certification programs and guidelines that include theological knowledge, mental health knowledge, and supervised practice. States do not generally regulate, certify, nor license pastoral counseling, but often, pastoral counselors also carry master's or doctoral-level mental health licenses or certifications, and are therefore accountable to the licensure requirements and to ethics codes of other professional organizations to which they may belong.

While the direct inclusion of spiritual or faith concerns in counseling does not necessarily make the counseling into "pastoral counseling," many professionals wish to openly identify with particular religious or spiritual affiliations. The American Association of Christian Counselors (AACC) is open to any mental health professional who wishes to fully identify with the Christian faith in their work. Their ethics code can be found at http://www.aacc.net/About_us/media/ethics.pdf.

ACA has a division called the Association for Spiritual, Ethical, and Religious Values in Counseling (ASERVIC). It began in 1974. The website at http://www.aservic.org/ notes that this is an organization that "is devoted to professionals who believe that spiritual, ethical, religious, and other human values are essential to the full development of the person and to the discipline of counseling."

Similarly, the APA has Division 36, Psychology of Religion, which "promotes the application of psychological research methods and interpretive frameworks to diverse forms of religion and spirituality; encourages the incorporation of the results of such work into clinical and other applied settings; and fosters constructive dialogue and interchange between psychological study and practice on the one hand and between religious perspectives and institutions on the other. The Division is strictly nonsectarian and welcomes the participation of all persons who view religion as a significant factor in human functioning." This can be found at: http://www.apa.org/about/division/div36.html Homepage: www.apa.org/divisions/div36 Feb. 9, 2006.

It is important to distinguish professional pastoral counseling from what has come to be known as spiritual direction. We will discuss the activity of spiritual direction later in this chapter. For now, it is important to note that they are not the same thing.

Specific Ethical Concerns and Challenges

Religion and spirituality have not necessarily always been welcomed into the practice of counseling and/or psychotherapy. As we mentioned earlier in the text, mental health professionals have sometimes been called the secular priesthood, and suspicion has been leveled in both directions—from faith systems toward secular counselors, and from secular counselors toward faith systems. These suspicions contribute to the overall ethical dimensions of pastoral counseling.

Competence.   Pastoral counselors walk between two worlds and must have rudimentary competence in both to work ethically. For centuries, literature has exploited supposed linkages between spirituality and madness. People suffering from serious mental illness may firmly believe their struggles are spiritual—the result of sin, or of Satan's influence. Competent pastoral counselors have the task of presenting clients with biological explanations and potential referrals to physicians, psychological explanations and potential solutions, *and* spiritual explanations and solutions. The portions of the poem in Digressions for Deliberation 12.3 express the gravity of this calling better than we could ever do in prose.

Knowing how and when to refer is a core component of competency in any profession. It is especially important for pastoral counseling because the profession itself has a limited focus, with overt connects to both faith and mental health. Therefore, it could easily appeal to people struggling with character pathology or serious mental illnesses whose needs exceed the training or skills of the pastoral counselor.

Confidentiality and multiple roles.   The limits of confidentiality covered in Chapter 6 apply to credentialed mental health professionals. In many states, clergy and attorneys are exempt from some of these legally mandated limits for counselors. In fact, some faith systems have explicit instruction regarding not sharing confidences. In an article entitled *Confidences and Their Limits in Rabbinic Counseling* Elliot Dorff (2001) writes:

> All Jews, however, are governed by strict Jewish laws requiring the keeping of confidences. Specifically, the Torah prohibits not only spreading falsehoods about other people (sheker, lying), but also spreading true but negative facts about someone else that the hearer has no need to know—that is, lashon ha-ra, "speech about the bad"—and even spreading neutral facts that the hearer has no need to know—that is, rekhilut, gossip. The Talmud takes this further, insisting that even if there is no harm intended or anticipated, a person may not reveal a private conversation to an outside party unless the original speaker gives explicit permission to do so. (p. 6)

Because of the potential confusion over what information can be kept confidential in the context of pastoral counseling, a pastoral counselor must research applicable state and federal laws as well as church and faith expectations. Informed consent is an absolutely essential component of ethical pastoral counseling. Clients seeking pastoral counseling might have widely varying assumptions and expectations about confidentiality and relationship boundaries. They deserve to understand these issues clearly.

For pastoral counselors who are in the same faith community as their clients, confidentiality and multiple roles can become complicated in ways similar to addictions counselors who attend the same support groups. The mutuality expected in faith communities and support groups runs counter to the one-way intimacies of counseling. The concerns that lead to ethical prohibitions against multiple relationships are intensified in the "small communities" of faith and/or support groups. Most likely the multiple roles cannot be avoided, but the majority of the responsibility for their management falls directly on the counselor, not the client.

Seismic Shocks

Pauline Lenore Larson (1979)

So—I need help.
And I have sought it.
The psychiatrists say—
> *What was your childhood like?*
> *How do you relate to your parents?*
> *What about sex?*
> *How is your id?*

And they advise—
> *Control yourself.*
> *Relax. Relax.*
> *Let go.*
> *It's all in your mind.*

Some Christian friends say—
> *Your faith is too small.*
> *True Christians don't feel like that.*
> *You are resisting the Spirit.*
> *Rebuke Satan.*
> *Let God heal you.*
> *It's all in your heart; get your heart right.*

I say—
> *Not mind or heart, but mind and heart and body.*
> *The seismic shocks that shake my mind and soul*
> *are physical.*
> *The Word was made flesh, so flesh must be important.*
> *Why is no attention paid to mine*

. . .

> *Where is help for it?*
> *I love my counselors and I trust my God—usually—*
> *But where is help for me?*

. . .

> *Dogs barking in the night—*
> *I remember*
> *Bands of coyotes howling*
> *As I slept with my parents*
> *Under the stars in the Texas sage.*
> *Dogs barking in the night—*
> *Hounds baying at my heart's portals.*
> *They savage my serenity.*
> *Now no stars, no sleep,*
> *Just pain.*

Pauline ended her life with a medication overdose shortly after writing this poem. Her journal said, "Dare I hope that God will let me enter His Kingdom when I have so knowingly gone against His will? How I pray that He will! He knows, of course, how little I am deserving of it. But please, God" (pp. 77–78).

==

=== **Deepening Diversity 12.3** ===

Peter's Diversity Vision

So when Peter went up to Jerusalem, the circumcised believers criticized him, saying "Why did you go to the uncircumcised men and eat with them?" Then Peter began to explain it to them, step by step, saying, "I was in the city of Joppa praying, and in a trance, I saw a vision. There was something like a large sheet coming down from heaven, being lowered by its four corners; and it came close to me. As I looked at it closely I saw four-footed animals, beasts of prey, reptiles, and birds of the air. I also heard a voice saying to me, 'Get up, Peter; kill and eat.' But I replied, 'By no means, Lord; for nothing profane or unclean has ever entered my mouth.' But a second time the voice answered from heaven, 'What God has made clean, you must not call profane.' This happened three times; then everything was pulled up again to heaven. At that very moment, three men, sent to me from Caesarea, arrived at the house where we were. The Spirit told me to go with them and not to make a distinction between them and us." Acts 11: 2–12a (Metzger & Murphy, 1994, p. 177)

What do we make of this story? God asked Peter to eat food that had clearly been forbidden in Hebrew Scripture. Depending on your background and belief systems, you may hear different messages and predict different outcomes. It's not a vegetarian-friendly sort of story—but it does aptly capture the all-too-human self-assuredness about what is wrong to do and who belongs in the inner circle. As writer Anne Lamott (1994) has said, "You can be pretty sure you've built God in your own image if you are sure that God hates all the same people you hate."

==

Faith, sin, and salvation.   Although other specialties do not use these words, pastoral counseling is not alone in accommodating "true believers" who, in their fervor, are tempted to impose *their* solutions and life-meanings on vulnerable others. While it is certainly not ethical to impose a set of beliefs on the unsuspecting client, there are ways that informed consent could allow certain belief-system baselines to be made known, allowing the consumer/client to make choices. For instance, a Christian pastoral counselor might make a point of indicating her stance on gay marriage, whether her stance is supportive, or one that questions the nature of homosexual orientation. However, informed consent cannot justify the use of questionable therapeutic techniques to ferret out or change "sinful" ways of being. This is simply incompetent and unethical. Consider the wording in the code example.

American Association of Pastoral Counseling *Code of Ethics*

Principle III

> We make only realistic statements regarding the pastoral counseling process and its outcome. . . . We show sensitive regard for the moral, social, and religious standards of clients and communities. We avoid imposing our beliefs on others, although we may express them when appropriate in the pastoral counseling process.

This explicit principle, as well as competency concerns, would argue against any use of the controversial *conversion therapy* for sexual reorientation by counselors of any specialty. Conversion therapy has not been shown to be effective, and "appears to be an expression of homophobia and multicultural insensitivity" (Southern, Smith, & Oliver, 2005, p. 464).

BEYOND SPECIALTY

There are many professions that utilize the skills and truths of the mental health professions, but are not considered specializations within the mental health or counseling professions. Some of these are well-established professions such as teaching, nursing, coaching, personnel management, and even parenting(!). Others are newer endeavors and forms of helping that, in some cases, have grown out of the mental health professions, or share related professional goals, such as professional mediation, or breath and body work associated with trauma recovery or personal growth. We discuss two of these helping relationships in the following paragraphs—personal coaching and spiritual directing. While many with advanced college degrees are choosing to pursue these areas and skills, these activities are not legally regulated; thus, a wide range of people are free to refer to themselves as spiritual directors or personal coaches.

Pause for Reflection

You may wonder, as we have occasionally, about why we chose to include these related helping endeavors in this text. Perhaps it is a fascination with how specialties come into being (or fail to do so). Perhaps it is to help you with your discernment process about what is and is not currently considered professional counseling. Perhaps we would secretly rather be personal coaches or spiritual directors. Are these areas harbingers of things to come? Do they constitute a clever way to step away from the medical model implicit in most counseling professions? We don't have the answers, but something tells us these are areas worth considering.

Personal Coaching

Personal coaching would not be considered a counseling specialty at present, but it has attracted a number of counselors and psychologists who have subsequently changed professions. You might wonder why these professionals don't simply add personal coaching to their list of services, and perhaps some do. However, some aspects of personal coaching diverge sharply from traditional mental health practices and thus the activities may not be covered by the practitioner's professional insurance. Further, personal coaching is a clear move away from any sort of medical model. Those who hire personal coaches are not diagnosed, their health insurance is not billed, and they are coached, as opposed to counseled or treated.

One personal coach who describes himself as a therapist-turned-coach stated, "The basic philosophy behind life coaching is that we humans have immeasurable resources of energy, wisdom, ability and genius waiting to be set in motion" (P. Williams, 2002).

There are national and international organizations for personal coaching. The International Coaching Federation's web page (http://www.coachfederation.org) has the following mission statement:

> The mission of the International Coach Federation is to be the global forum for the art and science of coaching, where we inspire transformational conversations, advocate excellence, and expand awareness of the contribution coaching is to the future of humankind.

This organization has a thoughtful ethics code that addresses boundaries, informed consent, confidentiality, and competence. It defines the overall goals of the professional activity. However, the reach of this code is simply to the membership of this organization. The website urges professional coaches to adhere to high professional standards with the hope that the profession can remain self-regulated, rather than state regulation.

Pause for Reflection

What are the benefits and/or problems associated with helping professions that self-regulate? Does the current state of professionalism with personal coaching sound appealing to you? Exciting? A new frontier? Or does it sound, as the English say, "a bit worrying?"

Professional, or personal, coaches envision themselves as partners with their clients—helping them improve their performances at work, or fulfill their callings, or capitalize on their gifts. Coaches use listening skills, performance enhancement skills, and team-building skills in order to bring about positive change. They do not diagnose people or problems, and they do not necessarily work within the 50-minute hour. They might accompany clients to work or to other activities. They might meet weekly, monthly, or even less often. While they use many counseling skills, coaches have clearly stepped away from some of the core definitions of counseling.

Spiritual Direction

Although enjoying a recent resurgence in popularity, it would not be accurate to describe spiritual direction as a newer profession. In fact, it predates mental health professions by 1700 years or so (Armstrong & Gertz, 2005). Many faiths and organizations offer forms of spiritual direction. For example, the organization Spiritual Directors International described itself on its web page as "a global learning community of people from many faiths and many nations who share a common concern, passion and commitment to the art and contemplative practice of spiritual direction" (SDI, 2005).

While Spiritual Directors International serves people from any faiths, and has a focus on more ecumenical contemplative practices, there are many spiritual directors who focus quite clearly on one faith system. Consider this quote from *Christianity Today:* "Christian counselor and popular author Larry Crabb took the trouble to earn a Ph.D. in clinical psychology. But now he believes that in today's church, therapy should be replaced by another, more ancient practice—spiritual direction. . . . Spiritual direction is a voluntary relationship between a person who seeks to grow in the Christian life and a director. The latter is not, notice, a counselor or therapist. Rather, he or she is a mature Christian who helps the directee both to discern what the Holy Spirit is doing and saying and to act on that discernment, drawing nearer to God in Christ" (Armstrong & Gertz, 2005).

Whether a narrow or broader definition of the Divine is used, the focus of spiritual direction is on relationship with things spiritual, not on psychological diagnoses or problems. The Spiritual Directors International website says "Spiritual direction is not psychotherapy, counseling, or financial planning."

Eugene Peterson (1996) defines spiritual direction as spiritual friendship, with the attention focused in conversation and prayer on the spiritual being of the other person. He encourages people to read about this sort of work done by the elders and masters of the trade.

There are many variants on the spiritual direction theme, including retreat centers, vision quests, and other opportunities for soul work in group or individual formats (Plotkin, 2003). The popularity of the rediscovered mystic Muslim poet, Rumi (Helminski, 2000), the numerous best-selling books by the Dali Lama, Thomas Moore's *The Care of the Soul,* (Moore, 1994), and the wide readership of many such works points to a hunger for greater spiritual understanding of ourselves and life in our culture.

Similar to personal coaches, spiritual directors are not regulated by state or federal law. Whereas the term "buyer beware" may be applicable to personal coaches, it may be more appropriate to say "seeker beware" with regard to spiritual direction. Either way, both of these professional helping relationships hold promise and offer interesting contrasts to the more developed, and thus more regulated, mental health professions.

CHAPTER WRAP-UP

If your only tool is a hammer, everything looks like a nail.

—Unknown

Specialties within counseling and psychotherapy will probably always have some degree of fluidity and controversy. Specialties can reflect extensive knowledge of

- the treatment needs and concerns of a certain population, such as a particular age group
- varied techniques and strategies required to treat certain problem areas, such as sexual abuse survivors
- a specific theoretical orientation, such as Gestalt or cognitive-behavioral
- a specific worldview orientation, such as wellness or pastoral counseling

There can be specialties within specialties, such as a counselor who specializes in treating families and couples within the addictions field, or a Jungian therapist who works exclusively with late mid-life adults.

Some professional organizations have guidelines for certification of specialization, or indicate an expected knowledge base. Certain larger specialties have numerous professional organizations that enhance professional identity, provide particular ethical guidance, serve as a conduit for research and continuing education, and can thereby influence public policy and practice.

There are tracks or entire degrees for the larger specialties, such as mental health, school, or marital and family counseling, but there are many professional opportunities for further specialization at the master's level. Most doctoral programs in psychology train for general counseling or clinical practice, with opportunities to focus during training, on internship, or at the post-doctoral level.

The choice to specialize has many factors—the needs in a given location, job demands and opportunities, personal preferences, and educational opportunities. Each area of potential specialization has its own unique ethical concerns, which will continue to evolve, just as the profession itself evolves.

Chapter Thirteen

TEACHING, MENTORING, SUPERVISION

> *For apart from inquiry . . . individuals cannot be truly human. Knowledge emerges only through invention and re-invention, through the restless, impatient, continuing, hopeful inquiry human beings pursue in the world, with the world, and with each other.*
> —Paulo Freire, *Pedagogy of the Oppressed*

CHAPTER ORIENTATION

Ethical professionals will be lifelong learners, and directly or indirectly, many will be or become teachers, mentors, role models, and/or supervisors. We also need to be explorers who continually assess what we are taught and examine what we assume to be true. We have an overabundance of ever-changing knowledge, which makes time and attention into very scare resources (Pór, 2000). Both knowledge itself and the manner in which it is taught have moral ramifications. In this chapter, we urge you to consider both the process and content of what you have been taught and are being taught. There are many forces and choices involved in lifelong questioning, exploring, learning, and professional development.

Specifically, in this chapter you will have the opportunity to reflect on the following:

- a review of moral philosophy through the lenses of teaching and supervision;
- the ethical responsibilities of those who teach in the mental health professions; and
- the ethical responsibilities of those who offer mental health supervision.

ALPHA, OMEGA: BEGINNING AND END

The topics in this chapter are the last in the book because teaching and supervision are the means by which the helping professions propagate their species. The transmission of the essential knowledge and skills of our vocation to the next generation of professionals is entrusted to teachers and supervisors. Throughout this text, one constant refrain has been "when in doubt, seek further education, consultation, and supervision." This, of course, is more easily written than enacted. And to make matters worse, our refrain should have been more explicit: seek cutting edge, research-informed education; insightful, compassionate, and knowledgeable consultation; and seasoned, highly skilled supervision.

Probably not surprisingly, we also believe that more is better. The lifelong supervision required in the United Kingdom seems a wise practice for the helping professions. At the very least, establishing consistent mutual consulting relationships, in ongoing groups or through regular contact with other professionals seems essential to sanity, balance, and ethical practice.

Just as counseling relationships have dimensions that recapitulate fundamental aspects of our most formative and meaningful relationships (parents, siblings, early teachers, and other caretakers), so do teaching, mentoring, and supervisory relationships. You might find yourself reacting to professors and supervisors in ways that are similar to your usual reaction to authority figures, or that remind you of your relationship with your parents. In some of these relationships, this will be true in only the smallest, unacknowledged way, but in others, it may be quite significant. You may struggle to keep certain negative reactions in check with some, and on the other hand, you may come to think of certain individuals as your "mothers" or "fathers" in the field.

You will not always have the opportunity to choose your teachers or supervisors. When you do, perhaps the contents of this chapter will enable you to choose well. Further, believe it or not, you will someday (maybe sooner than you feel ready) become a teacher, mentor, or supervisor of your colleagues-in-the-making. We hope this chapter will provide you with foundational guidelines and heights to aspire toward in those endeavors and duties.

Pause for Reflection

Consider your reactions to the last two paragraphs. Can you already identify the supervisors and professors who most remind you of your parents or other important authority figures in your life? Are there some you would like to emulate, and others you find difficult, at best? What are the attributes that matter to you? Do you think your answers to this query will change in 10 years?

ACA *Code of Ethics*

Section F Introduction

Counselors aspire to foster meaningful and respectful professional relationships and to maintain appropriate boundaries with supervisees and students. Counselors have theoretical and pedagogical foundations for their work and aim to be fair, accurate, and honest in their assessments of counselors-in-training.

NASW *Code of Ethics*

3.02 Education and Training

(a) Social workers who function as educators, field instructors for students, or trainers should provide instruction only within their areas of knowledge and competence and should provide instruction based on the most current information and knowledge available in the profession.

APA *Ethical Principles*

7.01 Education and Training

Psychologists responsible for education and training programs take reasonable steps to ensure that the programs are designed to provide the appropriate knowledge and proper experiences, and to meet the requirements for licensure, certification, or other goals for which claims are made by the program.

MORAL PHILOSOPHY AND PROFESSIONAL ELDERHOOD

The basic moral positions we covered in Chapter 2 hold great wisdom both for those seeking to find the best possible supervision, and for those seeking to provide the same. In this next section, we consider supervision and teaching through three of those classic perspectives. We do so to emphasize the many morally relevant dimensions of teaching and supervision. Each moral theory offers a different lens. Sometimes, there is concurrence; sometimes, contradiction. As we've noted, moral philosophy has yet to produce a comprehensive moral theory that when properly used would always yield the perfect, highest moral solution or set of rules. This should not stop us from using the dominant moral theories to compare and contrast the moral considerations each brings to light.

Deontological Dimensions

Doing one's duty as a supervisor or teacher includes tolerating the *redundancy* of the basics, always seeking *renewal* of enthusiasm, *relishing the rewards* of nurturing growth and development, shouldering *responsibilities* of discernment and assessment, devoting oneself to lifelong *regeneration* of knowledge and ongoing *renovation* of style and technique. And that's just the beginning. Supervisors and teachers have many important duties that are essential to ethical practice. Not only must they know and stay current in the theories, practices, and procedures of our profession, they must be able to enact these practices effectively and have the skills necessary to teach others how to do so as well. In short, they need to be able to not only talk the talk, they have to be able to walk the walk.

We will cover more specific ethical duties for supervision and teaching in later sections of this chapter, but we want to stress the primary importance of *duty* in supervision and teaching. Brilliance and insight are nice. Devotion is comforting, and dramatic presentation can be inspiring. But without attention to basic duties, supervision and teaching can come unhinged and actually be quite dangerous and/or destructive to the developing professional (Ladany, Friedlander, & Nelson, 2005; Metcalfe & Matharu, 1995).

Utilitarian Usefulness

Teachers and supervisors affect the lives and well-being of many generations of students. It is of paramount importance that they consider the greatest good for the greatest number, consciously aware of the possible effects of their actions. They are instructing or supervising people who will, in turn, impact the lives of many individuals. Like the stone thrown into still water, their teachings and supervisory guidance will move out in ever-widening concentric circles. Our own instructors and supervisors, now retired, live on in the ways we work with clients and students, and in the ways we write and promote ideas. Teachers and supervisors would do well to heed the advice attributed to the Iroquois Nations: In all our deliberations, we must consider the effects of our decisions on the next seven generations (Seventh Generation Fund, 2004).

What might be some practical considerations from a utilitarian perspective?

- **Playing favorites:** Even though we all enjoy being someone's favorite, teachers or supervisors who play favorites are not acting ethically or wisely, if for no other reason than this: They are spread too thinly to have favorites without then also neglecting others. There are other ethical concerns related to playing favorites. We are confident you can think of some.

- **Neglecting "generic" basics:** It might be fun, or ego-enhancing, to teach highly specialized, but rarely applicable interventions, but teachers and supervisors must make sure they teach and model the basics—highly developed listening skills, solid diagnostic skills, multicultural skills, and an ongoing determination to address bigotry and narrow-mindedness—and of course, ethics!

- **Avoid the Peter Principle** (Peter, 1984). In essence, the Peter Principle is this—We will rise to our level of incompetence. This usually means that people with awesome counseling skills will assume that those skills alone will make them awesome teachers or supervisors. The clear truth is this: there are separate skills and gifts necessary for effective teaching and supervision. The Peter Principle posits that once one rises to a level beyond their capabilities, they will stagnate there.

- **Avoid the Vertical Arabesque:** This is a grim extension of the Peter Principle. Sometimes, people rise *beyond* their level of incompetence. They don't stagnate, they keep getting promoted! We are aware of an agency supervisor who recognized that a given individual was a very unpopular counselor. Clients would only see him a few times, and then drop out. Those who knew the score coming in would request anyone but him. So, you guessed it. Because of the difficulties of actually firing him, the agency director "promoted" him to supervisor. In the short run, this might have inflicted less harm on clients. In the long run, though, situations like this represent a great loss for many affected individuals. In teaching, the old adage, "Those who can, do; those who cannot, teach; and those who cannot teach consult" is another ironic expression of vertical arabesque.

Character Concerns

As Aristotle so aptly pointed out, in order to become virtuous, we must *practice* the virtues. And in order to become a master at whatever profession or craft we were intended to become, we need to apprentice ourselves to the very best mentors and teachers available. Students want both excellent skills and well-developed virtues exemplified in teachers and supervisors.

Instruction and development in the artistic realms often involves periods of time during which developing artists, writers, musicians, or poets mimic the style and voice of the great masters. They try on the style, not with the hope of becoming a clone of the master, but with the hope of absorbing something from the master that will add to, transform, and mature the unique gifts of the aspiring artist. Counseling is an art that draws on science, or a science that draws on art (Gladding, 2005a; Hubble, Duncan, & Miller, 1999).

As expressions of character, the midlevel ethical principles we discussed in Chapter 2 are as important to teaching and supervision as they are to the therapeutic relationship. They are certainly relevant aspects to consider regarding the character of the supervisor or teacher in question. You should be able to see evidence of fidelity, benevolence, nonmaleficence, justice, and honoring of autonomy in those who teach and supervise. This should be evident in their professional practice and teaching, and in their ways of being with you as a supervisee. These are very high standards. No one is truthful, loyal, kind, just, respectful, and avoidant of harm at all times and in all places. Therefore, two more aspects of character emerge as relevant: humility (or the ability to admit mistakes) and compassion (or the ability to forgive mistakes).

In the next portions of this chapter, we separate supervision from teaching. There are obvious overlaps in the ethical and professional concerns of each, but there are distinct differences in knowledge base as well.

TEACHING: THE TRANSFORMING FORCE OF KNOWLEDGE

Who is this that darkens counsel by words without knowledge?

—Job 38:2

Ethical teachers are proficient in the skills they teach, passionate about their subject areas, and respectful of the professional role they play in the lives of their students. Mental health professionals will often find themselves teaching their clients, whether overtly in the form of psychoeducational groups, or more subtly and/or spontaneously as needed. There are many other parallels between the counseling relationship and the teaching relationship, with a few notable exceptions. The exceptions help elucidate the uniqueness of each, and the similarities underline the fact that both counseling and teaching involve relationships with significant power differentials.

Pause for Reflection

Who was your favorite teacher in the first 12 years of your education? From whom did you learn the most? Did you name the same person for questions 1 and 2? What do you think makes a great teacher? Is teaching a learned skill, or are people born with the gift of teaching?

Client Welfare

In Chapter 1, and throughout this text, we have emphasized that the person in need of the counseling services is the client. In contrast to supervisors, professors who teach skills for a wide variety of human interactions do not usually interact directly with clients. Does this nullify their ethical responsibility to these unseen future clients? We think not. In fact, this is one of the moral disconnects between knowledge and practice that we believe is harming our society. As we discussed in Chapter 9, there are serious ethical concerns when knowledge is morally disconnected from its application. This is true for counselor educators, professors in psychology, and professors in social work. Teachers *are* responsible to the clients their students will eventually see when those students are using strategies taught by the teacher in question.

Teaching Competence

Teaching competence has many dimensions. Excellent teachers know their material *and* know how to effectively and respectfully transmit the knowledge to students (Freire, 1993). In addition, like supervisors, professors must be able to fairly and accurately evaluate academic performance and applied skills.

Knowing the material.　　There may be a few rare faculty persons who are only expected to teach their very favorite courses, but we aren't acquainted with them. Most of us have our favorite courses and our tolerable courses. Unfortunately, due to the realities of academia, many of us also have our "Okay, fine. I'll teach it if no one else will" courses. Regardless, faculty members need to be current in the course-related research and literature of every course they teach. In a field that changes as rapidly as ours, this requires updated materials every time the course is taught.

Effective teaching.　　Teaching, like counseling, is both science and art—requiring hard work, honest self-appraisal, and an authentic presence in the classroom. The academic podium is not a bully pulpit for the professor's point of view (B. M. Fisher, 2001). The effective instructor is able to present all valid points of view, and continuously elicit the wisdom present in the students.

> The classroom ought to be just such a place: where students are taught to recognize a de facto code, to decode and recode it in their newly found voices. I always assume that my students have a voice, whether they know it or not. What I don't know is to what use this voice will be put. (Felman, 2001, p. 34)

At the end of most college courses, students are given a chance to evaluate the course and the instructor. Although important, this process has a number of concerns associated with it (Adamson, O'Kane, & Shevlin, 2005; Beran & Violato, 2005; Brems, Baldwin, Davis, & Namyniuk, 1994; McCormack, 2005). Some of these include:

- Evaluations tend to directly correlate with grades. Those who believe they are receiving high marks rate the course and instructor positively. This has many problematic implications, including grade inflation.
- Evaluations are anonymous, but in small classes in graduate programs, comments might still identify the evaluator, thus inflating the evaluations toward the positive out of fear of later retribution.

- Evaluations are done at the end of the term; the professor cannot therefore improve the course for those doing the evaluation.
- Due to the anonymity and lack of process involved, evaluations can be unnecessarily vicious without consequence or accountability.

Even though there are problems with the course evaluation process, it is important for teachers to have feedback about their competence, and an obvious source for some of this feedback is the students themselves.

Some faculty have experimented with midterm course feedback options (Center for Teaching and Learning, 2005) and many of us, taking advantage of the lessons of feminist pedagogy (Tetrault, 1994) make it a practice to invite continual feedback and commentary about the course content, assignments, and grading systems.

Ethical evaluation.   In graduate training programs, grades remain important, but other forms of evaluation become relevant as well. Evaluative feedback hopefully shapes and inspires student growth and development. Assessing something as multi-faceted as counseling skill development is challenging. Remley and Herlihy (2005) recommend the following three practices for assessing skills-related course work in an ethically and legally defensible manner:

- Use specific behavioral terms to describe the skills to be learned in the course.
- Provide regular, clear feedback regarding the students' development of the skills.
- Use grades or numeric ratings as part of the feedback and final marks. (p. 297)

Teaching Relationship

Even though students most often pay for their instruction, and are in this sense the employer of their instructor, the power in the relationship lies primarily with the instructor. Power differentials in relationships always trigger a set of fiduciary responsibilities for the one holding the power.

Pause for Reflection

Students sometimes sign honor pledges or endorse other codes of behavior or ethics. In graduate professional programs, students are expected to abide by state and national laws, university policies, and program guidelines. What other possible ethical guidelines might students consider in terms of:

- *their relationships with each other?*
- *behaviors in class?*
- *their relationships with teachers and supervisors?*

Students often have concerns about and frustrations with peers who they perceive to be impaired (Oliver, Bernstein, Anderson, Blashfield, & Roberts, 2004). What ethical responsibilities do you think you might have if you had similar concerns?

Informed consent.   The teaching relationship in competitive graduate education programs begins long before faculty and students actually meet. In graduate training programs, faculty members determine the curriculum, teaching materials, and supervisory practices, often in conjunction with accreditation requirements. They develop the literature that allows prospective students to determine if the program is a good fit for them. Analogous to informed consent, the materials about the program, specific class expectations, and practicum and internship opportunities should all be available to anyone wishing to assess the program.

Most programs that train mental health professionals now have websites and relevant links to other aspects of the learning institutions in which they are housed. These websites, as well as any written literature, need to accurately reflect the many central aspects of the program. These include, but are not limited to:

- required coursework
- required GPA during the program
- practicum and Internship expectations
- suggestions or requirements for personal counseling experiences
- requirements for participation in experiential learning, retreats, and so on
- extra or "hidden" costs, such as fees for practicum lab, supervision, graduate fees, or extra tuition fees specific to the program

Pause for Reflection

What did you know about your program before seeking admission? Are there gaps in the information you received? If so, can you think of ways you might offer your observations to program directors in the spirit of continual improvement?

Confidentiality.   A famous (or infamous, depending on your point of view) study done some years ago revealed that troubled students rated their college professors to be as good as, or better than, psychotherapists at helping them with their personal problems (Strupp, 1979). These might lead some to assume that certain college professors are not only helpful, but that they would make good mental health professionals—and with the right training, they might. However, as we noted in Chapter 1, hairdressers and bartenders are also helpful listeners, but they are not mental health professionals. They have a different set of ethical obligations.

In our experience, students and faculty alike sometimes mistakenly assume that teacher/student interactions, or even student/classroom interactions, can be kept confidential. This is not necessarily true. Teachers have many responsibilities and answer to many constituents. Obviously, they are never free to use student information for gossip or party entertainment, but they are also obliged to act in the best interest of the public, their teaching institution, and their colleagues. If a student in any field shared their dangerous fantasies, racist hatred, or illegal activities, most faculty members would feel an obligation to seek consultation, or call the authorities.

Professors in graduate mental health training programs must be especially careful in this domain. Because most are mental health professionals themselves, they or their students might become confused about ethical obligations. This is one of the many reasons that faculty should never be their students' counselors. They cannot provide students the same level of confidentiality or impartiality that counselors provide their clients. For example, students who share racist or homophobic beliefs, or disclose substance abuse problems or addictions, or treat classmates manipulatively or cruelly must be confronted. This will most likely be done after careful faculty deliberations, and will involve more than one faculty person. Because of their responsibilities to future generations of clients, graduate faculty must consider all they hear and observe about students in their evaluations of goodness-of-fit for the field. A faculty person seeing a current student for therapy constitutes a profound conflict of interests and duties.

Multiple roles and boundaries.   Faculty members who teach in the helping professions are almost always either sequentially or simultaneously teachers, supervisors, and mentors to their students. These roles last various lengths of time. As students mature and finish their training, faculty and former students might also become colleagues, consultants, and friends. Such sequential roles are not unethical. However, some roles have duties associated with them that outlast the roles themselves. For instance, a supervisor might come to know a student's worst adequacy fears. Later, this student might be a colleague in the community. It would be highly unethical and disrespectful to later use this knowledge to confront or manipulate this colleague in any way, or to share this information with others.

In small communities, it is also possible that applicants to the local counseling graduate program may be former clients of faculty persons. Trust us. This *can* happen. In our program, members of the selection committee can recuse themselves from commenting on or rating a certain applicant without explaining why. Former clients certainly have a right to apply to the only program within 200 miles, and they have the right for their previous counseling relationship with a given faculty person to remain confidential. Our practice has been to offer the former client a free check-in time, to talk over the issues and concerns in such a situation. It is not an easy situation, but is one that can be carefully managed to avoid harm to the former client.

Graduate students and faculty will usually have occasion to attend the same social events. Being friendly and socially interactive does not usually present ethical problems. However, on occasion, it can.

Case Example: Donna, a single 20-something Caucasian, was in her second year as a counselor education student. Her program's student handbook clearly stated that faculty would provide students with overall progress evaluations every semester, based on any and all contact that faculty had with students. One of the faculty members invited all other faculty and all graduate students to a holiday event in her backyard. She did not serve alcohol, but some guests brought beer and wine. Donna got drunk and behaved inappropriately—yelling, accusing one male student of leading her on, and making negative racial comments about a Japanese exchange student.

Five faculty and many students witnessed Donna's behaviors. The faculty agreed there was a need to meet with Donna and confront this behavior. In addition to the meeting, Donna's social behaviors were noted in her semester evaluation. Donna was humiliated. She apologized profusely. Over the holidays, she apparently reconsidered her career choice, and withdrew from the program. The faculty attempted to contact Donna, but she did not return phone calls, and did not respond to a letter inviting her to talk.

Problems such as those presented in the previous case example are infrequent but obviously disturbing. More common, but also problematic, are faculty who allow themselves to become friends with certain students while the students are still in the graduate program. The loss of objectivity is significant. The enjoyment of the friendship does not outweigh the potential damage to the student, or to other students who witness the apparent partiality.

Finally, the power differential between teachers and students argues against even consensual romantic relationships. Sexual harassment, sex-traded-for-grades, and other egregious misbehaviors are obviously unethical. Two single people, one a professor and one a student, expressing sexual attraction to each other may seem more innocent— but it is fraught with ethical troubles such as lack of objectivity and fairness to other students (Caldwell, 2003). It is also fraught with potential legal difficulties, should the romance end and the student come to feel manipulated or used. The one with the power is responsible for setting and keeping the boundaries. No matter how open or seductive a student might be, it will not be the student facing a ruined reputation, legal charges, and/or civil suits if the relationship breaks up in a destructive way.

Teaching and Technology

Stunning amounts of information are available in our culture, and methods of information delivery continue to become faster and have greater reach. Of course, simply making information available is not teaching, but teachers are responsible for both method and materials of instruction. From occasional distance-learning courses, to Internet based instruction, to fully accredited online degrees, there are many ethical dimensions to consider. Interestingly, the core concerns remain the same (Creed, 1997), but the application, practicalities, and relative risks shift significantly. For instance, while possible, Internet romantic relationships between faculty and students are less likely. However, issues in assessing student competence may be more salient and teaching competence will certainly involve different factors and skills.

The Association for Counselor Education and Supervision (ACES) has developed guidelines for online instruction that address the following domains:

- course quality
- course content and objectives
- instructional support
- faculty qualifications
- instructor and course evaluation
- technology standards

Applications 13.1

Questions to Consider When Using Technology

- In what ways will this technology change what I communicate and teach?
- How will my communications and teaching be enhanced or hampered?
- How can I address these changes, capitalize on the strengths, and compensate for the weaknesses?
- In what ways will this technology affect confidentiality of grades and feedback?
- What safeguards are in my control?
- If Internet skills or online courses are required, is our program informing all applicants?
- Are my students able to use the technology in ways that will not compromise their rights to adequate understanding and feedback?
- Is my own level of technological competence adequate to address any difficulties that might come up?
- Do I have a back-up system for times the technology fails or is unavailable?
- Can I accurately describe what I am offering with this technology?
- If I am offering coursework or supervision utilizing telephones or the Internet in a way that replaces traditional face-to-face interactions, have I attended to issues of equivalency?

These domains help organize practical and ethical reflections regarding the adequacy and appropriateness of a given online instructional opportunity. In addition, read the considerations listed in Applications 13.1 and review the guidance offered in the ACA and APA Codes of Ethics. This list, while specific to teaching and supervision, shares much common ground with the lists in previous chapters.

SUPERVISION: UNDERGIRDING AND OVERSIGHT

In the wild and distant 1960s, everyone who was anyone had a guru. If you find this hard to believe, find a 50-something friend or relative who still eats granola or drives an older-model Volkswagen van and make discreet inquiries. It was a time of loosened boundaries, questioned authority, and, paradoxically, gurus who were supposed to guide their followers to the true meaning of life. Gurus were wise beings from exotic places who, like Dr. Science (Dr. Science, 2005), knew more than we did.

Whether we admit it or not, most of us long for the perfect parent, the impeccable advocate, the sage elder who will guide us, shelter us, and bring us, painlessly, into self-sufficiency and maturity. Needless to say, supervisors can't measure up. It is no surprise that our supervisors catch a fair amount of transference and projection, whether positive or negative or both. Perfection aside, there are some high standards we should expect from our supervisors, and from ourselves when we begin offering supervision. The ethics codes address these standards.

NASW *Code of Ethics*

3.02 Education and Training

(b) Social workers who function as educators or field instructors for students should evaluate students' performance in a manner that is fair and respectful.

ACA *Code of Ethics*

F.1. Counselor Supervision and Client Welfare

F.1.a. Client Welfare

A primary obligation of counseling supervisors is to monitor the services provided by other counselors or counselors-in-training. Counseling supervisors monitor client welfare and supervisee clinical performance and professional development. To fulfill these obligations, supervisors meet regularly with supervisees to review case notes, samples of clinical work, or live observations. Supervisees have a responsibility to understand and follow the *ACA Code of Ethics.*

F.1.b. Counselor Credentials

Counseling supervisors work to ensure that clients are aware of the qualifications of the supervisees who render services to the clients.

APA *Ethical Principles*

7.06 Assessing Student and Supervisee Performance

(a) In academic and supervisory relationships, psychologists establish a timely and specific process for providing feedback to students and supervisees. Information regarding the process is provided to the student at the beginning of supervision.

(b) Psychologists evaluate students and supervisees on the basis of their actual performance on relevant and established program requirements.

Client Welfare

As mental health professionals, educators, and/or supervisors, our highest calling from that timid or bravado-filled greeting we offer our first client in our first practicum to the last thoughts we have about our professional work just before we depart this world is the welfare of our clients—their happiness, well-being, safety, healing, and growth. Even though supervisors have a central set of obligations to their supervisees, their *primary* obligation is to the clients of those supervisees. There are practical requirements that flesh out this obligation. Supervisors need to meet regularly with supervisees, review case notes, watch videotapes, hear summaries, and/or observe the counseling directly.

At the very least, they need to make sure that clients understand the professional educational background and developmental stage of the supervisee, and ensure that clients have been involved in a thorough informed consent process. This should include knowledge of the supervisory relationship, and in our opinion, the identity of the supervisor.

While supervisors cannot guarantee positive outcomes for their supervisee's clients, they can assist the supervisee in choosing tools and directions that stand a reasonable chance of being helpful. Supervisors must make sure no harm comes to clients, and that their basic needs are understood and attended to.

Pause for Reflection

Put yourself in the client's seat and consider how much you would want to know about your counselor's supervision. Of course, you are far more informed than the average layperson, and might want to know more as a result. Would you want to know the supervisor's name? Training? Credentials? If an entire practicum class was going to view your counseling sessions on videotape, what would you want to know about these people and the process?

Supervision Dimensions and Competencies

Supervision skills are not the same as applied counseling, therapy, or helping skills. There are theories and practices specific to supervision (Bernard & Goodyear, 2004; Haynes, Corey, & Moulton, 2003). Your supervisor should have training in these practices and theories, and should stay current by reading, attending continuing education training, and seeking feedback from supervisees as to their effectiveness as a supervisor. They should also be open to hearing about areas that might need attention.

As your supervision begins, you should have the opportunity to understand how your supervisor supervises. Professionals-in-training deserve to know and benefit from knowing the developmental process their supervisors have gone through on the path to becoming an effective supervisor. Supervision style has been shown to be related not only to supervisee skill attainment, but also to supervisee satisfaction and ultimate self-efficacy (Fernanado & Hulse-Killacky, 2005).

Haynes et al. (2003) provide a summary of supervisory competencies. They write that competent supervisors:

- are trained in supervision and keep their knowledge current by seeking continuing education;
- are trained specifically in the skills, theories, and treatment areas in which they are supervising;
- have effective interpersonal skills, and are able to listen, challenge, confront, provide feedback, and set careful, ethical boundaries around the supervisor/supervisee relationship;
- realize that supervision has component parts that are interactive and always in flux, which include the supervisor, the supervisee, the client(s), and the setting(s); Skilled supervisors adapt and modify as needed;
- are flexible and able to assume a variety of necessary roles and responsibilities as the situation dictates;
- have a broad knowledge of applicable ethics codes and mental health laws and regulations, and keep this knowledge current;

- stay centered and focused on the fact that client welfare is the primary concern;
- are willing and able to provide evaluation and feedback about their supervisees abilities and needs;
- document their supervisory activities in a timely manner; and
- empower their supervisees. They assist supervisees in problem-solving and teach and consult in a manner that allows supervisees to grow and develop their skills and their identities as autonomous professionals. (p. 159)

This is a helpful and thorough list. An attitude of respect and positive regard is evident in the duties and in the ways the duties are stated. From flexibility, to knowledge, to focus, to documentation—the obvious concern is for supervisee growth and development in the context of caring for clients.

Supervisors are role models, sometimes overtly, and sometimes, inadvertently. The care, or lack of care, with which they enact the basic professional responsibilities can impact and shape supervisees as much as the actual duties. It is a matter of both attitude and action. In addition to the overall functions of supervision covered thus far, the truly ethical supervisor cheerfully and thoroughly attends to the following basic, but important duties.

Informed consent. Supervisors provide an informed consent process for supervisees, detailing:

- theoretical orientation, and educational background
- timing and duration of supervision sessions
- other relevant policies and procedures
- supervisory record-keeping practices
- ways and means of evaluation
- contact information
- legal and ethical concerns
- what to do in case of an emergency
- when to anticipate supervisory absences, and who will be on-call
- an explanation of the supervisees rights to terminate the supervisory relationship

In one study, nearly 10% of the supervisees reported that their supervisors had not taken the time to explain what was expected of the supervisee (Ladany & Melincoff, 1999). Building a foundation that includes a thorough informed consent is a relatively new expectation. If you find yourself receiving supervision from someone who is not trained in supervision, or who is not engaging in any kind of informed consent process, you should consider your options carefully. You may be able to ask the most important questions from the previous list in a way that allows you to feel comfortable with the supervision. You may be able to ask a trusted professor or former supervisor about how to handle the situation. If these suggestions are not realistic options, you may want to consider seeking a different supervisor. For many reasons, including those in the following paragraphs, you deserve to seek the best possible supervision for your own professional development.

Discernment and growth.   Supervisors identify areas in need of growth, or limitations in the developing professional, and are prepared to assist the supervisee in finding ways to grow and/or overcome these limits. Although the concepts need continued definition and development, those who teach and supervise are charged with assessing both personal and professional development (Hensley, Smith, & Thompson, 2003). When a supervisor does notice deficiencies, and recommends some kind of counseling or remediation, the supervisor must either communicate this to program faculty responsible for such actions, or make sure the supervisee follows through—or both.

In the event that remediation isn't possible, supervisors have the difficult duty to make sure the proper faculty or licensing boards know of these deficits. This is probably one of the all-time least favorite duties supervisors face. When necessary, they recommend dismissal from training programs, or refusal to recommend that a student sit for licensure. This takes great courage, and should not be done without consultation and careful documentation. However, this kind of tough love can actually prove rewarding in some cases. In others, the only solace is that such actions are essential for the protection of clients and the integrity of our profession.

Case Example: Clara began her counseling training in her late 30s. She had recently published a very popular book that sold so well that she had the luxury of studying anything she wanted to study. She had always dreamed of being a counselor, and had very well-developed fantasies of exactly how she would make dramatic differences in the lives of young women. She loved her counseling classes and got excellent grades, but in practicum, she was difficult. She only wanted to see young women, and she could not stop herself from giving copious amounts of insistent advice to these vulnerable clients. She began having videotape "malfunctions" and her faculty supervisor began to suspect Clara was giving advice, but then erasing that part of the session. After a number of meetings and lengthy discussions that included Clara, her practicum supervisor, her faculty advisor, and the mental health team leader, it was determined that Clara would not get a passing mark for her practicum work. She was asked to consider seeking counseling to explore her own development, her ideas about clients and their needs, and so on.

Clara was devastated. She was angry, indignant, and alternated between threatening lawsuits and quitting the program. Fortunately, she did neither. She found a wonderful mental health professional and worked for over a year on her issues, which included a very difficult set of losses in early childhood, an overcontrolling mother, an abusive sibling, and three early miscarriages. Two years from the time of this stop-out, Clara began practicum again—a changed and grateful person. She finished her program and happily began working as a mental health counselor.

This is a happy ending. Can you imagine other endings? What kinds of fears or relief do you feel as you consider this account?

At times, it is difficult to sort out competence concerns from diversity issues. As we stated at the beginning of the chapter, program faculty and supervisors are the experts who select and train the next generation of all types of mental health professionals. We need to be alert to the human tendencies to gravitate toward the familiar, overvaluing those who are just like we are. Consider the dynamics in the next case example.

Case Example: Luke drove his classmates crazy. He used every classroom activity or sharing time to tell of his faith and his belief that everyone who had not accepted Christ as Lord and Savior was doomed to hell. Luke complained about the quality of instruction. Early on, he indicated that he planned to do his thesis research on the "horrific psychological damage" that young women incurred by having an abortion. The faculty in Luke's program tried to be tolerant, but Luke bothered many of them. Two of the faculty identified themselves as Christian. They volunteered to meet with Luke to try and help him integrate his faith and his studies more maturely. Luke accused them of undermining his faith. He inquired about their church communities, and declared they were not true believers. Further, he requested that his pastoral-led prayer group be allowed to meet his required group experience.

Things came to a crisis point when Luke, in his first practicum, proposed that he pair himself with a local pastor to offer a group to gays and lesbians who wished to explore the option of changing their sexual orientation. The practicum class erupted in groans of dismay. One woman burst into tears as she attempted to tell Luke how offended she felt. Practicum class was dismissed early, and Luke was asked to stay and talk with the instructor. The instructor remembered a recent graduate who had consistently spoken of her deep Christian faith, but with a kind of maturity and gentleness that allowed her to be heard and accepted in the general student body. He suggested that perhaps, Luke could meet with this recent graduate to discuss the integration of faith with generalist secular training. Luke refused.

What do you believe should happen next? Do you see mistakes that Luke's supervisors or instructors might have made? How would you handle this situation? What if Luke had been Muslim? Would this change your reactions?

Multicultural Competence

Disappointing as it is to point this out, one area of competency commonly lacking in supervisors is multicultural competence (Sanchez-Hucles & Jones, 2005). There are at least two levels of concern. First, supervisors must be able to help their supervisees develop the fledgling multicultural competencies that students hopefully began attaining in their coursework (M. T. Brown & Landrum-Brown, 1995; Handelsman, Gottlieb, & Knapp, 2005; Utsey, Gernat, & Hammar, 2005). Second, supervisors must be able to offer culturally sensitive and skilled supervision for supervisees from cultural, racial, or religious backgrounds different than themselves (Estrada, Frame, & Williams, 2004; Flores & Obasi, 2005), and for those with sexual orientations different than themselves (Bidell, 2005).

Of the topics in human discourse that students find difficult to talk about in detail and depth, sex, race, and disability probably top the list. The awkwardness and resulting silence allow ignorance and fear to fester, infecting clinical and supervisory work with shallowness and stereotypes that perpetuate cultural insularity and oppression (Tatum, 2002).

=== Deepening Diversity 13.1 ===

Issues Front and Center: A Guatemalan Exchange

by Mary Alice Bruce

Recently, I had the good fortune to be a visiting professor at a private university in Guatemala City, where I taught a practicum course in the master's counseling program as well as provided individual and triadic supervision for the practicum students. Juanita, one of my practicum students, was counseling Maria, a 26-year old unmarried woman who was living at the family home with her father, mother, two older brothers, and their wives and children. Maria was in counseling at the insistence of her father. He wanted her to work through her feelings of hostility because he disapproved of her relationship with her boyfriend. The father was paying for the counseling, but what he didn't know was that Maria was pregnant.

In Guatemala, two of the most powerful dynamics that influence thought and behavior are patriarchy and religion. Specifically, the father is the head of the family, and for many families, the church provides the overarching guiding values for mind, body, and spiritual decisions. In addition, it is common for extended families to live in the same physical compound with the father having the dominant role.

Naturally, my student-counselor, Juanita, was very concerned about her role. Who, exactly, was her client? Was it Maria's father who was paying for the counseling and expressing concern about Maria's relationship with her boyfriend? Or was the client Maria, who had significant depressive symptoms based upon the religious pressure because of her pregnancy as well as her violation of the moral values of her father? Or both?

Juanita's conflicts created ethical and professional issues for me as her practicum supervisor and as an American Caucasian female with different religious convictions than Juanita or Maria and her family. Initially, I was aggravated with Maria's father. Who was he to control and make decisions about his 26-year-old daughter? I was also frustrated with Juanita, whom I felt was being controlled by the father. On the other hand, I realized that the father was paying for the counseling without which Maria would not have the opportunity to address her conflicts. Of even greater importance, I recognized the cultural importance of the father as the head of the family as well as the powerful influence of the church.

So, what to do? I took the following steps in my thinking:

1. I worked on being consciously aware of and accepting of all of my feelings.
2. I reminded myself that I was a guest in a foreign country with different values than my own.
3. I dedicated myself to providing support and clarification for Juanita relative to her primary treatment goals for Maria.

The counseling continued, and eventually, Maria moved in with her boyfriend and had the baby. Maria's father had a hard time accepting these decisions, but the extended family's love of the baby has helped heal some of the wounds.

As a student, if you, your client(s), and/or your supervisor are from cultural or racial backgrounds different than each other, you have a golden opportunity to try and break through the silence and awkwardness. Of course, there are risks associated with bringing up the topic—fears of being misunderstood, offensive, ignorant, or demanding are common for most people trying to bridge these gaps (Utsey, Gernat, & Hammar, 2005). Supervisors have these fears as well. While we need to be gentle with each other, we also need to initiate and/or deepen these conversations.

Supervisory Relationships

Concerns about professional boundaries extend quite clearly to supervisor-supervisee relationships. Romance and sex are disallowed completely. These very human emotions and attractions are too powerful. They cannot be neatly contained in a way that allows objectivity and professional care (O'Connor Slimp & Burian, 1994). Research has shown (K. S. Pope, Levenson, & Schover, 1979) and continues to show that faculty teachers and supervisors ignore this ethic and engage in sexual relationships with students (Barnett-Queen, 1999). However, the vast majority of those surveyed in a recent study also indicated that this was inappropriate behavior (Caldwell, 2003).

Forbidden, too, is any kind of sexual harassment. Seemingly innocent flirtation and sexual innuendo, when introduced into relationships with power differentials, are usually neither appropriate nor ethical. There are plenty of perfectly acceptable places in our society for flirting and expressing appreciation for the sensual qualities of someone's dress, hair, perfume, make-up, or physique. The supervisory relationship is not one of those places (Jorgenson, 1995). You, or your supervisor, may genuinely believe that such banter is harmless, but when the power dynamics are not equal, the recipient is not free to react without fear of reprisal or obligation. There are ways to be warm and caring that stay safely away from sexual domains.

Friends, relatives, and lovers should be off the A-list of potential supervisors or supervisees. The codes do not absolutely forbid such arrangements, but this particular form of multiple roles should be avoided if at all possible. The professional discussions or consultations between friends or relatives who happen to share the same occupation can certainly be helpful. However, in formal supervisory relationships, the supervisor must assume an evaluative role, and put the supervisee's clients' welfare ahead of the welfare of the supervisee. You can probably imagine the awkwardness, or even outright impossibility, of this set of duties taking precedent over preserving the primary relationship in question.

Case Example: Dr. Mildred, a counseling psychologist, was proud when her daughter, Tosha, became a mental health counselor. Among many other professional activities, Dr. Mildred provided supervision for counselors getting their post-degree hours for licensure. Tosha had taken out many student loans for her graduate education. Her mother offered to provide the required post-degree supervision at no cost. Tosha was hesitant, but she respected her mother's work, and thought things would be fine. Tosha had a different last name than her mother, and lived in an urban area 50 miles from her mother's practice.

At first things went smoothly. However, Tosha began working with Bob, a young man with serious anger problems and a history of partner violence. Dr. Mildred's supervision took a decidedly protective turn. She cautioned Tosha about when to schedule appointments, called to check on Tosha on days she was seeing Bob, and in general, hovered. Tosha resented the hovering behavior, but at the same time, it made her feel just a little bit frightened of Bob. She knew her mother was being overprotective, but she began to wonder if she really wanted to work with Bob, or conversely, if she really wanted her mother to be her supervisor. It was difficult to imagine changing either relationship.

It would be easy to write similar scenarios featuring lovers, cousins, friends, or in-laws. The potential for drama and messiness increases logarithmically with such multiple roles. Both the NASW and the APA Ethical Principles address the basic responsibility of supervisors to do no harm to their supervisees, and follow this with cautions about multiple relationships. The risk of potential harm and loss of objectivity is cited as a reason to avoid dual or multiple roles.

After the ACA code specifically cautions against supervising or being supervised by a relative, family member, or friend, the code has the general ethical caution against multiple relationships, framed in the new, somewhat challenging language. As you may remember from Chapter 7, ACA has addressed this traditional caution against multiple roles in a paragraph with the heading *Potentially Beneficial Relationships.* Instead of simply cautioning against, or banning, multiple relationships in supervision, the supervisor is instructed to weigh the costs and benefits, with an eye to the welfare of the supervisee, and one would assume, the welfare of the supervisee's clients as well. Before entering into other forms of relationships with a supervisee, the supervisor must openly consider the added contact or role *with* the supervisee. The supervisor is responsible to identify the valuable and/or hazardous possibilities inherent in the additional contact or role, discuss these fully, and document the discussion.

Some of the roles could actually predate the supervisory relationship, such as belonging to the same professional or community organization. The same scrutiny should then be applied before entering into the supervisory relationship. In some cases, supervisors and supervisees are members of the same faith community. The proposed supervisor would be responsible to explore what it might be like for the supervisee to attend the same mosque, synagogue, or spiritual gathering as the supervisor. There might be benefits and there might be costs. The ethics code is clear: both the benefits and the possible harms should be thoroughly, openly explored and documented, and it is the *supervisor's* job to take the lead in this process.

Besides sex and romance, another forbidden "intimate" activity is this: supervisors are not to provide counseling to their supervisees. Certainly, well-done supervision can bring about insight, growth, and change. The relationship can be mutually respectful, close, and caring. Excellent supervision can even be therapeutic. But supervisors have evaluative duties that require a very different orientation than that of one's counselor. A mental health professional should be fully, 100% *there* for each client. Supervisors should be fully present to their supervisees, invested in their growth and development, but ultimately, they are responsible for the welfare of all the supervisee's current and future clients.

Technology and Supervision

As technology continues to become more available and sophisticated, forms of supervision have evolved. The same ethical principles and concerns remain, but like teaching, they might take on different levels of likelihood or saliency. The reach of the Internet has expanded the possibilities of supervision a number of ways. No longer is the new counselor practicing in a remote area forced to travel great distances for "live" supervision. Supervisors can be present in the room via web cam connections, and be sitting in the room next-door or half-way around the globe. Sessions can be digitally recorded and electronically mailed to the supervisor's computer. Intern groups can gather around their computers or telephones and engage in group supervision from ten different locations.

Resources and technological savvy are necessary for the scenarios described. More importantly, technology presents a challenging version of the old "is versus ought" distinction in ethical consideration. The fact that it is possible to do something makes it neither mandatory nor automatically right. Before using any form of technology for supervision, counselors, supervisors, and instructors should consider all possible ethical ramifications. Again, consider the generic issues listed in Applications 13.1.

CHAPTER WRAP-UP

The poet, Rumi, wrote, "What is bounty without a beggar? Generosity without a guest? Be beggar and guest; for beauty is seeking a mirror, water is crying for a thirsty man" (Helminski, 2000, p. 94). Teaching and supervision only have meaning when students and supervisees take what is offered and are informed, inspired, and benefited by it. Students and supervisees offer meaningful mirrors back to those of us who are privileged to teach and supervise. The power differentials may disguise this truth, but each side of the equation needs the other to be fully invested, ethical, and authentic in the respective roles.

Teachers have a responsibility to stay current in their knowledge base, and to use teaching methods that facilitate learning and retention. They need to attend to the diversity concerns in our world, and find ways to bring many cultures and divergent points of view into the classroom, eliciting everyone's voice, guiding, balancing, and empowering.

The skills involved in supervision are advanced and specialized. (Hopefully) gone are the days when supervisors just signed off a few clinical notes every week and patted supervisees on the back for all their hard work at the end of the term. Supervisors help new counselors make the move from knowledge to application, finding their stride and their voice as they develop into helping professionals. Supervisors must examine their own cultural encapsulation and push themselves toward greater and greater multicultural sophistication. Both teachers and supervisors must balance: the welfare of future clients, the overall development of our profession, and the needs of each developing student. This is a difficult but essential balancing act—one that needs the instructive and corrective feedback only students can provide.

Epilogue

As "the therapeutic" increasingly supplants religion as the accepted guide for human conduct, the psychotherapist becomes the de facto moral teacher in contemporary American society. The problem with the therapist being cast in the role of moral teacher, of course, is that therapists have done their best to stay out of the morality business. A cornerstone of all the mainstream models of psychotherapy since Freud has been the substitution of scientific and clinical ideas for moral ideas.

—William Doherty

A LIFE-LONG BALANCING ACT

Ethics and professional development courses can be a bit disconcerting—even nerve-wracking for students. This is a good thing. Being completely unfazed by the topics covered in this book would be a symptom of either extreme naïvete or professional narcissism. The descriptor "ethical professional" is not an end-state, but rather describes an exhilarating life-long process. It is process fraught with gray areas, indecision, ambiguity, fears, missteps, and sometimes, a rewarding sense of peace and well-being. Becoming ethical and professional requires self-tolerance as well as tolerance of others, as they (and we) struggle to grow and develop professionally and as human beings.

NO ONE IS PERFECT

Few seasoned mental health professionals would have the temerity to claim they had never behaved unethically. It would be an impossible claim to prove or assess because our codes include aspirational components that require lifelong maturation. On the other hand, most of us are trying and will continue to try to live ethical lives, both personally and professionally—and sometimes, we will fail. We might find ourselves in a terrible situation, trying to determine the best course of action from among three or four imperfect actions. We might allow ourselves to grow weary and bitter, or to fall in love, or in some other way lose objectivity. We might be overwhelmed and get lazy or careless with details. We might have financial setbacks that tempt us to take on the wrong client, or over-extend in some other way.

There are a number of ways you might wrestle with unethical conduct in your professional life. Briefly, we discuss each in the following.

Unreported, Unaccused, but Unethical

We have yet to hear of professionals filing complaints against themselves, but we know of many professionals who look back with chagrin at unethical behaviors they engaged in. And though the professional may experience internal shame or angst, it is often the client who suffers the more obvious consequences of unreported unethical behavior. The impoverished client who is hastily pushed aside, the gorgeous young woman who endures her therapist's sexual innuendos, the embarrassed or indignant client who hears details of his own case discussed in a public setting, the anxiety-ridden client who is treated with a paradoxical intervention that makes her life significantly worse— these are but a tiny fraction of the kinds of client suffering caused by unethical professional behaviors.

If you have behaved unethically, of course, you do not have to officially report yourself. However, from a moral perspective, you do have to try and repair the damage. Honest mistakes, when handled properly, can be therapeutic for clients and helping professionals alike. Similar to Winnicott's (1965) conception of the "good enough" parent, we have to forgive ourselves for mistakes, and realize that while we will not be perfect professionals, we can strive to be good enough. Clinical judgment is necessary as you decide how to handle an ethical mistake. In some cases, you may only burden the client further by bringing up your error. Obtain the best collegial consultation possible as you decide how to proceed.

Even if an erring helping professional has no guilty conscience, we happen to believe in a sort of cosmic karma. There may be no readily apparent consequences to the counselor, but unethical behavior diminishes the professional and our profession.

If You Are Accused

Being accused of ethical or illegal misconduct is a universally dreaded event in any professional's life. Whether warranted or not, the accusation can be devastating. There are a number of things you might do to partially alleviate the emotional pain and legal difficulties you might face. The first thing to do is take a deep breath, step back from the situation, and get your bearings. In Medical First Responder Training, people are taught to pause and assess before acting, even when someone is in acute medical distress. Impulsive responses can cause further damage. Below are some dimensions to consider.

Who is making the complaint?   Complaints can be made by clients, colleagues, supervisors, administrators, or the general public. When clients make an official complaint, they are waiving their rights to confidentiality within the confines of the complaint jurisdiction. They are not waiving them completely. You must still be very careful about protecting client information because you will probably be angry, and therefore tempted to talk with colleagues or others in ways that might reveal more about the client than is warranted.

If others are making the complaint, you cannot break confidentiality to defend yourself, at least initially, without client permission. However, you can address and/or deny the complaint. You will need an attorney to sort this out if the complaint is made formally.

Where is the complaint being directed? Clients and/or colleagues might come directly to you with their concern. You might then have the opportunity to directly work through the complaint, which is oftentimes best for all concerned (T. Remley & Herlihy, 2005). Complaints can be filed with your professional organization's ethics committee, your supervisor or administrator, or your state licensing board.

Probably the most feared and difficult ethical complaint processes are those that involve licensing or credentialing bodies. These bodies usually have ethics subcommittees to review complaints, and have the authority to require remediation, issue sanctions, and/or ultimately remove someone's license to practice.

Beyond ethics complaints, clients can also pursue legal recourse. They can bring a civil malpractice suit, or seek criminal charges against a counselor. Professional insurance companies offer workshops and literature designed to raise professional awareness of the most likely areas for legal and/or ethical complaints. While unsettling, these are usually workshops worth attending.

Each of these possibilities would dictate a different response from you. Keeping the appropriate people informed is as important as being careful not to disclose too much in the wrong places. In many cases, it will be wise to inform your supervisor of an accusation or potential complaint. In almost all cases, you should inform your malpractice insurance carrier. Many policies include assistance with legal fees, and most require immediate notification.

If You Know of Unethical Behavior

In most professional communities, people become familiar with each other's practices. Your professional peer group will most likely include people you respect and are proud to associate with. It might also include people who practice in ways you would not endorse. While we are not each other's ethics police officers, we do have moral and code-specified responsibilities to try and address collegial unethical behaviors. If we witness unethical behavior on the part of colleagues, supervisors, or teachers, ethics codes urge us to consider taking action. Assuming we have not been told of the unethical behavior in the context of a confidential relationship, the first action to consider is approaching our colleague with an attitude of concern and openness. Remember, things are not always as they seem, and you would certainly want the same courtesy, should someone believe you were behaving unethically. You can find prototypes of letters you might consider sending in an article by Brodsky and McKinzey (2002).

Both in the research literature (K. Pope & B. A. Vetter, 1992) and in our own experiences, one of the ways mental health professionals are informed of collegial unethical behavior is by current clients who are working through the pain or anger of earlier unethical treatment. If a client tells us of unethical behaviors by a colleague, we cannot break confidentiality without our client's written permission. Clients who formally accuse their counselors of unethical behavior give up their rights to confidentiality. This can be a step many are understandably unwilling to take. Therefore, they might bring it up in counseling, hoping to sort out their emotions and make decisions about what to do without risking public exposure.

Pause for Reflection

You will most likely hear of colleagues behaving unethically. What is your natural response to observed wrong-doing? Were you more likely the family tattle-tale or the family instigator? Do you avoid conflict? Do you lie awake nights saddened by the wrong-doing and injustice in the world? Do you consider whistle-blowers to be irritating or heroic? These are important, core personality traits and values to consider as you join the professional world.

BEST PRACTICES AND LIKELY CONCERNS

Surveys of professional members and state licensing boards over the years reveal important information about the patterns of ethical problems and complaints (Neukrag, Healy, & Herlihy, 1992; Neukrag, Milliken, & Walden, 2001; K. Pope & V. A. Vetter, 1992). First, state licensing boards receive more complaints than professional organizations. Second, most complaints have to do with inappropriate dual relationships, incompetence, and sexual relationships. Third, at least some data indicate that most complaints do not proceed all the way through to sanctions (American Psychological Association, 2000).

Attorney and psychologist Bryant Welch (2004), has identified twelve liability risks for mental health professionals. He divided them into six treatment risks and six administrative risks, and these were published by the American Professional Agency, a liability insurance company. These risks are:

- *Treatment Risks*
  - the completed suicide of a client
  - working with families, especially in forensic situations
  - working with clients who meet the diagnosis for Borderline Personality Disorder
  - responding to state licensing boards and ethics committees
  - working with managed care and treatment limitations
  - managing personal events in the life of the counselor
- *Administrative Risks*
  - inadequate record-keeping procedures
  - the overall impact of HIPAA
  - failing to do good disclosure and informed consent processes
  - handling subpoenas
  - failing to stay current and aware of ethical principles

- failing to carry the right types and levels of insurance, especially licensing board insurance

It is helpful to know that certain areas represent more liability risks than others, and to therefore take more precautions in these areas. Of course, professional organizations and insurance companies have a vested interest in helping mental health professionals practice a in safe, legal, and ethical manner. Therefore, staying in touch with these entities is wise.

Below, we provide a paraphrased list of cautions (D. Smith, 2003). The original list is available on the web at http://www.apa.org/monitor/jan03/10ways.html.

=== **Epilogue Applications** ===

Guidance for Avoiding Ethical Complaints

1. Multiple Relationships: If you choose to be in a multiple relationship, you must be extremely careful that you do not exploit clients and can document that you have not lost your clinical objectivity. If you cannot avoid a multiple relationship, take every precaution available to protect your client's welfare, and document this protection.

2. Maintain confidentiality: Many people and institutional entities can try to obtain client information in seemingly innocent ways. Do not make any client information available to anyone without first considering the laws and ethics involved.

3. Use comprehensive and comprehensible informed consent processes: Promote and respect the autonomy of your clients. Let them know how the process works, the limits of confidentiality, and state and federal laws that affect your practice.

4. Know your supervisory responsibilities: Supervisors are often surprised that ethics complaints about their supervisees will directly implicate them as well. Supervisors need to comply with state of the art supervision practices.

5. Identify your client and role: Be careful when working with couples, families, and groups—there can be competing interests among the people involved, each of whom is a client expecting you to act in his or her best interest. Be very clear from the beginning how your clinical practices and legal duties interact.

6. Keep very clear and professional records. Include every contact, attempts to get supporting documentation, fees and billing, treatment plans, summaries, test reports, signed informed consent forms, and any efforts you made to try and contact a client who disappears. Never deliberately alter a record because a complaint has been filed. If you need to add something to a record, add it and date the addition. It is illegal to retroactively alter a record.

7. Stay within the boundaries of your competence: Attend to the basics, and as you grow and develop, get supervision, seek continuing education, and make use of the interactive technologies available. If you are in a situation that demands your assistance in areas you do not feel competent (emergencies or rural settings), document your efforts to stay within ethical bounds.

Epilogue Applications (continued)

8. Make sure you end your counseling relationships as professionally as possible. You can terminate clients ethically and legally if they cannot reasonably be expected to benefit from continued therapy or they pose a threat to you or themselves. It is important to let clients know what alternatives might be available and how they might access them.

9. If asked to testify in court, offer only factual information. Do not volunteer more than asked and do not offer your opinion.

10. When billing clients or third-parties, be absolutely accurate. Use correct dates, procedure and diagnosis codes, and reflect payments made.

A FOND FAREWELL

We would like to extend our thanks to you for reading this book and considering the material. We wish you the best in your professional development, and trust that you will find your own, unique path to a moral and satisfying life. As our final offering, we share a poem that seems especially apropos.

In the evening we shall be examined on love

—St. John of the Cross

And it won't be multiple choice,
though some of us would prefer it that way.
Neither will it be essay, which tempts us to run on
when we should be sticking to the point, if not together.
In the evening there shall be implications
our fear will change to complications. No cheating,
we'll be told, and we'll try to figure the cost of being true
to ourselves. In the evening when the sky has turned
that certain blue, blue of exam books, blue of no more
daily evasions, we shall climb the hill as the light empties
and park our tired bodies on a bench above the city
and try to fill in the blanks. And we won't be tested
like defendants on trial, cross-examined
until one of us breaks down, guilty as charged. No,
in the evening, after the day has refused to testify,
we shall be examined on love like students
who don't even recall signing up for the course
and now must take their orals, forced to speak for once
from the heart and not off the top of their heads.
And when the evening is over and it's late,
the student body asleep, even the great teachers
retired for the night, we shall stay up

and run back over the questions, each in our own way:
what's true, what's false, what unknown quantity
will balance the equation, what it would mean years from now
to look back and know
we did not fail.

—Thomas Centolella, *Lights and Mysteries*

References

Abbott, T. K. (1998). Fundamental principles of the metaphysic of morals. In S. M. Cahn & P. Markie (Eds.), *Ethics: History, theory, and contemporary issues.* New York: Oxford University Press.

Ackerman, S. J., Benjamin, L. S., Beutler, L. E., Gelso, C. J., Goldfried, M. R., Hill, C., et al. (2001). Empirically supported therapy relationships: Conclusions and recommendations for the Division 29 Task Force. *Psychotherapy: Theory, Research, Practice, Training, 38*(4), 495–497.

Adams, J. L., Jaques, J. D., & May, K. M. (2004). Counseling gay and lesbian families: Theoretical considerations. *Family Journal: Counseling and Therapy for Couples and Families, 12*(1), 40–42.

Adamson, G., O'Kane, D., & Shevlin, M. (2005). Students' ratings of teaching effectiveness: A laughing matter? *Psychological Reports, 96,* 225–226.

Adler, A. (1956). *The individual psychology of Alfred Adler.* New York: Basic Books.

Adler, A. (1964). *Social interest: A challenge to mankind* (J. Linton & R. Vaughan, Trans.). New York: Capricorn.

Al-Krenowi, A., & Graham, J. R. (2005). Marital therapy for Arab Palestinian couples in the context of reacculturation. *Family Journal: Counseling and Therapy for Couples and Families, 13*(3), 300–310.

Albert, E., Denise, T., & Peterfreund, S. (1975). *Great traditions in ethics* (3rd ed.). New York: D. Van Nostrand.

Alexander, F., & French, T. M. (1946). *Psychoanalytic psychotherapy.* New York: Ronald.

Alexander, K., & Alexander, D. (2005). *American public school law* (6th ed.). Belmont, CA: Thomson West.

Alexander v. The Superior Court of Los Angeles. (2002). Cal. App. Unpub. LEXIS 253.

Allport, G. W. (1954). *The nature of prejudice.* New York: Doubleday/Anchor.

Altman, I. (1993). Challenges and opportunities of a transactional world view: Case study of contemporary Mormon polygynous families. *American Journal of Community Psychology, 21*(2), 135–163.

American Association of Marital and Family Therapists. (2002). About AAMFT. Retrieved November 8, 2005, from http://www.aamft.org/about/Aboutaamft.asp

American Counseling Association. (1995). *Code of ethics and standards of practice.* Alexandria, VA: Author.

American Counseling Association. (2002). Cross-cultural competencies and objectives. Retrieved October 7, 2005, from http://www.counseling.org/Content/NavigationMenu/RESOURCES/MULTICULTURALANDDIVERSITYISSUES/Competencies/Competencies.htm

American Group Psychotherapy Association (AGPA). (2002). *Ethical guidelines.* Retrieved December 7, 2005, from http://www.agpa.org/group/ethicalguide.html

American Psychiatric Association. (2000). *Diagnostic and statistical manual of mental disorders* (4th ed., text revision). Washington, DC: Author.

American Psychological Association (APA). (1994). Guidelines for Child Custody Evaluations. *American Psychologist, 49*(7), 677–680.

American Psychological Association (APA). (2000). Report of the Ethics Committee, 1999. *American Psychologist, 55,* 938–945.

American Psychological Association (APA). (2003). Guidelines on multicultural education, training, research, practice, and organizational change for psychologists. *American Psychologist, 58,* 377–402.

American Rehabilitation Counseling Association. (2005). Webpage Home. Retrieved December 4, 2005, from http://www.arcaweb.org/

Anchin, J. C. (2005). Introduction to the Special Section on Philosophy and Psychotherapy Integration and to the Inaugural Focus on Moral Philosophy. *Journal of Psychotherapy Integration, 15*(3), 284–298.

Anderson, P. (1991). *Great quotes from great women.* Lombard, IL: Celebrating Excellence Publishing.

Annas, J. (1991). Ethics and morality. In L. C. Becker & C. B. Becker (Eds.), *Encyclopedia of ethics* (Vol. 1, pp. 329–331). New York: Garland.

Aponte, H. J. (2002). Spirituality: The heart of therapy. In T. D. Carlson & M. J. Erickson (Eds.), *Spirituality and family therapy* (pp. 13–27). New York: Haworth Press.

Aquinas, S. T. (1993). *Commentary on Aristotle's Nicomachean ethics* (C. I. Litzinger, Trans.). South Bend, IN: Dumb Ox Press.

Aristotle. (1955). *The ethics of Aristotle: The Nichomachaen ethics* (J. K. Thomson, Trans. Revised ed.). New York: Viking.

Aristotle. (1980). *Nicomachaen ethics* (D. Ross, Trans.). New York: Oxford University Press.

Armstrong, C., & Gertz, S. (2005, Week of April 28). Got your "Spiritual Director" yet? *Christianity Today.* Retrieved from http://www.christianitytoday.com/ct/2003/117/51.0.html

Asai, A. (1996). Barriers to informed consent in Japan. *Eubios Journal of Asian and International Bioethics, 6,* 91–93.

ASCA. (2003). *The ASCA national model: A framework for school counseling programs.* Alexandria, VA: American School Counseling Association.

ASCA. (2005). The role of the professional school counselor. Retrieved December 9, 2005, from http://www.schoolcounselor.org/content.asp?pl=325&sl=133&contentid=240

Association for Specialists in Group Work (ASGW). (1998). *Best practices.* Retrieved June 2, 2006, from http://www.asgw.org/best.html

Athey, J., & Moody-Williams, J. (2003). Developing cultural competence in disaster mental health programs: Guiding principles and recommendations [Electronic Version], DHHS Publication No. SMA 3828. Retrieved on December 22, 2005, from http://www.mentalhealth.samhsa.gov/publications/allpubs/SMA03-3828/

Atkinson, D. R., Bui, U., & Mori, S. (2001). Multiculturally sensitive empirically supported treatments—an oxymoron? In J. G. Ponterotto, J. M. Casas, L. A. Suzuki, & C. M. Alexander (Eds.), *Handbook of multicultural counseling* (pp. 542–574). Thousand Oaks, CA: Sage.

Avnet, J., Kerner, J. (Producers), & Mandoki, L. (Writer). (1994). *When a man loves a woman* [Motion picture]. United States: Touchstone Pictures.

Ayantayo, J. K. (2005). *African traditional ethics and transformation: Innovations and ambivalence involved, and modifications necessary for sound 21st century African intellectual scholarship.* Ibadan, Nigeria: University of Ibadan.

Baca, L., & Cervantes, H. T. (1984). *The bilingual special education interface* (1st ed.). St. Louis, MO: Times Mirror/Mosby College Publishing.

Bailey, D. F. (2005). Response to the EGAS approach. *Professional School Counseling, 8,* 398.

Baker, S. B., & Gerler, E. R. J. (2004). *School counseling for the twenty-first century.* Upper Saddle River, NJ: Merrill Prentice Hall.

Bakker, A. B., Schaufeli, W. B., Sixma, H. J., Bosveld, W., & Van Dierendonck, D. (2000). Patient demands, lack of reciprocity, and burnout: A five-year longitudinal study among general practitioners. *Journal of Organizational Behavior, 21*(4), 425–441.

Baldwin, J. (2005). Sunbeams. *The Sun, August,* 48.

Bankart, C. P. (1997). *Talking cures: A history of Western and Eastern psychotherapies.* Pacific Grove, CA: Brooks/Cole.

Barad, J., & Roberson, E. (2001). *The ethics of Star Trek.* New York: Perennial.

Barak, A. (2005). Sexual harassment on the Internet. *Social Science Computer Review, 23,* 77–92.

Bardick, A. D., Bernes, K. B., McColloch, M. A. R., Witko, K. D., Spriddle, J. W., & Roest, A. R. (2004). Eating disorder intervention, prevention, and treatment: Recommendations for school counselors. *Professional School Counseling, 8,* 168–75.

Barnett-Queen, T. (1999). Sexual relationships with educators: A national survey of masters-level practitioners. *Clinical Supervisor, 18*(1), 151–72.

Bartley, A. E., Biles, K., Low, L. L., Nakazawa-Hewitt, M., & Windish, B. L. (2003). Evidence based research: Implications for counselor educators. *ERICdocs, July,* 9p.

Bassman, R. (2005). Mental illness and the freedom to refuse treatment: Privilege or right? *Professional Psychology: Research and Practice, 36*(5), 488–497.

Beahrs, J. O., & Gutheil, T. G. (2001). Informed consent in psychotherapy. *American Journal of Psychiatry, 158,* 4–10.

Beale, A. V., & Scott, P. C. (2001). "Bullybusters": Using drama to empower students to take a stand against bullying behavior. *Professional School Counseling, 4*(4), 300–305.

Beauchamp, T., & Childress, J. (1979). *Principles of biomedical ethics.* New York: Oxford University Press.

Beauchamp, T., & Childress, J. (1994). *Principles of biomedical ethics* (4th ed.). New York: Oxford University Press.

Beauchamp, T., & Childress, J. (2001). *Principles of biomedical ethics* (5th ed.). New York: Oxford University Press.

Beck, A. T., Ward, C. H., Mendelson, M., Mock, J., & Erbaugh, J. (1961). An inventory for measuring depression. *Archives of General Psychiatry, 4,* 561–571.

Beck, J. C. (Ed.). (1990). *Confidentiality versus the duty to protect: Foreseeable harm in the practice of psychiatry.* Washington, DC: American Psychiatric Press.

Beck, J. S. (1995). *Cognitive therapy: Basics and beyond.* New York: Guilford.

Bekhit, N. S., Thomas, G. V., & Jolley, R. P. (2005). The use of drawing for psychological assessment in Britain: Survey findings. *Psychology and Psychotherapy: Theory, Research and Practice, 78,* 205–17.

Bellah, R. N., Madsen, R., Sullivan, W., Swindler, A., & Tipton, S. M. (1996). *Habits of the heart.* Berkeley: University of California Press.

Belsler, K. R. (1999). Anger management: Immediate intervention by counselor coach. *Professional School Counseling, 3,* 81–90.

Benjamin, A. (1981). *The helping interview.* Boston: Houghton Mifflin.

Benjamin, L. S. (2003). *Interpersonal reconstructive therapy: Promoting change in nonresponders.* New York: Guilford.

Benyakar, M., & Collazo, C. (2005). Psychological interventions for people exposed to disasters. In J. J. Lopez-Ibor, G. Christodoulou, M. Maj, N. Sartorius, & A. Okasha (Eds.), *Disasters and mental health* (pp. 81–97). New York: Wiley.

Beran, T., & Violato, C. (2005). Ratings of university teacher instruction: How much do student and course characteristics really matter? *Assessment & Evaluation in Higher Education, 30,* 593–601.

Bernal, M. E., & Castro F. G. (1994). Are clinical psychologists prepared for service and research with ethnic minorities? Report of a decade of progress. *American Psychologist, 49,* 797–805.

Bernard, J. M., & Goodyear, R. K. (2004). *Fundamentals of clinical supervision* (3rd ed.). Boston: Allyn & Bacon.

Bernstein, B. E., & Hartsell, T. L. J. (2000). *The portable ethicist for mental health professionals.* New York: Wiley.

Bernstein, B. E., & Hartsell, T. L. J. (2004). *The portable lawyer* (2nd ed.). New York: Wiley.

Berry, J. W. (2003). Conceptual approaches to acculturation. In K. M. Chun, P. B. Organista, & G. Marin (Eds.), *Acculturation: Advances in theory, measurement, and applied research* (pp. 17–37). Washington, DC: American Psychological Association.

Beutler, L. E. (1998). Identifying empirically supported treatments: What if we didn't? *Journal of Consulting & Clinical Psychology, 66,* 113–120.

Beutler, L. E. (2000). Empirically based decision making in clinical practice. Prevention & Treatment. Retrieved November 12, 2005, from http://journals.apa.org/prevention/volume3/pre0030027a.html

Bickford, L., Herskovitz, M., Zwick, E. (Producers), & Soderbergh, S. (Writer). (2000). *Traffic* [Motion picture]. United States: USA Films.

Bidell, M. (2005). The Sexual Orientation Counselor Competence Scale: Assessing attitudes, skills, and knowledge of counselors working with lesbian, gay, and bisexual clients. *Counselor Education & Supervision, 44*(4), 267–279.

Bidell, M., Turner, J. A., & Casas, J. M. (2002). First impressions count: Ethnic/racial and lesbian/gay/bisexual content of professional psychology application materials. *Professional Psychology: Research and Practice, 33*(1), 97–103.

Bierce, A. (1911/1998). *The devil's dictionary* (reissued ed.). New York: Oxford University Press.

Binet, A., & Henri, V. (1896). Psychologie individuelle. *Annee Psychologie, 3,* 296–332.

Bodenhorn, N. (2005). American School Counselor Association ethical code changes relevant to family work. *Family Journal: Counseling and Therapy for Couples and Families, 13*(3), 317–320.

Bodenhorn, N. (in press). Common and challenging ethical dilemmas experienced by school counselors: An exploratory study. *Professional School Counseling.*

Bohart, A. C., O'Hara, M., & Leitner, L. M. (1998). Empirically violated treatments: Disenfranchisement of humanistic and other psychotherapies. *Psychotherapy Research, 8*(2), 141–157.

Bok, S. (2002). *Common values.* Columbia: University of Missouri Press.

Bonanno, G. A. (2004). Loss, trauma and human resilience. *American Psychologist, 59*(1), 20–28.

Bond, T. (2002). *Standards and ethics for counselling in action* (2nd ed.). London: Sage.

Bootzin, R. R., & Bailey, E. T. (2005). Understanding placebo, nocebo, and iatrogenic treatment effects. *Journal of Clinical Psychology, 61*(7), 871–880.

Bopp, J., Bopp, M., Brown, L., & Lane, P. J. (1985). *The sacred tree* (2nd ed.). Twin Lakes, WI: Lotus Press.

Borys, D. S., & Pope, K. S. (1989). Dual relationships between therapist and client: A national survey of psychologists, psychiatrists, and social workers. *Professional Psychology: Research & Practice, 20,* 283–293.

Boucher, M. (2002). Ethical implications regarding minors and the therapeutic relationship: The appropriate age of consent [Electronic Version]. *Family Clinic,* 1–6. Retrieved November 30, 2005, from http://www.yourfamilyclinic.com/pro/ageconsent.html

Boyd, J. (Ed.). (1950). *Thomas Jefferson to Thomas Law, 1814* (Vol. 14, Memorial Edition). New Jersey: Princeton.

Bradley, L. J., Sexton, T. L., & Smith, H. B. (2005). The American Counseling Assocation practice network: A new research tool. *Journal of Counseling and Development, 83,* 488–491.

Brannigan, M. C. (2000). *Striking a balance: A primer in traditional Asian values.* New York: Seven Bridges Press.

Brannigan, M. C. (2005). *Ethics across cultures.* Boston: McGraw Hill.

Braun, S. A., & Cox, J. A. (2005). Managed mental health care: Intentional misdiagnosis of mental disorders. *Journal of Counseling and Development, 83,* 425–433.

Brems, C., Baldwin, M., Davis, L., & Namyniuk, L. (1994). The imposter syndrome as related to teaching evaluations and advising relationships of university faculty members. *Journal of Higher Education, 65*(2), 183–193.

British Association for Counselling (BAC). (1990). *Code of ethics and practice for counsellors.* Rugby, England: Author.

British Association for Counselling and Psychotherapy (BACP). (2002). *Ethical framework for good practice in counselling and psychotherapy.* Rugby, England: Author.

Broderick, B. B., & Schrader, S. S. (1991). The history of professional marriage and family therapy. In A. S. Gurman & D. P. Kniskern (Eds.), *Handbook of family therapy* (Vol. 2, pp. 3–40). New York: Bruner/Mazel.

Brodsky, S. L., & McKinzey, R. K. (2002). The ethical confrontation of the unethical forensic colleague. *Professional Psychology: Research and Practice, 33*(3), 307–309.

Brody, B. A., McCullough, L. B., & Sharp, R. R. (2005). Consensus and controversy in clinical research ethics. *Journal of the American Medical Association, 294*(11), 1411–1414.

Brooks, A. (1886). Philosophy of the kindergarten. *Journal of Education, XXIV,* 103–108.

Brooks, G. (1970). *Family pictures.* Detroit, MI: Broadside Press.

Brown, L. S. (2001). Feelings in context: Countertransference and the real world in feminist therapy. *Journal of Clinical Psychology, 57*(8), 1005–1012.

Brown, M. T., & Landrum-Brown, J. (1995). Counselor supervision: Cross-cultural perspectives. In J. G. Ponterotto, J. M. Casas, L. A. Suzuki, & C. M. Alexander (Eds.), *Handbook of multicultural counseling* (pp. 263–286). Thousand Oaks, CA: Sage.

Brownlee, K. (1996). The ethics of non-sexual dual relationships: A dilemma for the rural mental health professional. *Community Mental Health Journal, 32*(5), 497–503.

Bruce, D. W. (2000). *The thru-hiker's handbook.* Hot Springs, NC: Center for Appalachian Trail Studies.

Bryant, J., & Milsom, A. (2005). Child abuse reporting by school counselors. *Professional School Counseling, 9,* 63–71.

Burchac, J. (1978). *Entering Onondaga.* Austin, TX: Cold Mountain.

Burcke, J. R. (2001). Ethical issues in pastoral counseling. *Perspective on the Professions, 21*(1), 7–8.

Burham, G. (2004). One teammate's journey with PTSD. *The Blast,* 36–38.

Burtness, J. H. (1999). *Consequences: Morality, ethics and the future.* Minneapolis, MN: Fortress Press.

Byock, I. (1997). *Dying well: The prospect for growth at the end of life.* New York: Riverhead Books.

CACREP. (2005). Accreditation standards. Retrieved November 8, 2005, from http://www.cacrep .org/

Caffo, E., & Belaise, C. (2005). Children and adolescents' psychopathology after trauma: New preventive psychotherapeutic strategies. In K. V. Oxington (Ed.), *Psychology of stress* (pp. 145–63). Hauppauge, NY: Nova Biomedical Books.

Caldwell, L. W. (2003). *Sexual relationships between supervisors and supervisees during psychology graduate training* (Vol. 63 [10B]): Dissertation Abstracts International: Section B: The Sciences and Engineering.

Campbell, C., & Dahir, C. A. (1997). *The national standards for school counseling programs.* Alexandria, VA: American School Counselor Association.

Campbell, D., & Fiske, D. (1959). Convergent and discriminant validation by the multitrait-multimethod matrix. *Psychological Bulletin, 54,* 81–105.

Capuzzi, D. (2002). Legal and ethical challenges in counseling suicidal students. *Professional School Counseling, 6*(1), 36–45.

Carey, J. (2000). Center for School Counseling Outcome Research. Retrieved December 13, 2005, from http://www.umass.edu/schoolcounseling/

Casey, W. M., & Burton, R. V. (1982). Training children to be consistently honest through verbal self-instructions. *Child Development, 53,* 911–919.

Center for Teaching and Learning. (2005/January 30, 2001). Midterm Course Evaluations. Retrieved November 21, 2005, from http://ctl.unc.edu/tfiapa.html

Chambless, D. L., Baker, M. J., Baucom, D. H., Beutler, L. E., Calhoun, K. S., Crits-Christoph, P., et al. (1998). Update on empirically validated therapies, II. *The Clinical Psychologist, 51,* 3–16.

Chaplin, W. F., Phillips, J. B., Brown, J. D., Clanton, N. R., & Stein, J. L. (2000). Handshaking, gender, personality and first impressions. *Journal of Personality and Social Psychology, 79*(1), 110–117.

Cheong, E. S. (2001). A theoretical study on the application of choice theory and reality therapy in Korea. *International Journal of Reality Therapy, 20*(2), 8–11.

Chiang, H.-H., Lu, Z.-Y., & Wear, S. E. (2005). To have or to be: Ways of caregiving identified during recovery from the earthquake disaster in Taiwan. *Journal of Medical Ethics, 31,* 154–158.

Christakis, N. A. (1992). Ethics are local: Engaging cross-cultural variation in the ethics for clinical research. *Social Science and Medicine, 35,* 1079–1091.

Christians, C. G. (2000). Ethics and politics in qualitative research. In N. K. Denzin & Y. S. Lincoln (Eds.), *Handbook of qualitative research* (2nd ed., pp. 133–155). Thousand Oaks, CA: Sage.

Christopher, J. C. (1999). Situating psychological well-being: Exploring the cultural roots of its theory and research. *Journal of Counseling & Development, 77,* 141–52.

Chuang Tzu. (1970). *The complete works of Chuang Tzu* (B. Watson, Trans.). New York: Columbia Press.

Clance, P. R., & Imes, S. A. (1978). The imposter phenomenon in high achieving women: Dynamics and therapeutic interventions. *Psychotherapy: Theory, Research & Practice, 15,* 241–247.

Clark, M. A., & Amatea, E. (2004). Teacher perceptions and expectations of school counselor contributions: Implications for program planning and training. *Professional School Counseling, 8,* 132–140.

Coffin, W. S. (1999). *The heart is a little to the left: Essays on public morality.* Hanover, NH: University Press of New England.

Cohen, S., & Wills, T. A. (1985). Stress, social support, and the buffering hypothesis. *Psychological Bulletin, 98*(2), 310–357.

Collins, B. G., & Collins, T. M. (2005). *Crisis and trauma: Developmental-ecological intervention.* Boston: Lahaska Press.

Collogon, L., Tuma, F., Dolan-Sewell, R., Borja, S., & Fleishman, A. R. (2004). Ethical issues pertaining to research in the aftermath of disaster. *Journal of Traumatic Stress, 17*(5), 363–372.

Conant, J. B. (1959). *The American high school today: A first report to interested citizens.* New York: McGraw Hill.

Constantine, M. G., & Yeh, C. J. (2001). Multicultural training, self-construals, and multicultural competence of school counselors. *Professional School Counseling, 4*(3), 202–207.

Cook, A. S., Ford, J., Lanktree, C., Blaustein, M., Cloitre, M., et al. (2005). Complex trauma in children and adolescents. *Psychiatric Annals, 35*(5), 390–398.

Corey, G. (2005). *Theory and practice of counseling and psychotherapy* (7th ed.). Belmont, CA: Brooks/Cole.

Corey, G., Corey, M. S., & Callanan, P. (2003). *Issues and ethics in the helping professions* (6th ed.). Pacific Grove, CA: Brooks/Cole.

Corey, M. S., & Corey, G. (2002). *Groups: Process and practice* (6th ed.). Pacific Grove, CA: Brooks/Cole.

Corsini, R., & Wedding, D. (Eds.). (2000). *Current psychotherapies* (6th ed.). Itasca, IL: F. E. Peacock.

Cottone, R. R., & Tarvydas, V. M. (2003). *Ethical and professional issues in counseling* (2nd ed.). Upper Saddle River, NJ: Merrill, Prentice Hall.

Covey, S. (1990). *The 7 habits of highly effective people* New York: Free Press.

Cowley, M. (Ed.). (1958). *Writers at work.* New York: Viking.

Craig, K. M. (2002). Examining hate-motivated aggression: A review of the social psychological literature on hate crimes as a distinct form of aggression. *Aggression and Violent Behavior, 7,* 85–101.

Creed, T. (1997). PowerPoint, No! Cyberspace, Yes [Electronic Version]. *The National Teaching and Learning Forum, 6,* 1–4, on December 13, 2005, from http://www.ntlf.com/html/pi/9705/creed_1.htm

Creswell, J. W. (2003). *Research design: Qualitative, quantitative, and mixed method approaches* (2nd ed.). Thousand Oaks, CA: Sage.

Croarkin, P., Berg, J., & Spira, J. (2003). Informed consent for psychotherapy: A look at therapists' understanding, opinions, and practices. *American Journal of Psychotherapy, 57*(3), 384–400.

Croxton, T. A., Churchill, S. R., & Fellin, P. (1988). Counseling minors without parental consent. *Child Welfare League of America, LXVII*(1), 3–14.

Csikszentmihalyi, M. (2000). The contribution of flow to positive psychology: Scientific essays in honor of Martin E. P. Seligman. In J. E. Gillham (Ed.), *The science of optimism and hope* (pp. 387–395). Philadelphia: Templeton Foundation Press.

Cuellar, I., & Paniagua, F. A. (Eds.). (2000). *Handbook of multicultural mental health: Assessment and treatment of diverse populations.* New York: Academic Press.

Cummings, A. L. (2000). Teaching feminist counselor responses to novice female counselors. *Counselor Education and Supervision, 40*(1), 47–57.

Cutchin, M. P., & Churchill, R. R. (1997). Scale, context, and causes of suicide in the United States. *Social Science Quarterly, 80,* 97–114.

Dass-Brailsford, P. (2003). A golden opportunity in supervision: Talking about countertransference. *Journal of Psychological Practice, 8*(1), 56–64.

Davidson, F. (Producer/Writer). (1995). On old age: A conversation with Joan Erikson at 90 [Motion picture]. United States: Davidson Films. (Available from Davidson Films, 668 Marsh Street, San Luis Obispo, CA 93401)

Davis, P. (2005). Licensed (fill in the blank) psychologist. *MPA Newsletter Addendum, Fall,* 1–4.

Davis, T. (2005). *Exploring school counseling: Professional practices and perspectives.* Boston: Lahaska Press.

Dearing, R. L., & Maddux, J. (2005). Predictors of psychological help seeking in clinical and counseling psychology graduate students. *Professional Psychology: Research and Practice, 36*(3), 326–329.

Deegear, J., & Lawson, D. M. (2003). The utility of empirically supported treatments. *Professional Psychology: Research & Practice, 34,* 271–277.

Denkowski, K. M., & Denkowski, G. C. (1982). Client–counselor confidentiality: An update of rationale, legal status, and implications. *Personnel and Guidance Journal, 60,* 371–375.

Dillard, A. (1974). *Pilgrim at Tinker Creek.* New York: Harper's Magazine Press.

Doherty, W. J. (1995). *Soul searching: Why psychotherapy must promote moral responsiblity.* New York: Basic Books.

Donley, C., & Buckley, S. (Eds.). (1996). *The tyranny of the normal.* Kent, OH: Kent State University Press.

Dorff, E. (2001). Confidences and their limits in rabbinic counseling. *Perspectives on the Professions, 21*(1), 5–7.

Dr. Science. (2005/2003). *Ask Dr. Science.* Retrieved October 13, 2005, from http://www.drscience.com/

Duncan, B. L., & Miller, S. D. (2000). *The heroic client: Doing client-centered, outcome-informed therapy.* San Francisco: Jossey-Bass.

Eagle, G. (2005). Therapy at the cultural interface: Implications of African cosmology for traumatic stress intervention. *Journal of Contemporary Psychotherapy, 35*(2), 199–209.

Eliade, M. (1985). *History of religious ideas, Volume 2: From Gautama Buddha to the triumph of Christianity* (W. R. Trask, Trans.). Chicago: University of Chicago Press. (Originally published 1982)

Elliott-Boyle, D. (1985). A conceptual analysis of codes of ethics. *Journal of Mass Media Ethics, 1,* 22–26.

Emerson, S. (1995). A counseling group for counselors. *Journal for Specialists in Group Work, 20*(4), 222–231.

Emerson, S., & Markos, P. A. (1996). Signs and symptoms of the impaired counselor. *Journal of Humanistic Education and Development, 34,* 108–117.

Enochs, W. K., & Etzbach, C. A. (2004). Impaired student counselors: Ethical and legal considerations for the family. *Family Journal: Counseling and Therapy for Couples and Families, 12*(4), 396–400.

Epstein, R. S. (1994). *Keeping boundaries: Maintaining safety and integrity in the psychotherapeutic process.* Washington, DC: American Psychiatric Press.

Erford, B. (2003). *Transforming the school counseling profession.* Upper Saddle River, NJ: Merrill Prentice Hall.

Erikson, E. H. (1963). *Childhood & society* (2nd ed.). New York: W. W. Norton.

Estrada, D., Frame, M. W., & Williams, C. B. (2004). Cross-cultural supervision: Guiding the conversation toward race and ethnicity. *Journal of Multicultural Counseling and Development, 32,* 307–319.

Evans, K. M., Kincade, E., Marbley, A., & Seem, S. R. (2005). Feminism and feminist therapy: Lessons from the past and hopes for the future. *Journal of Counseling and Development, 83,* 269–277.

Fakhry, M. (1994). *Ethical theories in Islam* (2nd ed.). Leiden, Holland: Brill.

Farber, B. A., Berano, K. C., & Capobianco, J. A. (2004). Clients' perceptions of the process and consequences of self-disclosure in psychotherapy. *Journal of Counseling Psychology, 51*(3), 340–346.

Farberman, R. K. (1997). Public attitudes about psychologists and mental health care: Research to guide the American Psychological Association Public Education Campaign. *Professional Psychology: Research and Practice, 28*(2), 128–136.

Fasching, D. J., & deChant, D. (2001). *Comparative religious ethics: A narrative approach.* Malden, MA: Blackwell.

Fay, A. I. (2002). The case against boundaries in psychotherapy. In A. A. Lazarus & O. Zur (Eds.), *Dual relationships and psychotherapy* (pp. 146–168). New York: Springer.

Felman, J. L. (2001). *Never a dull moment.* New York: Routledge.

Fels, A. (2005). *Necessary dreams: Ambition in women's changing lives.* New York: Anchor.

Fernanado, D. M., & Hulse-Killacky, D. (2005). The relationship of supervisory styles to satisfaction with supervision and the perceived self-efficacy of master's level counseling students. *Counselor Education & Supervision, 44*(4), 255–266.

Festinger, L., Pepitone, A., & Newcomb, T. (1952). Some consequences of deindividuation in group. *Journal of Abnormal and Social Psychology, 47,* 382–389.

Fine, M., Weis, L., Weseen, S., & Wong, L. (2000). For whom? Qualitative research, representations, and social responsibilities. In N. K. Denzin & Y. S. Lincoln (Eds.), *Handbook of qualitative research* (pp. 107–133). Thousand Oaks, CA: Sage.

Fischer, L., & Sorenson, G. P. (1996). *School law for counselors, psychologists, and social workers* (3rd ed.). White Plains, NY: Longman.

Fisher, B. M. (2001). *No angel in the classroom: Teaching through feminist discourse.* Lanham, MD: Rowman & Littlefield Publishers.

Fisher, D. B. (2005). Empowerment model of recovery from severe mental illness: An expert interview with Aniel B. Fisher, MD, PhD. *Medscape Psychiatry & Mental Health, 10*(1), 1–3.

Fishman, D. B., & Franks, C. M. (1997). The conceptual evolution of behavior therapy. In P. L. Wachtel & S. B. Messer (Eds.), *Theories of psychotherapy: Origins and evolution* (pp. 131–180). Washington, DC: American Psychological Association.

Flannery, D. J., Vazsonyi, A. T., Liau, A. K., Guo, S., Powell, K. E., Atha, H., et al. (2003). Initial behavior outcomes for the PeaceBuilders Universal School-Based Violence Prevention Program. *Developmental Psychology, 39,* 292–308.

Fletcher, J. (1966). *Situation ethics: The new morality.* Philadelphia: The Westminster Press.

Flores, L. Y., & Obasi, E. M. (2005). Mentors' influence on Mexican American students' career and educational development. *Journal of Multicultural Counseling and Development, 33,* 146–164.

Foa, E. B. (2000). Psychosocial treatment of posttraumatic stress disorder. *Journal of Clinical Psychiatry Special Issue: Focus on Posttraumatic Stress Disorder, 61*(Suppl 5), 43–51.

Foa, E. B., Rothbaum, B. O., & Furr, J. M. (2003). Augmenting exposure therapy with other CBT procedures. *Psychiatric Annals, 33*(1), 47–53.

Foster, M. S. (1993). A question of jobs—the two-career couple. *BioScience, 43*(4), 237–248.

Frank, J. D., & Frank, J. B. (1991). *Persuasion and healing* (3rd ed.). Baltimore: Johns Hopkins University Press.

Frankl, V. (1963). *Man's search for meaning.* Boston: Beacon.

Freire, P. (1993). *Pedagogy of the oppressed.* New York: Continuum Publishing Company.

Freud, S. (1949). *An outline of psychoanalysis.* New York: Norton.

Freud, S. (1957). The future prospects of psycho-analytic therapy. In J. Strachey (Ed. & Trans.), *The standard edition of the complete works of Sigmund Freud* (Vol. 11, pp. 3–55). London: Hogarth Press. (Originally published 1910)

Freud, S. (1958). On the beginning of treatment: Further recommendations on the technique of psychoanalysis. In J. Strachey (Ed. & Trans.), *Standard edition of the complete psychological works of Sigmund Freud* (Vol. 12, pp. 122–144). London: Hogarth Press. (Originally published 1910)

Freud, S. (1966). The dynamics of transference. In J. Strachey (Ed. & Trans.), *Standard edition of the complete psychological works of Sigmund Freud* (Vol. 12, pp. 97–108). London: Hogarth Press. (Originally published 1910)

Froeschle, J., & Moyer, M. (2004). Just cut it out: Legal and ethical challenges in counseling students who self-mutilate. *Professional School Counseling, 7,* 231–235.

Fromm, E. (1964). *The heart of man.* New York: Harper and Row.

Fullerton, C. S., & Ursano, R. J. (2005). Psychological and psychopathological consequences of disasters. In J. J. Lopez-Ibor, G. Christodoulou, M. Maj, N. Sartorius, & A. Okasha (Eds.), *Disasters and mental health.* New York: Wiley.

Furr, S. R., & Barret, B. (2000). Teaching group counseling skills: Problems and solutions. *Counselor Education & Supervision, 40*(2), 94–104.

Galton, F. (1879). Psychometric experiments. *Brain, 2,* 149–162.

Gamst, G., Dana, R. H., Der-Karabetian, A., & Kramer, T. (2004). Ethnic match and treatment outcomes for child and adolescent mental health center clients. *Journal of Counseling and Development, 82,* 457–465.

Garfield, S. L. (1998). Some comments on empirically supported treatments. *Journal of Consulting & Clinical Psychology, 66*(1), 121–125.

Garrod, A., & Beal, C. (1993). Voices of care and justice in children's responses to fable dilemmas. In A. Garrod (Ed.), *Approaches to moral development.* New York: Teacher's College Press.

Gelso, C. J., & Hayes, J. A. (1998). *The psychotherapy relationship: Theory, research, and practice.* New York: Wiley.

Gerber, S., & Terry-Day, B. (1999). Does peer mediation really work? *Professional School Counselor, 2,* 169–171.

Gert, B. (2004). *Common morality.* New York: Oxford University Press.

Gibbs, J. C. (2003). *Moral development and reality: Beyond the theories of Kohlberg and Hoffman.* London: Sage.

Gillham, N. (2001). *A life of Sir Francis Galton.* New York: Oxford.

Gilligan, C. (1977). *In a different voice.* Cambridge, MA: Harvard University Press.

Gilroy, P. J., Carroll, L., & Murra, J. (2002). A preliminary survey of counseling psychologists' personal experiences with depression and treatment. *Professional Psychology: Research & Practice, 33,* 402–407.

Giorgi, A. (1986, July). *Theoretical justification for the use of descriptions in psychological research.* Paper presented at the International Association for Qualitative Research, Pittsburgh, PA.

Gladding, S. T. (2002). . . . From Pier 94, near Ground Zero, New York City. In D. D. Bass & R. Yep (Eds.), *Terrorism, trauma, and tragedies: A counselor's guide to preparing and responding* (pp. 7–9). Alexandria, VA: American Counseling Association Foundation.

Gladding, S. T. (2004). *Counseling: A comprehensive profession.* Upper Saddle River, NJ: Pearson/Merrill Prentice Hall.

Gladding, S. T. (2005a). *Counseling as an art: The creative arts in counseling.* Alexandria, VA: American Counseling Association.

Gladding, S. T. (2005b, October). *Essential of ethics.* Paper presented at the Association for Counselor Education and Supervision, Pittsburgh, PA.

Gladwell, M. (2005). *Blink: The power of thinking without thinking.* New York: Little, Brown.

Glass, L. (2003). The gray areas of boundary crossings and violations. *American Journal of Psychotherapy, 57*(4), 429–444.

Glasser, W. (1998). *Choice theory: A new psychology of personal freedom.* New York: HarperCollins.

Glasser, W. (2000). *Reality therapy in action.* New York: HarperCollins.

Glasser, W. (2002). *Unhappy teenagers: A way for parents and teachers to reach them.* New York: HarperCollins.

Glosoff, H., Herlihy, B., & Spence, E. B. (2000). Privileged communication in the counselor-client relationship. *Journal of Counseling & Development, 78,* 454–462.

Glosoff, H., & Pate, R. H. (2002). Privacy and confidentiality in school counseling. *Professional School Counseling, 6,* 20–27.

Goldenberg, I., & Goldenberg, H. (2004). *Family therapy: An overview* (4th ed.). Belmont, CA: Thomson Brooks/Cole.

Goldfried, M. R., & Davison, G. C. (1976). *Clinical behavior therapy.* New York: Holt, Rinehart & Winston.

Goleman, D. (2003). *Destructive emotions: How can we overcome them?* New York: Bantam Books.

Gottlieb, M. (1993). Avoiding exploitive dual relationships: A decision-making model. *Psychotherapy, 30,* 41–48.

Greenberg, K. R. (2003). *Group counseling in k–12 schools.* Boston: Allyn & Bacon.

Greenberg, L. S. (2002). Integrating an emotion-focused approach to treatment into psychotherapy integration. *Journal of Psychotherapy Integration, 12*(2), 154–189.

Greenberg, L. S., Watson, J. C., Elliot, R., & Bohart, A. C. (2001). Empathy. *Psychotherapy: Theory, Research, Practice, Training, 38*(4), 380–384.

Greenwood, E. (1983). Attributes of the professions. In B. Baumrin & B. Freedman (Eds.), *Moral responsibility and the professions.* New York: Haven Publications.

Groth-Marnat, G. (2003). *Handbook of psychological assessment* (4th ed.). Hoboken, NJ: Wiley.

Gurman, A. S., & Fraenkel, P. (2002). The history of couple therapy: A millennial review. *Family Process, 41*(2), 199–260.

Hackney, A. (2005). Teaching students about stereotypes, prejudice, and discrimination: An interview with Susan Fiske. *Teaching of Psychology, 32*(3), 196–199.

Haddix, K., & Gurung, J. B. (1999). "Excess Women": Non-marriage and reproduction in two ethnic Tibetan communities of Humla, Nepal. *Himalayan Research Bulletin, 19*(1), 56–65.

Hagglund, K., & Frank, R. G. (1996). Rehabilitation psychology practice, ethics, and a changing health environment. *Rehabilitation Psychology, 41*(1), 19–32.

Hahn, W. K. (1998). Gifts in psychotherapy: An intersubjective approach to patient gifts. *Psychotherapy: Theory, Research, Practice, Training, 35*(1), 78–86.

Haley, J. (1977). A quiz for young therapists. *Psychotherapy, 14*(2), 165–168.

Handelsman, M., Gottlieb, M., & Knapp, S. (2005). Training ethical psychologists: An acculturation model. *Professional Psychology: Research & Practice, 36*(1), 54–65.

Hanson, S. L., Kerkhott, T. R., & Bush, S. S. (2005). *Health care ethics for psychologists.* Washington, DC: American Psychological Association.

Harcourt, D., & Conroy, H. (2005). Informed assent: Ethics and processes when researching with young children. *Early Child Development and Care, 175*(6), 567–577.

Harris, L. K., VanZandt, C. E., & Rees, T. H. (1997). Counseling needs of students who are deaf and hard of hearing. *School Counselor, 44*(4), 271–279.

Hartmann, L. (2005). Psychotherapy for children and adolescents: Evidence-based treatments and case examples [Book Review]. *American Journal of Psychiatry, 162,* 1231–1232.

Haslam, D., & Harris, S. (2004). Informed consent documents of marriage and family therapists in private practice: A qualitative analysis *American Journal of Family Therapy, 32*(4), 359–374.

Hatch, T. (2005). School counselor roles and responsibilities. In American School Counseling Association (Ed.), *School counseling fundamentals: Foundations and basics* (pp. 183–186). Alexandria, VA: American School Counselor Association.

Hattie, J. A., Myers, J. E., & Sweeney, T. J. (2004). A factor structure of wellness: Theory assessment, analysis, and practice. *Journal of Counseling & Development, 82*(3), 354–364.

Hauerwas, S. (1981). *A community of character.* South Bend, IN: University of Notre Dame.

Haverkamp, B. E. (2005). Ethical perspectives on qualitative research in applied psychology. *Journal of Counseling Psychology, 52*(2), 146–155.

Haynes, R., Corey, G., & Moulton, P. (2003). *Clinical supervision in the helping professions: A practical guide.* Pacific Grove, CA: Brooks/Cole.

Healy, D., Langmaack, C., & Savage, M. (1999). Suicide in the course of the treatment of depression. *Journal of Psychopharmacology, 13,* 106–111.

Helminski, K. (Ed.). (2000). *The Rumi collection.* Boston: Shambala Classics.

Henggeler, S. W. (2003). Advantages and disadvantages of multisystemic therapy and other evidence-based practices for treating juvenile offenders. *Journal of Forensic Psychology Practice, 3*(4), 53–59.

Henggeler, S. W., & Schoenwald, S. K. (2002). Treatment manuals: Necessary, but far from sufficient: Commentary. *Clinical Psychology: Science & Practice, 9*(4), 419–420.

Hensley, L. G., Smith, S., & Thompson, R. W. (2003). Assessing competencies of counselors-in-training: Complexities in evaluating personal and professional development. *Counselor Education and Supervision, 42,* 219–230.

Heppner, P. P., Kivlighan, D. M., Wright, G. E., Pledge, D. S., et al. (1995). Teaching the history of counseling: Training the next generation. *Journal of Counseling & Development, 73,* 337–341.

Herlihy, B., & Corey, G. (1997). *Boundary issues in counseling: Multiple roles and responsibilities.* Alexandria, VA: American Counseling Association.

Herman, D. A., & Hazler, R. J. (1999). Adherence to a wellness model and perceptions of psychological well-being. *Journal of Counseling & Development, 77,* 39–43.

Herman, J. L. (1992). *Trauma and recovery: The aftermath of violence—from domestic abuse to political terror.* New York: Basic Books.

Herring, R. D. (1996). Synergetic counseling and Native American Indian students. *Journal of Counseling & Development, 74,* 542–547.

Hershenson, D. B., & Power, P. W. (1987). *Mental health counseling: Theory and practice.* New York: Pergamon.

Heyward, C. (1994). *When boundaries betray us: Beyond illusions of what is ethical in therapy and life.* San Francisco: HarperCollins.

Hillier, D., Fewell, F., Cann, W., & Shephard, V. (2005). Wellness at work: Enhancing the quality of our working lives. *International Review of Psychiatry, 17*(5), 419–431.

Hobson, S. M., & Kanitz, H. M. (1996). Multicultural counseling: An ethical issue for school counselors. *School Counselor, 43*(4), 245–255.

Hodges, K. (2004). Using assessment in everyday practice for the benefit of families and practitioners. *Professional Psychology: Research and Practice, 35*(5), 449–456.

Holcomb-McCoy, C. (2004). Assessing the multicultural competence of school counselors: A checklist. *Professional School Counseling, 7,* 178–186.

Holcomb-McCoy, C. (2005a). Empowerment groups for urban African American girls: A response. *Professional School Counseling, 8,* 390–392.

Holcomb-McCoy, C. (2005b). Investigating school counselors' perceived multicultural competence. *Professional School Counseling, 8,* 414–423.

Holloway, I., & Todres, L. (2003). The status of method: Flexibility, consistency, coherence. *Qualitative Research, 3*(3), 345–357.

Holmes, T. H., & Rahe, R. H. (1967). The Social Readjustment Scale. *Journal of Psychosomatic Research, 11,* 213–218.

Houghton, A. B., Stricklin, K., & Morris, M. B. (1992). *Private choices, public consequences: A discussion on ethical choices using Gandhi's seven sins as challenges & guides.* Cinncinnati, OH: Forward Movement Publications.

Hubble, M. A., Duncan, B. L., & Miller, S. D. (Eds.). (1999). *The heart and soul of change.* Washington, DC: American Psychological Association.

Hughey, K. F., Gysbers, N. C., & Starr, M. (1993). Evaluating comprehensive school guidance programs: Assessing the perceptions of students, parents, and teachers. *School Counselor, 41*(1), 31–35.

Hunt, C., Shochet, I., & King, R. (2005). The use of e-mail in the therapy process. *The Australian and New Zealand Journal of Family Therapy, 26*(1), 10–20.

Hutman, S., Jaffe, J., Segal, R., Kemp, G., & Dumke, L. F. (2005). Burnout: Signs, symptoms and prevention [Electronic Version]. *Helpguide.* Retrieved December 7, 2005, from http://www .helpguide.org/mental/burnout_signs_symptoms.htm

Hyde, J. S. (2005). The Gender Similarities Hypothesis. *American Psychologist, 60*(6), 581–592.

International Association for Marriage and Family Counseling. (2005). Ethical codes. Retrieved November 8, 2005, from http://www.iamfc.com/ethical_codes.html

Irwin, T. (1985). *Aristotle: Nicomachean ethics.* Indianapolis, IN: Hackett.

Ivey, A. E., D'Andrea, M., Ivey, M. B., & Simek-Morgan, L. (2002). *Theories of counseling and psychotherapy: A multicultural perspective* (5th ed.). Boston: Allyn & Bacon.

Jablensky, A., Sartorius, N., Ernberg, G., Anker, M., Korten, A., Cooper, J. E., et al. (1992). Schizophrenia: Manifestations, incidence and course in different cultures. A World Health Organization ten-country study. *Psychological Medicine Monograph Supplemental, 20,* 1–97.

Jackson, G., & Cook, C. G. (1999). *Disaster mental health: Crisis counseling programs for the rural community.* Retrieved December 14, 2005, from http://www.mentalhealth.samhsa.gov/publications/allpubs/sma99-3378/crisiscounseling_ch2.asp

James, G. W. (1920). *Indian blanket and their makers.* Chicago: M.A. Donahue and Co.

Janoff-Bulman, R. (2004). Posttraumatic growth: Three explanatory models. *Psychological Inquiry, 15,* 30–34.

Jensen, L., & Buhanan, K. (1974). Resistance to temptation following three types of motivational instructions among four-, six-, and eight-year-old female children. *Journal of Genetic Psychology, 125,* 51–59.

Jerrel, J. M. (1995). The effects of client-counselor match on service use and costs. *Administration and Policy in Mental Health, 23,* 119–126.

Johnson, J. A., Musial, D. L., Hall, G. E., Gollnick, D. M., & Dupuis, V. L. (2004). *Introduction to the foundations of American education* (13th ed.). Boston: Allyn & Bacon.

Johnson, N., Sacuzzon, D., & Koen, W. (2005). Child custody mediation in cases of domestic violence: Empirical evidence of a failure to protect. *Violence Against Women, 11*(8), 1022–1053.

Johnson, S., Johnson, C., & Downs, L. (2006). *Building a RESULTS-BASED student support program.* Boston: Lahaska Press.

Jones, E. E. (2000). *Therapeutic action: A guide to psychoanalytic therapy.* Northvale, NJ: Jason Aronson.

Jones, M. C. (1924). The elimination of children's fear. *Journal of Experimental Psychology, 8,* 382–390.

Jordan, K. (2002). Clinical training of graduate students: The need for faculty to balance responsibility and vulnerability. *Clinical Supervisor, 21*(1), 29–38.

Jorgenson, L. M. (1995). Sexual contact in fiduciary relationships. In J. C. Gonsiorek (Ed.), *Breach of trust: Sexual exploitation by health care professionals and clergy* (pp. 237–283). Thousand Oaks, CA: Sage.

Kabat-Zinn, J. (2005). *Coming to our senses: Healing ourselves and the world through mindfulness.* New York: Hyperion.

Kant, I. (1963). *Lectures on ethics* (L. Infield, Trans.). Indianapolis, IN: Hackett. (Originally published 1762–94)

Kaplan, L. (2001). Dual relationships: A call for open discourse. *Professional Ethics, 9*(1), 3–29.

Kavathatzopoulos, I. (2005). Making ethical decisions in professional life. In H. Montgomery, R. Lipshitz, & B. Brehmer (Eds.), *How professionals make decisions* (pp. 277–288). Mahwah, NJ: Erlbaum.

Kessler, L. E., & Waehler, C. (2005). Addressing multiple relationships between clients and therapists in lesbian, gay, bisexual, and transgender communities. *Professional Psychology: Research and Practice, 36*(1), 66–73.

Kilbourne, J. (1999). *Can't buy my love.* New York: Simon and Schuster.

Kim, B. S. K., Hill, C. E., Gelso, C. J., Goates, M. K., Asay, P. A., & Harbin, J. M. (2003). Counselor self-disclosure, East Asian American client adherence to Asian cultural values, and counseling process. *Journal of Counseling Psychology, 50*(3), 324–332.

Kim, B. S. K., & Omizo, M. M. (2005). Asian and European American cultural values, collective self-esteem, acculturative stress, cognitive flexibility, and general self-efficacy among Asian American college students. *Journal of Counseling Psychology, 52*(3), 412–419.

Kinnes, T. (2004). Bhagavad gita. Retrieved October 3, 2005, from http://oaks.nvg.org/ys6ra8 .html#13

Kissinger, H. (2005). Kissinger quotes. Retrieved November 20, 2005, from http://www.quotedb .com/quotes/1477

Kitchener, K. S. (2000). *Foundations of ethical practice, research, and teaching in psychology.* Mahwah, NJ: Erlbaum.

Kivlighan, D. M. J. (2002). Transference, interpretation, and insight: A research-practice model. In G. S. Tryon (Ed.), *Counseling based on process research: Applying what we know* (pp. 166–196). Boston: Allyn & Bacon.

Kobasa, S. C. (1979). Stressful life events, personality, and health: An inquiry into hardiness. *Journal of Personality and Social Psychology, 37,* 1–11.

Koger, S. M., Schettler, T., & Weiss, B. (2005). Environmental toxicants and developmental disabilities: A challenge for psychologists. *American Psychologist, 60*(3), 243–255.

Kohlberg, L. (1979). *Measuring moral judgment.* Worcester, MA: Clark University Press.

Kohut, H. H. (1984). *How does analysis cure?* Chicago: University of Chicago Press.

Koocher, G., & Keith-Spiegel, P. S. (1990). *Children, ethics, and the law.* Lincoln: University of Nebraska Press.

Kottler, J. A., & Brown, R. W. (1996). *Introduction to therapeutic counseling.* Pacific Grove, CA: Brooks/Cole.

Kottow, M. (2004). The battering of informed consent. *Journal of Medical Ethics, 30,* 565–569.

Krebs, D. L., & Denton, K. (2005). Toward a more pragmatic approach to morality: A critical evaluation of Kohlberg's model. *Psychological Review, 112*(3), 629–649.

Kreisler, J. (2005). Professions and their identities: How to explore professional development among (semi-) professions. *Scandinavian Journal of Educational Research, 49,* 335–357.

Ladany, N., Friedlander, M., & Nelson, M. (2005). *Critical events in psychotherapy supervision: An interpersonal approach* Washington, DC: American Psychological Association.

Ladany, N., & Melincoff, D. S. (1999). The nature of counselor supervisor nondisclosure. *Counselor Education & Supervision, 38*(3), 191–204.

Lal, V. (1997, December 12, 2002). Gandhi and the Nobel Peace Prize. *India and its neighbors.* Retrieved December 9, 2005, from http://www.sscnet.ucla.edu/southasia/MAIN/site.html

Lally, S. J. (2003). What tests are acceptable for use in forensic evaluations?: A survey of experts. *Professional Psychology: Research and Practice, 34,* 491–498.

Lamb, D. H., & Catanzaro, S. J. (1998). Sexual and nonsexual boundary violations involving psychologists, clients, supervisees, and students: Implications for professional practice. *Professional Psychology: Research and Practice, 29*(498–503).

Lamb, D. H., Catanzaro, S. J., & Moorman, A. S. (2004). A preliminary look at how psychologists identify, evaluate and proceed when faced with possible multiple relationship dilemmas. *Professional Psychology: Research and Practice, 35*(3), 248–254.

Lambert, M. J. (1992). Implications of outcome research for psychotherapy integration. In J. C. Norcross & M. R. Goldstein (Eds.), *Handbook of psychotherapy integration* (pp. 94–129). New York: Basic Books.

Lambert, M. J., & Barley, D. E. (2002). Research summary on the therapeutic relationship and psychotherapy outcome. In J. C. Norcross (Ed.), *Psychotherapy relationships that work: Therapist contributions and responsiveness to patients* (pp. 17–32). London: Oxford University Press.

Lambert, M. J., & Bergin, A. E. (1994). The effectiveness of psychotherapy. In A. E. Bergin & S. L. Garfield (Eds.), *Handbook of psychotherapy and behavior change* (4th ed., pp. 143–189). New York: Wiley.

Lancaster, W. (1998). The code of conduct: Whose code, whose conduct? *Journal of Humanitarian Assistance.* http://www.jha.ac/articles/a038.htm (Posted June 3, 2000), 1–10.

Langs, R. (1980). *The technique of psychoanalytic psychotherapy.* New York: Jason Aronson.

Larson, P. L. (1979). *Broken arcs: A young poet's search for connection.* Chicago: Covenant Press.

Latham, E. C. (Ed.). (1979). *The poetry of Robert Frost.* New York: Holt Rinehart and Winston.

Lawrence, G., & Kurpius, S. E. R. (2000). Legal and ethical issues involved when counseling minors in nonschool settings. *Journal of Counseling & Development, 78*(2), 130–136.

Lazarus, A. A. (1994). How certain boundaries and ethics diminish therapeutic effectiveness. *Ethics & Behavior, 4*(3), 255–261.

Lazarus, A. A. (2005). Boundary crossing vs. boundary violations. *Annals of the American Psychotherapy Association, 6*(1), 25–26.

Lazarus, A. A., & Zur, O. (Eds.). (2002). *Dual relationships and psychotherapy.* New York: Springer.

Lazerson, M. (1971). Urban reforms in the schools: Kindergartens in Massachusetts, 1870–1915. *History of Education Quarterly, 11*(2), 115–142.

Leflar, R. B. (1997). The cautious acceptance of informed consent in Japan. *Medical Law, 16*(4), 705–720.

Leslie, L. K., Gordon, J. N., Lambros, K., Premji, K., Peoples, J., & Gist, K. (2005). Addressing the developmental and mental health needs of young children in foster care. *Journal of Developmental & Behavioral Pediatrics, 26*(2), 140–151.

Lester, D. (1997). Communitarianism and suicide prevention: Proposals for the year 2000. *Crisis: The Journal of Crisis Intervention and Suicide Prevention, 18,* 118–123.

Levine, M., & Doueck, H. J. (1995). *The impact of mandated reporting on the therapeutic process: Picking up the pieces.* Thousand Oaks, CA: Sage.

Levoy, G. (1997). *Calling: Finding and following an authentic life.* New York: Three Rivers Press.

Lewis, N. (Ed.). (1946). *Roget's international thesaurus* (9th ed.). New York: Thomas Y. Cromwell.

Liegeois, A., & Van Audenhove, C. (2005). Ethical dilemmas in community mental health care. *Journal of Medical Ethics, 31,* 452–456.

Linehan, M. M. (1993). *Skills training manual for treating borderline personality disorder.* New York: Guilford.

Linehan, M. M. (2000). The empirical basis of dialectical behavior therapy: Development of new treatments versus evaluation of existing treatments. *Clinical Psychology: Science & Practice, 7*(1), 113–119.

Litwack, T. R. (2001). Actuarial versus clinical assessments of dangerousness. *Psychology, Public Policy, and Law, 72*(2), 409–443.

Long, J. E. (2005). Power to prescribe: The debate over prescription privileges for psychologists and the legal issues implicated. *Law and Psychology Review, 29*(Spring), 243–260.

Longfellow, H. (1882). Elegiac verse. *In the harbor.* Retrieved May 31, 2006, from http://en .wikisource.org/wiki/Elegiac_Verse

Lopez, B. (1986). *Arctic dreams: Imagination and desire in a northern landscape.* New York: Charles Scribner's Sons.

Lowe, S. M. (2005). Integrating collectivist values into career counseling with Asian Americans: A test of cultural responsiveness. *Journal of Multicultural Counseling and Development, 33,* 134–145.

Luborsky, L. (1984). *Principles of psychoanalytic psychotherapy: A manual for supportive-expressive treatment.* New York: Basic Books.

Luborsky, L., & Crits-Christoph, P. (1998). *Understanding transference: The Core Conflictual Relationship Theme method* (2nd ed.). Washington, DC: American Psychological Association.

Luborsky, L., Singer, B., & Luborsky, L. (1975). Comparative studies of psychotherapies: Is it true that "Everybody has won so all shall have prizes?" *Archives of General Psychiatry, 32,* 995–1008.

Ludka v. O'Brien-Brick 1995 Wisc. App. 1670. (1995).

Luhrmann, T. H. (2000). *Of two minds.* New York: Afred A. Knopf.

MacFarlane, M., & Nierman, M. (2005, 2005). Discovering Psychology. Retrieved December 3, 2005, from http://www.learner.org/discoveringpsychology/history/history_nonflash.html

MacIntyre, A. (1998a). After virtue. In S. M. Cahn & P. Markie (Eds.), *Ethics: History, theory, and contemporary issues* (pp. 653–658). New York: Oxford.

MacIntyre, A. (1998b). Introduction: Historical sources. In S. M. Cahn & P. Markie (Eds.), *Ethics: History, theory and contemporary issues* (pp. 1–2). New York: Oxford.

Maher, F. A., & Tetrault, M. K. T. (Eds.). (1994). *The feminist classroom.* New York: Harper-Collins.

Mahoney, M. J. (1991). *Human change processes.* New York: Basic Books.

Mahoney, M. J. (2003). *Constructive psychotherapy.* New York: Guilford.

Mahoney, M. J. (2005). Suffering, philosophy, and psychotherapy. *Journal of Psychotherapy Integration, 15*(3), 337–352.

Maniar, S. D., Curry, L. A., Sommers-Flanagan, J., & Walsh, J. A. (2001). Student athlete preferences in seeking help when confronted with sport performance problems. *Sport Psychologist, 15*(2), 205–223.

Mann, T. (1994). Informed consent for psychological research: Do subjects comprehend consent forms and understand their legal rights? *Psychological Science, 5*(3), 140–143.

Maramba, G. G., & Hall, G. C. N. (2002). Meta-analyses of ethnic match as a predictor of dropout, utilization, and level of functioning. *Cultural Diversity and Ethnic Minority Psychology, 8,* 290–297.

Marcussen, K., & Piatt, L. (2005). Race differences in the relationship between role experiences and well-being. *Health: An Interdisciplinary Journal for the Social Study of Health, Illness and Medicine, 9*(3), 379–402.

Marlatt, G. A. (Writer). (1998). Cognitive-behavioral relapse prevention for addictions [Videotape]. Washington, DC: American Psychological Association.

Maslach, C., & Jackson, S. E. (1981). The measurement of experienced burnout. *Journal of Occupational Behaviour, 2,* 99–113.

Masson, J. M. (1988). *Against therapy: Emotional tyranny and the myth of psychological healing.* New York: Atheneum.

Mazurana, D. E., & McKay, S. A. (2001). Women, girls, and structural violence: A global analysis. In D. J. Christie, R. V. Wagner, & D. D. Winter (Eds.), *Peace, conflict, and violence* (pp. 130–138). Upper Saddle River, NJ: Prentice Hall.

McCormack, C. (2005). Reconceptualizing student evaluation of teaching: An ethical framework for changing times. *Assessment & Evaluation in Higher Education, 30*(5), 463–476.

McDonald, C. (2003). Will the "secular priesthood" of bioethics work among the sinners? *American Journal of Bioethics, 3*(2), 36–39.

McFarland, W. P., & Dupuis, M. (2001). The legal duty to protect gay and lesbian students from violence in school. *Professional School Counseling, 4,* 171–179.

McGee, V. C. (2004). Sunbeams. *The Sun, July,* 48.

McGrath, M. C. (1923). A study of the moral development of children. *Psychological Monographs, 32,* 161.

McGuire, S. R., & Cottone, R. R. (2003). Addiction counseling. In R. R. Cottone & V. M. Tarvydas (Eds.), *Ethical and professional issues in counseling* (2nd ed., pp. 378–386). Upper Saddle River, NJ: Merrill Prentice Hall.

McIntosh, P. (1998). White privilege: Unpacking the invisible knapsack. In M. McGoldrick (Ed.), *Re-visioning family therapy: Race, gender and culture in clinical practice.* New York: Guilford.

Mehlman, E., & Glickauf-Hughes, C. (1994). The underside of psychotherapy: Confronting hateful feelings toward clients. *Psychotherapy: Theory, Research, Practice, Training, 31*(3), 434–439.

Menski, W. (1996). Hinduism. In P. Morgan & C. Lawton (Eds.), *Ethical issues in six religious traditions* (pp. 1–51). Edinburgh, Scotland: Edinburgh University Press.

Merlone, L. (2005). Record keeping and the school counselor. *Professional School Counseling, 8,* 372–376.

Metcalfe, D. H., & Matharu, M. (1995). Students' perception of good and bad teaching: Report of a critical incident study. *Medical Education, 29*(3), 193–197.

Metzger, B. M., & Murphy, R. E. (Eds.). (1994). *The new Oxford annotated Bible.* New York: Oxford University Press.

Meyers, C. J. (1991). Where the protective privilege ends: California changes the rules for dangerous psychotherapy patients. *Journal of Psychiatry and the Law, 19,* 5–31.

Michels, R. (2001). Treatment of depression in the new health care scene. In M. M. Weissman

(Ed.), *Treatment of depression: Bridging the 21st century* (pp. 47–54). Washington, DC: American Psychiatric Publishing.

Middleton, R. A., Rollins, C. W., Sanderson, P. L., Leung, P., Harley, D. A., Ebener, D., et al. (2000). Endorsement of professional multicultural rehabilitation competencies and standards: A call to action. *Rehabilitation Counseling Bulletin, 43,* 219–240.

Mill, J. S. (1912). *"The subjection of women" in three essays.* London: Oxford University Press.

Mill, J. S. (1992). The subjugation of women. In J. Gray (Ed.), *On liberty and other essays* (pp. 472–582). New York: Oxford University Press.

Miller, E. T., Neal, D. J., Roberts, L. J., Baer, J. S., Cressler, S. O., Metrik, J., et al. (2002). Test–retest reliability of alcohol measures: Is there a difference between internet-based assessment and traditional methods? *Psychology of Addictive Behaviors, 16*(1), 56–63.

Miller, T. R., Scott, R., & Searight, H. R. (1990). Ethics for marital and family therapy and subsequent training issues. *Family Therapy, 17,* 161–171.

Miller, W. R., & Rollnick, S. (2002). *Motivational interviewing: Preparing people for change* (2nd ed.). New York: Guilford.

Milton, J. (2003). *Paradise lost.* New York: Penguin. (Originally published 1667)

Mitchell, C. W., Disque, J. G., & Robertson, P. (2002). When parents want to know: Responding to parental demands for confidential information. *Professional School Counseling, 6,* 156–161.

Mohr, D. C., Hart, S. L., Julian, L., Catledge, C., Honos-Webb, L., Vella, L., et al. (2005). Telephone-administered psychotherapy for depression. *Archives of General Psychiatry, 62,* 1007–1014.

Mohr, J. J., Gelso, C. J., & Hill, C. E. (2005). Client and counselor trainee attachment as predictors of session evaluation and countertransference behavior in first counseling sessions. *Journal of Counseling Psychology, 52*(3), 298–309.

Moore, T. (1994). *Care of the soul.* New York: Perennial.

Moreau, D., Mufson, L., Weissman, M. M., & Klerman, G. L. (1991). Interpersonal psychotherapy for adolescent depression: Description of modification and preliminary application. *Journal of the American Academy of Child & Adolescent Psychiatry, 30*(4), 642–651.

Morrison, J. (1994). *The first interview (revised for the DSM-IV).* New York: Guilford.

Motta, R. W., Chirichella, D. M., Maus, M. K., & Lombardo, M. T. (2004). Assessing secondary trauma. *Behavior Therapist, 27*(3), 54–57.

Mumford, M., Connelly, M. S., & Leritz, L. (2005). Integrity in professional settings: Individual and situational influences. In S. Shohov (Ed.), *Advances in psychology* (Vol. 34, pp. 221–257). New York: Nova Science Publishers.

Munely, P. H., Lidderdale, M. A., Thiagarajan, M., & Null, U. (2004). Identity development and multicultural competence. *Journal of Multicultural Counseling and Development, 32,* 283–295.

Mustaine, E. E., & Tewksbury, R. (2005). Southern college students' cheating behaviors: An examination of problem behavior correlates. *Deviant Behavior, 26*(5), 439–461.

Myers, J. E., & Harper, M. C. (2004). Evidence-based effective practices with older adults. *Journal of Counseling & Development, 82,* 207–218.

Myers, J. E., Sweeney, T. J., & Witmer, J. M. (2000). The wheel of wellness counseling: A holistic model for treatment planning. *Journal of Counseling & Development, 78,* 251–266.

Myers, L. J., Speight, S. L., Highlen, P. S., Cox, C. I., Reynolds, A. L., Adams, E. M., et al. (1991). Identity development and worldview: Toward an optimal conceptualization. *Journal of Counseling and Development, 70,* 54–63.

National Association of Social Workers (NASW). (2006). Webpage. Retrieved November 17, 2005, from http://www.naswdc.org/

National Career Development Association. (2005, 2003). Webpage. Retrieved December 3, 2005, from http://www.ncda.org/about/polccc.html

National Rehabilitation Association. (2005). Webpage Introduction. Retrieved October 13, 2005, from http://www.nationalrehab.org/website/history/index.html

Nell, W. C. (1852). On the current political parties (letter to William Lloyd Garrison). *The Liberator,* December 10.

Nelson, H. L. (2001). Identity and free agency. In P. DesAutels & J. Waugh (Eds.), *Feminists doing ethics* (pp. 45–62). Lanham, MD: Rowman & Littlefield.

Nemec, P. B. (2004). Evidence-based practice: Bandwagon or handbasket? *Rehabilitation Education, 18,* 133–135.

Neukrag, E., Healy, M., & Herlihy, B. (1992). Ethical practices of licensed professional counselors: An updated survey of state licensing boards. *Counselor Education & Supervision, 32,* 130–141.

Neukrag, E., Milliken, T., & Walden, S. (2001). Ethical complaints made against credentialed counselors: An updated survey of state licensing boards. *Counselor Education & Supervision, 41,* 57–70.

Nichols, G. (2005). Boston's Little Italy: 1900–Today. Retrieved December 9, 2005, from http://www.northendboston.com/history5.htm

Nichols, M. P. (2004). *Family therapy: Concepts and methods.* Boston: Allyn & Bacon.

Nickel, M.-B. (2004). Professional boundaries: The dilemma of dual and multiple relationships in rural clinical practice. *Counseling and Clinical Psychology, 1*(1), 17–22.

Nietzsche, F. (1982). Twilight of the idols. In W. Kaufmann (Ed. & Trans.), *The portable Nietzsche* (pp. 463–563). New York: Penguin. (Originally published 1895)

Norcross, J. C. (Ed.). (2002). *Psychotherapy relationships that work.* New York: Oxford University Press.

Norris, R., & Kaniasty, K. (1996). Received and perceived social support in times of stress: A test of the social support deterioration deterrence model. *Journal of Personality and Social Psychology, 71,* 498–511.

Northey, W. F. (2002). Characteristics and clinical practices of marriage and family therapists: A national survey. *Journal of Marriage and Family Therapy, 28*(4), 487–494.

Nouwen, H. J. M. (2000). *Life of the beloved.* New York: Crossroads.

O'Connor Slimp, P. A., & Burian, B. K. (1994). Multiple role relationships during internship: Consequences and recommendations. *Professional Psychology: Research & Practice, 25*(1), 39–45.

O'Neill, O. (2004). Some limits of informed consent. *Journal of Medical Ethics, 30,* 171–175.

Oliver, M. N. I., Bernstein, J. H., Anderson, K. G., Blashfield, R. K., & Roberts, M. C. (2004). An exploratory examination of student attitudes toward "impaired" peers in clinical psychology training programs. *Professional Psychology: Research and Practice, 35*(2), 141–147.

Olkin, R. (2004). Making research accessible to participants with disabilities. *Journal of Multicultural Counseling and Development, 32,* 332–343.

Otto, R. (2000). Assessing and managing violence risk in outpatient settings. *Journal of Clinical Psychology, 56,* 1239–1262.

Owen, J. P. (2004). *Cowboy ethics: What Wall Street can learn from the Code of the West.* Ketchum, ID: Stoeckleinm Publishing.

Oxford English Dictionary (Compact ed. Vol. I). (1981). Oxford, UK: Oxford University Press.

Paivio, S. C., & Greenberg, L. S. (1995). Resolving "unfinished business": Efficacy of experiential therapy using empty-chair dialogue. *Journal of Consulting & Clinical Psychology, 63*(3), 419–425.

Paniagua, F. A. (2001). *Diagnosis in a multicultural context.* Thousand Oaks, CA: Sage.

Parsons, F. (1909). *Choosing a vocation.* Boston: Houghton Mifflin.

Patton, W., & Burnett, P. C. (1993). The Children's Depression Scale: Assessment of factor structure with data from a normal adolescent population *Adolescence, 28*(110), 315–324.

Pearlman, L. A., & MacIan, P. S. (1995). Vicarious traumatization: An empirical study of the effects of trauma on trauma therapists. *Professional Psychology: Research & Practice, 26,* 558–565.

Pelham, W. E. J., Fabiano, G. A., & Massetti, G. M. (2005). Evidence-based assessment of attention deficit hyperactivity disorder in children and adolescents. *Journal of Clinical Child and Adolescent Psychology, 34,* 449–476.

Perrett, R. W. (1998). *Hindu ethics: A philosophical study.* Honolulu: University of Hawai'i Press.

Peter, L. (1984). *Why things go wrong, or the Peter principle revisited.* New York: William Morrow & Co.

Peterson, E. (1996). *Take and read: An annotated bibliography.* Grand Rapids, MI: Wm. B. Eerdmans.

Peterson, J. S., Goodman, R., Keller, T., & McCauley, A. (2004). Teachers and non-teachers as school counselors: Reflections on the internship experience. *Professional School Counseling, 7,* 246–255.

Petroff, E. A. E. (1986). *Medieval women's visionary literature.* New York: Oxford University Press.

Pidcock, B. W., & Polansky, J. (2001). Clinical practice issues in assessing for adult substance use disorders. In E. Welfel (Ed.), *The mental health desk reference* (pp. 128–135). New York: Wiley.

Pipes, R. B., Holstein, J., & Aguiree, M. G. (2005). Examining the personal-professional distinction: Ethics codes and the difficulty of drawing a boundary. *American Psychologist, 60*(4), 325–335.

Pirsig, R. (1984). *Zen and the art of motorcycle maintenance: An inquiry into values.* New York: Bantam.

Pistole, M. C. (2004). Mental health counseling: Identity and distinctiveness. Retrieved November 22, 2005, from http://www.ericdigests.org/2002-4/mental-health.html

Plotkin, B. (2003). *Soulcraft: Crossing into the mysteries of nature and psyche.* Novato, CA: New World Library.

Pojman, L. P. (1995). *Ethics: Discovering right and wrong.* Belmont, CA: Wadsworth.

Pomerantz, A., & Handelsman, M. (2004). Informed consent revisited: An updated written question format. *Professional Psychology: Research & Practice, 35,* 201–205.

Pope, K. (1988). How clients are harmed by sexual contact with mental health professionals. *Journal of Counseling & Development, 67,* 222–226.

Pope, K. (1990a). Indentifying and implementing ethical standards for primary prevention. *Prevention in Human Services, 8*(2), 43–64.

Pope, K. (1990b). Therapists' sexual feelings and behaviors: Research, trends, and quandaries. In L. Szuchman & F. Muscarella (Eds.), *Psychological perspectives on human sexuality* (pp. 603–658). New York: Wiley.

Pope, K., & Vasquez, M. (1998). *Ethics in psychotherapy and counseling: A practical guide* (2nd ed.). San Francisco, CA: Jossey-Bass/Pfeiffer.

Pope, K., & Vetter, V. A. (1991). Prior therapist-patient sexual involvement among patients seen by psychologists. *Psychotherapy, 28,* 429–438.

Pope, K., & Vetter, V. A. (1992). Ethical dilemmas encountered by members of the American Psychological Association. *American Psychologist, 47,* 397–411.

Pope, K. S., Levenson, H., & Schover, L. R. (1979). Sexual intimacy in psychology training: Results and implications of a national survey. *American Psychologist, 38,* 682–689.

Pór, G. (2000, May 23). *Knowledge, intelligence, wisdom: Essential value chain of the new economy.* Paper presented at the Consultation Meeting on the Future of Organizations and Knowledge Management of the European Commission's Directorate-General Information Society Technologies, Brussels. Retrieved December 11, 2005, from http://www.co-i-l.com/coil/knowledge-garden/kd/kiwkeynotes.shtml

Prabhavanada, S., & Isherwood, C. (Trans). (2002). *Bhagavad-Gita: The song of God.* New York: Signet Classics.

Prochaska, J. O., & DiClemente, C. C. (1982). Transtheoretical therapy: Toward a more integrative model of change. *Psychotherapy, 19,* 276–278.

Prout, S. M., & Prout, H. T. (1998). A meta-analysis of school-based studies of counseling and psychotherapy: An update. *Journal of School Psychology, 36,* 121–136.

Quattrocchi, M. R., & Schopp, R. F. (2005). Tarasaurus rex: A standard of care that could not adapt. *Psychology, Public Policy, and Law, 11*(1), 109–137.

Rachels, J. (1986). *The elements of moral philosophy.* Philadelphia: Temple University Press.

Rainer, J. (1996). Introduction to the special issue on psychotherapy outcomes. *Psychotherapy, 33,* 159.

Raven, B. H. (1983). Interpersonal influence and social power. In B. H. Raven & J. Z. Rubin (Eds.), *Social psychology* (pp. 399–443). New York: Wiley.

Rawls, J. (1998). A theory of justice: The main idea of the theory of justice. In S. M. Cahn & P. Markie (Eds.), *Ethics: History, theory, and contemporary issues* (pp. 621–640). New York: Oxford University Press.

Ray, O. (2004). How the mind hurts and heals the body. *American Psychologist, 59*(1), 29–40.

Redlich, F. C., & Pope, K. (1980). Ethics of mental health training. *Journal of Nervous and Mental Disease, 168,* 709–714.

Reese, R. (2003). Filial piety in Chinese religion. Retrieved September 15, 2005, from http://writing .lantenengo.com/filialpiety.php

Remley, T. (1995). A proposed alternative to the licensing of specialties in counseling. *Journal of Counseling & Development, 72,* 157–158.

Remley, T., & Herlihy, B. (2005). *Ethical, legal, and professional issues in counseling.* Upper Saddle River, NJ: Pearson.

Remley, T. P. J., Hermann, M. A., & Huey, W. C. (Eds.). (2003). *Ethical and legal issues in school counseling* (2nd ed.). Alexandria, VA: American School Counselor Association.

Renik, O. (1993). Analytic interaction: Conceptualizing technique in light of the analyst's irreducible subjectivity. *Psychoanalytic Quarterly, 62,* 553–571.

Rest, J. R., & Narvaez, D. (Eds.). (1994). *Moral development in the professions: Psychology and applied ethics.* Hillsdale, NJ: Erlbaum.

Richard, S. A., Rawal, S., & Martin, D. K. (2005). An ethical framework for cardiac report cards: A qualitative study [Electronic Version]. *BMC Medical Ethics, 6.* Retrieved November 30, 2005, from http://www.biomedcentral.com/1472-6939/6/3

Richards, P. S., & Bergin, A. E. (Eds.). (2000). *Handbook of psychotherapy and religious diversity.* Washington, DC: American Psychological Association.

Richardson, B. G. (2001). *Working with challenging youth: Lessons learned along the way.* Philadelphia: Brunner-Routledge.

Richardson, C. D., & Rosen, L. A. (1999). School-based interventions for children of divorce. *Professional School Counseling, 3*(1), 21–26.

Ridley, M. (1996). *The origins of virtue.* New York: Penguin.

Rifkin, J. (2004). For the experiences of a lifetime, sign on the dotted line. *Missoulian, April 5,* 5.

Roberts, L. W., Warner, T. D., & Hammond, K. G. (2005). Ethical challenges of mental health clinicians in rural and frontier areas. *Psychiatric Services, 56*(3), 358–359.

Robinson, A. (2003). The ethics of dual relationships: Will the real boundary violations please stand up? *Counselor: The Magazine for Addiction Professionals, 4*(6), 24–27.

Rodgers, R., & Hammerstein, O. (Writers). (1949). South Pacific [Motion picture]. United States: Sony.

Rodman Aronson, K. M., & Schaler Bucholz, E. (2001). The post-feminist era: Still striving for equality in relationships. *American Journal of Family Therapy, 29*(2), 109–124.

Rodolfa, E., Bent, R., Eisman, E., Nelson, P., Rehn, L., & Ritchie, P. (2005). A cube model for competency development: Implications for psychology educators and regulators. *Professional Psychology: Research and Practice, 36*(4), 347–354.

Rogers, C. R. (1957). The necessary and sufficient conditions of therapeutic personality change. *Journal of Consulting Psychology, 21,* 95–103.

Rogers, C. R. (1958). The characteristics of a helping relationship. *Personnel and Guidance Journal, 37,* 6–16.

Rogers, C. R. (1959). A theory of therapy, personality, and interpersonal relationships, as developed in the client-centered framework. In S. Koch (Ed.), *Psychology: A study of a science* (pp. 184–256). New York: McGraw-Hill.

Rogers, C. R. (1961). *On becoming a person.* Boston: Houghton Mifflin.

Rooney, P. (2001). Gender and moral reasoning revisited: Reengaging feminist psychology. In P. DesAutels & J. Waugh (Eds.), *Feminists doing ethics* (pp. 153–166). Lanham, MD: Rowman & Littlefield.

Rose, S., Bisson, J., Churchill, R., & Wessely, S. (2002). Psychological debriefing for preventing post traumatic stress disorder (PTSD). *The Cochrane Database of Systematic Reviews, Art. No.: CD000560*(2), 1–55.

Rosenberg, S. (2004). Face. Retrieved October 13, 2005, from http://www.beyondintractability .org/m/development_conflict_theory.jsp

Rosenstein, D. (2004). Decision-making capacity and disaster research. *Journal of Traumatic Stress, 17*(5), 373–381.

Rosenthal, R. (1994). Science and ethics in conducting, analyzing, and reporting psychological research. *Psychological Science, 5*(3), 127–134.

Rosenthal, R., & Rosnow, R. L. (1991). *Essentials of behavioral research: Methods and data analysis* (2nd ed.). New York: McGraw-Hill.

Rowell, L. I. (2005). Collaborative action research and school counselors. *Professional School Counseling., 9,* 28–36.

Rubin, L. R. (2003). Wilhelm Reich and Anna Freud: His expulsion from psychoanalysis. *International Forum of Psychoanalysis., 12*(2–3), 109–117.

Rutland, A., Cameron, L., Milne, A., & McGeorge, P. (2005). Social norms and self-presentation: Children's implicit and explicit intergroup attitudes. *Child Development, 76*(2), 451–466.

Ryan, M. K., David, B., & Reynolds, K. (2004). Who cares? The effect of gender and context on the self and moral reasoning. *Psychology of Women Quarterly, 28,* 246–255.

Sabella, R. A., & Booker, B. L. (2003). Using technology to promote your guidance and counseling program among stake holders. *Professional School Counseling, 6*(3), 206–213.

Sadler, J. (2002). *Descriptions and prescriptions: Values, mental disorders, and the DSMs.* Baltimore: Johns Hopkins University Press.

Sain v. Cedar Rapids Community School District (626 N.W.2d 115 [Iowa]). (2001).

Sanchez-Hucles, J., & Jones, N. (2005). Breaking the silence around race in training, practice, and research. *The Counseling Psychologist, 33*(4), 547–558.

Savage, T. A., Harley, D. A., & Nowak, T. (2005). Applying social empowerment strategies as tools for self-advocacy in counseling lesbian and gay male clients. *Journal of Counseling and Development, 83*(Spring), 131–137.

Scaturo, D. J. (2002). Fundamental dilemmas in contemporary psychotherapy: A transtheoretical concept. *American Journal of Psychotherapy, 56*(1), 115–131.

Scheoner, G., & Gonsiorek, J. C. (1988). Assessment and development of rehabilitation plans for counselors who have sexually exploited their clients. *Journal of Counseling & Development, 67,* 227–232.

Schmidt, J. (2005). Credentials. In American School Counseling Association (Ed.), *School counseling principles: Foundations and basics* (pp. 46–48). Alexandria, VA: American School Counselor Association.

Schmidt, J. J. (2003). *Counseling in schools: Essential services and comprehensive programs* (4th ed.). Boston: Allyn & Bacon.

Scott, C. (2000). Ethical issues in addiction counseling. *Rehabilitation Counseling Bulletin, 43*(4), 209–215.

Scott, J. (1998). *Seeing like a state: How certain schemes to improve the human condition have failed.* New Haven, CT: Yale University Press.

Sebre, S., Sprugevica, L., Novotni, A., Bonevski, D., Pakalniskiene, V., Popescu, D., et al. (2004). Cross-cultural comparisons of child-reported emotional and physical abuse: Rates, risk factors and psychosocial symptoms *Child Abuse & Neglect, 28*(1), 113–127.

Seligman, M. E. P. (1995). The effectiveness of psychotherapy: The Counsumer Reports study. *American Psychologist, 50,* 965–974.

Selye, H. (1974). *Stress without distress.* New York: Signet.

Sevenhuijsen, S., Bozalek, V., Gouws, A., & Minnaar-McDonald, M. (2003). South African social welfare policy: An analysis using the ethic of care. *Critical Social Policy, 23*(3), 299–321.

Seventh Generation Fund. (2004). Webpage. Retrieved July 7, 2005, from http://www.7genfund .org/#about

Sexton, T. L., & Liddle, M. C. (2001). Practicing evidence-based mental health: Using research and measuring outcomes. In E. R. Welfel & E. R. Ingersoll (Eds.), *The mental health desk reference* (pp. 387–392). New York: Wiley.

Shavers, V. L., Lynch, C. F., & Bermeister, L. F. (2000). Knowledge of the Tuskegee Study and its impact on the willingness to participate in medical research studies. *Journal of the National Medical Association, 92*(12), 563–572.

Shelton, C. F., & James, E. L. (2005). *Best practices for effective secondary school counselors.* Thousand Oaks, CA: Corwin Press.

Sherman, M. D., & Thelen, M. H. (1998). Distress and professional impairment among psychologists in clinical practice. *Professional Psychology: Research and Practice, 29,* 79–85.

Shermer, M. (1997). *Why people believe weird things: Pseudoscience, superstition, and other confusions of our time.* New York: W. H. Freeman.

Shin, S. H. (2005). Need for and actual use of mental health service by adolescents in the child welfare system. *Children and Youth Services Review, 27*(10), 1071–1083.

Shinfuku, N. (2005). The experience of the Kobe earthquake. In J. J. Lopez-Ibor, G. Christodoulou, M. Maj, N. Sartorius, & A. Okasha (Eds.), *Disasters and mental health* (pp. 127–136). New York: Wiley.

Shoham-Salomon, V., & Rosenthal, R. (1987). Paradoxical interventions: A meta-analysis. *Journal of Consulting and Clinical Psychology, 55,* 22–28.

Shuman, D. W., & Foote, W. (1999). Jaffee v. Redmond's impact: Life after the Supreme Court's recognition of a psychotherapist–patient privilege. *Professional Psychology: Research & Practice, 30*(5), 479–487.

Sigelman, C. K., & Rider, E. A. (2006). *Lifespan human development* (5th ed.). Belmont, CA: Thomson Wadsworth.

Silverman, W. H. (1996). Cookbooks, manuals, and paint-by numbers: Psychotherapy in the 90's. *Psychotherapy, 33,* 207–215.

Simi, N. L., & Mahalik, J. R. (1997). Comparison of feminist versus psychoanalytic/dynamic and other therapists on self-disclosure. *Psychology of Women Quarterly, 21,* 465–483.

Singer, P. (1993). *Practical ethics* (2nd ed.). Cambridge, UK: Cambridge University Press.

Singleton, J. (Writer). (1991). *Boyz n the hood* [Motion picture]. United States: Columbia TriStar Home Entertainment.

Skovholt, T. M. (2001). *The resilient practitioner.* Boston: Allyn & Bacon.

Slack, C. M., & Wassenaar, D. R. (1999). Ethical dilemmas of South African clinical psychologists: International comparisons. *European Psychologist, 4*(3), 179–186.

Smail, D. (1984). *Illusion & reality: The meaning of anxiety.* London: Constable and Company, Ltd.

Smedley, A., & Smedley, B. D. (2005). Race as biology is fiction, racism as a social problem is real: Anthropoloical and historical perspectives on the social construction of race. *American Psychologist, 60*(1), 16–26.

Smith, B. H. (1988). *Contingencies of value.* Boston: Harvard University Press.

Smith, D. (2003, January, 2003). Ten ways practitioners can avoid frequent ethical pitfalls. Retrieved November 14, 2005, from http://www.apa.org/monitor/jan03/10ways.html

Smith, D. S., & Fitzpatrick, M. (1995). Patient-therapist boundary issues: An integrative review of theory and research. *Professional Psychology: Research & Practice, 26,* 499–506.

Smith, H. B. (2002). The American Red Cross: How to be part of the solution, rather than part of the problem. In D. D. Bass & R. Yep (Eds.), *Terrorism, trama, and tragedies: A counselor's guide to preparing and responding* (pp. 37–39). Alexandria, VA: American Counseling Association Foundation.

Smith, M. L., & Glass, G. V. (1977). Meta-analysis of psychotherapy outcome studies. *American Psychologist, 32,* 752–760.

Smith, M. L., Glass, G. V., & Miller, T. I. (1980). *The benefits of psychotherapy.* Baltimore: Johns Hopkins University Press.

Smith, R. L. (1991). Ethical issues in marital and family therapy: Who is the client? *The Family Psychologist, 7,* 16.

Smolar, A. (2002). Reflections on gifts in the therapeutic setting. *American Journal of Psychotherapy, 56*(1), 27–45.

Somer, E., & Saadon, M. (1999). Therapist-client sex: Clients' retrospective reports. *Professional Psychology: Research & Practice, 30,* 504–509.

Sommers-Flanagan, J., & Sommers-Flanagan, R. (1989). A categorization of pitfalls common to beginning interviewers. *Journal of Training & Practice in Professional Psychology, 3*(1), 58–71.

Sommers-Flanagan, J., & Sommers-Flanagan, R. (1997). *Tough kids, cool counseling: User-friendly approaches with challenging youth.* Alexandria, VA: American Counseling Association.

Sommers-Flanagan, J., & Sommers-Flanagan, R. (1998). Assessment and diagnosis of conduct disorder. *Journal of Counseling & Development, 76*(2), 189–197.

Sommers-Flanagan, J., & Sommers-Flanagan, R. (2003). *Clinical interviewing* (3rd ed.). Hoboken, NJ: Wiley.

Sommers-Flanagan, J., & Sommers-Flanagan, R. (2004a). *The challenge of counseling teens: Counselor behaviors that reduce resistance and facilitate connection* [Videotape]. North Amherst, MA: Microtraining Associates.

Sommers-Flanagan, J., & Sommers-Flanagan, R. (2004b). *Counseling and psychotherapy theories in context and practice: Skills, strategies, and techniques.* New York: Wiley.

Sommers-Flanagan, R., Elander, C., & Sommers-Flanagan, J. (2000). *Don't divorce us!: Kids' advice to divorcing parents.* Alexandria, VA: American Counseling Association.

Sommers-Flanagan, R., Elliott, D., & Sommers-Flanagan, J. (1998). Exploring the edges: Boundaries and breaks. *Ethics & Behavior, 8*(1), 37–48.

Sommers-Flanagan, R., Sommers-Flanagan, J., & Davis, B. (1993). What's happening on music television? A gender role content analysis. *Sex Roles, 28*(11–12), 745–753.

Southern, S., Smith, R. L., & Oliver, M. (2005). Marriage and family counseling: Ethics in context. *Family Journal: Counseling and Therapy for Couples and Families, 13*(4), 459–466.

Spengler, P. M. (1998). Multicultural assessment and a scientist-practitioner model of psychological assessment. *Counseling Psychologist, 6,* 930–938.

Spiritual Directors International (SDI). (2005). Home Webpage. Retrieved November 23, 2005, from http://www.sdiworld.org/

Spitzform, M. (2004). Why I became a psychoanalyst. In J. Sommers-Flanagan & R. Sommers-

Flanagan (Eds.), *Counseling and psychotherapy in context and practice* (p. 69). New York: Wiley.

Stapp, H. (1993). *Mind, matter, and quantum mechanics.* London: Springer-Verlag.

Starr, P. (1982). *The social origins of professional sovereignty.* New York: Basic Books.

Steigerwald, F., & Forrest, A. (2004). An examination of gender and ethics in family counseling—part 2: A case study approach using a social constructivism model of ethical decision making. *Family Journal: Counseling and Therapy for Couples and Families, 12*(3), 278–281.

Stein, J., Bock, J., & Harnick, S. (1964). *Fiddler on the roof.* New York: Minskoff Theatre.

Stevens, P., Baltimore, M., Birdsall, B., Erickson, S. H., Miller, L. D., Thomas, A., et al. (1999). The ethical code illustrated. In P. Stevens (Ed.), *Ethical casebook for the practice of marriage and family counseling* (pp. 43–70). Alexandria, VA: American Counseling Association.

Stevenson v. Johnson 32 Va. Cir. 157. (1993).

Stiffman, A. R., & Brown, E. (2005). Cultural and ethical issues concerning research on American Indian youth. *Ethics and Behavior, 15*(1), 1–14.

Stone, C. B. (2000). Advocacy for sexual harassment victims: Legal support and ethical aspects. *Professional School Counseling, 4,* 23–30.

Stone, C. B. (2002). Negligence in academic advising and abortion counseling: Court rulings and implications *Professional School Counseling, 6,* 28–35.

Stone, C. B. (2004). *Legal and ethical issues in working with minors in schools.* Paper presented at the Annual meeting of the American School Counselor Association, Reno, NV.

Stone, C. B. (2005a). Cutting, eating disorders and confidentiality. *ASCA School Counselor, 43*(2), 6–7.

Stone, C. B. (2005b). *School counseling principles: Ethics and law.* Alexandria, VA: American School Counselor Association.

Stone, C. B. (2005c). Ethics/law. In American School Counselor Association (Ed.), *School counseling fundamentals: Foundations and basics* (pp. 50–51). Alexandria, VA: American School Counselor Association.

Stone, C. B., & Dahir, C. A. (2004). *School counselor accountability: A measure of student success.* Upper Saddle River, NJ: Lahaska Press.

Stone, C. B., & Dahir, C. A. (2006). *The transformed school counselor.* New York: Lahaska Press.

Strean, H. S. (1993). *Therapists who have sex with their patients: Treatment and recovery.* New York: Brunner/Mazel.

Stricklin-Parker, E., & Schneider, B. A. (2005). Ann: A case study. *Clinical Case Studies, 44*(4), 315–328.

Strupp, H. H. (1979). Specific vs nonspecific factors in psychotherapy: A controlled study of outcome. *Archives of General Psychiatry, 36,* 1125–1136.

Strupp, H. H., & Binder, J. L. (1984). *Psychotherapy in a new key.* New York: Basic Books.

Stein, J. (2001). *Substance abuse: The nation's number one health problem.* New York: Institute for Health Policy, Brandeis University.

Sue, D. W., & Sue, D. (2003). *Counseling the cuturally diverse: Theory and practice* (3rd ed.). New York: Wiley.

Sue, S. (1998). In search of cultural competence in psychotherapy and counseling. *American Psychologist, 53,* 440–448.

Sullivan, H. S. (1953). *The interpersonal theory of psychiatry.* New York: Norton.

Sullivan, J. R., Ramirez, E., Rae, W. A., Razo, N. P., & George, C. A. (2002). Factors contributing to breaking confidentiality with adolescent clients: A survey of pediatric psychologists. *Professional Psychology: Research and Practice, 33*(4), 396–401.

Tannen, D. (1990). *You just don't understand me: Women and men in conversation.* New York: Ballantine Books.

Task Force on Promotion and Dissemination of Psychological Procedures. (1995). Training in and dissemination of empirically-validated psychological treatments: Report and recommendations. *The Clinical Psychologist, 48*, 3–23.

Tatum, B. (2002). Breaking the silence. In P. S. Rothenberg (Ed.), *White privilege: Essential readings on the other side of racism* (pp. 115–120). New York: Worth Publishers.

Taylor, K. (1995). *The ethics of caring.* Santa Cruz, CA: Hanford Mead Publishers.

Taylor, L., & Adelman, H. S. (2001). Enlisting appropriate parental cooperation and involvement in children's mental health treatment. In E. Welfel & R. E. Ingersoll (Eds.), *The mental health desk reference.* New York: Wiley.

Teitelbaum, L. M., & Carey, K. B. (2000). Temporal stability of alcohol screening measures in a psychiatric setting. *Psychology of Addictive Behaviors, 14*(4), 401–404.

Temple, W. (1934). *Nature, man, and God.* New York: The McMillan Company.

Tenzin Gyatso (the 14th Dalai Lama). (1999). *Ethics for a new millenium.* New York: Penguin Putnam.

Teyber, E. (1997). *Interpersonal process in psychotherapy: A relational approach* (3rd ed.). Pacific Grove, CA: Brooks/Cole.

Thomas, S. R. (2005). The school counselor alumni peer consultation group. *Counselor Education & Supervision, 45*(1), 16–29.

Thompson, C., & Rudolph, L. (2000). *Counseling children.* Belmont, CA: Wadsworth Brooks/Cole.

Thornicroft, G., & Tansella, M. (2005). Growing recognition of the importance of service user involvement in mental health serve planning and evaluation. *Epidemiologia e Psichiatria Sociale, 14*(1), 1–3.

Thurston-Hicks, A., Paine, S., & Hollifield, M. (1998). Functional impairment associated with psychological distress and medical serverity in rural primary care patients. *Psychiatric Services, 49*(7), 951–955.

Timmerman, G. (2003). Sexual harassment of adolescents perpetrated by teachers and by peers: An exploration of the dynamics of power, culture, and gender in secondary schools. *Sex Roles, 48*, 231–244.

Tjeltveit, A. C. (1999). *Ethics and values in psychotherapy.* New York: Routledge.

Tulkin, S. R., & Stock, W. (2004). A model for predoctoral psychopharmacology training: Shaping a new frontier in clinical psychology. *Professional Psychology: Research & Practice, 35*, 151–157.

Tutu, D. (1999). *No future without forgiveness.* New York: Doubleday.

Twain, M. (1963). Consistency. In C. Neider (Ed.), *The complete essays of Mark Twain* (pp. 576–583). New York: Da Capo Press.

Ullom-Minnich, P. D., & Kallail, K. J. (1993). Physicians' strategies for safeguarding confidentiality: The influences of community and practice characteristics. *Journal of Family Practice, 37*(5), 445–448.

United Nations. (1948). Universal Declaration of Human Rights. Retrieved May 31, 2006, from http://www.un.org/Overview/rights.html

Urofsky, R., & Sowa, C. (2004). Ethics education in CACREP-accredited counselor education programs. *Counseling and Values, 49*, 37–47.

Ursano, R. J., Fullerton, C. S., Vance, K., & Kao, T.-C. (1999). Posttraumatic stress disorder and identification in disaster workers. *American Journal of Psychiatry, 156*, 353–359.

U.S. Center for Disease Control. (1994). *Growing Up Tobacco-Free: Preventing Nicotine Addiction in Children and Youths.* Retrieved October 23, 2005, from http://www.cdc.gov/tobacco/research_data/youth/ythiom.htm

U.S. Department of Education. (1973). *Information on Family Educational Rights Privacy Act.* Washington, DC: Family Policy Compliance Office.

Utsey, S. O., Gernat, C. A., & Hammar, L. (2005). Examining White counselor trainees' reactions to racial issues in counseling and supervision dyads. *The Counseling Psychologist, 33*(4), 449–478.

Valencia-Weber, G., & Zuni, C. P. (1995). Domestic violence and tribal protection of indigenous women in the United States. *St. John's Law Review, 69,* 69–170.

Van Sant, G. (Producer & Writer), & Yost, D. (Producer). (1989). *Drugstore cowboy* [Motion picture]. United States: Avenue Entertainment, Image Entertainment.

Vasquez, M. J. T. (1991). Sexual intimacies with clients after termination: Should a prohibition be explicit? *Ethics & Behavior, 1,* 45–61.

Violanti, J. M. (2000). Scripting trauma: The impact of pathogenic intervention. In J. Violanti, D. Paton, & C. Dunning (Eds.), *Posttraumatic stress intervention: Challenges, issues, and perspectives* (pp. 153–65). Springfield, IL: Charles C. Thomas Publisher.

Voelkl, J. E., & Ellis, G. D. (1998). Measuring flow experiences in daily life: An examination of the items used to measure challenge and skill. *Journal of Leisure Research, 30*(3), 380–389.

Wagenfeld, M. O., Murray, J. D., Mohatt, D. F., & DeBruyn, J. C. (1997). Mental health service delivery in rural areas: Organizational and clinical issues. *NIDA Res Monograph, 168,* 418–437.

Walker, M. U. (2001). Seeing power in morality: A proposal for feminist naturalism in ethics. In P. DesAutels & J. Waugh (Eds.), *Feminists doing ethics* (pp. 3–15). Lanham, MD: Rowman & Littlefield.

Wampold, B. E., Lichtenberg, J. W., & Waehler, C. A. (2005). A broader perspective: Counseling psychology's emphasis on evidence. *Journal of Contemporary Psychotherapy, 35,* 27–38.

Warner, D. (1991). Undergraduate psychology students' views of counselors, psychiatrists, and psychologists: A challenge to academic psychologists. *Professional Psychology: Research & Practice, 22,* 138–140.

Warner, T. D., Monaghan-Geernaert, P., Battaglia, J., Brems, C., Johnson, M. E., & Roberst, L. W. (2005). Ethical considerations in rural health care: A pilot study of clinicians in Alaska and New Mexico. *Community Mental Health Journal, 41*(1), 21–33.

Warner, T. D., & Roberts, L. W. (2004). Scientific integrity, fidelity and conflicts of interest in research. *Current Opinion in Psychiatry, 17*(5), 381–385.

Warnke, M. A. (2001). Family counseling competencies. In E. R. Welfel & R. E. Ingersoll (Eds.), *The mental health desk reference* (pp. 379–383). New York: Wiley.

Warren, K. J. (1991, August). *Working paper: Taking empirical data seriously: An ecofeminist perspective on woman-nature connections.* Paper presented at the North American Society for Social Philosophy, Colorado Springs, CO.

Weaver, J. (1995). *Disasters: Mental health interventions.* Saraota, FL: Professional Resource Press.

Weine, S. M., & Henderson, S. W. (2005). Rethinking the role of posttraumatic stress disorder in refugee mental health services. In T. A. Corales (Ed.), *Trends in posttraumatic stress disorder research* (pp. 157–183). New York: Nova Science Publishers.

Weinrach, S. G., Thomas, K. R., & Fong, C. (2001). The professional identity of contributors to the *Journal of Counseling & Development:* Does it matter? *Journal of Counseling & Development, 79,* 166–170.

Welch, B. (2004). The twelve biggest liability risks for psychologists. *Insight, 1,* 1–5.

Welch, S., Gruhl, J., Comer, J., & Rigdon, S. (2004). *American Government* (9th ed.). Belmont, CA: Thomson Learning, Inc.

Welfel, E. R. (2001). *Ethics in counseling and psychotherapy* (2nd ed.). Pacific Grove, CA: Brooks/Cole.

Welfel, E. R. (2006). *Ethics in counseling and psychotherapy* (3rd ed). Belmont, CA: Brooks/Cole.

Welfel, E. R., & Heinlen, K. T. (2001). The responsible use of technology in mental health practice. In E. R. Welfel & R. E. Ingersoll (Eds.), *Mental health desk reference: A practice-based guide to diagnosis, treatment, and professional ethics* (pp. 484–489). New York: Wiley.

Wesley, T. (1979). *Oxford dictionary of quotations.* Oxford, England: Oxford Press.

Westen, D., Novotny, C. M., & Thompson-Brenner, H. (2004). The empirical status of empirically supported psychotherapies: Assumptions, findings, and reporting in controlled clinical trials. *Psychological Bulletin, 130,* 631–663.

Westen, D., Novotny, C. M., & Thompson-Brenner, H. (2005). EBP does not equal EST: Reply to Crits-Christoph et al. (2005) and Weisz et al. (2005). *Psychological Bulletin, 131,* 427–433.

Whiston, S. C. (2003). Outcomes research on school counseling services. In B. T. Erford (Ed.), *Transforming the school counseling profession* (pp. 435–447). Upper Saddle River, NJ: Merrill Prentice Hall.

Whiston, S. C., & Sexton, T. L. (1998). A review of school counseling outcome research: Implications for practice. *Journal of Counseling and Development, 76,* 412–426.

Whiston, S. C., Sexton, T. L., & Lasoff, D. L. (1998). Career intervention outcome: A replication and extension. *Journal of Counseling Psychology, 45,* 150–165.

White, M. (1988). The process of questioning: A therapy of literary merit? *Dulwich Centre Newsletter,* 8–14.

White, T. I. (1988). *Right and wrong: A brief guide to understanding ethics.* NJ: Prentice Hall.

White, W. L. (2000). The history of recovered people as wounded healers: From Native America to the rise of the modern alcoholism movement. *Alcoholism Treatment Quarterly, 18*(1), 1–23.

White, W. L. (2004). The historical essence of addictions counseling. *Counselor: The Magazine for Addiction Professionals, 5*(3), 43–48.

Wiger, D. E. (2005). *The psychotherapy documentation primer* (2nd ed.). Hoboken, NJ: Wiley.

Wiggins, J. G., & Wedding, D. (2004). Prescribing, professional identity, and costs. *Professional Psychology: Research & Practice, 35,* 148–150.

Williams, C. C. (2005). Ethical considerations in mental health research with racial and ethnic minority communities. *Community Mental Health Journal, 41*(5), 509–520.

Williams, M., Parker, R., Baker, D., Parikh, N., Pitkin, K., Coates, W., et al. (1995). Inadequate functional health literacy among patients at two public hospitals. *Journal of American Medical Association, 274*(21), 1677–1682.

Williams, P. (2002). Life coaching in addiction counseling: How to get the most from the 12 steps [Electronic Version]. *Counselor: The Magazine for Addiction Professionals.* Retrieved September 15, 2005, from www.counselormagazine.com

Williams, T. T. (1991). *Refuge: An unnatural history of family and place.* New York: Vintage Books.

Wilmot, W., & Hocker, J. (2000). *Interpersonal conflict* (6th ed.). Boston: McGraw Hill.

Wilson, N. S. (1986). Counselor interventions with low-achieving and underachieving elementary, middle, and high school students: A review of literature. *Journal of Counseling and Development, 64,* 628–634.

Winneg, K., Kenski, K., & Jamieson, K. H. (2005). Detecting the effects of deceptive presidential advertisements in the spring of 2004. *American Behavioral Scientist, 49*(1), 114–129.

Winnicott, D. W. (1965). *The maturational process and the facilitating environment.* New York: International Universities Press.

Winston, A. S. (Ed.). (2004). *Defining difference: Race and racism in the history of psychology.* Washington, DC: American Psychological Association.

Withers, B. (1972). Lean on me. Retrieved August 17, 2005, from http://www.billwithersmusic.com/

Wolpe, J. (1958). *Psychotherapy by reciprocal inhibition.* Stanford, CA: Stanford University Press.

Woods, H. (2004). The truth about women and power. In *Feminist frontiers* (6th ed.). New York: McGraw Hill.

Woodward, B., & Bernstein, C. (1994). *All the President's men* (2nd ed.). New York: Simon and Schuster.

Woody, R. H. (1998). Bartering for psychological services. *Professional Psychology: Research and Practice, 29*(2), 174–178.

Woolf, H. B. (Ed.). (1973). *Webster's new collegiate dictionary* (9th ed.). Springfield, MA: G. & C. Merriam Company.

Worell, J., & Remer, P. (2003). *Feminist perspectives in therapy: Empowering diverse women* (2nd ed.). New York: Wiley.

Wright, R. (1994). *The moral animal: Evolutionary psychology and everyday life.* New York: Vintage Books.

Yalom, I. D. (1995). *Theory and practice of group psychotherapy.* New York: Basic Books.

Ybarra, M. L., & Eaton, W. W. (2005). Internet-based mental health interventions. *Mental Health Services Research, 7*(2), 75–87.

Yehuda, R., & Bierer, L. M. (2005). Re-evaluating the link between disasters and psychopathology. In J. J. Lopez-Ibor, G. Christodoulou, M. Maj, N. Sartorius, & A. Okasha (Eds.), *Disasters and mental health* (pp. 65–80). New York: Wiley.

Young-Eisendrath, P. (1993). *You're not what I expected: Breaking the "he said–she said" cycle.* New York: Touchstone.

Younggren, J. N., & Gottlieb, M. (2004). Managing risk when contemplating multiple relationships. *Professional Psychology: Research & Practice, 35*(3), 255–260.

Zeckhausen, W. (2002). Ideas for managing stress and extinguishing burnout. *American Academy of Family Physicians, April,* 35–38.

Zeuschner, R. B. (2001). *Classical ethics: East and West.* New York: McGraw Hill.

Zins, J. E. (1993). Enhancing consultee problem-solving skills in consultative interactions. *Journal of Counseling and Development, 72,* 185–190.

Zunker, V. (2002). *Career counseling: Applied concepts of life planning* (6th ed.). Pacific Grove, CA: Brooks/Cole.

Universal Declaration of Human Rights

On December 10, 1948, the General Assembly of the United Nations adopted and proclaimed the Universal Declaration of Human Rights, the full text of which is included in this appendix. Following this historic act the assembly called upon all member countries to publicize the text of the declaration and "to cause it to be disseminated, displayed, read, and expounded principally in schools and other educational institutions, without distinction based on the political status of countries or territories." (http://www.un.org/Overview/rights.html)

PREAMBLE

- Whereas recognition of the inherent dignity and of the equal and inalienable rights of all members of the human family is the foundation of freedom, justice, and peace in the world,
- Whereas disregard and contempt for human rights have resulted in barbarous acts which have outraged the conscience of mankind, and the advent of a world in which human beings shall enjoy freedom of speech and belief and freedom from fear and want has been proclaimed as the highest aspiration of the common people,
- Whereas it is essential, if man is not to be compelled to have recourse, as a last resort, to rebellion against tyranny and oppression, that human rights should be protected by the rule of law,
- Whereas it is essential to promote the development of friendly relations between nations,
- Whereas the peoples of the United Nations have in the Charter reaffirmed their faith in fundamental human rights, in the dignity and worth of the human person, and in the equal rights of men and women and have determined to promote social progress and better standards of life in larger freedom,
- Whereas Member States have pledged themselves to achieve, in co-operation with the United Nations, the promotion of universal respect for and observance of human rights and fundamental freedoms,
- Whereas a common understanding of these rights and freedoms is of the greatest importance for the full realization of this pledge,

Now, Therefore THE GENERAL ASSEMBLY proclaims THIS UNIVERSAL DECLARATION OF HUMAN RIGHTS as a common standard of achievement for all peoples and all nations, to the end that every individual and every organ of society, keeping this Declaration constantly in mind, shall strive by teaching and education to promote respect for these rights and freedoms and by progressive measures, national and international, to secure their universal

Appendix A (continued)

and effective recognition and observance, both among the peoples of Member States themselves and among the peoples of territories under their jurisdiction.

Article 1.

All human beings are born free and equal in dignity and rights. They are endowed with reason and conscience and should act towards one another in a spirit of brotherhood.

Article 2.

Everyone is entitled to all the rights and freedoms set forth in this Declaration, without distinction of any kind, such as race, colour, sex, language, religion, political or other opinion, national or social origin, property, birth, or other status. Furthermore, no distinction shall be made on the basis of the political, jurisdictional, or international status of the country or territory to which a person belongs, whether it be independent, trust, non-self-governing, or under any other limitation of sovereignty.

Article 3.

Everyone has the right to life, liberty, and security of person.

Article 4.

No one shall be held in slavery or servitude; slavery and the slave trade shall be prohibited in all their forms.

Article 5.

No one shall be subjected to torture or to cruel, inhuman, or degrading treatment or punishment.

Article 6.

Everyone has the right to recognition everywhere as a person before the law.

Article 7.

All are equal before the law and are entitled without any discrimination to equal protection of the law. All are entitled to equal protection against any discrimination in violation of this Declaration and against any incitement to such discrimination.

Article 8.

Everyone has the right to an effective remedy by the competent national tribunals for acts violating the fundamental rights granted him by the constitution or by law.

Appendix A (continued)

Article 9.

No one shall be subjected to arbitrary arrest, detention, or exile.

Article 10.

Everyone is entitled in full equality to a fair and public hearing by an independent and impartial tribunal, in the determination of his rights and obligations and of any criminal charge against him.

Article 11.

(1) Everyone charged with a penal offence has the right to be presumed innocent until proved guilty according to law in a public trial at which he has had all the guarantees necessary for his defence.

(2) No one shall be held guilty of any penal offence on account of any act or omission which did not constitute a penal offence, under national or international law, at the time when it was committed. Nor shall a heavier penalty be imposed than the one that was applicable at the time the penal offence was committed.

Article 12.

No one shall be subjected to arbitrary interference with his privacy, family, home, or correspondence, nor to attacks upon his honour and reputation. Everyone has the right to the protection of the law against such interference or attacks.

Article 13.

(1) Everyone has the right to freedom of movement and residence within the borders of each state.

(2) Everyone has the right to leave any country, including his own, and to return to his country.

Article 14.

(1) Everyone has the right to seek and to enjoy in other countries asylum from persecution.

(2) This right may not be invoked in the case of prosecutions genuinely arising from non-political crimes or from acts contrary to the purposes and principles of the United Nations.

Article 15.

(1) Everyone has the right to a nationality.

(2) No one shall be arbitrarily deprived of his nationality nor denied the right to change his nationality.

Article 16.

(1) Men and women of full age, without any limitation due to race, nationality, or religion, have the right to marry and to found a family. They are entitled to equal rights as to marriage, during marriage, and at its dissolution.

(2) Marriage shall be entered into only with the free and full consent of the intending spouses.

(3) The family is the natural and fundamental group unit of society and is entitled to protection by society and the State.

Article 17.

(1) Everyone has the right to own property alone as well as in association with others.

(2) No one shall be arbitrarily deprived of his property.

Article 18.

Everyone has the right to freedom of thought, conscience, and religion; this right includes freedom to change his religion or belief, and freedom, either alone or in community with others and in public or private, to manifest his religion or belief in teaching, practice, worship, and observance.

Article 19.

Everyone has the right to freedom of opinion and expression; this right includes freedom to hold opinions without interference and to seek, receive, and impart information and ideas through any media and regardless of frontiers.

Article 20.

(1) Everyone has the right to freedom of peaceful assembly and association.

(2) No one may be compelled to belong to an association.

Article 21.

(1) Everyone has the right to take part in the government of his country, directly or through freely chosen representatives.

(2) Everyone has the right of equal access to public service in his country.

(3) The will of the people shall be the basis of the authority of government; this will shall be expressed in periodic and genuine elections which shall be by universal and equal suffrage and shall be held by secret vote or by equivalent free voting procedures.

Article 22.

Everyone, as a member of society, has the right to social security and is entitled to realization, through national effort and international co-operation and in accordance with the organization and resources of each State, of the economic, social, and cultural rights indispensable for his dignity and the free development of his personality.

Article 23.

(1) Everyone has the right to work, to free choice of employment, to just and favourable conditions of work, and to protection against unemployment.

(2) Everyone, without any discrimination, has the right to equal pay for equal work.

(3) Everyone who works has the right to just and favourable remuneration ensuring for himself and his family an existence worthy of human dignity, and supplemented, if necessary, by other means of social protection.

(4) Everyone has the right to form and to join trade unions for the protection of his interests.

Article 24.

Everyone has the right to rest and leisure, including reasonable limitation of working hours and periodic holidays with pay.

Article 25.

(1) Everyone has the right to a standard of living adequate for the health and well-being of himself and of his family, including food, clothing, housing, and medical care and necessary social services, and the right to security in the event of unemployment, sickness, disability, widowhood, old age, or other lack of livelihood in circumstances beyond his control.

(2) Motherhood and childhood are entitled to special care and assistance. All children, whether born in or out of wedlock, shall enjoy the same social protection.

Article 26.

(1) Everyone has the right to education. Education shall be free, at least in the elementary and fundamental stages. Elementary education shall be compulsory. Technical and professional education shall be made generally available and higher education shall be equally accessible to all on the basis of merit.

(2) Education shall be directed to the full development of the human personality and to the strengthening of respect for human rights and fundamental freedoms. It shall promote understanding, tolerance, and friendship among all nations, racial, or religious groups, and shall further the activities of the United Nations for the maintenance of peace.

(3) Parents have a prior right to choose the kind of education that shall be given to their children.

========== Appendix A (continued) ==========

Article 27.

(1) Everyone has the right freely to participate in the cultural life of the community, to enjoy the arts, and to share in scientific advancement and its benefits.

(2) Everyone has the right to the protection of the moral and material interests resulting from any scientific, literary, or artistic production of which he is the author.

Article 28.

Everyone is entitled to a social and international order in which the rights and freedoms set forth in this Declaration can be fully realized.

Article 29.

(1) Everyone has duties to the community in which alone the free and full development of his personality is possible.

(2) In the exercise of his rights and freedoms, everyone shall be subject only to such limitations as are determined by law solely for the purpose of securing due recognition and respect for the rights and freedoms of others and of meeting the just requirements of morality, public order, and the general welfare in a democratic society.

(3) These rights and freedoms may in no case be exercised contrary to the purposes and principles of the United Nations.

Article 30.

Nothing in this Declaration may be interpreted as implying for any State, group, or person any right to engage in any activity or to perform any act aimed at the destruction of any of the rights and freedoms set forth herein.

Author Index

Subject Index

About the DVD

INTRODUCTION

This appendix provides you with information on the contents of the DVD that accompanies this book. For the latest and greatest information, please refer to the ReadMe file located at the root of the DVD.

SYSTEM REQUIREMENTS

- A computer running Windows XP or Mac OSX.
- A DVD-ROM drive and DVD Video player software.

The two clickable hot links in the web links section are formatted as DVD@CESS links. Most Macintosh computers have DVD@CESS built into the system DVD player but may require enabling DVD@CESS in the DVD player's preferences menu. Windows PCs with newer DVD player applications may have DVD@CESS built in. Those that don't can install the included DVD@CESS software that is contained on the ethics DVD.

USING THE DVD WITH WINDOWS AND OSX

1. Insert the DVD into your computer's DVD-ROM drive.
2. If you are using a PC, the disc should autoplay. If you have autoplay disabled, use your DVD player software to begin playing the DVD. The steps for this will vary depending on which software you use to play DVDs.
3. If you are using Mac, the disc should autoplay. If it doesn't, launch DVD player to begin using the DVD.

The included hotlinks for this DVD should work with most current DVD player software. If they do not, you may install the version of DVD@CESS that we have included on the disc.

WHAT'S ON THE DVD

New copies of *Becoming an Ethical Helping Professional* come bound with a complimentary Video-Based DVD. The DVD was created to offer readers live and interactive perspectives on ethical considerations in professional helping. Video clips include a group discussion with the authors about moral philosophy; a conversation with a Buddhist monk; a conversation with an Islamic scholar; and a conversation with a Latina counselor. Hot links to ACA and APA ethics codes are also provided on the DVD so that you can easily access these important codes over time.

Customer Care

If you have trouble with the DVD-ROM, please call the Wiley Product Technical Support phone number at (800) 762-2974. Outside the United States, call 1(317) 572-3994. You can also contact Wiley Product Technical Support at **http://support.wiley.com.** John Wiley & Sons will provide technical support only for installation and other general quality control items. For technical support on the applications themselves, consult the program's vendor or author.

To place additional orders or to request information about other Wiley products, please call (877) 762-2974.